SOCIONOMIC STUDIES OF SOCIETY AND CULTURE

HOW SOCIAL MOOD SHAPES TRENDS FROM FILM TO FASHION

Socionomics — The Science of History
and Social Prediction, Volume 4

Robert R. Prechter, Ed.

Socionomics Institute Press

Socionomic Studies of Society and Culture—How Social Mood Shapes Trends from Film to Fashion

Copyright © 2017 Robert R. Prechter

Printed in the United States of America

First Printing, 2017

ISBN: 978-1-946597-04-5
Library of Congress Control Number: 2017914483

Publisher: Socionomics Institute Press
Gainesville, Georgia USA
Address for comments: institute@socionomics.net

The Socionomics Institute
www.socionomics.net

COVER GRAPHICS:
Top panel:
Roller Coaster: Andyd/E+/Getty Images

Miniskirt: Dean Mitchell/Getty Images/iStockphoto

Car: Alexandre Prévot, Nancy, France, Ferrari California; Uploaded by High Contrast, CC BY-SA 2.0, commons.wikimedia.org

Taylor Swift: Prayitno, flickr.com

Kingdom Tower: Fair use, Wikipedia

Mary Poppins: © Disney

Beatles: Ingen uppgift - Scanpix, Public Domain, commons.wikimedia.org

Bottom panel:
CBGB sign: flickr.com/photos/thenails1

Johnny Rotten: Plismo - Own work, CC BY-SA 3.0, commons.wikimedia.org

The Mummy: Fair use, wikipedia.org

Face masks: David de la paz/XinHua/Xinhua Press/Corbis

Long skirt: Megan Tintari/Flickr

Handcuffs: MagMos/Getty Images/iStockphoto

Airplane Crash: By Greg L; originally posted to Flickr as Plane crash into Hudson River, CC BY 2.0, https://commons.wikimedia.org/w/index.php?curid=5723340

Back cover background:
Roller Coaster: Aneese/Getty Images/iStockphoto

CONTENTS

SOCIONOMIC STUDIES OF SOCIETY AND CULTURE

HOW SOCIAL MOOD SHAPES TRENDS FROM FILM TO FASHION

Socionomics — The Science of History
and Social Prediction, Volume 4

Robert R. Prechter, Ed.

Socionomics Institute Press

Printed in the United States of America

First Printing, 2017

ISBN: 978-1-946597-04-5
Library of Congress Control Number: 2017914483

Publisher: Socionomics Institute Press
Gainesville, Georgia USA
Address for comments: institute@socionomics.net

The Socionomics Institute
www.socionomics.net

COVER GRAPHICS:
Top panel:
Roller Coaster: Andyd/E+/Getty Images

Miniskirt: Dean Mitchell/Getty Images/iStockphoto

Car: Alexandre Prévot, Nancy, France, Ferrari California; Uploaded by High Contrast, CC BY-SA 2.0, commons.wikimedia.org

Taylor Swift: Prayitno, flickr.com

Kingdom Tower: Fair use, Wikipedia

Mary Poppins: © Disney

Beatles: Ingen uppgift - Scanpix, Public Domain, commons.wikimedia.org

Bottom panel:
CBGB sign: flickr.com/photos/thenails1

Johnny Rotten: Plismo - Own work, CC BY-SA 3.0, commons.wikimedia.org

The Mummy: Fair use, wikipedia.org

Face masks: David de la paz/XinHua/Xinhua Press/Corbis

Long skirt: Megan Tintari/Flickr

Handcuffs: MagMos/Getty Images/iStockphoto

Airplane Crash: By Greg L; originally posted to Flickr as Plane crash into Hudson River, CC BY 2.0, https://commons.wikimedia.org/w/index.php?curid=5723340

Back cover background:
Roller Coaster: Aneese/Getty Images/iStockphoto

CONTENTS

The Authors

Robert Prechter is President of the Socionomics Institute, the Socionomics Foundation and Elliott Wave International and editor of *The Elliott Wave Theorist.*

Peter Kendall is co-editor of *The Elliott Wave Financial Forecast.*

Mark Galasiewski is editor of *The Asian-Pacific Financial Forecast.*

Alan Hall, Euan Wilson, Chuck Thompson and Lynda Edwards are/were researchers at the Socionomics Institute.

Gary Grimes works with Elliott Wave International.

Peter Atwater is President of Financial Insyghts and author of *Moods and Markets* (2012).

Murray Gunn is Head of Technical Analysis at HSBC Bank.

Rosen Ivanov is an independent financial consultant in Bulgaria.

Foreword

Suppose you could predict which genres of stars would rule music and movies; what types of TV shows would be popular; trends in the attendance and viewership of sporting events; the next big thing in fashion; what styles, sizes and colors of cars people would buy; when and where epidemic diseases would be likely to strike; the ups and downs of the economy; when a country would be peaceful and when it would be beset with labor strikes, protest demonstrations, terrorist attacks and war.

How much would such abilities be worth to artists, entertainers, companies, governments, cultural leaders and everyday people? How much would they be worth to you?

It is no accident that futurists of all types fail at prediction. They get excited at extremes in positive social expression and predict all kinds of wonderful things, just when a downturn is imminent. They get cynical at extremes in negative social expression and predict doom and gloom when in fact an upturn is just around the corner. As a result,

— investors expand their portfolios at major tops and pull in their horns at major bottoms;

— individuals, companies and governments spend too much money in boom times and have too little money to spend in bad times;

— record companies, movie studios, sports franchises, auto designers, fashion designers and public health officials are blindsided by changing tastes and new developments;

— armed forces are bloated and girded for battle at the onset of peaceful times, and they are dilapidated and unprepared when wars break out.

In each such case, participants should be doing the opposite of what comes naturally. The failure of futurists to anticipate change and especially their long record of predicting the opposite of what actually occurs has immense social and personal costs.

The problem with almost all social predictions is that they are based upon the linear extrapolation of present trends into the future. The approach always fails, because social trends continually fluctuate. All that has been wrong with social prediction is due to one simple error: the presumption that social trends persist unless events shock them into changing. This assumption is erroneous, as demonstrated with respect to financial markets in Part I of *The Socionomic Theory of Finance* (2016).

Being a successful futurist requires recognizing that changes in social mood bring about changes in the character of social actions. The natural, fractal fluctuations in shared mood are the primary cause of trends in areas as diverse as the arts, entertainment, the economy and politics. It is stunning to realize that social activities are but physical expressions that social mood animates. Its invisible influence makes crowds of people dance or fight. This book is mostly about the dancing part. For coverage of the fighting part, read our companion book, *Socionomic Causality in Politics*.

The recognition of socionomic causality has opened up a whole new approach to social forecasting and established a new foundation for the fields of finance, macroeconomics, sociology, politics and history. It has the potential to bring social science further into the realm to which its second name aspires. *The Wave Principle of Human Social Behavior and the New Science of Socionomics* (1999), and our more recent book, *The Socionomic Theory of Finance* (2016), provide theoretical grounding in this field.

Socionomic Studies in Society and Culture and *Socionomic Causality in Politics*, the fourth and fifth entries in our socionomics book series, focus not on socionomic theory but on its practical application. These collections pick up where *Pioneering Studies in Socionomics* (2003) left off, with new explorations conducted by the Institute and its associates from 2004 through 2016. They demonstrate how you can use socionomic causality to anticipate social trends. We hope this book will inspire new socionomists to join us in this exhilarating endeavor, at once both delightfully fun and deadly serious.

For this book, Angela Hall and Sally Webb handled the colossal task of production and layout, and Cari Dobbins co-designed the book jacket. Chapter headers include original publication dates and sources. In-house publications are indicated as follows: *The Socionomist* (TS), *The Elliott Wave Theorist* (EWT), *The Elliott Wave Financial Forecast* (EWFF), *The European Financial Forecast* (EFF) and *The Asian-Pacific Financial Forecast* (APFF). All original articles are available from the Socionomics Institute.

This is not just a collection of essays but a flowing book. The pieces are arranged in thematic order and have been edited for precision of meaning and to maintain socionomic accuracy. Superfluous text was trimmed, as were technical terms relating to specific degrees of waves under the Elliott wave model. A few of the charts retain their Elliott wave labels in the form of numbers and letters for easy orientation to textual narratives. A smattering of labels have been adjusted to current thinking so as to remain consistent with those in the *Socionomic Theory of Finance*. Wave analysis is incidental to this book's purpose, so we do not elaborate on it. You can learn the subject by reading *Elliott Wave Principle* (1978). Some of the incidentally implied market interpretations within the original pieces have been genericized (so that "in the current bear market" might become "in the next bear market") so as to remain accurate with regard to socionomic causality. When a bold market forecast was a key element of a thesis, as in Chapter 76, it remains intact, as do all other germaine forecasts, including those still open.

The authors use aggregate stock prices as a benchmark sociometer—the primary meter of social mood. As explained in previous volumes, social mood fluctuates on its own, and it prompts some members of society to revalue overall stock prices up and down while simultaneously inducing other expressions of social mood in the realms of politics, business and culture. As you will see throughout this compilation, using stock indexes as benchmark sociometers allows for useful anticipation of all kinds of social activity. It is important to understand that the graphs of social trends plotted alongside those benchmark sociometers are themselves newly identified sociometers, which fluctuate in concert with each other as expressions of overall social mood.

This book is designed to be of interest to nearly everyone, from professionals to the average person who cares about life and culture. Whether your interests are reflected in *Scientific American, The Wall Street Journal, Cosmopolitan, Rolling Stone* or *Variety*, you will find a whole new world in the field of socionomics.

—Robert Prechter

Five Tenets of Socionomics

1. Social mood motivates social actions, not the other way around.

2. Social mood is endogenously regulated, not prompted by outside forces.

3. Social mood is constantly fluctuating according to a hierarchical, robust fractal called the Wave Principle. Robust fractals are patterned but quantitatively variable.

4. Social mood is unconscious and unremembered.

5. Waves of social mood arise when humans interact socially. The process appears to be related to the herding impulse.

Applying Socionomics

Socionomics explains shifts in the character of social events. It is not a crystal ball for forecasting specific social or individual actions.

Some social actions—such as buying and selling stocks—express social mood almost instantaneously. Others—such as economic and political actions—lag substantially due to the varying times it takes for people to implement decisions made under the influence of social mood. Leading actions forecast lagging actions.

There is always a mix of positive and negative actions in society, but their quantity and intensity vary with social mood.

Extreme expressions of social mood tend to occur near the end of a positive or negative trend. The breadth and intensity of expressive social actions correspond to the degree of the largest wave that is ending.

Conventional statements of social causality are backwards. For example, leaders and pop stars do not influence social mood; waves of social mood influence which leaders and pop stars society chooses and how their performances are perceived.

Large groups cannot act independently of social-mood impulses, but individuals can learn to act contrarily to impulses arising from social mood.

Part I:

SOCIAL MOOD AND STARDOM

Chapter 1

Social Mood Regulates the Popularity of Stars
Case in Point: The Beatles

Robert Prechter

July 16, 2010 (EWT)

Reporter: "Can you explain why these kids do it?"
Ringo: "No. Every day, we've been asked that, and we still don't know why."
Reporter: "Do you think you'd have to be a sociologist, a psychologist, of the times?"[1]

"Why the mayhem started, and why it was necessary to those causing it, *will forever remain a mystery*, defying social psychologists and historians then as now."[3]

A sociologist, of the times or not, cannot shed much light on the appearance and disappearance of the mass adoration of certain people, much less on the changes from adoration to vilification and (sometimes) back again. But a socionomist can.

The extreme popularity and unpopularity that some people achieve in society is regulated by social mood. Social mood trends have outlets of expression, and one of them is the creation of, and then the adoration and/or vilification of, public figures. When the public finds individuals or ensembles (such as sports teams or musical groups) upon whom they can project their positive or negative feelings, those people become public figures.

The public does not choose such individuals entirely by chance. They have characteristics that allow people to project their feelings onto them. People who become popular representatives of positive social mood might be intelligent, lovable, talented, clever, funny, urbane, handsome, beautiful or sexually attractive, or have several of these traits. People who become popular representatives of negative social mood might be intelligent, provocative, driven, rebellious, daring, harsh, arrogant, melancholy, comforting or vulnerable. Fame rarely lights on just anyone. At the same time, however, millions of people share such traits, and they do not become famous. The combination of *ambition, circumstance* and trends in *social mood* work to place certain people in the public eye. Exertion alone cannot do it; many people try and fail to become famous. Circumstance alone is rarely enough; talent and effort must be part of the package. But once these factors combine for a person at the right time with respect to the trend of social mood, he or she can achieve fame. Thereafter, such a person's popularity is strongly, if not exclusively, buffeted by social mood.

One can link the fortunes of dozens of stars to social mood trends. Whether the individual is Carol Burnett, Bill Clinton, Perry Como, Bill Cosby, Miley Cyrus, John Edwards, Herbert Hoover, Michael Jackson, Michael Jordan, Marilyn Monroe, Richard Nixon, Elvis Presley, Ronald Reagan, Franklin Roosevelt, Shakespeare, Frank Sinatra, Britney Spears, John Travolta, John Wayne or any other such public personality, one can observe the waves of social mood shaping their periods of success and failure. The ultimate star-maker is the public, and how the public feels determines how it views, and treats, its stars.

There are positive-mood stars and negative-mood stars. Positive-mood stars tend to be more revered, because positive mood encourages more love and loyalty than does negative mood. Almost no person or ensemble is consistently popular through positive and negative trends in mood. Social mood regulates people's choice of media heroes, and when mood changes, so does the focus of people's adoration or vilification.

On rare occasion, an object of acclaim can succeed in both positive and negative-mood environments, but some change in social mood usually ushers in the popularity. Rodney Dangerfield, for example, toiled in obscurity for many years until his sad-sack, "I don't get no respect" routine caught on in the negative mood period of the late 1960s to the early 1980s. Yet by skewing his image to that of a lovable guy, he stayed popular through the positive mood period of the 1980s. Most comedians, in contrast, clearly represent positive or negative mood. Bill Cosby was riding high in the positive-mood decade of the 1960s, when he recorded popular comedy albums and starred in two TV shows, and again in the positive-mood decade of the 1980s, when his *Bill Cosby Show* was the highest ranking sitcom of all time. Richard Pryor, on the other hand, was a negative-mood comedian, who was popular throughout the 1970s until the end of the 16-year bear market in PPI-adjusted stock prices in 1982, the year he won the last of his five Grammys. The vast majority of public figures are either "positive-mood" or "negative-mood" heroes, as they embody and reflect society's dominant positive or negative feelings.

The rarest of stars have a feel for the public's mood and know when to press their cases. It is said that after Napoleon's initial period of success had ended, a rabid fan approached him and demanded that he return to prominence and lead France again; Napoleon replied, "While my star is rising, nothing can stop me; while my star is falling, nothing can save me."[27] When reporters asked Jerry Seinfeld why he announced retirement when his show was so popular, he simply said, "[I] want to go out on top. It's time."[30] Most stars overstay their welcomes, and when the trend of social mood shifts, they become has-beens. Others achieve relatively unstained immortality by conveniently (for their legacy, at least) dying near their peaks in popularity, as did John Kennedy, Marilyn Monroe, Jimi Hendrix and Cleopatra.

In 1985, "Popular Culture and the Stock Market" (reprinted in *Pioneering Studies in Socionomics*) first proposed the socionomic regulation of famous people's public experience. To illustrate this idea in detail, I can choose few better examples than the most popular band of the past half-century. Many people living today have a relationship with the Beatles. Such readers will be able to hear and feel—as opposed to simply read about—the band's story and its connection to social mood.

The Beatles were a quintessential positive-mood band. Their hit-songwriting, pop-performing counterparts to a lesser degree, the Beach Boys in the U.S. and Francoise Hardy in France, experienced nearly identically timed records of early struggle and success, except that their stars faded after the trend toward positive mood ended in 1966, while the Beatles outlasted them by reinventing their sound and personas for pop music's artsy period during the positive-mood rebound of 1967-1969. In order to contrast the Beatles' era of popularity with that of a negative-mood hero, I thereafter review the fortunes of another performer: John Denver.

Ambition and Effort

The Beatles were ambitious and aimed high. They repeatedly stated out loud to themselves their ultimate goal: to reach "the toppermost of the poppermost." During the early years of frustrated goals, the Beatles' single-mindedness was a key ingredient in letting their talent develop and producing the ultimate result.

The Beatles also put forth the effort. Norman Chapman, the Beatles' drummer for a few gigs in 1960, later recalled, "Everything they did and said was directed at making their sound better and better, day by day."[32:132] Sam Leach, Liverpool music promoter, wrote, "The Beatles kept up a blistering pace…. John and Paul pushed each other to the limit."[18:76-77] Alf

Bicknell, their driver from 1964 to 1966, wrote in his diary, "They never stop those two.[4g] ...there was always something to do and I could not actually say that I had a full free day."[4b] Tony Bramwell, personal assistant to the Beatles' manager Brian Epstein, said, "I don't think anyone worked as hard as the Beatles. They hardly ever had time off, hardly ever had a holiday...."[6:113, 228] Derek Taylor, former press officer for the band, quoted one of them as saying, "The reason we were twice as good as anyone else is we worked twice as hard as anyone else."[13:56] Paul added later, "God bless their little cotton socks, those boys *worked*! They worked their little asses off! Here I am talking about an afternoon off and we're sitting there writing! We just loved it so much. It wasn't work.... We were always pushing ahead.[13:56,167] If you look at any of those books that say where the Beatles were working, you find we hardly ever had a day off."[2:v4] Ringo: "We put in a thousand percent."[2:v8] "We never stopped.... We didn't know how to stop this band."[2:v2] Their efforts paid off, not only in the musicianship and songwriting but also in the recordings: "It is extremely difficult to think of a remake of any Beatles song that is superior to the original."[13:301] Obsessive focus and hard work built the foundation upon which they could fulfill a role as pop icons of their age.

Circumstance

Circumstance was the second important factor in the mix. In November 1960, England terminated its program requiring two years of National Service in the military. "Given their age difference[s], the Beatles could never have existed had National Service been maintained."[24:55] Or consider: Had the Beatles been as few as five years older when they met in 1957-1958, they surely would have given up on careers as pop stars before 1963 arrived. Many musicians and singers, trying to repeat Elvis Presley's success, followed just such a path to oblivion.

Other happy circumstances are well documented: the bizarre string of chance events[32:99-151] that led to the Beatles' booking in Hamburg, which pushed them to improve; their exposure to the young German exis (existentialists, a loose cultural group akin to American beatniks) and their peculiar haircut, which the Beatles amended to their own taste; a teenager's request for an obscure foreign 45 (on which the Beatles played back-up) coupled with store owner Brian Epstein's fussy determination to fill every customer request; Epstein's decision to see the Beatles perform; his homosexuality, which charged his attraction to them; his fortunate encounter with the last available record label in London, whose parent company had already rejected the group; George's cheeky joke at George Martin's expense that turned the company's potential dismissal of the band into a mutual bonding session; Martin's musical knowledge and keen pop sense despite having never recorded pop music; and Ringo's last-minute availability.

Some important circumstances were of a personal nature. Their shared addiction—to alcohol and other drugs, a common trait of charismatic people[37]—both bound them together and set them apart from others. (Their manager was an addict as well.) To a man, the Beatles disdained traditional behavior; every member of the pre-Beatles incarnation of the band—the Quarry Men—who quit or were dismissed wanted normal lives. But the Beatles—even Paul, who had top grades and a bright academic future—quit school to play music, without a clue as to where such rash decisions would lead them. The group's democratic choice of a collective name, rather than one featuring a leader ("X and the So-and-So's," a construction popular at the time), would allow fans to identify with any one of them, paving the way for their broad appeal. Their wit, candor, self-assurance and engaging personalities are well known and documented, and without them they could not have won over Brian Epstein (who noted "their personal charm"[31e]), George Martin (who found their intelligence and laconic humor sufficient reason to work with them) and the worldwide press (to whom the Beatles always gave honest or humorous responses to questions instead of show-biz clichés). The Beatles had a cocky stubbornness in insisting upon writing their own singles, and once they began, they "definitely had an eternal curiosity for doing something different."[20:4] Other important circumstances were their compatibility and closeness. George: "Oh, yeah, we were *tight*...you know, as friends...we were very, very close to each other."[2:v2] Paul: "We work well together. That's the truth of it. It's a very special thing." Ringo: "It was magical. There were some really loving, caring moments between four people...a really amazing closeness, just four guys who really loved each other."[2:v8] Performers without such bonds might not have been able to work so closely or to handle the pressure.

The Mood of the Sixties

The third and most important factor in the mix was society's drive toward a major peak in positive mood during the 1960s. A time of "Love, Hope and Fun,"[11a:221] the mood of the Swinging Sixties is famous:

> The spirit of that era disseminated itself across generations, suffusing the Western world with a sense of rejuvenating freedom comparable to the joy of being let out of school early on a sunny afternoon.... That there was indeed something unusual in the air can still be heard

from many of the records of the period: a light, joyous, optimism with a tangible spiritual aura and a thrillingly fresh informality.... The Sixties seem like a golden age to us because, relative to now, they were.[22:1,15,34]

Bill Harry, founder of *Mersey Beat*, placed the Beatles' popularity squarely within the context of overall social mood:

> we were carried along not only with the Beatles *but with the whole essence of the '60s*. We thought anything would happen; we thought everyone could go to the top of the tree. *We thought the whole world was wonderful, and it was going to be better and better and better.*[42]

Such expressions convey the extent of positive social mood at the top of a bull market in stocks of 24 years' duration and what may be labeled, in real-money terms by the Dow/gold ratio, as a peak in social mood of much higher degree. That the Beatles' music was exceptionally energetic and joyful fit the mood. On August 23, 1966, a New York fan enthused, "The Beatles bring joy to the world. The happiness! We can forget our cares when we listen to Beatle records."[2:v6]

Based utterly on the fallacy of *post hoc ergo propter hoc*, sociologists have long claimed that the assassination of President John Kennedy was some sort of causal factor in the Beatles' success. Never mind that hundreds of preceding and subsequent political events have produced no such outcome. Others cite "the ability of four young musicians to spark such mass spontaneous joy and excitement around the world...."[13:96] But socionomic causality is different; it is expressed as *the ability of four young musicians to serve as a focal point for the mass spontaneous joy and excitement that were welling up around the world.*

According to the Beatles themselves, their songwriting fell into the same category: "Lennon once said that he and McCartney...were merely vehicles that 'the music of the spheres...' passed through on its way into the world. One had to be open to it—'You have to be in tune,' John said—but in the end, he and Paul were just 'channels' for music that was not really theirs. The trick was to get into the flow...."[13:118-119] Such comments may be substantially nonsense, but there is no question that these particular songwriters expressed—evidently by sharing—the trends in social mood prevailing during their time. For example, when the stock market's trend changed from down to up in late 1962, the Beatles underwent an equally dramatic metamorphosis: They pretty much abandoned the raucous, anarchic, late-'50s, three-chord r&b rave-ups that brought the members of the band together in the first place (one can hear its final, wild expression on the Star Club tapes from December 1962) and changed the core of their repertoire to their own polished, "glorious," love-oriented pop songs expressing "freedom, energy, and sheer happiness."[13:211] Just before the stock market's trend changed from up to down/sideways in February 1966, they underwent another dramatic change in musical style, capturing the new thoughtful mood, though never without the hopeful, at times playful, attitude that colored the decade to its end.

In 1966, a fan, pestered by reporters demanding to know how soon the Beatles' popularity would fade, replied, "Well, I *wish* they'd last forever. They could bring happiness to everybody."[2:v6] But under socionomic theory, performers cannot bring mass happiness that isn't already there; they can only express and symbolize it.

The Mass Psychological Aspect of Beatlemania

Social mood propelled the Beatles to heights of adoration arguably never before achieved, as judged by the breadth (worldwide), intensity (extreme) and duration (nearly four years) of the ecstatic screaming that accompanied their performances from as early as November 1962 through August 1966, when they completed their final tour. Worship of the band and its members happened both because of them and despite them:

> Bridging nationalities, classes, and cultures, they became the common property of a generation of young people who idealized them, and then identified powerfully with that idealization of them—even as the Beatles themselves, in their music and their public lives, struggled to deflate those idealizations in an effort to retain their own grip on reality.[12:8]

Like Napoleon and Jerry Seinfeld, the Beatles were not naïve about their fame's reliance upon the fickle public. Several times in interviews conducted at the height of their popularity, members of the band referred to the public's adoration as surely a fleeting thing. In November 1963, Brian Epstein noted to a reporter,

> The Beatles are famous because they are good, but they are a cult because they are lucky. It was not my managerial cunning, not my tutelage at all, that has brought about this Beatlemania. *It is simply a kind of mass pathology*; they have an extraordinary ability to satisfy a certain hunger in the country.[12:162]

Some observers witnessed the dominance of unconscious, non-rational crowd psychology attending Beatlemania and recoiled in horror at it:

> In *The Neophiliacs*...writer Christopher Booker saw what was happening as a *mass-hysteria* based on a "vitality fantasy," describing the youth uprising and its leaders The Beatles as a manifestation of "evil."[22:26]

In 1964, the Beatles' first American tour, like virtually every tour beforehand and afterward, prompted the release of mass emotion:

> There was no precedent for the mayhem the Beatles provoked.... "I saw two girls fall to their knees at the roadside, biting their hands to stem the ecstasy of seeing the foursome." ..."exasperated sheriff's deputies" brought in police dogs to quell the "shrieking mob." Most of the kids unleashed another burst of "screaming, weeping ecstasy," keeping it up relentlessly throughout the entire performance. ..."*These people have lost all ability to think,*" complained a greatly agitated police inspector.... *The audience was asserting itself without even realizing what it was doing.*[28:520-533]

Demonstrating that social mood, not the Beatles themselves, were responsible for the exuberance, expressions of extremely positive social mood spread to other performers. Recalling an event on April 11, 1965, singer Madeline Bell recalled, "The experience of being at the *New Musical Express* Poll Winners' Concert, in London, in Wembley Arena [then called Empire Pool], was unbelievable. You could not hear yourself think. The screaming never stopped. Just like they did for the Beatles, literally they did this the whole day, be it Dusty [Springfield] or...The Who, the Rolling Stones, the Kinks...."[5]

Emotional expression at the Beatles' second American tour a year later, undertaken when the stock market was nearing its peak, was perhaps even more intense. The Shea Stadium concert of August 1965 elicited a pinnacle of positive-mood expression mirroring the enthusiasm that also showed up in the stock market:

> As the Beatles emerged from the dugout of the stage situated over second base, "mass hysteria" broke out. More than fifty thousand kids jumped to their feet and screamed, wept, thrashed, and contorted themselves in a tableau that, to some, must have personified pure bedlam. "Their immature lungs produced a sound so staggering, so massive, so shrill and sustained that it quickly crossed the line from enthusiasm into hysteria and was soon in the area of the classic Greek

meaning of the word pandemonium—the region of all demons," wrote the stunned reporter for *The New York Times*. Another compared the roar to "a dozen jets taking off." Mick Jagger, who, along with Keith Richards, was watching from a seat behind the first-base dugout, was visibly shaken by the crowd's behavior. "It's frightening," he told a companion. All this without a note of music.[28:577]

Individuals' participation in this "pathology" or "mass hysteria" is well communicated by one of Elvis Presley's young fans, reminiscing later about being at the foot of the stage at his Tupelo, Mississippi outdoor concert in 1956: "I do remember him coming on stage. I remember what he had on. I can't tell you the songs he sang. *I just remember being sort of mesmerized.*"[26]

On December 12, 1965, at the height of Beatlemania, John Lennon complained to Tony Bramwell, "Beatles concerts have nothing to do with music anymore. They're just bloody tribal rites."[6:164]

The non-rational thinking involved in fans' actions manifested in other ways. George Martin recalled, "Everywhere they went, they were brought cripples.... They'd wheel in all the paraplegics so they could touch them. It was like Jesus almost." The Beatles' press officer Derek Taylor added, "That situation did become nightmarish."[2:v4]

John and George, in contemplative moments, later placed the band's experience squarely in a socionomic context:

John: "We were figureheads for what was going on.... We *represented* the change rather than *instigated* the change."[41]

George: "Everyone got into the mania.[2:v4] *They used us as an excuse to go mad—the world did—and then blamed it on us.* [W]e were the ones trapped in the middle of it, while everybody else was going mad. We were actually the sanest people in the whole thing."[2:v5]

This is exactly what the theory of socionomics proposes: People unconsciously project their moods onto certain individuals or groups, making them public figures and regulating their success as such. The individuals on the receiving end are often perfectly capable of remaining rational.

Waves of Social Mood Regulated the Beatles' Success (see Figure 1)

A brief history of the Beatles as it relates to our benchmark sociometer—the stock market—should help elucidate the case for the socionomic regulation of the popularity of famous people. The main *general* point of this review is to show that the radical shifts in the Beatles' fortunes followed quite precisely the radical shifts in the stock market's fortunes. A

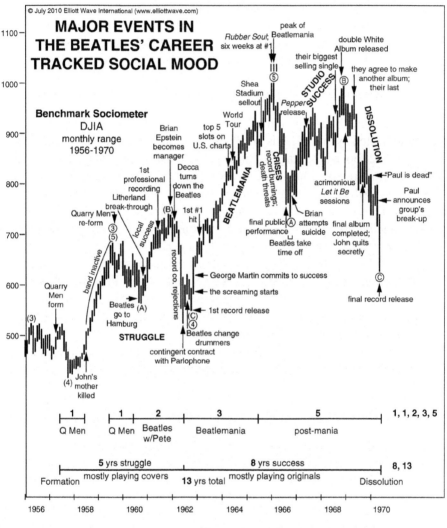

Figure 1

hidden influence, social mood, regulated both sets of changes. Contrast the years of struggle and frustration, ending at the bottom of the bear market of 1962, with their career-making breakout when the trend turned up. Contrast the spectacular rise in their fortunes as the stock market rose from 1963 through 1965 with the string of stunning setbacks during the bear market of 1966. Observe that the stock market advance of 1967-1968 reinvigorated the band's success, but, being a *bear market rally*, not a bull market wave as occurred in 1963-1965, it had plenty of stresses and negative aspects.

Finally, contrast the positive events attending the 1967-1968 stock market rise with the negative events of the 1969-1970 bear market. The changes in the group's experiences are so stark—and the role of society so obviously important—that one cannot fail to see the trends of social mood at work. Figure 1 summarizes this information, using the Dow Jones Industrial Average as a proxy for global social mood. For those interested in getting a more intimate flavor for each of these periods, as well as for those interested in the story itself, a detailed timeline follows. For those interested in an explanation of the durations noted at the bottom of Figure 1 and a related discussion, see the Appendix posted at www.socionomics.net/SCappx.

Note: Different sources list different dates for certain events. For example, Spitz (cited at 28) and other sources have Epstein first meeting with Martin on February 13, 1962, whereas Coleman and Hill (cited in 31e) peg the date as May 9. Lewisohn, the most meticulous source (cited at 38) records meetings on both dates. Other disputed dates usually differ by only a day.

Becoming Inspired as Individuals: 1956, at the Peak of Wave (3) of ③ (see Figure 2)

1956: John's mother Julia plays rock 'n' roll songs for John and teaches him some chords on the banjolele.

March-May 1956: John and George independently hear 'Heartbreak Hotel' and are inspired; Paul is inspired by Little Richard.

June 1956: Paul buys a guitar and begins to practice.

June-August 1956: Ringo begins playing rhythm on a tin box, then a washboard, for a makeshift skiffle band.

Circa September 1956: John picks up a guitar for the first time and transfers chords from the banjolele.

Circa October 1956: George buys a guitar and begins to practice.

October 31, 1956: Paul's mother dies of cancer.

Late 1956: Paul writes a song: 'I Lost My Little Girl'.

December 1956: Julia suggests to John and his friend Pete Shotton that they start a skiffle group.

The Early Playing Years: 1957-1962

Everything the young members of the Beatles did with respect to the band's career beginning in 1957 but especially from the summer of 1959 forward laid the groundwork that allowed them to benefit from the watershed event that came in October 1962, namely, the change in social mood from negative to positive at Primary degree.

Perusing the events of this initial five-year period gives one a feel for the shortcomings, roadblocks, difficulties, vacillations and failures that dogged the band's efforts through the end of the Primary wave ④ corrective formation in the stock market. In the early years through August 1960, the band members had no money, no drummer, one amp, shoddy guitars and few prospects. They were so broke that they would argue over whether to pay extra for jam on their toast. They could rarely afford to buy records; even as late as 1961 they were copping chords and lyrics of songs in the listening booth at the NEMS record store.

This period subdivides into three sections: one year of initial activity (1957-58), one year of inaction (1958-59) and three years of concerted effort (1959-62) against the headwind of a bear market. Figure 2 includes the first two periods; Figure 3 depicts the third.

Initial Activity/Inaction, 1957-1959 (2 years) (see Figure 2)

February 1957: John and Pete Shotton are suspended from school. They spend two weeks of daytimes hiding out at Julia's house, playing and learning banjo, skiffle and rock 'n' roll songs. John's Aunt Mimi buys him an acoustic guitar; he takes a couple of lessons.

Early March 1957: John's friend George Lee suggests starting a skiffle band. John and he assemble some friends, including Pete. Originally dubbed the Blackjacks, they change their name to the Quarry Men.

April 1957: The Quarry Men begin performing at private parties with John (then aged 16) singing lead. For the band's entire three-year life, it plays with either no drummer or a temporary one.

May 1957: The Quarry Men play a skiffle slot at a jazz venue called the Cavern Club. Against management's instructions, the group plays rock 'n' roll songs. They are banned from the club.

June 1957: The Quarry Men come in second at a skiffle talent show.

July 6, 1957: The Quarry Men play at St. Peter's Church garden fete in Woolton. A tape recorder captures portions of the band playing 'Puttin' on the Style' and 'Baby Let's Play House'. Paul (who had just turned 15) views the second set. After the set, a mutual friend introduces John and Paul to each other. Paul sings and plays five rock 'n' roll songs flawlessly on his guitar, and he and John form a bond over like taste in music. John starts practicing guitar seriously.

1957: "At the age of fourteen George formed the Rebels with one of his brothers and a few mates from school."[6:24] The Rebels play a gig in Speke.

July 1957: Ivan Vaughan invites Paul to join the Quarry Men.

August 1957: Paul performs in public for the first time. Billed as the McCartney Brothers, he and his brother Mike sing the Everly Brothers' 'Bye Bye Love' at Butlins Holiday Camp in Yorkshire.[24:29]

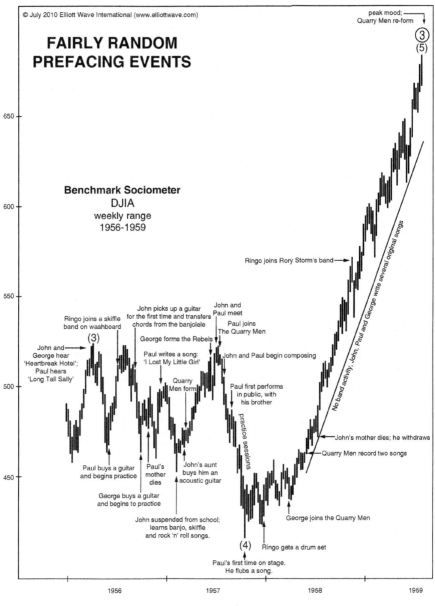

Figure 2

October 18, 1957: The Quarry Men play the Conservative Club. It is Paul's first time on stage. He flubs a song.

December 25, 1957: Ringo receives a used, rudimentary drum set for Christmas.

Summer 1957: Paul plays John 'I Lost My Little Girl'. John catches the songwriting bug.

Mid 1957-mid 1958: John and Paul begin writing songs, including 'Love Me Do', which will become their first record, 'Like Dreamers Do', 'I Call Your Name', 'I'll Follow the Sun' and 'The One After 909'.

Circa January 1958: Paul and George (age 14) meet and bond over mutual musical interests.

February 6, 1958: George travels to Garston to watch the Quarry Men play.

March 13, 1958: At a Quarry Men gig at The Morgue Skiffle Cellar, Paul invites John to hear George play an instrumental song on his guitar.

Mid-March 1958: Paul arranges for John to hear George play another instrumental.

Late March 1958: George joins the Quarry Men, and other members, who were in it for a lark, are dismissed.

May 1958: Paul and George play and sing at the Liverpool Art Institute.

June 1958: At George's instigation, the Quarry Men book a small studio and make a two-sided acetate of 'That'll Be the Day' and a Paul and George original, 'In Spite of all the Danger'.

June 1958: John, Paul and George wear jackets and ties when playing at Paul's Aunt Jin's house for his cousin Ian's wedding reception.

July 15, 1958: John's mother is killed when hit by a car. Paul later said, "This was a bond for us...both losing our mothers."[28:147]

July 1958-August 1959: Although John and Paul continue to compose, "John neglected the group and for the next fifteen [actually 13] months the Quarry Men had no commercial bookings."[24:50] Events that occur at peaks and troughs in social mood can generate social actions that constrain society later. An example is the Russian Revolution at the negative-mood extreme of 1917, which forced the society to live under communism for decades thereafter. In similar fashion, the death of John's mother threw him into an unproductive emotional state. In essence, John's mother's death and his subsequent withdrawal cheated the band out of the benefits of a 13-month run of positive social mood. The peak of positive mood in August 1959, however, will provide the impetus for them to re-form.

November 1958: Ringo begins playing with the Raging Texans, later Rory Storm and the Hurricanes.

1959: George begins playing with the Les Stewart Quartet.

August 3, 1959: The Dow ends wave ③ of III up. The extreme in positive social mood pulls John out of his funk; the band is about to re-form.

Persistent Activity and Struggle Coincide During an (A)-(B)-(C) Bear Market, 1959-1962 (3 years) (see Figure 3)*

Circa August 22, 1959: The Les Stewart Quartet, due to open the local Casbah Club a week later, argue and disband. George convinces John and Paul to have the Quarry Men play the newly opened slot.

August 29, 1959: The Quarry Men open the Casbah Club.

September-October 1959: The Quarry Men have a Saturday night "residency"[24:57] at the Casbah Club. Membership soars and the club is packed.

October 18, 1959: John, Paul and George enter the *Star Search* competition, performing as Johnny and the Moondogs. Top prize is a possible appearance on Corroll Lewis's *Discoveries* TV show.[24:51]

November 15, 1959: Johnny and the Moondogs perform again for the competition but fail to win the talent show. John steals his first electric guitar from another contestant.

"By 1960 the Quarry Men had a repertoire of over a hundred songs...."[24:47]

January 17, 1960: John's best friend Stuart Sutcliffe wins an art show and sells a painting for £75. John and Paul persuade Stuart to buy a bass guitar and join the Quarry Men. Throughout his stint, Stuart never learns to play his instrument adequately. Stuart starts booking the band.

February-April, 1960: The band members hang around the Jacaranda Club, doing odd jobs and playing off hours in its basement. Club owner and local booking agent Allan Williams drifts into becoming the group's manager.

February 3, 1960: Stuart comes up with the name Beetles, a play on Buddy Holly's bandmates, the Crickets. John alters the spelling to Beatals.

March 1960: Stuart and Bill Harry use Student Union funds to buy the band's first amplifiers, which are nominally for use by the school.

April 23-24, 1960: "[I]n another short-lived incarnation,"[24:51] John and Paul on acoustic guitars perform as the Nerk Twins at Paul's cousin's husband's bar in Caversham.

Spring and Summer, 1960: Members of the band play gigs as the Beatles, the Silver Beats, the Silver Beetles and the Silver Beatles.

*Underlined dates indicate daily closing extremes in the Dow unaccompanied by an intraday extreme.

Figure 3

May 10, 1960: The Silver Beetles compete with other bands at an audition to become Billy Fury's band. "They blew everyone away."[28:185] Fury's agent can see that Stuart can't play, so he wants the band without Stuart. John refuses, so they lose the assignment.

May 20-28, 1960: John, Paul, George and Stuart begin a tour through Scotland, performing as backup musicians for Johnny Gentle. The Silver Beetles do 40-minute sets of "kick-ass music that never let up for a beat [and would] steal the whole show."[28:190] The band settles on its name: The Beatles.

June 1960: The band's drummer for the Scotland tour quits. Booked earlier under their previous name, the Silver Beetles go on a second tour; but the new drummer quits, forcing them to return home.

July 2, 1960: The name "The Beatles" first appears in print. The Beatles find a competent and compatible drummer, but he is immediately called up for military service.

Early July 1960: The Beatles, grumbling about reaching rock bottom, back a stripper for a week.

Late July 1960: Allan Williams books the Beatles for a gig in the seedy red-light district of Hamburg, Germany.

August 12, 1960: The Beatles adopt their first full-time drummer, Pete Best.

August 16, 1960: The Beatles obtain student visas and depart England to play in Hamburg. The experience changes everything. "It was the 800 hours on stage in Hamburg that transformed them into a world-class act."[24:57]

August-October 1960: The Beatles move up the Hamburg circuit, from the shabby Indra—playing from 8:30 p.m. to 2:00 a.m. seven nights a week—to the Kaiserkeller and later to the Top Ten Club.

Circa September 1960: The Beatles go swimming in a Hamburg pool and return with their hair falling forward instead of slicked back; their exi friends tell them to keep it that way. They don't, but the idea takes root.

October 4, 1960: In Hamburg, the Beatles begin associating regularly with Ringo, then drumming with Rory Storm and the Hurricanes.

October 11, 1960: Astrid Kirshherr sees the Beatles at the Kaiserkeller and soon begins photographing them.

October 15, 1960: John, Paul, George and Ringo back Lu Walters of the Hurricanes on two cover songs in a tiny Hamburg recording studio. (The recordings are lost.) The Beatles want to record something of their own, but Williams insists they leave the studio to begin work on time.

October 25, 1960: The Dow reaches the bottom of wave (A).

November 20, 1960: The Beatles negotiate to play a better venue, the Top Ten Club, enraging their employer, who contacts the police. George is immediately arrested for working underage and violating a curfew for minors and is deported. This event occurs while social mood is still negative, less than a month after the stock market's low in wave (A).

December 1, 1960: Paul and Pete are arrested on trumped-up charges and deported. A week later, John returns to Liverpool. Broke and out of work, the band members feel like failures. "Each of the Beatles was convinced that his career in the band was over."[28:231] Paul gets a job as a truck driver's mate.

December 2, 1960: Williams opens his new club, the Top Ten, in Liverpool. He plans to make it the Beatles' main performance venue.

December 7, 1960: Williams' club is burned to the ground by thugs who had demanded protection money.

Wave (B), a powerful bear market rally carrying to new all-time highs, coincides with a positive change in fortunes.

December, 1960: Out of work, the Beatles bug Bob Wooler to find them a gig. He manages to get them squeezed onto the roster of bands due to play at the Litherland Town Hall Christmas dance. Neil Aspinall makes hundreds of posters proclaiming the return of the "Fabulous Beatles." Bob Wooler instructs him to add "Direct from Hamburg."

December 27, 1960: The Beatles, clad head to toe in black leather, play the Litherland Town Hall, unleashing all the energy, chops and stage antics they had honed in Hamburg. Instead of dancing, the 1000 teenagers in attendance watch, shout and clap. "But no one screamed."[6:4] "This concert is widely regarded as a turning point in the Beatles' career.... The first signs of Beatlemania had begun.... From now on they began to build a serious local following...."[24:73]

1961: The Beatles' popularity soars locally, following the upward trajectory of the stock market.

January 25, 1961: Local music promoter Sam Leach catches a Beatles performance at a dilapidated venue and tells them, "You know what, lads? One day, you'll be as big as Elvis."[19] They laugh. He begins booking them at clubs and ballroom shows.[19]

February 21, 1961: The Beatles play the Cavern Club for the first time. They play the club 274 times through August 3, 1963.

February 25, 1961: Local toughs, jealous that their girlfriends think Stuart is cute, ambush Stuart and beat him up.

March 1961: Stuart enrolls in the State College of Art in Hamburg. Pete takes over the role of booking agent.

March 10, 1961: Williams' final booking for the Beatles.

April 1, 1961: George having attained the age of 18, the Beatles return to Hamburg to play the Top Ten Club. They play seven hours a night, seven nights a week.

April 10, 1961: Stuart writes to Williams informing him that the Beatles will decline to pay his commission and that his services are no longer needed.

April 20, 1961: Williams threatens to ruin the Beatles' career if they don't pay his commission. He does not follow through on the threat.

Circa May 1961: Stuart shows up with the exis' *pilzen kopf* (mushroom head) haircut, styled by Astrid. Two days later, George follows.

Circa June 1961: Paul and Stuart fight on stage. Stuart quits the band. Paul switches from guitar to become the Beatles' bass player.

June 22-23, 1961: The Beatles, named the Beat Brothers for the session, back Tony Sheridan in a German studio on recordings for Polydor Records. The Beatles are allowed to record two songs on their own: George and John's original instrumental, 'Cry for a Shadow', and a version of 'Ain't She Sweet', sung by John.

July-August 1961: The Beatles play venues all over Liverpool, six or seven days a week and as often as three times a day. "They were booked, day and night, for weeks ahead. Incredible lines queued in Mathew Street for hours prior to Beatle performances."[17:622] An official Beatles Fan Club is formed.

October 1961: The track 'My Bonnie' (backed with [b/w] 'The Saints') by Tony Sheridan and the Beat Brothers is released in Germany and reaches #5 on the German Hit Parade. George receives a copy of the 45 in Liverpool. Flush with a birthday gift of £100 from John's uncle, John and Paul hitchhike to Paris.

Circa October 12, 1961: In Paris, John and Paul meet up with Hamburg friend Jurgen Vollmer, who cuts their hair in *pilzen kopf* style except that John and Paul want it long in back to avoid alienating their English "rocker" fans. The trio has created the Beatle haircut.

October 13, 1961: John and Paul return to Liverpool. George re-adopts the Beatle haircut. Pete declines.

October 28, 1961: Raymond Jones asks NEMS for a copy of 'My Bonnie' by Tony Sheridan, on which the Beat Brothers had played. Owner Brian Epstein spends a week locating the German disc and learns of the Beatles' existence. Sam Leach tells him, "the Beatles are the biggest thing in Liverpool."[18:126]

November 9, 1961: Brian Epstein goes to the Cavern Club to see the Beatles. He is as smitten with the Beatles as investors are with the stock market, which is selling at what will prove to be the highest P/E ratio of the century.

November 10, 1961: The Beatles and other Mersey bands break the all-time attendance record at New Brighton's Tower Ballroom. Leach, who had promoted this and other shows with the Beatles all year, recalled,

> I went back to the ballroom to watch the end of the Beatles' set and was confronted by a frenzied scene that beggared belief. The entire dance floor was crammed with ecstatic young girls crying and screaming, pushing forward to catch a glimpse of their idols. The noise was incredible, and I had to cover my ears. I was barely able to tell which song the lads were singing. Young girls sobbed uncontrollably. The girls nearer the back were standing on tables and chairs, waving their hankies and imploring their favourite Beatles to look at them. It was madness. [These] scenes…increased to quite frightening proportions during the second [set]. 'The first aid room [was] snowed under with young girls fainting. I had never seen anything like it before in my life…. *This was the night Beatlemania broke out.*[18:130-133]

The stock mania was just as feverish, as the year's stock market peak—at a new all-time high—was less than a week away.

November 16, 1961: **The DJIA registers its intraday high for wave (B).**

December 3, 1961: Epstein proposes to the Beatles that he manage them.

December 4, 1961: Top London promoter Tito Burns turns down Leach's offer to add the Beatles to his roster.

December 6, 1961: The Beatles agree to let Epstein manage them. He talks them into wearing suits, cleans up their stage presence and begins shopping them to record companies. He begins to raise the bar on their bookings, increasingly getting them on the bills of pop-music shows and eventually onto the cinema circuit.

December 9, 1961: Leach's promotion in Aldershot, designed to introduce the Beatles to London, falls through when the newspaper fails to run his ad. The flub ruins his last-ditch bid to become the band's manager.

December 13, 1961: **The DJIA registers its closing high for wave (B).**

January 1, 1962: The Beatles make a demo recording at Decca Records in London. They record eight covers and three originals: 'Like Dreamers Do', 'Hello Little Girl' and 'Love of the Loved'.

January 4, 1962: The Beatles win the "best band" poll in Liverpool's *Mersey Beat*.

January 5, 1962: The British version of 'My Bonnie' is released.

January 24, 1962: The Beatles sign a management contract with Epstein.

Wave (C) down ushers in disappointment, roadblocks and changes.

Circa February 4, 1962: Decca turns down the Beatles.

February 5, 1962: Pete falls ill, and Ringo fills in for him at the Cavern.

February 13, 1962: While on rounds through the London record companies, Epstein meets briefly with George Martin, a specialist in classical music and comedy albums. Nothing sparks.

February-April, 1962: Epstein exhausts all his record company possibilities and is rejected by every record company in London. He believes he has failed.

April 10, 1962: Stuart dies of a brain hemorrhage.

April 13-May 31, 1962: The Beatles return to Hamburg to play the Star Club. They write the first version of 'Please Please Me' and perform it live.

May 7, 1962: Epstein takes the train to London to make copies of the songs from the Decca audition tape in hopes of finding some other way to sell the group.

May 8, 1962: While making 78 rpm acetate copies of the Decca tape in EMI's public studios above a London record store, the engineer suggests to Epstein that he play the original songs for EMI's publishing company, which is in the same building. Epstein does so, and the publisher likes the originals enough to suggest that he meet with George Martin, the A&R man at Parlophone, a subsidiary of EMI. Brian does not tell either person that Martin and EMI had already passed on the group.

May 9, 1962: Epstein meets with Martin again. He promises Martin that the Beatles will be "bigger than Elvis" and plays him some songs from the Decca audition tapes. Martin is unconvinced but informs Epstein that the Beatles are eligible for a contingent contract, after which they would have to pass a recording audition in the studio.

June 2, 1962: The Beatles return to Liverpool. Cynthia tells John she's pregnant. He decides to "do the right thing" and marry her. He later said, "I thought it would be goodbye to the group."[28:314]

June 4, 1962: Back-office machinations trump Martin's indifference, and the Beatles sign a contingent contract with Parlophone.

June 6, 1962: The Beatles audition to tape at Abbey Road studios. In a tense session, they record four songs, including three originals: 'Love Me Do', 'Ask Me Why' and their first version of 'Please Please Me'. Martin is unimpressed with their songs and their drummer, but their wit and humor charm him.

June 25-26, 1962: The stock market makes its low within Primary wave ④. "Suddenly everything seemed to be breaking the Beatles' way."[28:319]

August 15, 1962: The Beatles convince Ringo to become their drummer.

August 16, 1962: The Beatles have Epstein fire Pete.

August 19, 1962: At the Cavern, Ringo begins playing with the Beatles. "[H]undreds of girls marched in the streets waving placards. They massed outside NEMS offices and chanted: '*Pete forever, Ringo never!*'"[6:74] The controversy quickly recedes.

"August 1962…was the single most crucial crossroads of their career. [T]hey were *turning the corner* rapidly toward inescapable fame."[10:118] The stock market was also turning a corner, from down to up at Primary degree.

September 4, 1962: The Beatles re-record 'Love Me Do', with Ringo on drums, and Mitch Murray's 'How Do You Do It'.

September 11, 1962: They record 'Love Me Do' a third time, with session drummer Andy White, who also drums on 'P.S. I Love You'. The Beatles beg George Martin not to release their version of 'How Do You Do It', a guaranteed hit song (soon to reach #1 for Gerry and the Pacemakers), and insist upon recording their own material for the next single. They demo 'Please Please Me' again to Martin, who suggests they speed up the "dreary" song and "work out some tight harmonies."[28:353]**

October 5, 1962: 'Love Me Do' b/w 'P.S. I Love You' is released. (*Dr. No* is released on the same day, kicking off the James Bond franchise. See April 2007 EWT [reprinted as Chapter 10 in this book].)

October 12, 1962: The Beatles play 'Love Me Do' for Radio Luxembourg.

October 17, 1962: The Beatles appear on TV on the first time, in a film made partly at the Cavern Club.

October 1962: 'Love Me Do' reaches #49 on the *Record Mirror* chart and #17 on the *Record Retailer* charts, thanks partly to purchases by Epstein and fans in Liverpool. Its persistence on the charts surprises Martin. The BBC declines to air the song.

October <u>23-24</u>, 1962: **The stock market ends Primary wave ④, and Primary wave ⑤ begins.**

Later, Ringo summed up the arc that was about to shift to a positive direction:

> "In '62, people were laughing at us. That's how our career started. They were laughing at us in Scotland and places like that. Then they got interested, and then they got to really listen and like us. And then, this screaming thing started."[2:v5]

**Anthology I* claims that an uptempo version of 'Please Please Me' with Andy White on drums was recorded at this session, but all other data contradict this claim. Below a YouTube posting of this rendition of the song, jasona9 states, "This is actually a recording from 27th November (one of 18 takes that day) and has Ringo on drums." No doubt this is true.

POSITIVE MOOD SUPPORTS BEATLEMANIA

'We Can Work It Out' #1; last of 6 consecutive #1 singles, a record

'Day Tripper' #1

Rubber Soul released; often voted their best album

Norman Smith's last session as recording engineer

Beatles receive MBEs

Beatles cartoon series debuts

'Yesterday' #1

record crowd Shea Stadium

Help! premiers

'Help' #1

Beatles made MBE

'Yesterday' recorded; all-time most covered song

'Ticket To Ride' #1

'Eight Days A Week' #1

Northern Songs on stock exchange

'I Feel Fine' #1

John reads poetry on TV

record crowd in Liverpool

'A Hard Day's Night' #1

A Hard Day's Night premiers

world tour; Beatlemania goes global

top 5 slots on American charts plus 9 more in Top 100

'Can't Buy Me Love' #1

Beatles play Carnegie Hall

Meet the Beatles released

'I Want To Hold Your Hand' #1 in America

Ed Sullivan Show record audience

'I Want To Hold Your Hand' #1 in Britain

Royal Variety performance

headline: BEATLEMANIA!

Royal Albert Hall

'She Loves You' #1

'From Me To You' #1

'Please Please Me' #1

Thank Your Lucky Stars TV show

'Please Please Me' released

final gig in Hamburg

'Please Please Me' recorded

girls scream at live radio performance

Beatles rework 'Please Please Me'

George Martin commits → to the Beatles' success

world tour

Benchmark Sociometer
DJIA
weekly range
1962-1966

© July 2010 Elliott Wave International (www.elliottwave.com)

④   ⑤

1962   1963   1964   1965   1966

Figure 4

The Positive Mood Trend of 1962-1966 Sparks Beatlemania (see Figure 4)

November 1-13, 1962: The Beatles fulfill an engagement at the Star Club in Hamburg. Working on their own, they revamp 'Please Please Me', turning it from a plaintive, negative-mood ballad into an upbeat, positive-mood pop song, changing its character right in line with the trend change in the stock market.

November 14, 1962: The Beatles perform before a live audience at EMI headquarters for a Radio Luxembourg show. Teenage girls in the audience, who had gotten to know the Beatles through their hundreds of live cinema performances, explode with emotion. Press agent Tony Barrow was there:

> "Immediately," Barrow recalls, "the kids started screaming." This caught him by surprise. "I'd never experienced anything like it before."

> What provoked such a reaction? It is difficult to say. 'Love Me Do' had received only scant airplay so far, not enough to spark a popular groundswell. Barrow suspects the APPLAUSE! sign had little to do with it, either, judging from the look on the kids' faces. "They were genuinely excited," he says. "They knew the song; they knew about the band. It had to be spontaneous, to some extent. But if you ask me, that special Beatles mystique was already at work." At the time, such a phenomenon was unknown, even puzzling. This was London, after all, not the provinces. Bands didn't simply wander into the city and take it by storm. But the jungle drums were already beating through cultural channels. Word of mouth traveled from town to town, from city to city, via teenagers who had seen the Beatles on the cinema circuit.[28:363]

November 16, 1962: A newly energized George Martin calls a meeting with Epstein and "the boys" and commits to their joint success.

November 26, 1962: The Beatles record their new version of 'Please Please Me.' The arrangement stuns Martin, who says, "Gentlemen, you've just made your first number one record." On this date their ages are between 19 and 22 (J 22, P 20, G 19, R 22).

2016 addition: The difference in the mood attending the sessions during the bear market and this new one in a bull market was as night and day. Lewishohn described it as follows:

> The Beatles' three previous Abbey Road sessions had a *hunched-shoulders feel* about them, the parties slightly kicking against each other, *reined in by restrictions, at odds* over material, beset by *nerves and frustrations*, working...but not working well.

> This was a restart. 'Love Me Do' 's impressive run up the charts and the November 16 office confab altered everything—the work was *efficient, energetic, exciting and harmonious*, the chemistry gelled, the jokes flew, *everything clicked*, and inside the allotted three hours

the Beatles-George Martin production line started rolling: "It went beautifully," George said. "The whole session was a joy."[38]

It was fundamentally not a song's modest success and a meeting that "altered everything" but the shift in social mood, which brought about both of those events and fostered the shared positive emotions evident at the later session.

December 18-31, 1962: The Beatles fulfill their final obligation in Hamburg.

January 11, 1963: 'Please Please Me' is released.

January 19, 1963: The Beatles appear on the *Thank Your Lucky Stars* TV show and perform 'Please Please Me'.

February 9, 1963: Audiences begin screaming before the Beatles even take the stage at the Empire Theatre, Durham. Kenny Lynch, one of the other acts on the bill, noted, "They were so different, so tight, so confident, really playing their hearts out."[28:371]

February 11, 1963: The Beatles record the entire album, *Please Please Me*, in a single session.

February 23, 1963: 'Please Please Me' hits #1 on BBC radio.

March 22, 1963: *Please Please Me* is released. It remains on the charts for six months.

April 1963: The Beatles take part in a BBC concert broadcast live from the Royal Albert Hall.

April 11, 1963: 'From Me To You' is released. In the first week it sells 200,000 copies, more than all the sales of 'Please Please Me'. It stays at #1 for a month.

"According to Mark Lewisohn's survey of local newspaper coverage, 'Beatles-inspired hysteria had definitely begun by the late spring [of 1963], some six months before it was brought to national attention by Fleet Street newspapers.'"[13:89]

June-July 1963: John and Paul write and arrange 'She Loves You'. Advance orders total "a staggering 225,000 copies."[28:422]

August 23, 1963: 'She Loves You' is released and touches off "a nationwide reaction the press immediately dubbed 'Beatles fever.'"[28:421-422] "The record's chart history is unprecedented and unmatched since,"[10:181] registering at #1 for seven weeks, at #1-4 for 13 weeks, and staying in the top ten for over five months, until February 1964. The "deliriously enthusiastic...mood"[13:52] of the song reflects the mood of society.

September 15, 1963: The Beatles play London's Royal Albert Hall.

Fall 1963: United Artists decides to do a film starring the Beatles. Richard Lester signs on as director.

October 13, 1963: The Beatles rehearse for the TV show, *Sunday Night at the London Palladium*. As they leave the building, a horde of 200 teenage girls releases "an incredible roar"[28:427] as they charge the Beatles' car. The *Daily Mirror* coins the term "BEATLEMANIA!" for its front-page headline. "[B]y show's end they were two thousand strong, all of them overcome with frenetic Beatles rapture. [S]creaming and sobbing seemed like the accepted way to act."[28:427]

October 1963: Fans camp out for days to be in line for Beatles show tickets. At a taping of *Thank Your Lucky Stars*, girls "fainted.... Thousands of girls battled with police. [A] stampede broke out, injuring sixty screaming teenage fans. [T]he Beatles had touched off what appeared to be a mass swoon. Girls of all classes were caught up in the screaming, love pledging, sobbing, hair pulling, and fainting that accompanied each show."[28:430] "[T]he national media's sudden saturation coverage could not help but amplify the underlying frenzy, creating a self-reinforcing process...."[13:89]

October 31, 1963: The Beatles return from a week-long tour of Sweden, and the airport is packed with fans. Ed Sullivan is at the airport to witness the scene.

November 4, 1963: The Beatles perform for the Queen at the Royal Variety Performance at the Prince of Wales Theater.

November 1963: Four Lennon-McCartney songs—two of them performed by other artists—are on the U.K. charts. One million copies of 'I Want To Hold Your Hand' are pre-ordered. Capitol Records agrees to promote 'I Want To Hold Your Hand' in the U.S.

November 22, 1963: *With the Beatles* is released in the U.K.

December 1963: The Beatles record their first Christmas fan-club record.

December 14, 1963: 'I Want To Hold Your Hand' hits #1 in Britain.

December 27, 1963: Capitol releases 'I Want To Hold Your Hand' in the U.S.

January 3, 1964: Jack Paar shows a clip of the Beatles on U.S. television.

January 20, 1964: *Meet the Beatles* is released in the U.S.

February 1, 1964: 'I Want To Hold Your Hand' hits #1 in the U.S.

February 9, 1964: The Beatles play on *The Ed Sullivan Show* to a record TV audience of 73 million people, sitting in front of "86% of all TVs on at the time."[8]

February 10, 1964: Many reviews of the performance are negative, but the Beatles charm a hostile New York press and win them over.

February 11, 1964: The Beatles play their first American concert at the Washington (D.C.) Coliseum. George Martin, a normally staid man, recalled, "[The entire] audience started singing with them[, and] Judy and I just found ourselves standing up and screaming along with the rest…swept up in that tremendous current of buoyant happiness and exhilaration."[13:91]

February 12, 1964: The Beatles play Carnegie Hall.

March 2 through mid-April, 1964: *A Hard Day's Night* is filmed on a budget of £175,000.

March 31-April 6, 1964: Beatles records fill the top five slots on the American charts.

April 4, 1964: 'Can't Buy Me Love' hits #1.

April 1964: The Beatles have 14 singles on the Hot 100 chart, "a record not likely to be approached again."[22:77]

June 4, 1964: The Beatles begin a world tour. Beatlemania goes global.

June 12, 1964: 300,000 people—a record crowd—greet the Beatles in Adelaide.

July 6, 1964: *A Hard Day's Night* premiers in London and earns $8 million the first week, "making it one of the most profitable films of all time."[24:166] Reviews are "profusely and apologetically enthusiastic."[12:244] Reflecting the power of positive social mood, *Newsweek* reports, "With all the ill-will in the world, one sits there, watching and listening—and feels one's intelligence dissolving into a pool of approbation and participation."[12:244]

July 25, 1964: 'A Hard Day's Night' hits #1.

August 19-September 20, 1964: The Beatles tour America.

October 24, 1964: Bicknell's diary: "I…just watched as they very skillfully handled the men from the press. I don't think I like a lot of the characters who show up at these places and some of their questions are so personal, I don't know how the boys cope so well."[4a]

November 8, 1964: Record crowds welcome the Beatles' return to Liverpool.

November 29, 1964: John reads some of his poetry on British television.

December 12, 1964: 'I Feel Fine' hits #1.

February 8, 1965: Northern Songs, the Beatles' publisher, is listed on the London stock exchange.

February 25, 1965: Filming begins on the Beatles' second film, *Help!*

March 13, 1965: 'Eight Days a Week' hits #1.

Late April, 1965: 'Ticket To Ride' hits #1.

June 12, 1965: The Beatles are made Members of the Order of the British Empire (MBE). Holders of the MBE protest and some of them return their medals, but most of the public agrees with the awards.

June 14/17, 1965: Paul and George Martin record 'Yesterday', later cited in the *Guinness Book of Records* as the most-covered song of all time.

July 29, 1965: *Help!* premiers in London.

August 1965: 'Help' hits #1.

August 14, 1965: The Beatles play at Shea Stadium amidst "mass hysteria"[28:577] among over 55,000 fans, at the time the largest crowd ever assembled for a concert.

August 31, 1965: Bicknell's diary: "this was…the only concert that I can remember, that the Beatles had to leave the stage due to the pandemonium and excitement of the people."[4c]

September 25, 1965: *The Beatles* TV cartoon series begins a four-year run.

October 9, 1965: 'Yesterday' hits #1.

October 16, 1965: At Buckingham Palace, the Beatles receive their MBEs.

October-November 1965: The Beatles record *Rubber Soul*, kicking off their thoughtful "middle period."

November 12, 1965: Norman Smith records his final session for the Beatles, completing his three-year stint behind the boards. He had "engineer(ed) 13 number-one hits for the Beatles"[6:88] throughout the wave of positively trending mood.

December 3, 1965: *Rubber Soul* is released. Reviews, for the first time, are positive from nearly all sources. Over time, this album is often cited as their best: "the Beatles' most unqualified triumph, the record claimed by their *Sgt. Pepper* faction and their Hamburg faction both."[13a:374] In 2003, *Rolling Stone* lists it as #5 among the "500 Greatest Albums of All Time." The album anticipates change: "*Rubber Soul* sets the pace for a major shift in pop-rock music. [The] late-1965 change in the Beatles' basic rhythms [toward] slower tempos…sets the stage for the remainder of their career and for those of other rock musicians."[10:311] The stock market, weeks from the peak of wave ⑤ of wave III, was also setting the stage for a major shift in social mood.

December 15, 1965: 'Day Tripper' hits #1.

January 21, 1966: George marries Pattie Boyd.

January 1966: 'We Can Work It Out' holds at #1 in the U.S. It is the last of the Beatles' six consecutive U.S. #1 single releases, setting a record. "The American version of *Rubber Soul* reached number one in the first week of January, 1966 and stayed at the top for six weeks,"[14a:7] a run that ends just a few days after top tick in the 1962-1966 bull market.

February 6, 1966: Primary wave ⑤—the bull market from 1962— ends.

Negative Mood from February to October 1966 Brings Multiple Crises (see Figure 5)

The following comment references two ways in which the change in social mood in 1966 affected the Beatles' output: "Whereas *the number of their products would drop off quickly in 1966*, Help! *and* Rubber Soul *usher in a period embodied by a new seriousness of purpose*."[10:339] The number of stocks rising would also "drop off quickly in 1966," and the fall in the stock market averages likewise indicated "a new seriousness" in social mood.

Circa February 1966: The Beatles begin taking LSD.

March 4, 1966: John and George speak incautiously—for the first time—to a member of the press. Bicknell's diary describes the atmosphere that led to the lapse of caution:

> A good interview with John, by Maureen Cleave, was in the *Evening Standard* tonight. I remember John telling me about it. They are really quite close John and Maureen, and she spends quite a lot of time with him whenever she can, as well as with the other lads. Anyway John said he just rambled on for about four hours with Maureen taking notes, at home of course where he feels comfortable. She had been doing a piece on all of the boys, with Brian's permission of course. It's quite difficult finding a member of the press you can trust, but she's one that you can.[4d]

In the article, John is quoted as saying, "We're more popular than Jesus now." He predicts that Christianity will "vanish and shrink…. I don't know which will go first—rock 'n' roll or Christianity." "Harrison seconded Lennon's remarks on the hypocrisy of religion: 'All of this love thy neighbor and none of them are doing it. If Christianity's as good as they say it is, it should stand up to a bit of discussion.'"[12:310] After the quotes appear in the *London Evening Standard*, radio stations in the Netherlands, Spain and South Africa ban Beatles songs from their playlists.

March 25, 1966: Reflecting the negative mood, the Beatles are photographed with chunks of meat and baby doll parts for the *Yesterday and Today* album cover. Bicknell's diary: "I found the whole thing quite distasteful…. It'll get them some bad publicity this I'm sure."[4e]

April 6, 1966: Geoff Emerick takes over engineering duties as recording begins on *Revolver*.

April 13, 1966: The *San Francisco Chronicle* runs Maureen Cleave's article, but there is no reaction in the U.S. The trend toward negative mood is still young.

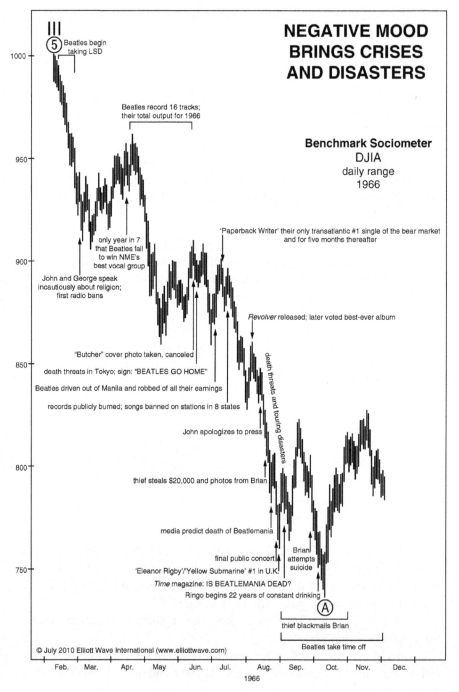

III

(5) Beatles begin
taking LSD

**NEGATIVE MOOD
BRINGS CRISES
AND DISASTERS**

1000 ─

Beatles record 16 tracks;
their total output for 1966

Benchmark Sociometer
DJIA
daily range
1966

950 ─

'Paperback Writer' their only transatlantic #1 single of the bear market
and for five months thereafter

only year in 7
that Beatles fail
to win NME's
best vocal group

John and George speak
incautiously about religion;
first radio bans

900 ─

Revolver released; later voted best-ever album

"Butcher" cover photo taken, canceled

850 ─

death threats in Tokyo; sign: "BEATLES GO HOME"

Beatles driven out of Manila and robbed of all their earnings

records publicly burned; songs banned on stations in 8 states

death threats and touring disasters

John apologizes to press

800 ─

thief steals $20,000 and photos from Brian

media predict death of Beatlemania

Brian
attempts
suicide

final public concert

750 ─

'Eleanor Rigby'/'Yellow Submarine' #1 in U.K.

Time magazine: IS BEATLEMANIA DEAD?

Ringo begins 22 years of constant drinking

(A)

thief blackmails Brian

Beatles take time off

© July 2010 Elliott Wave International (www.elliottwave.com)

Feb.　Mar.　Apr.　May　Jun.　Jul.　Aug.　Sep.　Oct.　Nov.　Dec.
1966

Figure 5

April 1966: This is the only year in the seven-year span from 1963 to 1969 that the Beatles fail to be voted the world's best vocal group in Britain's New Musical Express (NME) annual poll; they come in second to the Beach Boys.

April-June 1966: The bear market takes its toll on the Beatles' productivity, as "the sixteen songs completed between April and June would be the only new Beatles tracks in 1966."[14b:8] These 16 tracks are fewer than half the usual number of 33-34 per year that they had released in 1963, 1964 and 1965.

May 30, 1966: The Beatles release 'Rain' b/w 'Paperback Writer' and film the first promotional music videos.

June 3, 1966: Bicknell's diary: "The phone in the office didn't stop all day…. Those photos of the boys with all that meat and dolls and blood and such has been in the papers and it hasn't gone down well. I knew it wouldn't!"[4f] Capitol Records yanks the "butcher" photo, deeming it offensive, and replaces it with a bland photo.

June 17, 1966: The Beatles fly to Japan to begin a tour of Asia. Japanese conservatives are outraged that a foreign pop group will play at the hallowed Budokan hall. A banner greets them: "BEATLES GO HOME." "If they played there, it was said, they would not leave Tokyo alive."[28:616]

Late June, 1966: 'Paperback Writer' is the only Beatles record to hit #1 in both the U.S. and the U.K. during the 8-month bear market and for 5 months thereafter, a 13-month period.

July 3-4, 1966: The Beatles land in Manila, the Philippines. First Lady Imelda Marcos proposes to host a luncheon for the Beatles and 200 children. Epstein declines the offer without telling the band. Marcos arranges the event anyway. News reports accuse the Beatles of snubbing the dictator-President's wife. Brian tries to apologize in a TV interview, "but strangely, static interfered with the broadcast, stopping only when he stopped talking."[6:166] The government pulls its police escort and incites a mob to attack the Beatles' car after their stadium concert. Functionaries demand tax payments and bribes before issuing exit permits. The hotel staff disappears. The Beatles' entourage commandeers a car to escape to the airport. Police direct their car off the highway. Electricity is turned off at the airport, which is deserted. Two hundred Filipino men with guns and clubs arrive at the airport. Customs agents and police spit on the Beatles and push them around, from one person to another. Two members of the entourage are kicked and beaten. Eventually the touring party makes it across the tarmac to the plane. The plane is held as authorities force Epstein and two staffers off the plane in order to confiscate the Beatles' concert earnings. Finally, everyone gets out alive. "Manila added up to the single most frightening episode the Beatles had ever experienced on tour."[12:339]

July 1966: Datebook magazine runs a story on John's comments about Christianity, headlined "WE'RE MORE POPULAR THAN JESUS." By August, "The shit had hit the fan."[28:626]

> On *July 31*...Beatles records were being burned in Birmingham, Alabama. [D]isc jockeys at WAQY immediately banned the playing of all Beatles records and sponsored a community bonfire fueled by the offending LPs for *August 19*.... "Beatle Burnings" and boy-cotts spread to other...communities. KZEE, in Weatherford, Texas, damned their songs "eternally"; in Reno, KCBN broadcast an anti-Beatles editorial every hour; WAYX, in Waycross, Georgia, burned its entire stock of Beatles records; a Baptist minister in Cleveland threatened to revoke the membership of anyone in the congregation who played Beatles records; South Carolina's Grand Dragon of the Ku Klux Klan nailed several Beatles albums to a cross and set it aflame. Boycotts were announced by radio stations [in four southern states and] New York...Massachusetts, Connecticut, Michigan [and] Ohio.... "We were being told" through operatives in New York, says Tony Barrow, "that there were now religious zealots who were actu-ally threatening to assassinate John Lennon if the Beatles came to Memphis," one of the scheduled stops on the upcoming American tour.[28:627-628]

August 5, 1966: Revolver is released. Reflecting the negative trend in social mood, the album contains arguably the two morosest Beatles songs: 'Eleanor Rigby' and 'For No One'. Thirty years later, in 1996, *Mojo* magazine readers will vote *Revolver* number one among "The 100 Greatest Albums Ever Made." In 2003, *Rolling Stone* lists it as #3 among the "500 Greatest Albums of All Time."

August 12, 1966: The Beatles hold a press conference in Chicago to allow John to apologize for his remarks made in March. Their final American tour begins and becomes "a harrowing experience."[24:293] "The 1966 tour was plagued by mishaps, rain-outs, and an undercurrent of fear."[12:347] "The furor in America came as a revelation—'the first time we started to see *the power that could turn against us*,' Paul McCartney recalled...."[12:343] It was the power of social mood turning negative.

> [In] Memphis...the Beatles were loaded into the back of a specially armored minivan.... Paul later said, "there was this little blond-haired kid, he could have been no older than eleven or twelve, screaming

at me through the plate glass, banging the window with such vehemence." [H]ooded Ku Klux Klansmen...roamed the grounds of the Mid-South Coliseum.[28:635]

A series of accidents, incompetences, and circumstances.... Cincinnati was a disaster. It rained before showtime. [T]he stage was soaking.... Brian called off the show. [In] St. Louis...There were sparks flying all over the place. [They had] a frantic and narrow escape in the airless container of a chrome-paneled truck....[28:637]

Paul: "[T]he woman who predicted Kennedy's death said we were going to die on a flight into Denver."[24:294]

Only two or three concerts on the American tour had been sellouts, and...several promoters failed to make back their investment.[28:638]

George Martin: "All along this time, they were getting...death threats. It wasn't long since President Kennedy had been assassinated."[2:v6]

George: "I think the most important thing was the safety aspect... people threatening Ringo or threatening us, or 'the plane was going to crash', hurricanes hitting, race riots, student riots.... When we pulled into town, there was always some big thing going on, and we'd come in the middle of this mania. It would just be like chaos. So it was just becoming too difficult on the nervous system. That's what I felt."[2:v6]

August 17, 1966: A con man steals $20,000 cash from Brian Epstein's briefcase, along with a datebook and photos of his homosexual liaisons. Brian sinks into "a suicidal depression."

August 18, 1966: 'Eleanor Rigby' and 'Yellow Submarine', released on August 5, hit #1 in the U.K. on a two-sided single.

August 23, 1966: The Beatles play Shea Stadium again. News commentators predict the death of Beatlemania because the band sells "only" 45,000 tickets.

August 29, 1966: The Beatles play their final advertised public concert, at San Francisco's Candlestick Park. They vow never to tour again, and they don't.

September 2, 1966: *Time* magazine headlines, "Is Beatlemania Dead?" "From every perspective, it seemed as though the Beatles were in free fall."[28:654] In financial circles, from every perspective, it seemed as though the stock market were in free fall.

Early September 1966: Yoko Ono, living in New York, boards a plane for London.

September 26, 1966: Brian Epstein attempts suicide by prescription-drug overdose and is revived after having his stomach pumped. He remains hospitalized for a week.

September-October 1966: John takes time off, with Ringo in tow, to film *How I Won the War*. George travels to India to study sitar with Ravi Shankar. George Martin and Paul write soundtrack music for the film *In the Family Way* and later win an Ivor Novello award for their instrumental, 'Love in the Open Air'. The con man begins blackmailing Brian. Ringo begins what he later calls a "22-year bender."[43]

October 1966: Gerry and the Pacemakers, erstwhile contenders with the Beatles for the #1 slot on the British charts and unwilling or unable to change musical styles, become a casualty of the trend toward negative social mood and disband within days of the stock market low. Leader Gerry Marsden explained: "The whole scene was changing; the Beatles were changing. All new bands were coming in. We didn't really change."[23]

October 7/10, 1966: Primary wave A of the Cycle degree bear market ends.

November 6-19: Paul vacations in France and Kenya.

November 9, 1966: John meets Yoko Ono, his "soul mate," at an art show. She will be a factor in the breakup of his marriage and ultimately of the band.

> The year 1966 therefore marked the end of the first half of their career, the so-called touring years, and the start of the second half, the studio years.[13:88]

Positive Mood Supports a Powerful Bear Market Rally and Revives the Beatles' Success: October 1966 to December 1968 (see Figure 6)

November 19, 1966: Paul comes up with the idea of transforming the band into a new persona.

November 24, 1966: The band returns to the studio to record the next two-sided single and begins work on the *Sgt. Pepper* album.

February 16, 1967: 'Strawberry Fields' b/w 'Penny Lane' is released in the U.K. It is the first single, after 13 successive #1s (beginning with 'Please Please Me'), that does not make it to #1 in the U.K., but the reason is that the sales numbers are halved to represent each side of a two-sided single. The disc actually outsells the "#1" record by nearly double.

March 18, 1967: 'Penny Lane' hits #1 in the U.S.

May 1967: Epstein throws a party to celebrate the launch of three new companies: Apple Music, The Beatles & Company and Nemperor, Inc.

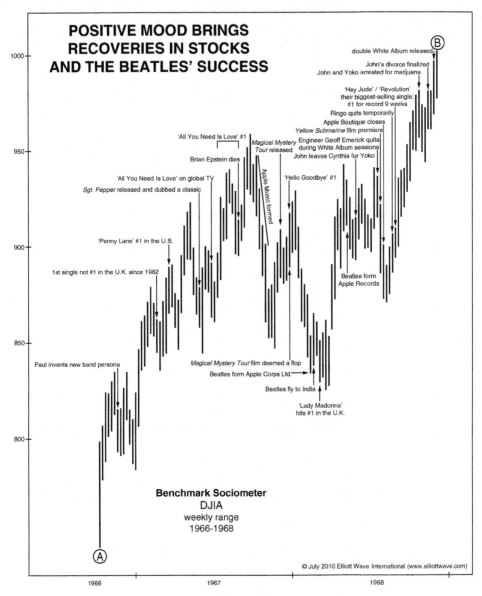

**POSITIVE MOOD BRINGS
RECOVERIES IN STOCKS
AND THE BEATLES' SUCCESS**

double White Album released Ⓑ
John's divorce finalized
John and Yoko arrested for marijuana

'Hey Jude' / 'Revolution'
their biggest-selling single;
#1 for record 9 weeks
Ringo quits temporarily
Apple Boutique closes
Yellow Submarine film premiers
Engineer Geoff Emerick quits
during White Album sessions
John leaves Cynthia for Yoko

'All You Need Is Love' #1

Magical Mystery Tour released

Brian Epstein dies

Apple Music formed

'All You Need Is Love' on global TV

'Hello Goodbye' #1

Sgt. Pepper released and dubbed a classic

'Penny Lane' #1 in the U.S.

1st single not #1 in the U.K. since 1962

Beatles form
Apple Records

Paul invents new band persona

Magical Mystery Tour film deemed a flop
Beatles form Apple Corps Ltd.

Beatles fly to India

'Lady Madonna'
hits #1 in the U.K.

**Benchmark Sociometer
DJIA
weekly range
1966-1968**

Ⓐ

© July 2010 Elliott Wave International (www.elliottwave.com)

1966   1967   1968

Figure 6

June 1, 1967: *Sgt. Pepper's Lonely Hearts Club Band*, widely considered a pop-music masterpiece, is released. It stays at #1 in the U.K. for 27 weeks. In 2003, *Rolling Stone* lists it #1 among the "500 Greatest Albums of All Time."

June 25, 1967: The Beatles represent Britain in performing 'All You Need Is Love' on "Our World," a global television broadcast seen by 400 million people in 26 countries. The song, with verses in tricky 7/8 time, orchestral accompaniment and inspired ad-libs at the end, is performed live after a single rehearsal. With other countries mostly featuring cattle ranchers, subway systems and folk dancers, the Beatles' segment is far and away the best of the show.

July 1967: The Beatles travel to Greece and buy an island. A few months later, after losing interest, they sell it.

July-August 1967: 'All You Need Is Love' hits #1.

August 25, 1967: Brian Epstein dies of an overdose of sleeping pills. Thereafter, John "lapsed into a state of lethargy…watching television, reading the papers, smoking pot or tripping."[24:562]

September 1967: The Beatles create the *Magical Mystery Tour* film and soundtrack.

Fall 1967: The Beatles' accountants inform them that with Britain's 96% tax rate, their £1m. worth of owed royalties would net them only £40,000 to split among the four of them. They are advised to blow money on quasi-business ventures. Over the next two years, Apple Music, Ltd. has a number of recording successes, but all its side businesses fail. With Epstein gone, business takes up more and more of the Beatles' time.

November 27, 1967: *Magical Mystery Tour* is released.

December 1967: 'Hello, Goodbye' hits #1. *Candy* is filmed, with Ringo in the cast.

December 26, 1967: The Beatles' low-budget, personally overseen, avant-garde film *Magical Mystery Tour* is shown in black & white on BBC television and is widely trashed. A U.K. headline reads, "Magic leaves Beatles with mighty FLOP!"

January 1968: The Beatles form Apple Corps Ltd.

February 16, 1968: The Beatles fly to India to study transcendental meditation. Over the next month they write most of the songs for the *The Beatles*, commonly called the White Album.

> Their togetherness, in fact, was so extreme that they seriously considered buying a Greek island where they would all live together with their wives and children. And, of course, the Indian trip was a communal adventure as well. In short, most of the evidence suggests that, as of the start of 1968, the Beatles were not, in fact, destined to break up. Not yet.[13:233]

The stock market was not ready to break apart, either.

March 1968: 'Lady Madonna' hits #1 in the U.K.

May 14, 1968: The Beatles launch their own label, Apple Records.

May 22, 1968: John leaves Cynthia for Yoko. He and Yoko are using heroin.

June 22, 1968: Paul announces to Capitol that all future Beatles songs would be released on Apple Records.

July 17, 1968: The cartoon film *Yellow Submarine* premiers to mostly positive reviews.

Summer of 1968: The Beatles record the White Album, mostly without George Martin's assistance.

July 1968: Engineer Geoff Emerick quits during the White Album sessions; Ken Scott completes the project.

July 30, 1968: The Apple Boutique, one of the Beatles' new businesses, fails and closes after seven months.

August 22, 1968: Ringo—the first band member to quit temporarily—feels ignored; he walks out of a session and takes his family to the Mediterranean.

September 9, 1968: Ringo returns to a flower-decked studio after receiving a telegram begging him to come back.

September-November 1968: 'Hey Jude' b/w 'Revolution' stays at #1 in the U.S. for nine weeks, the longest such period for any Beatles single. It sells 6 million copies worldwide, making it the band's most successful single. Its run on the chart carries to the peak of Primary wave Ⓑ in the stock market as the Value Line Composite index tops out at new all-time highs.

October 18, 1968: John and Yoko are arrested for marijuana possession.

November 8, 1968: John's divorce is finalized.

November 22, 1968: The two-record White Album is released to mostly positive reviews.

November 29, 1968: John and Yoko release *Two Virgins*, widely considered a visual and sonic disaster.

December 2, 1968: Apple releases George's *Wonderwall Music*, a film soundtrack performed on sitar and tabla.

The peak year of the social mood recovery supporting wave Ⓑ has another positive effect: "The Beatles released 34 new tracks in 1968, returning to the high level of productivity they had maintained from 1963 [through] 1965."[14c:22]

December 2-3, 1968: Primary wave Ⓑ upward ends.

George later recalled the transition:

"This was the period when everything was going up and up and up—and rosier—and suddenly it reached that point when it started to go down. Everything goes in a cycle, and once it starts going down—as anybody can tell you—when you get knocked to the ground, then they start kicking you."[2:v8]

A Period of Negative Mood from December 1968 to May 1970 Brings Dissolution (see Figure 7)

December 17, 1968: The film *Candy*, in which Ringo has a small part, is released. It is banned in several countries due to sexual content.

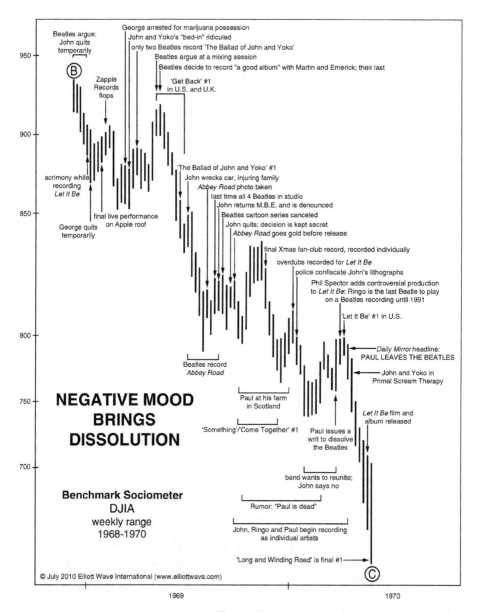

Figure 7

December 1968: The Beatles argue over future direction. John—the second band member to quit temporarily—announces, "I'm breaking up the group." But the others talk him into agreeing to "give it a couple of months."[28:805]

January 2, 1969: The Beatles begin making an album, later titled *Let It Be*, with cameras rolling at Twickenham Studios. They direct the project themselves. Acrimony among band members is caught on film. The recordings are not mixed for a year. John called the *Let it Be* sessions at Twickenham film studios "hell…the most miserable sessions on earth."[29:53] George called them "the low of all time."[21:310] Writers chalk up the bad feelings to the bare studio, the early morning schedule, Yoko's presence, and a number of other incidental things. But this is the first month of the new negative mood trend, and John later put matters closer to a socionomic perspective:

> "Like people do when they're together, they start picking on each other. It was like, 'It's because of you—you'd got the tambourine wrong—that my whole life is a misery.' …The manifestations were on each other, because we were the only ones we had."[2:v8]

January 10, 1969: George—the third band member to quit temporarily—walks out of a session.

January 13, 1969: George agrees to return only if certain conditions are met; they are.

January 18, 1969: John tells the press that Apple Records is losing money so fast that it will be broke in six months.

January 22, 1969: The Beatles resume recording *Let It Be*, at Apple.

January 30, 1969: The Beatles give their final live performance, an impromptu set on the roof of the Apple building, recorded for the *Let It Be* album and film. "It was the last time they played together as a unit."[6:310] John recalls, "We couldn't play the game anymore. It had come to the point where it was no longer creating magic." Though the Beatles had created the music, social mood had created the magic.

February 1969: The Beatles launch Zapple Records, designed to record and release beat poetry. It flops. The Beatles fight over whom to name as their accountant and legal representative. A depressed Paul "sank into a whiskey-soaked oblivion,"[44] but his girlfriend Linda Eastman helps him out of it.

February-March 1969: Despite Jagger and Richards' warning, the Beatles hire the abrasive Allen Klein to become their business manager. He cleans up Apple's finances but contributes to contention within the group.

March 12, 1969: Paul marries Linda. Drug police raid George's house and arrest him for marijuana possession.

March 20, 1969: John and Yoko fly to Gibraltar to get married. They fly to Amsterdam and stage a "bed-in for peace." They are widely ridiculed.

April 14, 1969: John and Paul record 'The Ballad of John and Yoko' without the other band members.

April 30, 1969: George overdubs a guitar solo on what will become the single version of 'Let It Be'.

May-June 1969: 'Get Back' hits #1 in U.S. and U.K.

May 9, 1969: The Beatles gather in the studio to mix *Let It Be* with George Martin, but an argument among band members about Allen Klein thwarts the session. They decide that mixing the 29 hours of *Let It Be* tapes is too daunting to undertake, so they temporarily shelve the project.

May 1969: At the top of a three-month recovery in the stock market, the Beatles invite George Martin to help them record "a good album." Martin agrees, providing they will work with him "like we used to."[28:835]

Summer 1969: John gets treatment for heroin addiction at the London Clinic.

June 1969: Peter Asher resigns from Apple.

June 1969: 'The Ballad of John and Yoko' hits #1.

July 1, 1969: John has a car wreck with his wife, her daughter and John's son aboard. They are all injured but survive.

July-August 1969: The Beatles record *Abbey Road*, "one of their most evocative and beautiful albums"[6:331] and sonically their best. Paul: "The session for *Abbey Road* went remarkably smoothly with only a few shouting matches."[24:551]

August 8, 1969: The famous cover photo for *Abbey Road* is taken.

August 20, 1969: The final track on *Abbey Road* is completed. "It was to be the last time that all four Beatles were together in the studio."[24:559] On this date their ages are between 26 and 29. (J 28, P 27, G 26, R 29).

> George: "...an all-time low. [But] I didn't know...it was the last Beatles record that we would make."[29:53,54]

> Ringo: "There was always a possibility that we could have carried on. We weren't sitting in the studio saying, 'O.K., this is it: last record, last track, last take.'"[2:v8]

> George Martin: "It was a very happy record. I guess it was happy because everybody thought it was going to be the last."[29:54] And, expressing the unconscious nature of social mood and the emotions it fosters: "Nobody *knew* for sure that it would be the last one, but everybody *felt* it was."[2:v8]

August 1969: "By this time the atmosphere at Apple had soured irredeemably."[24:557]

September 1, 1969: John returns his M.B.E. and is widely denounced for doing so.

September 1969: EMI agrees to pay the Beatles an unprecedented 25% of retail on U.S. records, "a far higher royalty than any other group had ever attained."[24:561]

September 7, 1969: *The Beatles* TV cartoon series is canceled.

September 13, 1969: John plays live, for the first time in three years, with a new lineup—the Plastic Ono Band—at the Toronto Rock and Roll Festival.

September 20, 1969: John announces at a band meeting, "I'm leaving the group." His decision is kept secret.

September 26, 1969: *Abbey Road* is released. In Britain, orders for the album set a new record. In the U.S., the album goes gold before it is released.

September 27, 1969: John records 'Cold Turkey' with the Plastic Ono Band.

October 10, 1969: A rumor begins: "Paul is dead." "A Detroit disc jockey reports a University of Michigan student's theory that Paul died in 1966 and was replaced by a stand-in. Every commercial radio station, joined by an army of impetuous college deejays, jumped on the story, sending hundreds of thousands of distraught fans scrambling to scour their Beatles records for clues."[28:843] The rumor persists for months.

October-November 1969: 'Something'/'Come Together' is released and hits #1.

Circa November 1969: The Beatles record their final Christmas fanclub record. The segments are recorded individually.

October-December 1969: Paul holes up at his farm in Scotland with his family.

January 3, 1970: For the *Let It Be* album, Paul, George and Ringo add overdubs to the basic track of George's 'I, Me, Mine', recorded a year earlier. "This final recording date…took place eight years to the day [actually 8 yrs + 2 days] from the Beatles' disastrous audition at Decca Records in 1962."[12:598]

January 4, 1970: Paul, George and George Martin do overdubs for 'Let It Be'. George records a second guitar solo, which will go on the album version of the song.

January 16, 1970: Police confiscate eight of John's lithographs, which were supposedly in violation of obscenity laws, from an exhibit. On April 27, they are ruled not obscene and are returned to him.

January 1970: Based on John's comments in interviews, "It did seem as if John was still unsure about the breakup."[24:565]

February 6, 1970: 'Instant Karma', by the Plastic Ono Band and produced by Phil Spector, is released.

February 18-19, 1970: Ringo records 'It Don't Come Easy', soon to be a hit.

February-March 1970: George and Ringo phone each other and then Paul to talk about whether they will get back together. Paul calls John, who says no.

March 18, 1970: "Paul was convinced that Klein was crooked and issued a writ to try to dissolve the Beatles partnership [as a] legal way [to] get rid of Klein and start again with a clean slate…. Years of lawsuits and wrangling began."[6:355] It was 13 years to the month after John had formed the Quarry Men.

March 27, 1970: Ringo releases *Sentimental Journey*, a solo album of standards.

April 1-2, 1970: At Allen Klein's direction, Phil Spector adds production elements to *Let It Be*—particularly harps, horns, an orchestra and a women's choir to 'The Long and Winding Road'—against George Martin and Paul's sensitivities and without their knowledge. Ringo adds a drum track, making this the last day, until the 1990s, that a Beatle plays on a Beatles recording.

April 11, 1970: 'Let It Be' hits #1 in the U.S.

April 1970: John and Yoko undergo Primal Scream Therapy at the Janov Institute in California.

April 17, 1970: Paul releases a solo album, *McCartney*. It includes a brief Q&A in which Paul is asked, "Do you foresee a time when Lennon-McCartney becomes an active songwriting partnership again?" His answer, making him the fourth band member to quit and the second to quit finally, is "No." The *Daily Mirror* headlines, "PAUL LEAVES THE BEATLES." John is angry that Paul "gets all the credit for it,"[28:854] but he confirms that the Beatles are no more.

May 8, 1970: *Let It Be* is released in the U.K.

May 13, 1970: The film *Let It Be* is released.

May 18, 1970: *Let It Be* is released in the U.S.

May 23, 1970: 'The Long and Winding Road' hits #1 in the U.S. It is the Beatles' last #1 single.

The band's final four #1 hits—'Hey Jude' from 1968, 'Something' from 1969, and 'Let It Be' and 'The Long and Winding Road' from 1970—show that the Beatles could compose popular negative-mood ballads as well as popular positive-mood pop songs. They were also able to write ugly and angry negative-mood material such as 'I Am the Walrus' from *Magical Mystery Tour* and 'Helter Skelter' and 'Yer Blues' from the White Album. So, their social-mood sensitivity, along with their talent, remained intact during the negative trend in social mood even as it ultimately tore them apart.

May 26, 1970: After nearly 18 months of decline in the stock market and following two months of crashing prices, Primary wave © of the bear market ends.

AFTERMATH

Key Events of the Negative Mood Period of 1970-1974 and Through the Mixed-Trend Period Until 1982 (see Figure 8)

> For a few years after the Beatles disbanded in 1970, pop critics tended to downplay their importance and compare their music unfavorably with the ruder styles of rock exemplified by their old rivals, the Rolling Stones.[12:9]

November 1970: George Harrison releases a triple album, *All Things Must Pass.*

January 19-28, 1971: The High Court puts the Beatles partnership in receivership to sort matters out. John, George and Ringo appeal but drop the appeal in April.

February 18, 1971: Paul sues for dissolution of the Beatles and a division of assets.

August 1, 1971: George plays at Madison Square Garden for the Concert for Bangladesh, which he and Ravi Shankar had organized.

August 1971: Paul forms Wings, which racks up hits throughout the negative mood period from 1972 to April 1980 (see Figure 11).

September 9, 1971: John releases *Imagine*, whose 'How Do You Sleep', with lyrics contributed by Yoko and Allen Klein, makes "a vitriolic attack"[24:584] on Paul.

March 6, 1972: The U.S. government begins proceedings to deport John. The battle goes on for four years.

April 19, 1973: The Beatles' *1962-1966* (the Red Album) and *1967-1970* (the Blue Album) are released. Reflecting the re-elevated social mood of January's new all-time high in the Dow and S&P, the Blue Album reaches #1 in *Billboard*, and the Red Album reaches #1 in *Cashbox*.

June 28, 1973: Allen Klein sues John for $508,000 after John and Yoko fire him.

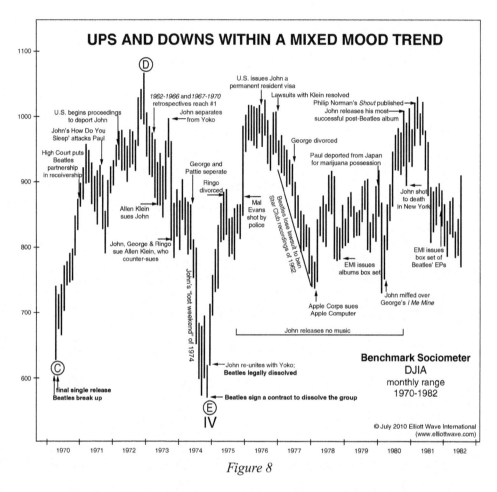

Figure 8

October 1973: John moves to Los Angeles and lives with May Pang through 1974, during the largest decline of the 8-year bear market.

November 3, 1973: John, George and Ringo sue Allen Klein for damages, and Klein counter-sues.

1974: John has a year-long "lost weekend," in which he records three albums and hangs out a lot with fellow alcoholics Harry Nilsson, Keith Moon and Jesse Ed Davis.

June 1974: George and Pattie separate.

December 6/9, 1974: Cycle wave IV comes to an end. So, legally, do the Beatles.

December 19, 1974: Due to tax concerns, John declines to attend a meeting in New York to sign a document dissolving the group. An angry George cancels John's appearance that night at his Madison Square Garden show.

December 20-28, 1974: Lawyers work out the final details of the dissolution document.

December 29, 1974: Twenty days after the wave IV low in the Dow, John signs, beneath the signatures of Paul, George and Richard Starkey (Ringo), a contract to dissolve the Beatles.

January 9, 1975: "The partnership of The Beatles & Co. is finally dissolved in the London high court."[9:620]

January 1975: As a new bull market lifts off, John re-unites with Yoko, who is "soon pregnant."[9:620]

John releases no music from late 1975 until late 1980, as real stock prices (see Figure 10) mostly continue to drag lower.

January 4, 1976: Beatles' former roadie Mal Evans, distraught and on drugs, is shot by police.

July 1, 1975: Ringo and Maureen divorce.

July 27, 1976: After the stock market nearly doubles, the government stops its deportation efforts and issues John a permanent resident visa.

January 1977: Lawsuits directing Klein to leave Apple are resolved with a payment to him of $4.2m.

1977: A German company releases a recording of a tape made of the Beatles at the Star Club in December 1962. The Beatles lose a lawsuit to ban the recording.

June 9, 1977: George and Pattie divorce.

1978: Apple Corps, the Beatles' holding company, enters into a 29-year trademark dispute with Apple Computer.

December 1978: EMI issues a box set of the Beatles' albums.

January 16, 1980: Paul is arrested for marijuana possession in Japan and spends nine days in jail. Paul recalled, "I was fully convinced that I would be imprisoned for nine or ten years. I was scared out of my wits."[6:404] Paul is deported on January 25, aborting the scheduled Wings tour of that country. The event takes place the exact week of the low in the real-money Dow (the Dow/gold ratio).

***January 21, 1980*: The real-money Dow (Dow/gold) bottoms.**

1980: "John and George's final disagreement came…when George published his autobiography *I Me Mine*…" and mentioned his former band leader "a mere eleven times."[24:584]

November 17, 1980: Ten months after a new bull market in the real-money Dow begins, John releases *Double Fantasy*, his most successful post-Beatles album.

December 8, 1980: In New York, a deranged fan shoots John, age 40, to death.

Other Bear-Market Rock 'n' Roll Deaths of the Period

The bear market years of 1969-1982 took a heavy toll on some other 1960s pop musicians:

July 1, 1969: Brian Jones (age 27), a drug addict, drowns in a swimming pool.

September 18, 1970: Jimi Hendrix (age 27) chokes to death while unconscious from drugs.

October 4, 1970: Janis Joplin (age 27) dies of a heroin overdose.

July 3, 1971: Jim Morrison (age 27) dies as a result of his addictions to alcohol, heroin and cocaine.

March 8, 1973: Ronald "Pigpen" McKernan (age 27) dies of a gastrointestinal hemorrhage, probably as a result of alcoholism.

August 16, 1977: Elvis Presley (age 42) dies from complications from an overdose of ten prescribed drugs.

September 7, 1978: Keith Moon (age 32) dies of alcoholism.

September 25, 1980: John Bonham (age 32) dies of alcoholism.

April 27, 1981: Wings disbands.

Early 1981: The first major Beatles biography, Philip Norman's *Shout*, is published. *The New York Times* calls it "definitive."

December 1981: EMI issues a box set of the Beatles' EPs.

August 9/_12_, 1982: The Dow/PPI bottoms, and a bull market by all measures begins.

December 1982: EMI issues a box set of the Beatles' singles.

A New Trend Toward Positive Mood Clears the Air (see Figure 9)

Not much happens for the Beatles until the bull market enters the third wave of the third wave, the "pivot point" at which social mood switches from less negative to more positive (see Chapter 8 of *The Socionomic Theory of Finance*). Suddenly the Beatles are back in the public's consciousness.

February 26-November 1987: The Beatles catalog is released on CD. The reissues are mostly completed by August 25, 1987, the date of the pre-crash stock market peak.

March 1987: 'Let It Be (Ferry Aid Song)', a remake of 'Let It Be', by the Charity Ensemble and featuring musical contributions from Paul along with his lead vocal track from 1970, reaches #1 in the U.K.

March 7, 1988: The *Past Masters* double CD is released, completing the CD song reissues.

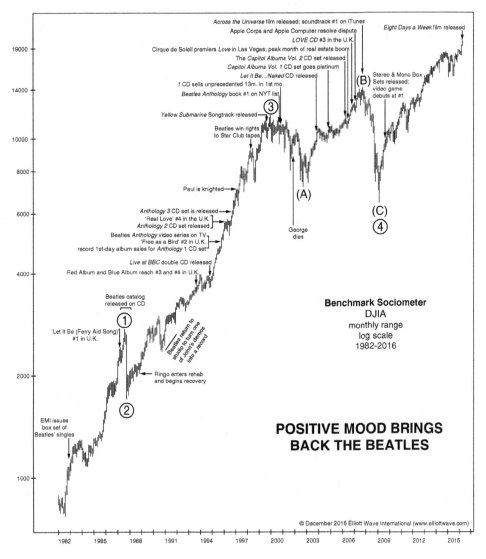

Across the Universe film released; soundtrack #1 on iTunes
Apple Corps and Apple Computer resolve dispute
LOVE CD #3 in the U.K.
Eight Days a Week film released
Cirque de Soleil premiers *Love* in Las Vegas; peak month of real estate boom
The *Capitol Albums Vol. 2* CD set released
Capitol Albums Vol. 1 CD set goes platinum
Let It Be...Naked CD released
1 CD sells unprecedented 13m. in 1st mo.
Beatles Anthology book #1 on NYT list
③
Stereo & Mono Box Sets released; video game debuts at #1
(B)
Yellow Submarine Songtrack released
Beatles win rights to Star Club tapes
Paul is knighted
(A)
Anthology 3 CD set is released
'Real Love' #4 in the U.K.
Anthology 2 CD set released
Beatles *Anthology* video series on TV
'Free as a Bird' #2 in U.K.
record 1st-day album sales for *Anthology 1* CD set
George dies
(C)
④
Live at BBC double CD released
Red Album and Blue Album reach #3 and #4 in U.K.
Beatles catalog released on CD
①
Beatles return to studio to turn one of John's demos into a record
'Let It Be (Ferry Aid Song)' #1 in U.K.
Ringo enters rehab and begins recovery
②
EMI issues box set of Beatles' singles

Benchmark Sociometer
DJIA
monthly range
log scale
1982-2016

**POSITIVE MOOD BRINGS
BACK THE BEATLES**

© December 2016 Elliott Wave International (www.elliottwave.com)

Figure 9

October 1988: As the Dow begins its recovery from the 1987 crash, Ringo enters rehab and begins life in recovery.

October 1988-October 1990: George records with the Traveling Wilburys.

November 15, 1988: The Beatles' CD box set is released.

1989: Ringo begins touring with his All-Starr Band (still active).

June 28, 1991: Paul's *Liverpool Oratorio* is premiered by the Royal Liverpool Philharmonic Orchestra. Reviews are mixed.

1992: Paul's contributions and efforts save the Liverpool Institute for Performing Arts.

September 1993: Apple reissues *1962-1966* (the Red Album) and *1967-1970* (the Blue Album) on CD. The Red Album reaches #3, the Blue Album #4 in the U.K.

February-March 1994: At George's suggestion, the surviving Beatles return to the studio to record 'Free as a Bird'. It is built from John's piano demo from 1977, with the other Beatles' contributions overdubbed.

November 30, 1994: The *Live at the BBC* double CD is released.

November 19-22, 1995: The Beatles *Anthology* video series is shown on U.S. television.

November 20, 1995: 'Free as a Bird', the first new Beatles single since 1970, is released. The song reaches #2 in the U.K. and #6 in the U.S.

November 21, 1995: The *Anthology 1* CD set is released. 450,000 copies sell on the first day, setting a record for the most album sales in one day.

March 4, 1996: 'Real Love', another John demo with overdubs by the other Beatles, is released. It reaches #4 in the U.K. and #11 in the U.S.

March 18, 1996: The *Anthology 2* CD set is released.

October 28, 1996: The *Anthology 3* CD set is released.

March 11, 1997: Paul is knighted.

May 9, 1998: The Beatles win the rights to the Star Club tapes of 1962.

September 17, 1999: The *Yellow Submarine* Songtrack CD of remixed songs is released.

October 2000: *The Beatles Anthology* book is released. It goes directly to #1 on *The New York Times* bestseller list. This event occurs one month after the NYSE Composite Index hits an all-time high prior to a nine-year bear market.

November 13, 2000: The Beatles' *1* CD is released. It sells "an unprecedented 13 million copies in the first month"[12:9] and becomes the best selling album of the decade.

2000-2002: The Mood Trend Turns Negative

2001-2002: Nothing happens musically with respect to the Beatles aside from the *Anthology* video series being transferred to DVD. See http://www.cyber-beatles.com/year2001.htm and associated pages. This period is a bear market in stocks.

November 29, 2001: George dies of lung cancer at age 58.

2003-2007: The Mood Trend Turns Positive

November 18, 2003: The *Let It Be...Naked* CD is released. It presents the album mixed as originally intended, without Spector's production.

November 15, 2004: The *Capitol Albums Vol. 1* CD set is released. It goes platinum within a month.

April 11, 2006: The *Capitol Albums Vol. 2* CD set is released.

July 1, 2006: Cirque de Soleil, in partnership with Apple Records, premiers the Beatles-themed show *LOVE* at the Mirage Resort and Casino, at the epicenter of the U.S. real estate boom, Las Vegas, Nevada, in the exact month (according to the S&P/Case-Shiller Composite-20 Home Price Index) of the national peak in real estate prices, another indication of historically elevated social mood.

November 21, 2006: The *LOVE* CD, produced by George and Giles Martin for Cirque du Soleil, is released. It reaches #3 in the U.K. and #4 in the U.S. and goes platinum.

February 5, 2007: Fifteen days before the all-time high in the KBW Bank Index and the year of a major top in the Dow, Apple Corps resolves its 29-year trademark dispute with Apple Computer.

October 12, 2007: *Across the Universe*, a musical film based on Beatles songs, is released the day after a longstanding all-time intraday high in the DJIA at 14,198. That month, the deluxe edition of the movie soundtrack "was the #1 downloaded album on iTunes."[31g]

October 9/11, 2007 - March 2009: Major Stock Market Decline

November 2007-early 2009: Nothing happens musically with respect to the Beatles. This period features a bear market in stocks and real estate.

Parallel Expressions of Elevated Social Mood (see Figure 10)

Figure 10 shows socionomic causality at work in the timing of the Beatles' productivity and fame in the 1960s and the resurgence of their productivity and popularity in the 1990s-2000s. The Beatles and their music are more appealing to people during periods of very positive social mood, so the past two times society enjoyed extremely positive social mood, the Beatles enjoyed successful products.

The parallels are rather striking. The Beatles began issuing new products in November 1994, when *Live at the BBC* came out. Although it is not readily apparent on the chart, that month ended a period of negative social mood (see Figure 1 in Chapter 12) that lingered on after the Primary degree correction of 1987-1990, which was much like the period of 1959-1962 that preceded the onset of their hit-making career. Echoing their intense productivity in 1963-1965, the Beatles tackled ten ambitious new projects from 1994 to 2000. Paralleling the peak of Beatlemania in early 1966, this period ended along with the bull market in 2000 when a CD re-issue of the Beatles' #1 hits sold an unprecedented 13 million copies in its first month. The Beatles then issued nothing as the market declined into 2002-2003,

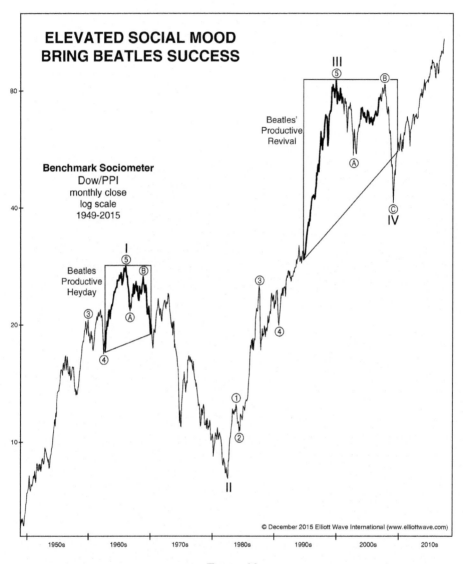

Figure 10

a period parallel to the 1966 bear market during which their productivity contracted by more than half. The band had resumed recording during the peak-area bear market rally of 1967-1968; the band likewise resumed issuing new material during the peak-area bear market rally of 2003 to 2007. This period brought a different mix of the *Let It Be* album with new snippets of audio, a song collage for Cirque du Soleil compiled by George Martin titled *LOVE*, and Capitol's reissue of early Beatles material, which went platinum.

In the first cycle, the Beatles kept working for eight months into the new bear market of 1968-1970 until the group dissolved. This time, they issued no product whatsoever in the bear market of 2007-2009.

2009 – ????: **Major Stock Market Advance**

September 9, 2009: *The Beatles Stereo Box Set* and *The Beatles Mono Box Set* of the band's remastered catalog are released. Sales are strong for the discs. "The Beatles, Rock Band" video game is released. The pricey game debuts at #1 for the month and makes the top ten for the year but sells shy of expectations. The stock market is only six months off its low.

Post-Production Update (Q2 2017)

November 16, 2010: After years of wrangling that did not stop until the bear market of 2000-2009 ended, the Beatles' catalog finally becomes available on iTunes. Here is a report on the first week of sales:

> Forty years after breaking up, The Beatles are flexing their digital sales muscle. They sold 450,000 albums and 2 million songs world-wide in their first week on iTunes, according to Apple Inc. The 1969 classic *Abbey Road*, the final album recorded before the band's breakup in 1970, topped album sales, and George Harrison's 'Here Comes The Sun' was the best-selling tune. …The $149 Beatles Box Set, with 13 remastered studio albums and loads of video extras, is No. 10 on iTunes' ranking of U.S. best-selling albums.[33]

September 2016: With U.S. stock indexes on the way to new all-time highs, a new Beatles movie hits the theaters. *Eight Days a Week*, Ron Howard's documentary on the band's touring years, is the first film to star the band since 1970's *Let it Be*. The two surviving Beatles participate in the film.

March 5, 2017: As U.S. stock indexes register another new high, Apple announces the June 1 release of a remixed, remastered, expanded version of *Sgt. Pepper's Lonely Hearts Club Band*.

May 2, 2017: As the S&P Composite index heads to another new all-time high amidst exceptionally positive social mood, SiriusXM announces the May 18 startup of an all-Beatles channel.

Fading and Potential Resurgence

What is the future of Beatlemania? Given that the stock market here in 2017 is poised to peak at Grand Supercycle degree and usher in the biggest bear market since the 1700s, it is likely that the Beatles' public appeal will fade. The Beatles were for the most part a positive-mood band, and it will take extremes in positive social mood—like the ones that supported them in the 1960s and 1990s—to make revivals of their popularity possible.

Postscript: The Beach Boys on a Similar Roll

On September 30, 2016, David Kirby of *The Wall Street Journal* reviewed two new books by individual Beach Boys. Kirby opined, "Given the longevity of the Beach Boys, *a chart of their career would resemble a graph of the Dow Jones Industrial Average* over several turbulent decades."[39] It certainly would. The Beach Boys started recording in 1961, a year before the Beatles did. Their stature peaked in 1966, the year of the end (in February) of wave III in the stock market (see Figure 1). That year they won the NME poll and released their most acclaimed album and single. Two manifestations of that year's negative mood, however (see Figure 5), were that the their album *Pet Sounds* comprised mostly melancholy songs and that in March 1967 'Good Vibrations' was denied a Grammy award for best rock song of 1966 in favor of 'Winchester Cathedral', a novelty throwback performed by session musicians. Beach Boy Mike Love was astute enough to recognize, "So much of the Beach Boys' early success was tied to the optimism of the era...."[40;119] The band's last single to chart in that era was issued in 1969, a year before the Beatles' last hit of the same era. Love related, "In March of 1970, I finally reached my own breaking point." [40;228] The following month Paul publicly confirmed the breakup of the Beatles. The month after that, the stock market bottomed. Overall, the Beach Boys' career reached a pinnacle in 1966, and they hit bottom in 1982, matching the years of the major turns in the Dow/PPI (see Figure 10).

Confirming the socionomic insight conveyed in Figures 1 and 4 of this chapter, Mike Love of the Beach Boys wrote, "Industry-wide, there was a pre- and post-psychedelic era—from 'I Want to Hold Your Hand' to 'Lucy in the Sky with Diamonds'. The years 1965 and '66 were more or less the dividing line, with the Beatles the most conspicuous agents of that transition. ...The year 1965 also marked a pivot in what was happening in the country."[40;158,119] The title and theme of Steve Tumer's *Beatles '66—The Revolutionary Year* (2016) likewise capture the sea change in the Beatles' music and activities illustrated graphically in Figures 1 and 4.

REFERENCES

[1] *The Beatles American Tour 1964*. DVD, "Interview at Kennedy Airport," Sept. 21, 1964, Disc 2, 1:38.

[2] *The Beatles Anthology*. (1995/2002). DVD set.

[3] *The Beatles—Beatles '63*. (2008). DVD, rear panel.

[4] Bicknell, Alf and Garry Marsh. (1989). *Baby, You Can Drive My Car*. Number 9 Books. a. 10/24/64; b. 10/27/64; c. 8/31/65; d. 3/4/66; e. 3/25/66; f. 6/3/66; g. 8/26/68

[5] Bell, Madeline. (2010). "Dusty Springfield—Once Upon a Time 1964-1969," *British Invasion*. DVD, Interview. Reelin' in the Years Productions.

[6] Bramwell, Tony (2005) *Magical Mystery Tours*. Thomas Dunne, New York.

[8] Clark, Cindy. (June 22, 2010). "Troll dolls are making a comeback." USA Today, p. D1.

[9] Coleman, Ray. (1985). *Lennon*. New York: McGraw-Hill.

[10] Everett, Walter. (2001). *The Beatles as Musicians: The Quarry Men through 'Rubber Soul'*. New York: Oxford University Press.

[11] Giuliano, Geoffrey. (1986). *The Beatles: A Celebration*. New York: St. Martin's Press. a. quoting Neil Innes, p. 221

[12] Gould, Jonathan. (2007). *Can't Buy Me Love: The Beatles, Britain, and America*. New York: Harmony Books.

[13] Hertsgaard, Mark. (1995). *A Day in the Life: The Music and Artistry of the Beatles*. New York: Delacorte Press.   a. quoting Christgau and Piccarella, p. 374

[14] Howlett, H. Kevin and Mike Heatley. (2009). "Historical Notes," *The Beatles Stereo Box Set*. a. *Rubber Soul* CD booklet, p. 7; b. *Revolver* CD booklet, p. 8; c. *White Album* CD booklet, p. 22

[17] Kessler, Jude. (2008). *Shoulda Been There*. Dothan, Ala: On the Rock Books, p. 622.

[18] Leach, Sam. (1999) *The Birth of the Beatles*. Pharaoh Press, Gwynedd.

[19] Leach, Sam. "Sam Leach," Interview, YouTube, Internet.

[20] Lewisohn, Mark. (2009). Notes for *Sgt. Pepper* booklet, *The Beatles Stereo Box Set*, p. 4.

[21] Lewisohn, Mark. (2000) *The Complete Beatles Chronicle*. Hamly, p. 310.

[22] MacDonald, Ian. (1994). *Revolution in the Head: The Beatles' Records and the Sixties*. New York: Henry Holt & Co.

[23] Marsden, Gerry. (2010). "Gerry & the Pacemakers—It's Gonna Be All Right 1963-1965," *British Invasion*. DVD, Interview. Reelin' in the Years Productions.

[24] Miles, Barry. (1997). *Paul McCartney: Many Years From Now*. New York: Henry Holt & Co.

[26] Reasons, Gloria Wedgeworth. (2008). "The Alamo Girls," *Elvis: Return to Tupelo*. DVD, bonus material.

[27] Source unknown.

[28] Spitz, Bob. (2005). *The Beatles: The Biography*. New York: Little Brown. (Note: Spitz's 10-page prologue is as much a tour-de-force as 'She Loves You'.)

[29] Thompson, Dave. (2010, June 4). "Breaking Up Is Hard To Do," *Goldmine*, p. 53.

[30] *TV Guide* (December 1997).

[31] Wikipedia, http://en.wikipedia.org/wiki/The_Beatles. a. "Live at the BBC" http://en.wikipedia.org/wiki/Live_at_the_BBC_(The_Beatles_album) b. "Twist and Shout" http://en.wikipedia.org/wiki/Twist_and_shout#The_Beatles.27_version c. "1 (The Beatles album)" http://en.wikipedia.org/wiki/1_(The_Beatles_album) d. "Anthology 3" http://en.wikipedia.org/wiki/Anthology_3 e. "Brian Epstein" http://en.wikipedia.org/wiki/Brian_Epstein f. "List of The Beatles' record sales" http://en.wikipedia.org/wiki/List_of_The_Beatles'_record_sales g. "Across the Universe (film)" http://en.wikipedia.org/wiki/Across_the_Universe_film

[32] Williams, Allan and William Marshall. (1975). *The Man Who Gave the Beatles Away*, New York: Ballantine Books, pp. 99-151.

[33] Clark, Cindy. (November 24, 2010). "The Beatles Enjoy a Big iTunes Debut." *USA Today*, p. D1.

[34] Caulfield, Keith, Gary Trust and Jessica Letkemann, "The Beatles' American Chart Invasion: 12 Record-Breaking Hot 100 & Billboard 200 Feats," billboard.com, February 17, 2014.

[37] Thorburn, Doug, *Drunks, Drugs and Debits*, 2000.

[38] Lewisohn, Mark, *The Beatles—All These Years: Tune In*, 2013, p. 772.

[39] Kirby, David, "New Memoirs by The Beach Boys," *The Wall Street Journal*, September 30, 2016.

[40] Love, Mike, *Good Vibrations—My Life as a Beach Boy*, Blue Rider Press, 2016.

[41] Interview with Howard Cosell, "Speaking of Everything," WABC radio, October 6, 1974.

[42] Bill Harry, "The Real John Lennon 2000" (documentary) September 2000; Director: Richard Denton

[43] Dougherty, Steve and Vistoria Balfour, "Ringo on the Rebound," *People*, August 28, 1989

[44] Sounes, Howard, *Daily Mail*, August 17, 2010.

Other Sources (not directly cited)

Epstein, Brian. (1984). *A Cellarful of Noise* (reprint ed.). Ann Arbor, MI: Pierian Press.

Howlett, Kevin. (1983). *The Beatles at the BEEB: The Story of Their Radio Career* (reprint ed.). Ann Arbor, MI: Pierian Press.

Norman, Philip. (1981). *Shout! The Beatles in Their Generation*. New York: Fireside Books.

Chapter 2

John Denver: Bear Market Hero

Robert Prechter

July 26, 2010 (EWT)

Negative social mood, as indicated by declining stock prices, brings about feelings of alienation, anger, depression and fear. This is why the 1970s and early 1980s supported morose-sounding bands such as Pink Floyd ("classic" period 1967-1979); noisy, angry-sounding bands such as Led Zeppelin (1968-1980) and Black Sabbath (heyday 1969-1977); the mellow, often melancholy musings of such performers as James Taylor (hits from 1970 to 1979), America (hits from 1972 to 1982), Barry Manilow (hits from 1974 to 1983) and Kansas (hits from 1974 to 1983); and the comforting messages of John Denver (success from 1971 to 1982). Despite their benign music and images, Wings (1971-1981) and ABBA (1973-1982) were also negative-mood performers, as was Linda Ronstadt in her "Queen of Rock" persona (major hits 1973-1982). (As first proposed in "Pop Culture and the Stock Market" (1985), women tend to become more dominant in society in negative mood periods.) Figure 1 shows these performers' times of success with respect to stock prices.

In 1993, I had the privilege of advising John Denver. He was in a slump and disappointed with an inability to rekindle his career. One of my friends was his personal assistant, and he arranged for us to meet at a hotel in Atlanta and again backstage after a concert. When I first thought about Denver's music, I assumed that its sunny, aw-shucks themes would fit a positive social mood. But an investigation of Denver's fortunes revealed precisely the opposite case. I took a day to study his history and found something interesting: He was unequivocally a hero for people suffering negative mood.

As the Beatles' career began to fracture, Denver's career began to gel. Denver had paid his dues during the first two waves (down and up) of the negative mood period of 1966-1968, first as a member of the Mitchell Trio

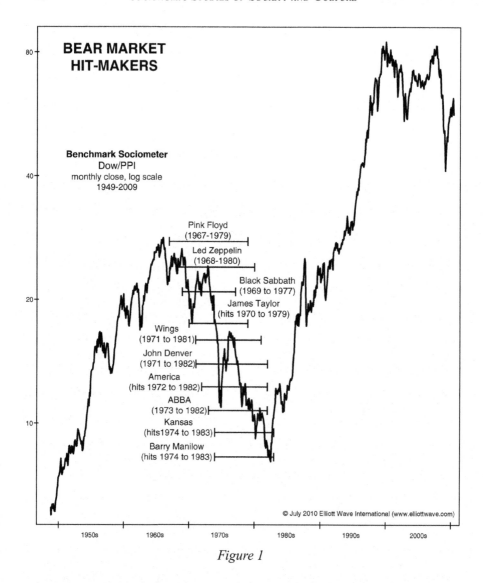

Figure 1

and then of its offshoot, Denver, Boise and Johnson. In early 1969, as the trend toward negative mood resumed in earnest, he quit the trio and began a solo career. His first album was released in October 1969, two months after the Beatles' last recording session. *Rhymes and Reasons* was only a modest success, but in December of that year, Peter, Paul and Mary took their version of his 'Leaving on a Jet Plane' to #1. Denver became a household name as a performer in 1971, when his 'Take Me Home, Country Roads' was played all spring and summer and reached #2. The popularity of his descriptions of bucolic settings in this and other songs is comparable to the popularity of earth tones among car buyers [see Chapter 29] in negative mood periods. In 1973, Denver hosted "The John Denver Show" for the BBC. His career peaked in 1974, when the stock market was crashing, inflation was raging, a recession was deepening, and the U.S. President was being hounded from office. In August, within days of Nixon's resignation, Denver set a record by selling out seven shows at the Universal Amphitheater in southern California in 24 hours. He had two #1 hits that year, both—appropriately for the social mood—wistful ballads: 'Sunshine on My Shoulders' in April and 'Annie's Song' in July, the latter song reaching #1 in Britain on October 12, 1974, the very week of the bottom in the S&P Composite index.

Just as the Beatles continued to have #1 songs for a year and a half after the stock market's second peak in 1968, Denver scored #1 hits and had other major successes for nearly a year after the bear market in nominal stock prices ended. His television special, "An Evening with John Denver," won an Emmy as the Best Musical Variety Special of the 1974-1975 season. The upbeat 'Thank God I'm a Country Boy' (recorded live at his popularity peak in August-September, 1974) captured the new trend toward positive mood, reaching #1 in April 1975. A melancholy ballad, 'I'm Sorry' (b/w 'Calypso'), reached #1 in October 1975, at the bottom of that year's stock market selloff. On October 13, 1975, the Country Music Association dubbed him Entertainer of the Year. In December 1975, with the market still depressed, his duet with Olivia Newton-John, 'Fly Away', recorded for his 1975 "Rocky Mountain Christmas" TV special, reached #13 on Billboard's chart. It was his sixth and final song to reach #1 on the Adult Contemporary chart.

On the first trading day of January, 1976, the stock market gapped upward, kicking off a ten-week, soaring advance borne of positive social mood. From that day forward, no Denver recording got higher than #29 on the charts. As usual, a general news magazine inadvertently put the tombstone on Denver's popularity: *Newsweek* on December 20, 1976 proclaimed him "the most popular pop singer in America," a year after it was no longer true.

Nevertheless, as the bear market in real stock values (as measured by the Dow/PPI, per Figure 2) continued, Denver continued to have some career successes. Six of his songs charted at the low end of the Top Forty through April 1982, four months before the end of the bear market in the Dow/PPI. In 1977, he starred in the film *Oh God* with George Burns. In 1978, an instrumental version of 'Annie's Song' reached #3 in Britain. In

February 1978 and February 1979, Denver hosted the Grammys. He made other TV appearances, including an acclaimed Christmas special with the Muppets on December 5, 1979. From 1978 to 1980, he was a member of Jimmy Carter's Presidential Commission on World and Domestic Hunger.

The negative mood eventually took a toll on Denver. In 1982, on the day of his 15th wedding anniversary, he and his wife decided to separate, and the following year they divorced.

After 1975, but especially after the upturn in the Dow/PPI in 1982, when social mood turned unequivocally toward the positive, Denver's

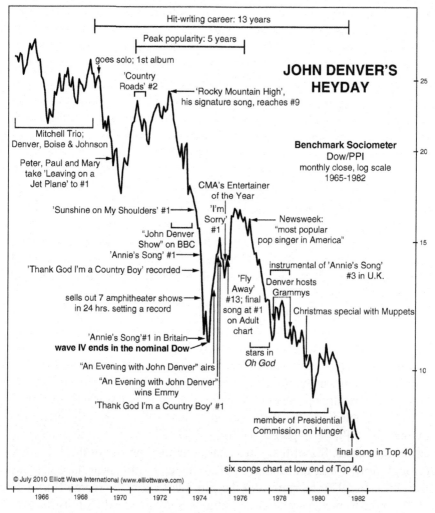

Figure 2

heartfelt musical style became passé, as record buyers no longer needed his messages of comfort and introspection. In the 1980s, upbeat pop songs came back into vogue. Denver still worked hard, but his public persona withered. Despite personal achievements and moments of triumph, he never approached his erstwhile level of popularity.

In our meeting, I told John that he would be struggling as long as the positive mood reigned but that he had an excellent chance of returning to a measure of popularity when the next trend toward negative social mood

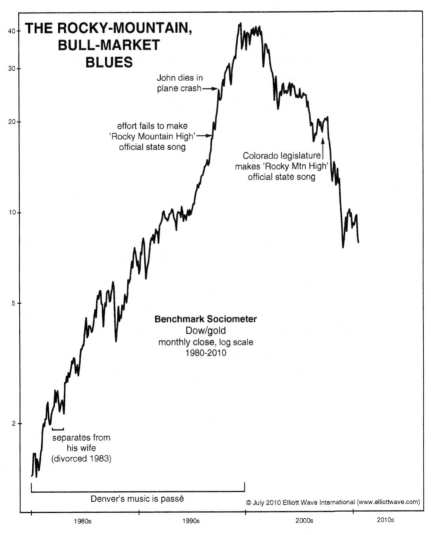

Figure 3

turned public tastes back toward his brand of music. On October 12, 1997, six months before the Value Line Composite index made its all-time high, John died when the plane he was piloting solo crashed. So, unfortunately, he was not around in 2006 when social mood—as indicated first by a reversal in real estate prices—finally turned strongly negative, staying there for three to six years depending on the measure.

In 1997, Kari Neuman tried to get Colorado to make 'Rocky Mountain High' an official state song. With a bull market rampaging toward a high, her effort failed. On March 12, 2007, after one year of slipping property prices and eight years of falling stock prices in real-money terms (per the Dow/ gold ratio, shown in Figure 3 to emphasize the hidden bear market), and one year after fellow negative-mood star Barry Manilow suddenly enjoyed a #1 album, the Colorado legislature passed a resolution making Denver's signature composition the state's second official song.

Chapter 3

Bad Times Were Good Times for Mickey Rooney

Chuck Thompson

April 25, 2014 (TS)

Actor Mickey Rooney, who died at age 93 on April 6, experienced "a seesaw of career tailspins and revivals."[1] But what's interesting to socionomists is that Rooney's most popular years, the late 1930s and early 1940s and his resurgence in the late 1970s and early 1980s, occurred in trends toward negative social mood.

In his study of the Beatles [see Chapter 1], Robert Prechter wrote, "Social mood trends have outlets of expression, and one of them is the creation of, and then the adoration and/or vilification of, public figures." Regarding negative-mood heroes such as John Denver [see Chapter 2], Prechter added,

> People who become popular representatives of negative social mood
> might be intelligent, provocative, driven, rebellious, daring, harsh,
> arrogant, melancholy, comforting [as in Rooney's case] or vulnerable.

He went on to note that stars in positive mood trends tend to be more revered, because positive mood encourages more loyalty than does negative mood. That was true of Rooney, who went from superstar to outcast when the trend in mood became positive again.

Rooney began his acting career as a toddler

Source: Classic Movie Stills

A Happy Ending Every Time: Rooney and Judy Garland in the 1940 film Andy Hardy Meets Debutante

in his parents' vaudeville act in the 1920s.[2] From 1927-1936 he appeared in a series of short films based on a comic strip character named Mickey McGuire.[3]

The Dow Jones Industrial Average completed a five-year bull market in 1937 and then began a five-year bear market (see Figure 1). The negative mood of that time was a boon to Rooney's career. In 1937, he won the lead role of Andy Hardy in the film *A Family Affair*, which spawned 15 Andy Hardy movies.[4] *USA Today's* Donna Freydkin called the series "such a smash that from 1939 to 1941, Rooney became the Tom Cruise of his time: the No. 1 box-office draw in the country."[5]

In 1939, Rooney received a special Juvenile Academy Award for his role in *Boys Town* (1938).[6] The following year he received an Academy Award nomination for "Best Actor in a Leading Role" for *Babes in Arms* (1939). In 1944, the Academy again nominated him for "Best Actor in a Leading Role" for his performance in *The Human Comedy* (1943).[7] That year, Rooney began 21 months of service in the military, entertaining more than 2 million troops as part of the "Jeep Theater," a traveling entertainment brigade that performed across Europe—usually on the front lines.[8]

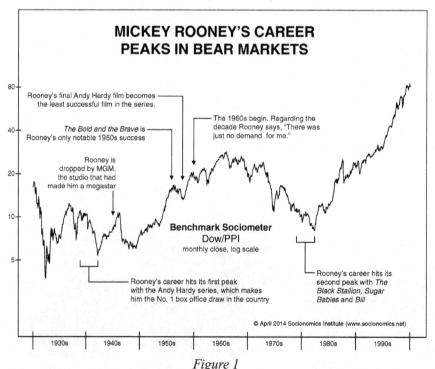

Figure 1

Rooney's "sunny spirits"[9] made him popular in tough times, much as John Denver's similarly "sunny, aw-shucks themes" were in big demand in the negative-mood period of the 1970s.

But social mood was trending positively when Rooney returned to Hollywood, and his status as an actor changed.

On the Front Lines: *Rooney entertains infrantrymen from the 44th Division at Kist, Germany, in April 1945*

In 1945, near the top of a four-year advance in stock prices, MGM, the studio that had turned him into a megastar, dropped him.

As Denver later did, Rooney worked hard but still watched his public persona wither. *Variety's* Carmel Dagan described the difficulties faced by the actor:

> Rooney made nightclub appearances as he rebuilt his career. His freelance movie assignments, such as *Quicksand* [1950], sank without a trace. Only *The Bold and the Brave* [1956], a WWII drama that brought him a third Oscar nomination, met with any success. The final Andy Hardy drama, 1958's *Andy Hardy Comes Home*, found him as a successful lawyer and a new head of the family. It was the final and least successful film in the series.[10]

The 1960s brought further challenges for Rooney. Looking back on those days in a 1988 interview with *The London Times*, he said, "the work was very sparse indeed: there was just no demand for me."[11]

After many years of minor parts and television roles, Rooney's career soared again during another negative mood trend: the late 1970s and early 1980s. In 1980, he received an Academy Award nomination for "Best Actor in a Supporting Role" for *The Black Stallion* (1979), in which he played a horse trainer. His role in the 1979 Broadway spectacle *Sugar*

Back in the Limelight: *Rooney with Kelly Reno in the 1979 film The Black Stallion*

Babies earned him a Tony nomination. In an interview that year, Rooney said, "I was a very famous has-been until this show. Now, it's almost like the resurrection of a career."[12]

Sugar Babies ran for almost three years, and during that period Rooney received an Emmy award for his role in the 1981 television movie *Bill*, about a mentally disabled man trying to live independently.[13] In 1983, he received an honorary Academy Award recognizing his versatility in a variety of film performances.

Turan notes that Rooney was a survivor.[14] Even in dry times he found some work. "I always say, 'Don't retire—inspire,'" said Rooney in 2008.[15] The following year he explained, "I keep going because if you stop, you stop."[16]

Fans will remember Rooney's wit, feistiness, and ability to get up after being repeatedly knocked down. The achievements by which he will be remembered most, however, are those that occurred in the late 1930s to early 1940s and again in the late 1970s to early 1980s—periods that were shaped by negative social mood.

NOTES AND REFERENCES

[1] McCartney, A. (2014, April 7). Iconic Hollywood Actor Mickey Rooney Dies at 93. *San Francisco Chronicle*.

[2] *Ibid.*

[3] Turan, K. (2014, April 7). Mickey Rooney, with Gumption and Grit, Put on a Show. *Los Angeles Times*.

[4] Bowles, S. (2014, April 7). Mickey Rooney's Five Top Performances. *USA Today*.

[5] Freydkin, D. (2014, April 7). Reports: Hollywood Legend Mickey Rooney Dies. WLTX.com.

[6] Arkin, D., & Blankstein, A. (2014, April 7). Hollywood Icon Mickey Rooney Dead at 93. *Today*.

[7] Mickey Rooney awards. IMDb.

[8] Hollywood Legend, USO Tour Vet Mickey Rooney Dies at 93. (2014, April 7). *On Patrol*.

[9] Guzman, R. (2014, April 7). Mickey Rooney Dead: Legendary Actor Known for Andy Hardy, 'The Black Stallion' and 'Bill'. *Newsday*.

[10] Dagan, C. (2014, April 6). Mickey Rooney, Legendary Actor, Dies at 93. *Variety*.

[11,12] See endnote 5.

[13] Duke, A., & Leopold, T. (2014, April 7). Legendary Actor Mickey Rooney Dies at 93. CNN.

[14] See endnote 2.

[15] See endnote 6.

[16] See endnote 13.

Chapter 4

Sinatra Swings to the
Rhythm of Social Mood

Peter Kendall
December 16, 2011 (EWT)

Elliott Wave International generally covers markets and cultural phenomena that express manifestations of social mood. *Elliott Wave Principle* (p. 156) proposed that "there is a natural psychodynamic in humans that generates form in social behavior" and added that it is "most important [to] understand that the form we describe is primarily social, not individual." Social units of both large and small size can reflect the influence of social mood.

It is our belief—developed over years of observing famous people's triumphs and tribulations—that social mood influences the fortunes of public personas quite immediately and over long periods of time. When the trend changes, "stars" in distinct cultural galaxies burn out, and new ones, uniquely suited to the emerging mood, burst onto the scene. Behind the rise and fall of cultural heroes we find the unmistakable influence of social mood as reflected in our benchmark sociometer, the stock market. In July and August 2010, *The Elliott Wave Theorist* offered a detailed profile of social mood expressing itself through swings in the public's attitudes toward the Beatles. This report will look at another musical star whose experiences reflected social mood trends, especially in the period from 1942 to 1974.

To begin, we return to the "Major Pop Music Crazes" chart, which initially appeared in the April 1991 issue of *The Elliott Wave Theorist* and then in *The Wave Principle of Human Social Behavior* (1999). Figure 1 illustrates the socionomic proposal that people express positive social mood by simultaneously creating pop-music icons and vigorous uptrends in the stock market. As Prechter wrote,

Figure 1

Young people are particularly prone to release ecstatic emotion by showering pop music performers with adoration. Therefore, one manifestation of major-degree ebullience is the excited and passionate idolization of pop musicians or singers by teenagers.

Five major instances of crowd euphoria—over Benny Goodman through the stock market peak of 1937, Frank Sinatra from 1942 to 1946, Elvis Presley in the mid-to-late-1950s, the Beatles in the 1960s and Michael Jackson from 1983 to 1987—continue to mark *the* musical frenzies of the great bull market up to that time. Our chart is essentially unchanged from its 1999 iteration although we have adjusted the wave labels to current opinion and widened the bracket for Benny Goodman to reflect the following entry for August 1935 from the *Chronicle of the 20th Century*: "Benny Goodman opens at Palomar Ballroom." The bracket for Sinatra was also extended slightly to include his debut as a solo act at the Paramount Theater on Times Square in December 1942.

The level of audience elation at each separate outbreak in popularity is not easily quantifiable, but the breadth, intensity and duration of participants' shared adulation appears unique within the 20th century to these five episodes. The veracity of this list is substantiated by a quote from Quincy Jones, who produced Jackson's *Thriller* album as Jackson's public image and the last great bull market of the 20th century lifted off in 1982. While producing Sinatra's last solo album, *L.A. Is My Lady*, in 1984, Jones introduced the two musical superstars to each other and made the following observation:

> It was astounding to see the two of them together because the real landmarks and pop phenomenon start with Sinatra and then Elvis Presley in the Fifties and the Beatles in the Sixties, the Seventies was skipped, and in the Eighties it was Michael. To see the beginning and the end gave me goose bumps.

Jones' observation, "the Seventies was skipped," fits socionomic theory to a T: That decade featured no musical hero of comparable stature because social mood was trending toward the negative. Jones excluded Goodman, but Goodman's swing music clearly set the stage for future fan expression. In fact, he did so on the very same stage as Sinatra, just six days from the peak of wave I on March 10, 1937. This article from the *Chronicle of the 20th Century* reveals the uncanny similarity between the hysteria Goodman orchestrated and the one that Sinatra would ignite six years later:

Goodman Swings as Teenagers Scream
March 4, 1937. The Benny Goodman Band is taking the country by storm.

If you were at the Paramount Theater in New York yesterday, you would know why. The crowned "King of Swing" not only had them tapping their feet and snapping their fingers, but dancing with wild abandon in the aisles.

It promised to be something special as early as 7 a.m., when the line outside stretched halfway around the block. As the day wore on, extra cops were called to contain the frenzied crowd.

The morning show began calmly enough with Goodman's theme song, 'Let's Dance'. By the time several more tunes were heard, pandemonium had broken loose with the kids stompin' in the aisles.

In 1984, Robert Prechter's "Popular Culture and the Stock Market" (reprinted in *Pioneering Studies in Socionomics*, 2003) first linked musical heroes to bull markets in stocks and therefore to positive trends in social mood. Since then, further research has revealed the depth of the connection as well as the tendency for the adoration of stars to rise and fall with trends in social mood for the duration of their lives and beyond. This is certainly true for Frank Sinatra. He got his first big break near the peak in stocks of 1937, at the front end of the multi-decade trend toward positive social mood, and he performed throughout it until his death in 1998. His longevity helped solidify his standing at the top of the pantheon of popular entertainers. *The New York Times'* obituary stated,

> Widely held to be the greatest singer in American pop history and one of the most successful entertainers of the 20th century, Sinatra was also the first modern pop superstar. He defined that role in the early 1940s when his first solo appearances provoked the kind of mass pandemonium that later greeted Elvis Presley and the Beatles.

Yet it was hardly a one-way ride for Sinatra. His fortunes vacillated, in nearly perfect time, with the trends in social mood as reflected by stock prices. We will now review that history.

Sinatra Flunks Out, Then Rallies in His First Wave Higher

According to Sinatra's own recollection in an early 1970s *Life* magazine article, he made his singing debut in the "late 1920s." As the Roaring Twenties culminated, Sinatra closed out the great bull market with a rendition of 'Am I Blue' at an Elizabeth, New Jersey hotel.[1] For both Sinatra and the stock market, it was downhill from there. In 1931, as the Dow Jones Industrial Average plunged, the future pride of Hoboken dropped out of high school and failed in a succession of jobs. In late 1932 or early 1933, as the Dow tested the July 1932 low that served as the launching pad for wave (V), Sinatra left Hoboken for the Big Apple where he tried to make a name for himself on Tin Pan Alley. "He crossed the river and failed miserably," says biographer James Kaplan in *Frank: The Voice*.

Sinatra possessed key traits that probably made him ideal for receiving and transmitting the positive mood behind a multi-decade bull market. In addition to being "gigantically ambitious" and musically gifted, Sinatra was a first-rate mimic, actively adapting his style and career to popular performers and other successful role models. In 1933, the most popular singer was Bing Crosby. According to Earl Wilson in *Sinatra: An Unauthorized Biography*, Sinatra witnessed Crosby's act that year (his daughter Nancy says the encounter occurred in 1935) and decided "he was going to be the next Crosby." In 1935, as the Dow plowed higher, he landed a weekly radio gig on a Jersey City radio station. In September 1935, Sinatra debuted with the Hoboken Four on a radio program called the *Major Bowes Original Amateur Hour*. Their performance went well enough to earn the group a spot in Bowes' touring company. In late 1936, near the end of wave I, Sinatra secured a 15-minute radio spot on WNEW in New York, and as social mood approached a positive extreme he "worked his way up to as many as 18 spots a week."

As they would in the wake of later stock market peaks, Sinatra's fortunes pushed higher after the March 1937 top. His unpaid radio

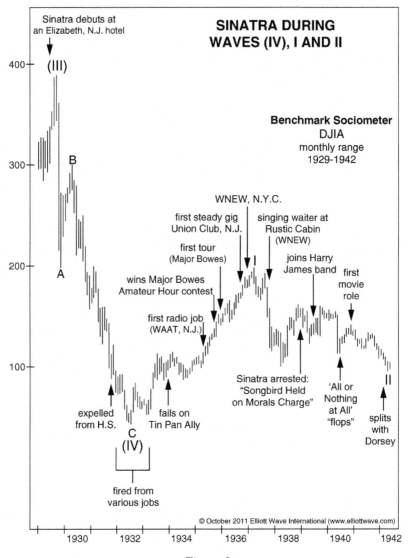

Figure 2

performances turned into a steady job as a singing waiter at a New Jersey nightclub, the Rustic Cabin.[2] But things turned down decisively for him as negative social mood led to a stock market crash in the second half of the year. Following the Dow's retreat back below 100 in 1938, Sinatra's domineering mother, Dolly, was arrested for performing abortions in the first of four Sinatra-family arrests over the next 20 months. "Strikingly, her arrests neatly bracketed Frank Sinatra's own arrests, in November and December 1938, for the then-criminal offenses (in the first case) of seduction and (in the second) adultery," wrote Kaplan. "Also remarkable is that all these Sinatra arrests would not have occurred today." A headline from the *Jersey Observer* of December 23, 1938 hints that Sinatra's burgeoning status as a musical celebrity factored into his arrest three days earlier:

Songbird Held on Morals Charge

In response to these events, in 1939 Sinatra's mother forced him into a marriage he did not want. Kaplan reported, "He felt stalled that spring," as the stock market stalled as well. "He had married in haste; he wasn't cut out for it. His career was going nowhere." When breakthrough opportunities presented themselves, The Voice literally lost his voice in impromptu auditions for Tommy Dorsey and Cole Porter.[3] But soon Sinatra's talent started to shine through, and he became known as he honed his craft. Coincident with a powerful countertrend rally in stocks in June 1939, Sinatra took a big step toward fame when he joined band leader Harry James and his Music Makers. But the time was not yet ripe, and even Sinatra could not carry the James band higher. The band had "a hard time making a go of it," reported Kaplan. Fronting the Music Makers, Sinatra recorded his first record, 'All or Nothing At All'. It would later become a signature song, but it failed to catch fire at the time. When it came out in June 1940, near the bottom of a one-month stock market crash and within 20 points of the Dow's upcoming low of 92.60 in April 1942, the song sold just 8,000 copies. But, upon its re-issue in the midst of the Sinatra-mania of 1943, it became a huge hit, selling a million copies and hitting No. 2 on the pop charts. "The world would fall at both men's feet in a few years," says Kaplan. "But not everyone was thrilled at first; both Sinatra and Harry James seemed ahead of their time."

Sinatra and Stocks Lift Off

In one of the few career divergences from the stock market's trend yet coincident with a rally in the second half of 1940, Sinatra joined Jimmy Dorsey's band and recorded his first hit song. In July 1940, 'I'll Never Smile Again' reached No. 1 and stayed there for 12 weeks, "turning Frank

Sinatra into a national star." In November 1940, he scored his first major movie role, singing three songs in an MGM musical, *Ship Ahoy*. In 1941, a down year for the Dow, Sinatra earned *DownBeat*'s male vocalist of the year award. From Dorsey, Sinatra learned by "example how to be a real star" and acquired a work ethic that would serve him well in later years.

Early on, Sinatra demonstrated a gift for timing, on stage as well as off. Sensing that the big band era was giving way to a new crooner phase, Sinatra determined that he would be the first member of the band to go solo. But the negative mood of the bear market bottom took its toll on his career, as his plan set him back considerably, both in financial and personal terms. As his break with Dorsey and the Dow's wave II low approached, Sinatra was a "wreck"; he was "almost tubercular," said companion Nick Sevano. "He was seeing all kinds of doctors.... He started talking a lot about death and dying. 'I get the feeling that I'm going to die soon,' he'd say." Sinatra's "disentanglement from one his most powerful relationships, his deep emotional and artistic bond with Dorsey, is complex and bewildering," wrote Kaplan. But as Kaplan also noted, "the story of Frank Sinatra's life is one of continual shedding of artistic identities." In February 1942, two months prior to the stock market's low, Sinatra finally asked to be let out of his contract.

Sinatra-Mania Begins Eight Months into the Bull Market

It took Sinatra most of 1942 to sever ties with Dorsey. On December 31, 1942, he went solo. Jack Benny introduced Sinatra at the Paramount Theater and later recalled, "I said, 'Here is Frank Sinatra.' I thought the god damn building was going to cave in. I never heard such a commotion with people running down to the stage, screaming and nearly knocking me off the ramp." A *Herald Tribune* critic wrote, "The spontaneous reaction corresponds to no common understanding relating to tradition or technique of performance, nor yet to the meaning of the sung text." Sinatra himself admitted to being "very confused. I had never seen it.... Nobody had ever heard that kind of reaction before." "Not since the days of Rudolph Valentino [during the bull market of the 1920s] has American womanhood made such unabashed love to an entertainer," *Time* magazine marveled.

Within a matter of days, Sinatra was on his way to superstardom. Kaplan called it "one of those hinges in time that come along periodically, a moment when everything simply *vaults forward*." The stock market, reflecting social mood, was doing precisely the same thing. The pandemonium lasted for the duration of the 1942-1946 bull market. As bobby-soxed teenage girls screamed, swooned and fainted, the rest of the population looked on with a mix of curiosity, bafflement and disapproval. The youthful, grassroots ecstasy was reflected in the stock market, where, as R.N. Elliott noted, young "speculators with more money than experience favored low-priced stocks instead of seasoned issues,"[4] driving them upward as much as 13,000%. By the end of 1943, Sinatra's own wave broadened as he "ascended from mere teen idol to bona fide American superstar," taking his first major motion picture role and gaining "unprecedented power and influence." In his first movie, he played himself in the appropriately titled *Higher and Higher*.

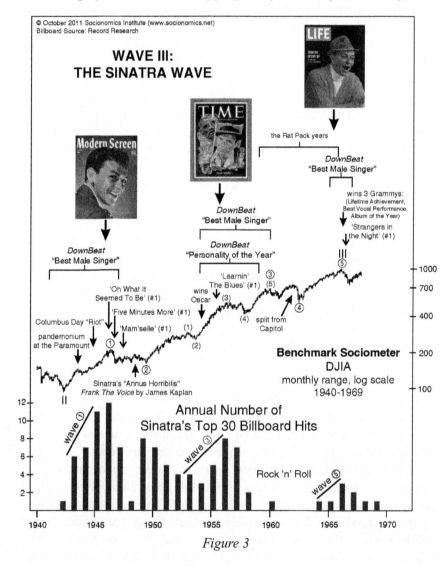

Figure 3

Third waves are generally the strongest within a five-wave sequence, and the sustained strength of the middle phase of the positive mood trend was evident in events surrounding his return to the Paramount Theatre in October, 1944: "The line began forming before dawn and soon swelled to approximately 20,000 fans, packed six abreast. Many members of the audience for the first show wouldn't leave, and the frustrated crowd outside went berserk in what became known as the Columbus Day Riot. Two hundred police, 421 police reserves, 20 radio cars and 2 emergency trucks were called in to control the rampaging, mostly teenage, girls."[5] As with most fifth waves, the audience's energy level dissipated somewhat near the stock market peak of 1946, but Sinatra always saved a big finish for the final high and its immediate aftermath: He had two No. 1 hits in 1946 and one in 1947.

"Mysterious" Setbacks During the 1946-1949 Bear Market

Some biographers have dated Sinatra's initial fall from public grace to the late 1940s, but a December 1948 *Modern Television & Radio* article, "Is Sinatra Finished?" reported that "Frank's troubles all started sometime in 1946," which happens to be the very year the stock market reversed direction from up to down. It was then that he began to argue with hecklers during his nightclub act. In early December, 1946, he "issued an edict barring fans under 21 from his broadcasts. The public outcry was noisier than anything he had to endure in the studio." Sinatra reversed the ban, but Kaplan says, "He seemed whipsawed at the end of that year," just as investors were. In April 1947, Sinatra was arrested for punching newspaper columnist Lee Mortimer. After the Mortimer incident, Sinatra's career came off the tracks: "Mysteriously, Frank's career went into a slow decline that quickened and became a historic nosedive for the hero of the great American success story. Everybody went after his throat, and his money." But the cause is not mysterious to socionomists; his public image was reflecting the trend toward negative social mood of 1946-1949.

Sinatra's image sank even deeper when he was associated "with pro-Soviet causes" and photographed in Cuba shaking hands with mobsters including Lucky Luciano, "considered the father of modern organized crime in America." For the first time since 1942, his annual income fell below $1 million. At a time when print media ruled, the largest chain of newspapers, the Hearst syndicate, was "snapping at his heels." On September 26, 1947, Westbrook Pegler, a Pulitzer-Prize-winning Hearst columnist, made the following comparison: "There is a weird light playing around Sinatra. Hitler affected many Germans much the same way and madness has been rife in the world." Even the U.S. government was after him, for unpaid taxes.

Sinatra's record sales also tanked. "He was putting more in and getting less out," said Kaplan. "America's tastes had simply changed." The last full year of the bear market, 1948, also marked the low in terms of Sinatra's Top 30 hits (see Figure 3). In May 1949, he lost his Lucky Strike radio show. In June, the month of the end of a 20-year bear market in the Dow/PPI, his *Frankly Sentimental* album debuted and "completely failed to chart, a bad first." Sinatra himself would later refer to this era as "The Dark Ages." Some writers date the end of this period to 1953, but its actual end coincided precisely with the nadir in stock prices. Another biography correctly called 1949 Sinatra's "rock bottom" year: "He was fired from his radio show. Soon, his personal life was falling apart as fast as his career. He and [his first wife] Nancy were splitting. His affair with Ava Gardner had become an open scandal. Columbia Records wanted him out." This was also the all-time, rock-bottom year for the stock market's price/earnings ratio, indicating record pessimism among investors. In 1950, Columbia succeeded in severing ties with Sinatra, and even his own agent, MCA, dumped him. According to one critic, "He was a has-been at 34."[6]

Nevertheless, as early as September 1949, a few months after stocks lifted off again, there were signs of revival after he returned to the radio with his own show. In December 1949, he "surprised himself and his agents by breaking records at the State Theater in Hartford." In 1950, Sinatra scored a new TV show (although it lasted less than a year). Through 1952, his film career enjoyed modest though unspectacular success, record sales improved, and his live performances remained popular.

"Going to Extremes with Impossible Schemes"

Influences barring Sinatra's climb back to the top abated in early 1953, when he signed with Capitol Records and landed the role of Maggio in *From Here to Eternity*. "The balance had shifted," wrote Gay Talese in a famous 1966 profile for *Esquire*. "Somewhere during this period Sinatra seemed to change from the kid singer, the boy actor in the sailor suit, to a man. Some flashes of his old talent were coming through—in his recording of *The Birth of the Blues*, in his Riviera nightclub appearance that jazz critics enthusiastically praised. There

was a trend now toward L.P.s. Sinatra's concert style would have capitalized on this with or without an Oscar." As the breaks finally started to roll his way again, the Dow approached 300 for the first time since 1930.

Still, 1953—which was also the final year for a lagging negative social action known as the Korean War—was a difficult year for Sinatra. His marriage to Ava Gardner ended, and chart hits did not come easily. Alan Livingston, who signed him to Capitol, said Sinatra's decline seemed to tame his tempestuous, superstar persona. "He was meek, a pussycat, humble. He had been through terrible times. He was broke. He was in debt. I was told he had tried to kill himself on occasion. He was at the lowest ebb of his life. Everybody knew it." Teaming with arranger Nelson Riddle, Sinatra produced a "gloriously exuberant" song 'I've Got the World on a String', but, Kaplan observed, "It was not a great year for Sinatra sales. The song hit No. 14, but stayed there for just two weeks." Sinatra would figuratively and almost literally die before breaking out again in 1954. After a failed suicide attempt in November 1953,[7] Sinatra was nominated for an Academy Award, now known as an Oscar. It was Maggio's death scene in *From Here to Eternity* that "got them," writes Kaplan. In the recording studio, Sinatra was suddenly in top form.

> A paean to rebirth, "Young at Heart" [was] the ideal soundtrack to Frank Sinatra's matchless comeback. Everything about this recording was perfect. New high fidelity recording tape and microphones brilliantly brought out Sinatra's diction, phrasing and pitch perfect tone. He truly had returned from the dead. But as would be the case with the movie, the real fruits of the recording would be delayed until the new year.

He won that Oscar in April 1954. At the end of the year, the Dow finally surpassed its September 1929 peak, and Sinatra's popularity likewise rose to one new all-time high after another. "All at once, he was hot as a pistol," said Kaplan. "There were nightclub dates, TV spots, and all kinds of movie offers." *Time* magazine placed him on its cover in August 1955, and he appeared on Edward R. Murrow's top-rated, celebrity interview show, *Person to Person*, in September 1956. "Getting on the cover of *Time* was an even higher pinnacle" than the Oscar, remarked Sinatra's valet George Jacobs in his book, *Mr. S.: My Life with Frank Sinatra*. "That *Time* cover combined with his being featured on the prestigious Edward R. Murrow television show *Person to Person*, was the Good Housekeeping seal of approval in American life in 1956." According to Jacobs, the recognition amounted to a "figurative talisman" that converted "naysayers into idolators." Jacobs added, "In the highest echelon of American life, Frank Sinatra was now a made man."

The quality of Sinatra's recordings rose to a new level of sophistication. "The band was hipper. The songs were better. Sinatra was astonishing," wrote Kaplan. "The voice was as magnificent as ever, but now he showed a rhythmic ease, a sense of play, that he hadn't shown since 1946. He'd been loose in 1946 and he was loose now, but with a new component added: maturity." This change fit perfectly with the stock market's wave pattern. *Elliott Wave Principle* (p. 80) describes third waves as "wonders to behold. They are strong and broad, and the trend at this point is unmistakable. Such points invariably produce breakouts, creating large gains in the market, depending on the degree of the wave." The stock market was then in a wave (3) of ③ of III, a third wave at three degrees of trend. Sinatra correspondingly moved into the most productive period of his life. According to another biography, it was precisely in the last 12 years of wave III that Sinatra's status as an entertainer carried to the level of "an American legend." In *Frank Sinatra*, Chris Rojek pinpointed this span of time:

> Between 1953 and 1965, Sinatra left behind all canards and innuendoes that he was a mere flash in the pan or wartime wonder. In these 12 years, he established himself as an enduring legend in 20th Century American popular culture. The span left most of his fellow stars of the day nonplussed. The auteur albums released in the Capital years (1953-1961), notably 'In the Wee Small Hours' (1955), 'Where are You?' (1957) and 'Only the Lonely' (1958), reconceptualized the long-playing record and set new standards in the creation of mood music. It was in the late 1950s and early 1960s that he engraved himself indelibly upon the public mind as the greatest living exponent of his art.

Sinatra broadened his star power by becoming a major force in motion pictures. His "remarkably industrious output" from 1955 to 1965 included 18 full-length feature films and 32 record albums. The string of successes secured his financial independence for the first time in his career; it also brought something rare among musical entertainers: political power. In early 1960, as wave ③ peaked in the Dow, Sinatra hosted the famous "Summit at the Sands," in which "an unimaginable pantheon of stars" turned out to take in Sinatra and his Rat Pack at a three-week series of shows at the Sands Hotel. The show turned into a campaign event on February 7, when presidential candidate John F. Kennedy showed up. Throughout 1960, Sinatra actively campaigned for the senator.[8] A special version of Sinatra's

'High Hopes' became the campaign theme song ("1960's the year for his high hopes/Come on and vote for Kennedy"). He also performed at the Democratic national convention and organized Kennedy's inaugural ball.

Sinatra remained a key figure in the Camelot story until March 1962, shortly after the stock market started plunging. The president's brother Robert unceremoniously cut all ties between Sinatra and JFK shortly after F.B.I. director J. Edgar Hoover discovered that Sinatra, JFK and mobster Sam Giancana shared the same girlfriend, Judith Campbell. In response, Sinatra famously took a sledge hammer to a helipad that had recently been installed to receive the president at his Palm Springs home.

The "Chairman of the Board" Phase

The "Top 30 Hits" bars at the bottom of Figure 3 show a clear ebb in Sinatra's popular-music appeal in 1959-1963 as the stock market underwent a corrective phase, but he continued to succeed as the consummate businessman/entertainer. He started a new record label, Reprise Records, in 1961. From its inception, Reprise reflected the waves of social mood with such precision that one observer with no knowledge of the Wave Principle seemed to recognize the socionomic dynamics behind its emergence. The following quote is from music critic Noel Murray:

> Sinatra's career in the '60s—and the fate of Reprise Records—would become a case study in how a savvy entertainer and businessmen can both coast and crash on waves he doesn't fully comprehend. Sinatra's spirits are bright on *Ring-A-Ding-Ding!*—almost aggressively so. He banished the ballads and served up the swing, almost exclusively, with the zip and optimism that people often associate with the early days of the Kennedy administration. Sinatra even revived a novelty number from his '40s act, 'The Coffee Song', about how there's so much coffee in Brazil that the natives don't drink anything else. The song is an indicator of how loose and ready to entertain he was feeling as this new adventure began. Like nearly everything else Sinatra was involved with circa 1961, *Ring-A-Ding-Ding!* was an unqualified success.

But the B-wave rise of 1960-1961 was part of a corrective pattern in the stock market, and tension with Capitol Records prompted Sinatra to split from the label. In a chapter called "Lonely Millionaire," *Sinatra: The Life* authors Anthony Summer and Robyn Swan described the negative side of Sinatra's separation from Capitol. The fourth-wave trend toward negative social mood fueled Sinatra's animus toward Capitol, but it cleared the way for further gains in wave five:

Though Capitol had been his label through the glory years of his recording career, the break had become inevitable.[10] He had established Reprise Records. He pronounced the word, however, not as "represe" but as in "reprisal." Some dubbed the new company Revenge Records. The aspiration was to bring Frank and the artists he contracted more creative freedom and more money. He saw his future "not so much as an entertainer but as a high level executive.... I've been getting fascinated with finances."

Sinatra's last recording for Capitol, *Point of No Return*, came out in March 1962, as wave (C) of ④ led stock prices into a crash while Kennedy confronted the steel companies in the U.S. and then the Russians in Cuba. Sinatra had residual trouble through much of 1963. He went hitless, and the Nevada Gaming Control Board revoked his gaming license for allowing an "outlawed person," mobster Sam Giancana, into the Cal-Nev Casino, of which Sinatra was part owner. In August 1963, a business deal finally put Sinatra back on track for one last rise to the pinnacle of popularity. With the sale of two-thirds of Reprise to Warner Brothers at "a time when everything seemed to be going wrong for him," Sinatra's fortunes reversed course. The deal was actually a "rescue-takeover" by Warner, but somehow Sinatra came out on top. His title of "special assistant" to Jack Warner was "a prestigious title in a mighty empire." Newspapers swirled with word of an eventual Sinatra move into the top spot at Warner Brothers. The expectation was so strong that Jack Warner issued a press release denying that Sinatra was taking over: "The association has led to a certain amount of speculation that I am considering Mr. Sinatra as my successor—or that Mr. Sinatra desires to be my successor. There is no evidence or reason for such speculation." The deal coincided with the first new all-time highs for the Dow since 1961 and renewed success for Sinatra:

By 1965, Frank was presiding over Reprise Records; two movie companies, Artanis—"Sinatra" spelled backward—Productions and Park Lake Enterprises; CalJet Airway, an airplane charter business; and Titanium Metal Forming, which made parts for aircraft and missiles. Frank's enterprises employed seventy-five people full-time.[11]

It was also in this phase that Sinatra began actively polishing his public image by lavishing gifts on charities and doing benefits, which began with the ten-country "World Tour for Children" in 1962.[12] By 1965, the last full year of positive social mood as wave III approached its peak, Sinatra was bigger than ever. "He was on top of the world, again,"[13] as was the stock market. The vibe around Sinatra was so positive that the press fawned over him with long articles in *Life*, *Look* and *Newsweek*, an 89-page "tribute" in *Billboard* and a highly rated November 17 CBS News documentary titled

Sinatra: An American Original. After following Sinatra around for six months, the CBS crew that would go on to become the core of the hard-hitting *60 Minutes* team offered a "highly flattering"[14] portrait. At one point, the documentary shows Sinatra recording 'It Was a Very Good Year' with the voice of Walter Cronkite interjecting, "When he sings, he makes it sound as if it all happened to him. It probably did all happen to him." The feature also includes a series of clips of the last recorded performance of the Rat Pack at a St. Louis benefit concert (pictured below).

Rat Pack benefit for Dismas House, May 1965, St. Louis

The Rat Pack, Inclusion and the Fading Strength of a Fifth Wave

Coalescing in the late 1950s and enjoying a brilliant, though fading, popular appeal through September 1965, the Rat Pack emerged and reached maximum glamour at the ends of two waves of positive social mood (see Figure 4). The Rat Pack debuted in January 1959 when Dean Martin joined Sinatra on stage at the Sands in Las Vegas. The group quickly grew to include comedian Joey Bishop, song and dance man Sammy Davis Jr. and actor Peter Lawford, John F. Kennedy's brother in law. As with the Beatles, one of their common bonds was addiction, especially to alcohol but also to other drugs. Bishop, the only non-addict in the group, later confessed that he was never treated as a "full-fledged member."[15] (On the plus side, he lived the longest.) The Rat Pack hit its peak of cultural influence a few days after the end of wave ③, at the famous "Summit at the Sands" in February 1960:

> The Rat Pack Summit capitalized on the buzz around the city and around the Sands, but it also helped create and spread it. It was the hottest ticket Las Vegas had ever seen, and probably the hottest ever.
> —*Rat Pack Confidential*, 1998

The night club act broadened into a movie franchise, as the group filmed the first and most successful Rat Pack movie, *Oceans 11*, during the Summit. This is the month in which presidential candidate John F. Kennedy appeared at one of their shows, after which the entire Pack went on to figure prominently in the campaign. "The association between politician and entertainers was so close that they were nicknamed the Jack Pack."

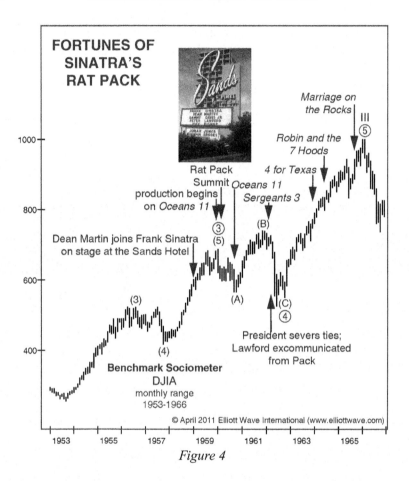

FORTUNES OF
SINATRA'S
RAT PACK

Marriage on
the Rocks

III
⑤

Robin and the
7 Hoods

Rat Pack   4 for Texas
Summit *Oceans 11*
production begins   *Sergeants 3*
on *Oceans 11*

③
(B)

Dean Martin joins Frank Sinatra   (5)
on stage at the Sands Hotel

1000

800

600

(3)

(A)

(C)
④

400

(4)

President severs ties;
Lawford excommunicated
from Pack

Benchmark Sociometer
DJIA
monthly range
1953-1966

© April 2011 Elliott Wave International (www.elliottwave.com)

1953   1955   1957   1959   1961   1963   1965

Figure 4

The Pack even sang the national anthem at the Democratic National Convention, "increasing [Kennedy's] popularity significantly."[16] At the outset of the wave (B) rally in stocks to a new all-time high, the group starred at the inaugural gala. A December 1998 *American Heritage* article, "Fly Me To the Moon," marked this event as a critical moment in the life of Frank Sinatra and his Rat Pack:

> On January 19, 1961, at a gala in Washington's National Armory on the eve of his inauguration, President-elect John Kennedy made a remarkable gesture. He rose to tell the crowd, "We're all indebted to a great friend—Frank Sinatra." It was an act of legitimation, Camelot's first knighting: it marked the official ascendancy of Sinatra and, through him, of the rakish group of confederates known as the Rat Pack. For a few brief years the Rat Pack would be the swinging minstrels of Camelot, and the values and aspirations they embodied

would have the imprimatur of presidential authority and enormous cultural cachet. They would be both actors in and emblems of the carnivalesque, Janus-faced period called the Swinging Sixties.

Another socionomic key to the Rat Pack's popularity is aspects of the act that reflected a positive social mood. A focal point of its appeal was the projection of a strong male sexual identity that typically prevails in periods of positive mood (see "Popular Culture and the Stock Market," 1985, republished in *Pioneering Studies in Socionomics*, 2003). Also reflecting positive mood, the tone of the act was relentlessly upbeat. "At its nucleus was the idea that fame and success could be attained through play," says Chris Rojek. "Sinatra's mantra was 'fun with everything and I mean fun.'" The Rat Pack "valued inclusion and extending participation," another trait that typically becomes dominant late in positive mood periods. According to *The Wave Principle of Human Social Behavior*, "A waxing positive social mood accompanies increased inclusionary tendencies in every aspect of society, including the cultural, social and political. Racial harmony is promoted in bull markets." With its blend of races and ethnicities, the Rat Pack reflected the broadening civil rights movement of the time. Here is one assessment from *American Heritage*:

> They were sign and symptom. The Rat Pack was a giddy version of multiethnic American democracy in which class was replaced by "class." The Rat Pack show featured—even flaunted—race and eth- nicity. Bishop, dressed as a Jewish waiter, warns the two Italians to watch out "because I got my own group, the Matzia." The night JFK showed up ringside, Dean picked Sammy up in his arms and held him out to the candidate: "Here. This award just came for you from the National Association for the Advancement of Colored People." Sammy: "I'm colored, Jewish, and Puerto Rican. When I move into a neighborhood, I wipe it out."

1961 was a peak year for both the Rat Pack and the stock market. But the glory days for Camelot's swinging minstrels came to a screeching halt in March 1962, when the Kennedys cut off all contact. In response, Sinatra excommunicated Peter Lawford from the Pack. The 20% reduction in the Pack's size resembled the Dow's decline of about 25% over the next three months.

In wave ⑤ of wave III, the Rat Pack re-united as a four-person act on stage, but its membership continued to fall over three more films. By September 1965, when wave ⑤ was just four months from its high, the last Rat Pack movie came out. It featured only Sinatra and Martin. *Marriage on the Rocks* bombed. Here's the review from *Rat Pack Confidential*: "1965: The last Rat Pack movie and a damned ugly way to go. It was clearly over."

Rat Pack Confidential mentions a final 1966 appearance at a "mini-summit" in Las Vegas, but we can find no other evidence of such an appearance. We do know that Sinatra tried and failed to re-unite the group in the late 1960s. The last recorded gathering, featuring Johnny Carson in place of Joey Bishop, is the St. Louis benefit concert of 1965 mentioned above. CBS's 1965 documentary, which contains footage from the same concert, describes the positive mood attending the event and hints at the violent reversal to come:

> No one had a better time than the performers. The actors' joy in their own performance is communicated to the crowd, that old black magic. Once again, Sinatra and friends have established that rare rapport that can be made to exist between entertainer and audience. What is there about Sinatra that gives him this magic quality? We asked author and social historian Leo Rosten: 'It's not just his talent, not just his voice that makes him a star. It's his supreme self-assurance and his absolute control. He has an animal tension, a suggestion of violence, even of danger, of a temper that might break through.

In a matter of months, the Dow would be heading lower. But the positive mood trend still had some rewards in store for Sinatra as a solo performer.

Sinatra Sets a Major Mood Reversal to Music

Sinatra once again struck the right chords through the peak of wave III and its aftermath. His solo career started to regain traction in 1964, when he scored his first Top 30 hit since 1960. In 1965 and 1966, as the Dow Jones Industrial Average approached a new all-time high near 1000, Sinatra returned to the top of the charts for the first time since the mid-1940s. In both years, he was *DownBeat*'s "Best Male Singer" as well as a Grammy winner for Album of the Year and for Best Vocal Performance. Shortly after the Dow's February 1966 peak, he claimed the Grammy Lifetime Achievement Award as well as his last solo No.1 hit, 'Strangers in the Night'. The album of the same name was one of Sinatra's two platinum efforts. His other was a compilation of greatest hits at the second peak of the double top, in 1968.

The Negative Mood Period of 1966-1974

Sinatra's talent was no match for the large-degree trend toward negative social mood that held sway from 1966 to 1974 and which persisted in milder form until 1982. There are many ways to capture the socionomic aspects of Sinatra's reversal from the 1966 peak, but one of the most compelling is to simply listen to the music he recorded as the turn approached. In "Popular

Culture and the Stock Market," Prechter explained that 1965 was the same year that the Beatles and the Rolling Stones tapped into the approaching negative mood with new styles of hit songs. The Beatles did it by introducing introspective lyrics in such songs as 'Help' and 'Yesterday' ("all my troubles seemed so far away...now it looks as if they're here to stay"), while the Stones harped on themes of dissatisfaction and rejection. For his part, Sinatra foreshadowed the bear market by slowing down the pace of his songs and emphasizing a thematic transition into a darker time. Sinatra finishes the dirge-slow 'It Was a Very Good Year', for instance, with "But now the days are short; I'm in the autumn of my years." In another languid song from the same album, 'September of My Years', Sinatra explores the same sentiment in much the same way: "One day you turn around and it's fall."

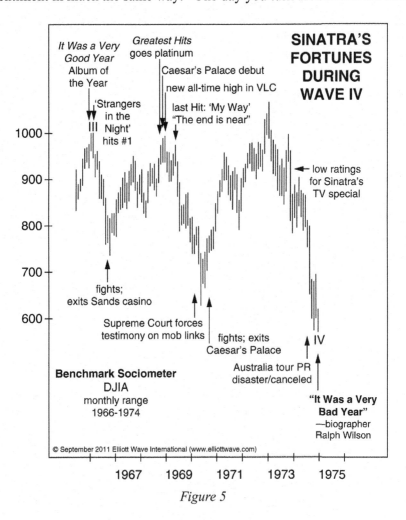

Figure 5

On *That's Life*, which came out at the end of the market's initial wave down in 1966, melodies still carry the optimism that rang through songs such as 'High Hopes' in 1959, but the lyrics, which were of supreme importance to Sinatra, are decidedly downbeat. In the title song, which was written specifically for him (by Dean Kay and Kelly Gordon), Sinatra responded wearily to the vicissitudes of stardom:

> You're riding high in April, shot down in May
> But if there's nothing shaking on this here July
> I'm gonna roll myself up in a big ball and die.

For the most part, his recordings after mid-1966 did not sell well. From the twelve full albums recorded over a period of six years between November 1966 and July 1974, Sinatra garnered just two hit songs.

In 1967, a duet with his daughter Nancy went to #1. But Sinatra insider George Jacobs wrote, "For Frank Sinatra, 1967 was a very bad year. His biggest career accomplishment was his throwaway song 'Something Stupid', the only father-daughter love song ever to hit No. 1 on the pop charts." In November 1968, Sinatra recorded *Cycles*, an album of contemporary hits of questionable merit by other artists, including 'Little Green Apples', 'Gentle on My Mind' and 'By the Time I Get to Phoenix'. The liner notes all but acknowledged Sinatra's slide: "Like the great American buffalo, the Sinatra brand of recording is diminishing." On the title track, Sinatra seemed to anticipate the exhaustion that would soon visit the stock market and economy:

> Although I'm kinda tired
> My gal just up and left last week
> Friday I got fired
> You know it's almost funny
> But things can't get worse than now
> —'Cycles', 1968

For Sinatra they did get worse, and he did not take his ill fortunes well. "The Mr. S. of 1968 was on the downhill slope from the pinnacle. He had become a world idol, but now at 52 he was on the border of old age. Mr. S. was coming to despise himself. He had sung and won, but he had also loved and lost. That crucial defeat in the game of life made him one sore loser, a frustrated, angry man. His days of hope were over," writes Jacobs. In August 1968, *The Wall Street Journal* "for the first time exposed details of Frank's mafia contacts."[17] Years later, Sinatra's daughter Tina recalled the depth of the blow: "One could almost understand such slander if it had appeared in a second-rate publication. But this was sanctioned by *The Wall Street Journal*, one of the most respected papers in America." Advisors to presidential candidate Hubert Humphrey distanced the candidate from Sinatra, "which hurt Frank deeply."

In conjunction with a speculative stock bounce in 1969 that propelled the Dow to within 2.5% of its all-time high and led the Beatles to agree to do one more album, Sinatra similarly managed to squeak out one more recorded high note. His anthem, 'My Way', which was written specifically for him by Paul Anka, became his last Top 30 hit. It dramatically and accurately depicted his status as a popular music star:

And now the end is near
And so I face the final curtain
　—'My Way,' 1969

By late 1969, Sinatra's public image was under siege. Mario Puzo's bestseller, *The Godfather*, raised the talk of mob associations to a higher pitch, which would intensify as the Oscar-winning movies, *The Godfather* and *The Godfather: Part II*, appeared in 1972 and 1974. "The singer and mafia protégé of the story was unmistakably based on Sinatra. *The Godfather* furor was just one element in a barrage of bad press."[18] In 1969, Sinatra was served with a subpoena to appear before a New Jersey commission investigating organized crime. He declined to appear. But in February 1970, with the Dow in the midst of a precipitous decline, the U.S. Supreme Court threatened him with a three-year jail term. Two decades earlier, in deference to his stature, Sinatra had been allowed to testify in secret during Senator Estes Kefauver's organized crime hearings of 1951. In his testimony, Frank admitted that he "knew" various mobsters "but that was it."[19] In 1970, Sinatra was given no such courtesy, and he damaged his reputation by refusing to acknowledge or deny any association with mobsters.

Negative Mood Grabs Sinatra "By the Throat"

Another way in which negative social mood invariably expressed itself in the life of Frank Sinatra was through outbreaks of physical violence along with concomitant negative portrayals in the media. As witnessed by an entourage of friends, press agents, lawyers and bodyguards, Sinatra was involved in several confrontational incidents. When mood was positive, none of them garnered much interest in the press. Yet trouble loomed. "It was predictable, if you got to know him. You could see the turn coming," said one bodyguard. "He had an enormous temper."[20] The first infamous outbreak had been his attack on columnist Lee Mortimer, covered above. That punch announced Sinatra's initial retreat from public adoration in 1947. With the return of more positive social mood in the 1950s, handlers were able to keep a lid on Sinatra's temper. *Sinatra: The Life* describes several violent outbursts that came ahead of the stock market peak's of 1966.[21] They include a 1958 New York City incident in which Sinatra's limousine struck a photographer; a 1962 wrestling match with a photographer in San Francisco; a 1964 charge and fine in Spain for disturbing the peace; and a 1965 incident in Israel when Sinatra "went out looking for trouble." If negative mood had dominated at these times, any one of these altercations could have risen to the level of an international incident. But the times were not yet ripe for that type of media treatment.

As social mood entered the negative trend of 1966-1974, things spun dangerously out of control. In June 1966, Sinatra's victim was an innocent businessman, art collector Frederick Weisman, who happened to be seated next to him at a Sinatra-organized birthday party for Dean Martin at the Polo Lounge in the Beverly Hills Hotel. After Weisman complained about the noise and crude language, Sinatra instigated and several henchman finished a beating that left their victim with a fractured skull. According to Kitty Kelly,[22] the beating marked the start of "the most violent period of Frank Sinatra's life." It was also the start of an 8-year bear market in stocks.

In 1967, Sinatra threw a legendary tantrum at the Sands. When pit bosses cut off his gambling credit, Sinatra smashed furniture, lit curtains on fire and crashed a baggage cart into the casino's front window. "I built this hotel from a sand pile," he shouted, "and before I'm through that's what it'll be again!" A few days later, he returned and got into a fight with casino manager Carl Cohen. After Sinatra dumped a pot of hot coffee in Cohen's lap, Cohen punched Sinatra, splitting his lips and knocking out two teeth.

Sinatra then moved to Caesar's Palace, where he made his debut in November 1968, just days ahead of the DJIA's December 1968 peak. The Dow trended lower, and in September 1970 an IRS investigation at Caesars Palace "targeted Sinatra."[23] The IRS determined that Sinatra was skimming "vast sums" in gambling markers and using the casino as a source of "easy money. We were concerned about his paying back markers," reported an IRS agent. "He said that when he sat down to gamble, he attracted enough big money around him so that the casino made out and profited enough so that they didn't need to collect from him." That logic squared with casino operators until 1970, shortly after a new low in the stock market. Suddenly the matter escalated into a confrontation between Sinatra and

Sam Waterman, the Caesars Palace manager. *The Daily Report*, an Ontario, California newspaper, offered the following account of the resulting scuffle:

Sinatra Clutched Man by the Throat

The casino executive who pulled a gun on Frank Sinatra still had the singer's finger marks on his throat when questioned later by deputies, says the district attorney.

Because of those marks, Dist. Atty. George Franklin said Wednesday he will not charge the casino man with assault with a deadly weapon.

—AP, September 18, 1970

In November 1970, Sinatra's film career reached its nadir with the release of *Dirty Dingus Magee*, a "comic anti-western" that *The New York Times* described as "a dreadful parody." The box office returns were "even more disappointing" than sales of his 1970 album *Watertown*, which numbered just 35,000 copies.[24] According to reviewer Stephen Thomas Erlewine, "The culminating effect of the songs is an atmosphere of loneliness without much hope or romance—it is the sound of a broken man." In March 1971, Sinatra finally surrendered, announcing his retirement from "the entertainment world and public life." "I've had enough," he told a *Life* magazine reporter. "Maybe the public's had enough, too." For months, "Frank did not sing. 'I wouldn't even hum. Not a sound did I make.'"[25]

Within the eight-year bear market, the Dow managed one more new high just above 1000 in January 1973. A few months later, Sinatra came out of retirement. "I know I said that I was leaving/ But I just couldn't say goodbye," he explained on 'Let Me Try Again'. Sinatra's "second comeback" turned out to be a mistake. Backed by a 45-piece orchestra with 20 violins, Sinatra announced his return on November 18 with "Ol' Blue Eyes Is Back," a television special and album. "Despite the carefully orchestrated special, ratings were poor and the reviews disappointing."[26]

A Low Ebb for Old Blue Eyes

In 1974, stocks fell hard, and Sinatra—like Richard Nixon at the same time—went to war with the media and his critics. In a June 1974 *Rolling Stone* article, Ralph Gleason lamented Sinatra's lost prowess:

> It is simply weird now to see him all glossed up like a wax dummy, that rug on his head looking silly, and the on stage movement, which used to be panther-tense, now a self-conscious hoodlum bustle.... What seemed a youthful bravado 25 years ago seems like perversity now. Today he behaves like an arrogant despot with a court of sycophants.

An Australian tour in July 1974 turned into "his most damaging public relations misadventure since he punched columnist Lee Mortimer in 1947."[27] After a "skirmish between guards, reporters and photographers," Sinatra lashed out, calling the Australian press "bums, parasites, hookers and pimps." Sinatra's political clout also abandoned him. His choice for sheriff of Las Vegas lost in the fall of 1974. Voters "seemed to resent Sinatra's intrusion. The local political experts repeated, 'Sinatra's support is the kiss of death.'" "Once you get Sinatra on your side in politics, you're out of business," cracked comedian Mort Sahl in 1974.[28]

The specter of violence accompanied Sinatra and his entourage down through the bitter end of the stock market decline. In May 1973, Frank Weinstock filed assault charges against Sinatra and several friends, including Sinatra confidante Jilly Rizzo. The case came to trial in September 1974. While the jury cleared Sinatra of assault and battery, Rizzo lost on the same charge and paid $101,000 in damages. "Although Sinatra won the battle, jibes from the press on other matters continued to pour in."[29] As the S&P Composite index reached its low in October, the critical savaging of Sinatra reached fever pitch. Columnist Rex Reed offered the following assessment of Sinatra's celebrity and talent:

> Somebody do something about Frank Sinatra. His public image is uglier than a first-degree burn, his appearance is sloppier than Porky Pig, his manners are more appalling than a subway sandhog's and his ego is bigger than the Sahara (the desert, not the hotel in Las Vegas). All of which might be tolerable if he could still sing. But the grim truth is that Frank Sinatra has had it. His voice has been manhandled beyond recognition, bringing with its parched croak only a painful memory of burned-out yesterdays.
>   —*Chicago Tribune*, November 3, 1974

In December 1974, the month of the wave IV low in the DJIA, the Hollywood Women's Press Club "went out of its way to give the Sour Apple

Award ('for least cooperation') to Sinatra." The title of the chapter covering 1974 in Wilson's biography, *Sinatra*, captures the nine-year, high-to-low transformation: "It Was A Very Bad Year."

The Return of Positive Mood Makes an Oldie Golden Once Again

From the outset of wave V dating from December 1974 in the Dow, no one satisfied the public desire to re-live positive mood moments as expertly as Sinatra. Ralph Wilson (*Sinatra*) records that within weeks of the low a "success compulsion" had "seized Sinatra" and "revived his ego." While he never regained his former popularity, Wilson identifies this as Sinatra's "Third Comeback," providing yet another demonstration of the importance of socionomic timing in the public life of Frank Sinatra. Sinatra's final comeback went much better than his decision to come out of retirement in 1973. By midsummer 1975, when the Dow was rising in a new bull market, Sinatra revived his career. Although his record sales would never again approach the stratospheric levels of the 1950s and 1960s, loyal fans packed increasingly larger venues and paid higher and higher ticket prices to hear "The Voice" in his golden years. In 1976, shows in New Haven and Providence set records. In England, where "they had been believing that the Sinatra magic was gone," the reviews and attendance "were excellent."[30]

There were setbacks along the way. A series of concerts at the Westchester Premier Theatre in 1976 and 1977 evolved into an open scandal in which Sinatra was implicated in a mob-run "skimming operation." No charges were brought. In March 1980, the Dow Jones Industrial Average touched a low of 740. A month later, in an echo of the Sinatra-mania that accompanied the stock market lift-off in 1942, Sinatra scored his last solo hit, 'Theme from New York, New York'. The song rose to No. 32 on the Billboard charts. That year he also completed his conversion to conservative politics, just in time to bask in the glow of Ronald Reagan's election and to organize another inaugural gala (followed by a second one for Reagan in 1984). In February 1981, he testified before another government commission and again "denied ever associating with members of organized crime," even though the same board had revoked his gaming license in 1963 for his having just such contacts. With the help of a character reference from the new president, the five-member Nevada Gaming Control Commission granted Sinatra a license. After a few perfunctory questions, the chairman of the commission turned the hearing into a testimonial in which "the commissioners rushed to vindicate Frank."[31]

In August 1984, he recorded his last solo album, *L.A. Is My Lady*, as the Dow left the 1100 level behind for good. Although in his final years Sinatra was "drinking a bottle of Jack Daniels a day,"[32] he managed to pull off two more albums, which were recorded midway through the extended stock market advance of the 1990s. On *Duets* (November 1993) and *Duets II* (November 1994), Sinatra sang many of his standards with popular entertainers ranging from Gloria Estefan to Bono to Willie Nelson to Julio Iglesias. The recordings garnered commercial success, rising to No. 2 and No. 9 on the Billboard album charts, respectively, but got mixed reviews. Many critics saw the efforts as another among Sinatra's "artistically questionable, often risible attempts to remain hip." In *Frank Sinatra*, Chris Rojek linked the efforts to a "psychological need" within mass culture and Sinatra. "He was incapable of breaking the umbilical cord with the public. [T]hroughout his career Sinatra was concerned not only to re-invent former recording glories but to keep up with the times. *Duets I* and *II* were moribund attempts, hugely successful it might be added, to bridge the gap by demonstrating that the octogenarian 'Voice' was still hip and that younger performers recognized Sinatra as the maestro."[33] At the age of 80 in 1996, *Duets II* won Sinatra his last Grammy, for Best Traditional Pop Vocal Performance. Social mood was positive, and Frank Sinatra reaped the benefits, just as he had in earlier such times.

Even in death, Sinatra's timing was impeccable. In April 1998, U.S. stock prices reached the front edge of a peaking process with a multi-year top in the Value Line Composite index. Sinatra died on May 14, 1998, right at the peak of positive social mood. *People* magazine, reflecting the euphoria of the time, gushed, "Francis Albert Sinatra was simply the greatest male vocalist in the history of popular music. Period." With the stock market mostly holding near historically high valuations ever since, no one has yet appeared to contest this assessment.

Why Sinatra?

> If the voice, more than any language, more than any other instrument of expression, can reveal to us our own hidden depths, and convey those depths to other souls of men, it is because voice vibrates directly to the feeling itself, when it fulfils its natural mission. To sing should always mean to have some definite feeling to express.
> —Clara Kathleen Rogers: *The Philosophy of Singing* (1893)

Most artists may not realize it, but from the perspective of socionomics, their ultimate goal is to express successfully the prevailing social mood.

No singer both reflected and benefitted from positive mood over a longer period of time than "The Voice." In a February 1963 interview with *Playboy*, Sinatra rooted his success to his capacity for expressing emotional extremes. "Being an 18-karat manic-depressive and having lived a life of violent emotional contradictions, I have an overacute capacity for sadness as well as elation." Sinatra continued,

> It's because I get an audience involved, personally involved in a song—because I'm involved myself. It's not something I do deliberately; I can't help myself. If the song is a lament at the loss of love, I get an ache in my gut, I feel the loss myself and I cry out the loneliness, the hurt and the pain that I feel. I've been there—and back. I guess the audience feels it along with me. They can't help it.

"Other singers could be placed in a mood; Frank became it," explained Shawn Levy in *Rat Pack Confidential*. In observing the phenomenon, writers frequently make the mistake of attributing audiences' moods to Sinatra, much as economists place the head of the Federal Reserve or the U.S. president at the helm of the economy. The 1965 CBS *American Original* documentary, for instance, depicts Sinatra as defining the trend: "He can make an audience feel he's their kind of guy. Anything Sinatra does is the thing to do. Any place he goes is the place to go." In "Frank Sinatra Has a Cold," the 1966 *Esquire* profile, Talese wrote,

Sinatra with a cold is Picasso without paint, Ferrari without fuel—only worse. For the common cold robs Sinatra of that uninsurable jewel, his voice, cutting into the core of his confidence, and it affects not only his own psyche but also seems to cause a kind of psychosomatic nasal drip within dozens of people who work for him, drink with him, love him, depend on him for their own welfare and stability. A Sinatra with a cold can, in a small way, send vibrations through the entertainment industry and beyond as surely as a President of the United States, suddenly sick, can shake the national economy.

But a socionomist knows better: These vibrations are endogenous to society, not the result of clever manipulation.

It is nearly impossible for a public person to ride a surge in positive social mood yet avoid getting dragged under during transitions to negative mood. Success in harnessing positive mood entails an elevated level of confidence. "If there was one thing [Sinatra] was absolutely sure of it was that he had big things coming to him," wrote Kaplan of Sinatra. "His large sense of himself derived from the Secret he entertained, the sounds he heard in his head." Shawn Levy put it a slightly different way: "He didn't know any theory—he could barely sight-read—but his instincts were impeccable, the best, perhaps of any singer of the century."

But Sinatra never understood the implications of negative mood periods. Each time the trend of social mood turned negative, his instincts failed him. In "Frank Sinatra Has a Cold," Talese described Sinatra nearly coming to blows with a young writer whose informal attire offended his formal taste. "I don't want anybody in here without coats and ties," Sinatra snapped. That was in November 1965, just a few weeks from the end of wave III. It was one of many battles Sinatra would lose as the 1970s closed in. For four years, Sinatra fought the new negative mood tooth and nail before temporarily retiring in 1971. As noted above, he failed to stay retired long enough. The too-early attempt at a comeback in 1973 turned out to be one of his biggest timing errors, which shows how hard it is, even for a veteran of earlier swings, to anticipate changes in social mood. Eventually, his determination saw him through to a respectable finish, although he never returned to his former heights.

The anguish Sinatra felt surrounding the negative mood nadir of 1974 could have been avoided. The best approach for public figures is to discern the direction of the social mood trend as indicated by Elliott waves in the stock market. Only those who know the position of social mood and the nuances of social life at comparable points in the past can figure out when to push and when to lay low. Based on the accounts of his daughters, Sinatra died a bitter man despite a vast fortune and more fame than almost anyone alive. Being born at the right time with a gift for the music of a golden age makes for an amazing life. But studying history and the Wave Principle is the only way to fully grasp the social influences at work in shaping the careers of public people. If Sinatra had known about socionomic causality, perhaps he would have been less bitter at the end.

NOTES AND REFERENCES

[1] Kaplan, James. 2010. *Sinatra: The Voice*, New York, Doubleday, p. 22.

[2] Kaplan did not offer a date for beginning of Sinatra's stint at the Rustic Cabin. Some biographers stated that he started there in 1938, but three separate sources—the book *Why Sinatra Matters* by Pete Hamill, the "Life of Sinatra" originally written by Gary Cadwallader for Seaside Music Theater, and a photo of a "Rustic Cabin 1937 WNEW Radio Show"—dated his start to some time in 1937. The book *Sinatra*, by Richard Havers, said it may have been as early as August 1937 that Sinatra first gained steady employment as a professional singer.

[3] *Sinatra: The Voice*, p. 64.

[4] Elliott, R.N. 1946/1993/2005. *Nature's Law*, ch. 27. New York: Self-published. Reprinted in *R.N. Elliott's Masterworks*, New Classics Library, 1980, p. 298.

[5] Lahr, John. 1997. *Sinatra: The Artist and the Man*, New York: Random House, p. 32.

[6] Internet, "Historical Account of the Rat Pack," www.ratpack.biz.

[7] Kaplan, *Sinatra: The Voice*, p. 667. It was the more serious of two suicide attempts as Sinatra's career struggled to get back on track after the stock market low of 1949. This time Sinatra slit his wrist and was hospitalized. Another somewhat lame attempt came in 1951. The suicidal mindset exemplifies the persistence of negative mood in the early stages of a bull market. The second attempt came despite the early box office success of *From Here to Eternity*, when Sinatra's career was clearly going well once again. History illustrates how fear and anguish resulting from negative mood sometimes manifest themselves through the early parts of the next positive phase; thus the continuance of World War II through the advance of 1942-46 and the Korean War through most of the rally of 1949-1952.

[8] Doyle, Jack. 2011. *The Jack Pack*, PopHistoryDig.com. This site offers a good overview of Sinatra's involvement in the Kennedy campaign. In 2000, Sinatra's daughter Tina confirmed what many people had long suspected, that her father was instrumental in delivering Kennedy a victory in the May 1960 West Virginia Primary. Challenger Hubert Humphrey dropped out of the race the next day. "Legendary crooner Frank Sinatra served as a liaison between John F. Kennedy's 1960 campaign for president and mobster Sam Giancana in a scheme to use Mafia muscle to deliver union votes," reported CBS in October 2000. It was probably the peak moment of influence for Sinatra, but he continued to surf the political waters almost as deftly as he did those musical. After working for liberal Franklin Delano Roosevelt in 1944, Sinatra backed the more moderate Democrat Kennedy in 1960 and organized his inaugural

bash. In 1968, during his own bear market, he backed the losing candidate, Hubert Humphrey. By 1980, when his star was rising again, he moved to the right and caught the wave of conservatism that took over as stocks started rising again and Ronald Reagan was elected president.

[9] Ironically, one of the most successful business deals in the history of these icons came when Michael Jackson purchased the Beatles' song catalog in 1985.

[10] The Beatles went through the same transition on the approach to the positive-mood peak of 1968, also moving from Capitol to their own label, Apple Records.

[11] Summers, Anthony and Swan, Robyn. 2006. *Sinatra: The Life*. New York: Vintage Books, p. 301.

[12] Jacobs, George and Stadiem, William. 2003. *Mr. S.: My Life with Frank Sinatra*. "In the face [of a] humiliating public rejection by the Kennedys and his equally public association with gangland," Sinatra chose to "rehabilitate his tarnished image" by becoming "a philanthropist. The singing philanthropist, Rockefeller with a tune." CBS's American Original documentary, which aired a few weeks before the peak of wave III in 1966, made the following observation about the situation: "At this affluent point in his career, he responds more quickly to the request for a benefit performance than to the opportunity to make money." Here Sinatra demonstrates a socionomic sensitivity. Elliott Wave International has observed that one of the classic traits of an aging fifth wave is an increased interest in philanthropy—"the ultimate luxury." At the end of wave III and during wave V, Sinatra burnished his image via "humanitarianism," much of which, it was continually stated, came in the form of anonymous contributions.

[13] Wilson, Earl. 1976. *Sinatra: An Unauthorized Biography*. New York: Macmillan Publishing Co., p. 216.

[14] Kelley, Kitty. 1986. *His Way: The Unauthorized Biography of Frank Sinatra*. New York: Bantam Books, p. 350.

[15] Severo, Richard. October 19, 2007. "Joey Bishop, Last of the Rat Pack, Is Dead," *The New York Times*.

[16] Internet, "Peter Lawford Biography," http://www.imdb.com.

[17] *Sinatra: The Life*, p. 344. "Sinatra hobnobs with the mafia's elite," reported the WSJ. This was ironic because, by this time, the mafia had also ended its "association" with Sinatra, disappointed by his inability to cash in on his contacts with JFK and losses associated with the Cal-Nev Casino. "It was ridiculous because all those connections had long ago disconnected from Sinatra," says Jacobs in *My Life With Frank Sinatra*, p. 253.

[18] *Sinatra: The Life*, p. 342.

[19] Van Meter, Jonathan. 2003. *The Last Good Time: The Rise and Fall of Atlantic City*. New York: Crown Publishing, p. 115.

[20] *Sinatra: The Life*, p. 328.

[21] *Ibid*., pp. 322-328.

[22] *His Way: The Unauthorized Biography of Frank Sinatra*, p. 350.

[23] *Ibid*, p. 380.

[24] *Ibid*, p. 403.

[25] *Sinatra: The Life*, pp. 344 and 346.

[26] *His Way: The Unauthorized Biography of Frank Sinatra*, p. 421.

[27] *Sinatra: An Unauthorized Biography*, p. 292.

[28] *His Way: The Unauthorized Biography of Frank Sinatra*, p. 530.

[29] *Sinatra: An Unauthorized Biography*, p. 303.

[30] *Ibid*, p. 232.

[31] *His Way: The Unauthorized Biography of Frank Sinatra*, p. 484.

[32] Internet. July 31, 2008. WENN, "Experts Reveal Sinatra was a Functioning Alcoholic," Contactmusic.com.

[33] Rojek, Chris. 2004. *Frank Sinatra*. Boston: Polity, p. 153.

APPENDIX

A RAT PACK REVIVAL

Sinatra is gone, but the relationship of his persona to trends in social mood remains strong. As the 1990s boom reached fever pitch near the positive mood peak of 2000, a Rat Pack revival occurred. In 1997, "the only known concert recording of the Rat Pack, capturing the on-stage antics and raucous camaraderie" at the 1965 St. Louis benefit concert, surfaced and became a popular DVD. The following year, a new incarnation of the Rat Pack appeared on the world stage:

The Year of the Rat (Pack) Movies:
Two films are in the works about the megastars who embodied the essence of cool at the height of a show-biz era
—Los Angeles Times, January 1998

Clooney to Lead Revived Rat Pack
—South China Morning Post, January 12, 2000

Rat Pack Is Back in Las Vegas
—Florida Times Union, May 28, 2000

Rat Pack Remake Brings Big Stars Scurrying to Roles
—San Diego Union-Tribune, May 30, 2000

Rat Pack Renaissance
—Wall Street Journal, August 25, 2000

The centerpiece of the revival was a remake of *Oceans Eleven*, which was announced in mid-January 2000, within days of the Dow's peak that year. As the topping process continued, *Oceans Eleven* and its two sequels stretched out across it.

"The Rat Pack is Back," a Las Vegas stage show featuring four Rat Pack impersonators, returned in 2000; it continues play at the Crown Theater in Las Vegas. "I get very nostalgic, particularly when I see those Rat Pack tribute shows," said Buddy Grecco, a 1960s lounge singer and occasional Rat Pack contributor, in a recent interview. "I remember what it felt like to walk into a lounge in Las Vegas with Frank, Dean and Sammy and watch the world stop. We were like gods." In some ways, the revival is bigger than the original act. "The Rat Pack is Back" is in its 11th year, giving it close to twice the life span of the original group. The Rat-Pack revival films—*Oceans Eleven* (2001), *Twelve* (2004) and *Thirteen* (2007)—brought in $1.1 billion, which is $157.5 million in 1960 dollars, ten times the $14.5 million earned by the Rat Pack's three biggest movies. When the stock market crashed in 2008, the revival movies ceased.

The Sands was torn down for a larger casino, the Venetian, but the name survives in the form of a company, the Las Vegas Sands Corp. (LVS), which achieved something in 2004 that no Vegas casino had dared to do in the 1960s: a public offering.

Figure 6 captures the change in Sinatra's corporate legacy as reflected by LVS's stock price. After rising dramatically to a peak in October 2007, LVS stock fell 99% into March 2009. The peak and trough coincided with the months of the high and low in the Dow. LVS has since recovered.

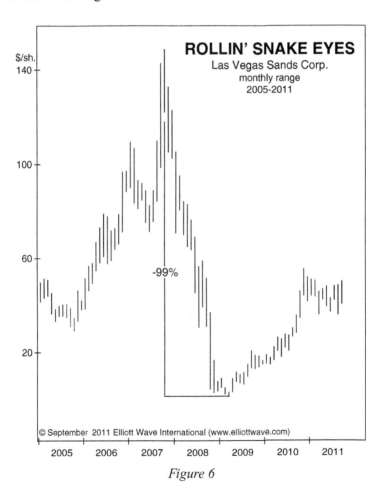

Figure 6

In recent days, every stick of furniture at the Sahara Hotel, another Rat Pack hangout, was sold in a three-month auction. Here's a headline announcing the auction that hints at a larger significance:

Everything Must Go as Rat Pack-Era Casino Closes
—Associated Press, June 3, 2011

Clearly, the trend back toward positive social mood has not quite ended, because the Rat Pack revival continues and Las Vegas remains a top tourist destination. In addition to the "Rat Pack Is Back," several Rat Pack variety shows are appearing in Vegas and other venues around the U.S. and England. The Fox Theatre in St. Louis is featuring "Christmas with the Rat Pack: Live at the Sands," December 6 through December 18, 2011. The winner of the latest "America's Got Talent" is a Frank Sinatra clone, Landau Eugene Murphy. Murphy won $1 million and a one-week headline show at Caesar's Palace. In a fitting finale, a new Sinatra CD, *Sinatra: Best of the Best* came out on November 1. The album, which hit #23 on Billboard's U.S. Top 100 Albums chart, marks the first compilation of hits from Sinatra's Capitol and Reprise Records periods. The first disc starts with 1953's 'I've got the World on a String' and ends with Sinatra's last three hits, 'Strangers in the Night', 'My Way' and 'Theme from New York, New York'. The reviews are solid with one critic saying, "Best of the Best" lives up to its title. "What makes this deluxe edition the one to get, though, is its second disc, *'57 In Concert*. Originally released as a live album and long since out-of-print, it boasts a complete performance recorded on June 9, 1957. Sinatra is exquisite, delivering one highlight after another with supreme cool and command."

The history detailed in this chapter allows us to predict that what remains of the public's love affair with the Rat Pack and Frank Sinatra will end in the next major, prolonged period of negative social mood. This type of analysis also works in reverse: By gauging the status of Sinatra's image and associated elements within the culture, we can get a bearing on the current state of social mood.

Chapter 5

Goldman Sachs—History of a Bull-Market Financial Star

Peter Kendall

October 30, 2009 / April 30, 2010 (EWFF)

At the Dow's peak in October 2007, Goldman Sachs Group, Inc. was the undisputed heavyweight champion of financial institutions. A year later, the company was on the ropes. Thanks to its bailout in 2008 by Warren Buffett and the U.S. Treasury as well as the liquidation of rivals Bear Stearns and Lehman Brothers, its reign lives on. At year-end 2009, earnings and bonuses will reputedly approach the record levels of 2007. If the stock market holds up, Goldman's good fortunes should continue. But when the next big stock market retreat grabs hold, Goldman Sachs, we predict, will experience an epic fall.

To understand the basis for this forecast, we need to review the firm's history in light of socionomics. At the beginning of the last century, Goldman Sachs originally made a name for itself with its first initial public offerings, United Cigar and Sears Roebuck. These deals came as the stock market made a multi-year top in 1906. Within months, the panic of 1907 was on, and the U.S. Interstate Commerce Commission's investigation of the Alton Railroad Company bond offering, in which Goldman participated, was in full swing. According to Charles Ellis' *The Partnership*, the deal was "long remembered as 'that unfortunate Alton deal.'" The bond issue allowed a considerable cash surplus to be paid out to shareholders in the form of a one-time dividend, a standard financial maneuver in the preceding bull market. In fact, the deal was unknown to the public until it came before the ICC in 1907. "Then, probably to the surprise of the syndicate, the verdict was practically unanimous against them. They were tried before the bar of public opinion and found guilty," said author William H. Lough in *Corporation Finance*. Lough added that syndicate members "ought not be too severely criticized for they merely acted in accordance with the custom of the period." So it

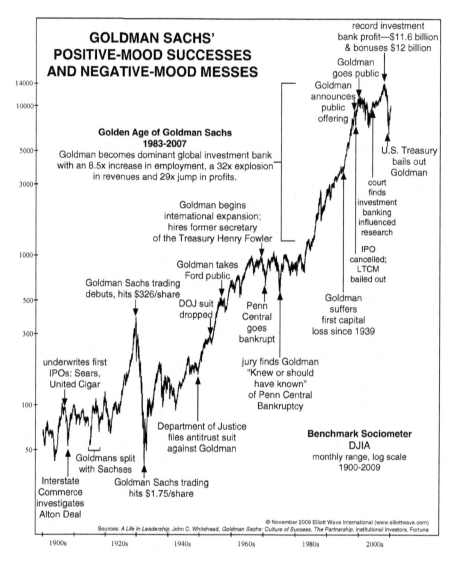

Figure 1

goes when social mood shifts toward the negative: Customary Wall Street devices are invariably recast as the instruments of evil financiers.

Negative mood also tears apart social units, and Wall Street firms are no less susceptible. From 1914 to 1917, a major rift emerged between the founding Goldman and Sachs families, and the Goldman side of the partnership left the firm. The tension endured through several generations, and as late as 1967 it was said that "hardly any Goldmans are on speaking terms with any Sachses."

Larger-degree social mood reversals lead to larger complications. The firm's biggest and most devastating setback came after the major stock market top of 1929. Goldman Sachs Trust Company had played a role in the 1920s financial mania similar to the one that hedge funds perform today. GSTC issued a quarter billion dollars' worth of new shares the month before the September 1929 peak, and with the help of successively higher levels of leverage the firm held many of them in its own account, leaving it dangerously exposed to the decline that followed. The firm survived only because a quick-witted former mailroom employee, Sidney Weinberg, took charge and used the stock market rally in early 1930 to jettison many of the firm's equity positions. Weinberg also turned out to be an investment banking savant. While the firm made no money for the next 16 years, he served on the war production board and carefully cultivated key relationships in business and government. In 1956, in the middle of a 24-year bull market, Goldman completed the largest IPO in history, delivering Ford Motor Company into the public's hands. Goldman was not yet a major force on Wall Street, but by hiring MBAs from top schools, fostering a reputation for fair dealing and maintaining a partnership structure that aligned the ownership of its principals with the long term success of the firm, Weinberg laid the foundation for rapid growth. In the words of Gus Levy, Weinberg's successor, Goldman Sachs was "long-term greedy." Another Levy secret was to be certain that positions exposing capital were "half-sold" before they were entered into.

Despite careful stewardship, Goldman's reputation faltered as stocks fell in 1969-1970 and social mood turned negative. When the Penn Central Railroad went under, it was revealed that Goldman had sold off most of its own Penn Central bonds before the June 1970 bankruptcy. This was another case of shifting standards, as Goldman's customers were all institutions dealing in unregistered commercial paper. They should have known the high odds of failure, as the railroad's stock was down almost 90% when the company finally went under. As the S&P touched its low in October 1974, however, a jury ruled that Goldman "knew or should have known" that the railroad was in trouble.

Goldman Sachs survived the adverse judgment and grew quickly as a new bull market took off in 1975. As Figure 1 shows, the company was exceptionally successful during the rise. During this period, Goldman "reinvented itself" as a "risk-taking principal." By 1994, *Goldman Sachs: The Culture of Success* (by Lisa Endlich) says that compensation policies had tilted so heavily toward risk-taking that one vice president noted, "everyone decided that they were going to become a proprietary trader." In that year, the firm suffered its first capital loss in decades as stocks sputtered, but within a year the Great Asset Mania was back in full force and Goldman's appetite for risk took off with that of the investment public. In 1999, the last year of a two-decade rise in stocks, Goldman Sachs, appropriately, went public, becoming the last major Wall Street partnership to do so. As *The Elliott Wave Theorist* said at the time, "Some of the most conspicuous cashing in has come from the brokerage sector, which has a long history of reaching for the brass ring near peaks."

The Partnership noted that by May 2006, when a nationwide embrace of ever-riskier financial investments was in its very late stages, Goldman had "the largest appetite and capacity for taking risks of all sorts, with the ability to commit substantial capital." As other firms felt the sting of an emerging risk aversion, Goldman profited by shorting the subprime housing market and putting the squeeze on its rivals. The firm earned $11.6 billion in 2007, more than Morgan Stanley, Lehman Brothers, Bear Stearns and Citigroup combined. Merrill Lynch lost $7.8 billion that year.

A former bull market initiative explains Goldman's relative strength since that time. It dates back to the hiring of a former U.S. Treasury Secretary as the Value Line Composite index peaked in 1968 (see Figure 1). This was the firm's first foray into the upper reaches of the U.S. government. In the 1980s and 1990s, the flow of talent went the other way, as executives regularly moved from Goldman to Washington. This process was aided in part by Goldman's policy of paying out all deferred compensation to any partner who accepts a senior position in the federal government. In May 2006, Henry Paulson, Goldman's chairman, left to become Secretary of the U.S. Treasury. These associations proved valuable to Goldman.

Another important late-cycle development has been Goldman's all-out effort to court, rather than to avoid, conflicts of interest. From the 1950s through the early 1980s, Goldman leaders assiduously avoided even the perception of a conflict of interest between the firm's positions and those of its clients. The atmosphere of the Great Asset Mania changed all that. Goldman's current leader, Lloyd Blankfein, "spends a significant part of his time managing real or perceived conflicts." Says Blankfein, "If major clients—governments, institutional investors, corporations, and wealthy families—believe they can trust our judgment, we can invite them to partner with us and share in the success."

These strategies paid off big in 2008 when Henry Paulson, who was still in charge at the Treasury, acted with other officials to use the public's money to rescue Goldman. According to a *Vanity Fair* article by Andrew

Ross Sorkin, Paulson had signed an ethics letter agreeing to stay out of any matter related to Goldman. In September 2008, however, he received a waiver that freed him "to help Goldman Sachs," which was faltering under the financial meltdown that accompanied the biggest bear market

in 76 years. Recent headlines reveal that another former Goldman Sachs chairman, Stephen Friedman, negotiated the "secret deal" that paid Goldman Sachs $14 billion for worthless credit-default swaps from a bankrupt AIG. He effected this clandestine scheme as chairman of the New York Fed while also serving on the board of Goldman Sachs. Without the force of the state, Goldman would have gone under.

In January 2008, our *Elliott Wave Financial Forecast* noted that Goldman's success relative to the rest of Wall Street pointed "to the eventual appearance of a much larger public relations problem in the future. In the negative mood times that accompany bear markets, conflict of interest charges will come pouring out." The recent revelations about Paulson's and Friedman's actions are the type to which we were referring. Additional claims against Goldman—including front-running its clients and profiting from inside information—are already too numerous to mention. With the market's recent advance, however, such transgressions have failed to capture the imagination of the public or the scrutiny of law enforcement. But in the next wave of negative social mood, Goldman's dealings will become a lightning rod for public discontent. Then the firm will attract scrutiny and scandal as easily as it brushed it off in the mid-2000s.

Chapter 6

The Rise and Fall of a Cable News Personality

Euan Wilson

June 6, 2011 (TS)

It's been a rough six months for Glenn Beck. After a meteoric rise to the top of cable news just two years ago, Fox News announced his show's end in early April. Beck wasn't involved in a scandal or other transgression that led Fox to relieve him of his duties. So, what brought about his show's spectacular decline? As Figure 1 illustrates, the answer is simple: A change toward positive social mood induced the public to cease caring for his message.

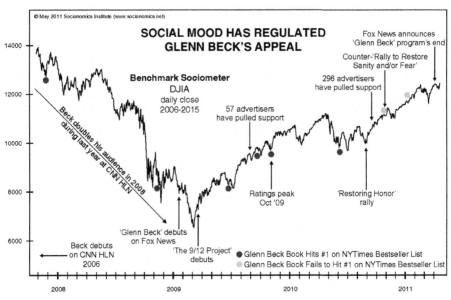

Figure 1

We have used socionomics to explain the rise and fall of celebrities. In *The Wave Principle of Human Social Behavior*, Robert Prechter discussed Benny Goodman, Frank Sinatra, Elvis Presley, the Beatles, Michael Jackson and even Franz Liszt as positive-mood heroes. We've given less press to negative-mood personalities, but they do exist, for example Roman Polanski, Hunter S. Thompson, Huey Long, Richard Pryor, George Carlin and the original combative talk-show host, Morton Downey, Jr. Glenn Beck is another negative-mood icon.

A negative-mood personality, like a positive-mood one, is charismatic. But positive-mood icons tend to be friendly, composed and agreeable, whereas negative-mood icons tend to be controversial, edgy and provocative. They excel at stirring things up. Beck has been all of these things, and his popularity has risen and fallen inversely with the stock market, our best indicator for social mood.

Glenn Beck: The TV Show

During negative mood trends, people who court controversy find ready listeners. Before Fox News picked up Beck's program, Beck had a similarly formatted (and named) show on CNN's Headline News channel. His tenure there lasted three years. During the stock market collapse that took place during his final full year with CNN in 2008, negative social mood helped Beck double his audience. By the time he moved to Fox, the Dow was nearing its low for the decade, and his Headline News program had the second-highest ratings of any show on the network.

Nielson ratings show that in March 2009, Beck's program was one of the highest-rated 5 p.m. cable news shows. TVbythenumbers.com reported that Beck's viewers outnumbered those of all his news competitors combined. By January 2011, however, Beck's numbers were down 39%, the steepest drop of any cable news show during the period.

The timing of Fox's decision to hire Beck in early 2009 was socionomically significant. At that time of widespread anger, fear and uncertainty, Beck had his finger on the pulse of the nation's mood and seemed to understand the what and how behind all those negative emotions. Fox's audience was initially grateful. But over the course of his program's run, as mood became less negative, advertisers steadily pulled their support. Five months into the stock market's recovery following the low of March 2009, Beck accused president Obama of racism. That accusation prompted 57 advertisers to boycott his show. As social mood continued to brighten over the next twelve months, more advertisers jumped ship. By last summer, *The New York Times* reported, 296 advertisers were gone.

Just 2¼ years after launching the *Glenn Beck Show*, Fox News announced on April 6, 2011 that Beck would be transitioning off the air. The announcement came after a nearly uninterrupted advance in the stock market from the March 2009 low. During the same two years, the Tea Party suffered a commensurate loss of popularity, as recounted in Chapter 30 of *Socionomic Causality in Politics* (2017).

Books

Beck played to his strength with catchy and provocative book topics. In times when social mood was negative, the strategy paid off. Six of Beck's books hit No. 1 on *The New York Times'* best seller list, including the latest in the spring of 2010 (see Figure 1). But Beck's two most recent books, one from last fall and another from early this year, have faltered. Why? Because a shift in mood has changed what people feel and therefore what they want to read.

A Disappointing Crowd

In November 2009, Beck announced his "Restoring Honor" rally. He originally planned to promote the rally as a vision-casting gathering and to announce a century-long political strategy for saving the country. As mood continued to become more positive, however, his favor waned and he changed the rally's theme "to [create] awareness and raise funds" for charity. As the rally drew closer and social mood waxed even more positive, fellow journalists began to attack and mock his efforts. The most reliable sources estimate that the August 2010 rally attracted an estimated 87,000 people, though some media reported as few as half that many and others as many as half a million.

By the time of the function, the positive mood trend was prompting more people to turn against Beck. In October, Jon Stewart and Stephen Colbert hosted a counter rally parodying Beck, titled the "Rally to Restore Sanity and/or Fear." The same media service that estimated 87,000 attendees at Beck's rally estimated 215,000 for Stewart and Colbert's event. By then, Beck's bleak predictions and agenda of urgency were so out of step with social mood that two and a half times as many people turned out to mock the former icon as did to support him. The new state of social mood explains the disparity.

Epitaph

What does the mainstream think about Beck's loss of popularity? James Downie of *The New Republic* summed up the change in Beck's fortunes:

"Beck built a following by making outlandish, conspiratorial claims—about ACORN, Obama, and so on. …Now, each new idea appears to be costing Beck both eyeballs and credibility." David Carr of *The New York Times* wrote, "The problem with 'Glenn Beck' is that it has turned into a serial doomsday machine that's a bummer to watch." Dana Milbank of the *Washington Post*, whose insights helped inspire this article, pointed out the following: "But as the recession began to ease, Beck's apocalyptic forecasts and ominous conspiracies became less persuasive, and his audience began to drift away. Beck responded with a doubling-down that ultimately brought about his demise on Fox."[1] All these changes were courtesy of social mood.

NOTES AND REFERENCES

[1] Milbank, D. (2011, April 6). Why Glenn Beck lost it. *The Washington Post.*

Chapter 7

Time's Person of the Year

Robert Prechter

January 17, 2007 (EWT)

For its 2006 "Person of the Year" cover, *Time* magazine chose no person in particular but an abstract internet user: "You." Immediately we recognized that this cover, celebrating all of humanity, echoes the "I love everyone" spirit identified in "Popular Culture and the Stock Market" in 1985 as a hallmark of positive social mood peaks. Then we read the following lines in an Associated Press report (December 16, 2006):

> It was not the first time the magazine went away from naming an actual person for its "Person of the Year." In 1966, the 25-and-under generation was cited; in 1975, American women were named; and in 1982, the computer was chosen.

Figure 1 shows that each of the years in which the magazine refrained from identifying a particular person or persons followed (by no more than 12 months) a major turning point in social mood. The 1966 cover, issued at peak positive mood, was an expression of inclusionism and a focus on youth. As *Prechter's Perspective* noted, "In every field, women gain dominance in bear markets," and the 1975 cover, published one year after the December 1974 bottom in the stock market, highlighted this theme by celebrating "American Women." *Time*'s cover of 1982, issued at the end of the 16-year bear market in PPI-adjusted terms, featured an inanimate object as Person of the Year, reflecting the feeling of alienation that attends extremes in negative social mood. The magazine's editors were apparently unable to reach a consensus on awarding the title to any member of humanity. Without doing it consciously, *Time*'s editors here in early 2007 may once again be reflecting the mood of a significant turning point in mood and the market—this time a peak—by honoring the collective "You."

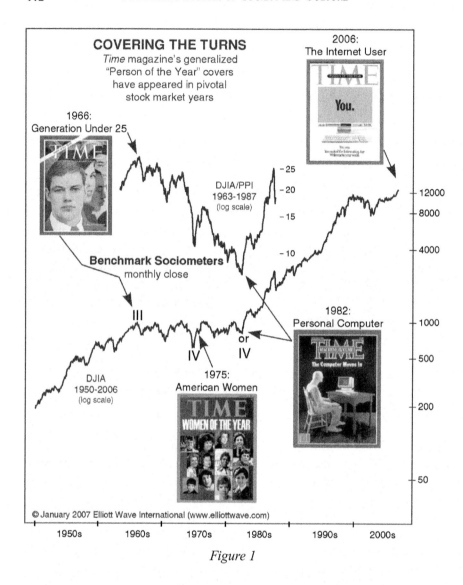

Figure 1

[*Real estate prices had peaked nine months before this report and underwent their biggest collapse in U.S. history. Stock prices topped nine months afterward and started their biggest decline since that of 1929-32.*]

Chapter 8

Positive Mood is the Fuel Boosting Taylor Swift's Skyrocketing Career

Chuck Thompson

July 31, 2015 (TS) / updated through December 2015

Taylor Swift's star couldn't shine any brighter these days. The BBC called her "the most powerful force in music."[1] *USA Today* said she "rules the world."[2] *The New York Times* noted that with just a tap of her fingers, even Apple retreated.[3]

A combined 165 million people follow Swift on Twitter, Instagram and Facebook,[4] and she has garnered a trove of awards, including seven Grammys, that would make many entertainers jealous.

Prechter's Perspective (1996) explained why some musicians become so popular:

> Pop cultural heroes are made by the public, so the public mood determines who's popular. The mood can also affect the creative direction of the heroes as well, so there are two effects.

The popularity of upbeat pop music rises when social mood is trending positively, and during the past several years Swift has been transforming herself from a country singer to a pop superstar. She made the full transition with her album *1989*, which was released in October 2014. It has become the fastest-selling album of the past decade.[5]

Riding the Wave: Taylor Swift performs in Charlotte, North Carolina during 2015's "The 1989 World Tour"

Billboard noted Swift's talent for appealing to the public and called her

> perhaps the sharpest, savviest, populist singer/songwriter of her
> generation, one who could harness the zeitgeist and turn it personal
> and, just as impressively, perform the reverse. These skills were
> evident in her earliest hits....[6]

Two music videos from Swift's *1989* album recently set new records on
Vevo, a video hosting service. "Bad Blood" had 20.1 million plays in only
one day, breaking Vevo's 24-hour viewing record. "Blank Space" became
the fastest video on the service to reach 1 billion plays.[7]

When Swift speaks, people listen. Even the leaders of the world's most
valuable company, Apple, which launched a subscription streaming music
service, Apple Music, on June 30, respond to her views. The company
decided that it would not pay royalties to musicians during a three-month
free trial of the new music service. In a blog post, Swift said that as a result
of the company's decision, she would withhold *1989* from Apple Music.
Within a day of the post, Apple announced on Twitter that musicians would
be paid during the three-month trial.[8] Swift then agreed to make the album
available on the service.[9]

This isn't the only case in which Swift changed a company's policies.
She recently gave $50,000 to a GoFundMe campaign for a girl with leu-
kemia. Because the website had a $15,000 donation limit, Swift gave the
money in four separate donations. GoFundMe followed up by changing its
donation limit to $50,000.[10]

As 2015 comes to a close, the accolades are flooding in. The Associated Press reported that Swift and Kendall Jenner dominated Instagram's
list of the top ten most-liked images of 2015.[11] Pollstar reported that Swift's
"1989 World Tour" outsold all other music tours last year, earning $250
million.[12] *USA Today* proclaimed that in the pop-music field, Swift has
"achieved world domination."[13]

In our November 2014 issue, we noted that Swift's *1989* "arrived with
the American markets on their way to all-time highs and social mood at its
most positive in more than five years."[14] But as Prechter pointed out in the
November 1998 issue of *The Elliott Wave Theorist*,

> one of the operative principles of social mood is that every bull market
> has its champions. These heroes are of their times, and their images
> become vulnerable when the wind changes.[15]

As long as the stock market is making new highs, Swift should do
well. A shift toward negative mood however, will be challenging for her.

If Swift's fortunes are as sensitive to social mood as we believe, it will be interesting to watch what happens when the prevailing mood eventually turns negative. Will we see her abandon upbeat pop and appear decked out in gothic threads with a Gibson Flying V, or will she simply fade from the limelight? Time will tell. But the striking extremity of her current popularity suggests that her star power is at or near the highest it will ever be.

NOTES AND REFERENCES

[1] Lee, D. (2015, June 22). Eddy cue: Apple's dad-dancing problem-solver. *BBC News*.

[2] Ryan, P. (2015, June 30). Her sick beat: Taylor rules the world. *USA Today*.

[3] *Ibid*.

[4] Sisario, B. (2015, June 22). With a tap of Taylor Swift's fingers, Apple retreated. *The New York Times*.

[5] Zumberge, M. (2015, July 8). Taylor Swift's "1989" becomes fastest-selling album of the last decade. *Variety*.

[6] Erlewine, Steven T., (2015, September 22). *Taylor Swift Bio*. Bill-Board.com.

[7] Goodman, J. (2015, July 7). Taylor Swift's "Blank Space" becomes fastest video to hit 1 billion plays on Vevo. *Entertainment Weekly*.

[8] Chen, B.X. (2015, June 28). Taylor Swift scuffle aside, Apple's new music service is expected to thrive. *The New York Times*.

[9] Rosen, C. (2015, June 25). Taylor Swift is putting 1989 on Apple Music. *Entertainment Weekly*.

[10] Guglielmi, J. (2015, July 10). Taylor Swift's $50,000 donation to cancer patient causes GoFundMe to raise giving limit. *People*.

[11] "Kendall Jenner, Taylor Swift most liked on Instagram in 2015." (2015, December 2). Associated Press.

[12] Fekadu, M. (2015, December 31). "Taylor Swift's '1989 World Tour' tops Pollstar's 2015 list with $250.4m grossed; AC/DC is 2nd." *US News & World Report*.

[13] Ryan, P. (2015, October 6). "6 pop stars who have checked into TV shows." *USA Today*.

[14] Thompson, C. (2014, November). Mood Riffs. Swift basks in limelight of pop success. *The Socionomist*.

[15] Prechter, R. (1998, November). Heroes under fire as the social mood changes. *The Elliott Wave Theorist*.

Chapter 9

Will Positive Mood Save Bill Cosby?

Chuck Thompson

January 29, 2016 (TS)

On December 30, just before the statute of limitations on an alleged 2004 offense would have run out, Bill Cosby was arraigned in Montgomery County, Pennsylvania, on one charge of aggravated indecent assault. The charge involves a former Temple University employee who alleges that Cosby drugged and violated her.[1]

Cosby's good fortunes have long depended on positive social mood, as noted a quarter century ago in the May 1992 issue of *The Elliott Wave Theorist*:

> Bill Cosby is a bull market personality. He hit it big in comedy records in the early 1960s and had a hit TV show in the late 1960s. Then he dropped nearly out of sight until the early 1980s. In 1984, he launched what *TV Guide* calls "the decade's most important program."

The Cosby Show debuted during a bull market and ran until 1992. It was television's biggest hit in the 1980s and "almost single-handedly revived the sitcom genre and NBC's ratings."[2]

Following the usual socionomic sequence, rumors of Cosby's impropriety had circulated for years, yet it was not until a surge of negative social mood over the past half year—as indicated by a deep setback in the NYSE index—that he formally faced charges. Cosby's attorneys succeeded in getting a defamation suit brought by another of his accusers dismissed in court, and they have also filed a dismissal motion in the Pennsylvania criminal proceedings.[3,4] Even if the motion is successful, the comedian faces accusations from about 50 women at a time when global stocks have lost $3.17 trillion in value, including $1.77 trillion in the U.S. in just six months.[5]

Post-Production Update: Much as a last-minute surge of positive mood saved Bill Clinton from impeachment (see Chapter 17 of *The Wave Principle of Human Social Behavior*), social mood turned more positive during Cosby's trial, and the defendant walked free. The Dow registered new all-time highs on three of the five days of jury deliberations covering June 12 to June 16, 2017, and the case ended in mistrial. It seems that historically positive social mood allowed Cosby to retain just enough of the Teflon coating that he has enjoyed through most of his career to get him off the hook. The accusers have vowed to continue their quest. Social mood will remain an important influence on their degree of success.

NOTES AND REFERENCES

[1] Schillaci, S., & Bueno, A. (2015, December 30). Bill Cosby Arraigned on Sexual Assault Charge, Bail Set at $1 Million. *Entertainment Tonight*.

[2] The Cosby Show. *TV Guide*.

[3] Melendez, P., & Ferrigno, L. (2016, January 22). Bill Cosby Wins in Pennsylvania Court; Defamation Lawsuit Dismissed. CNN.

[4] Ford, D. (2016, January 11). Bill Cosby's Lawyers Move to Dismiss Charges Against Him. *CNN U.S.*

[5] $3.17 Trillion Wiped Off Global Stocks So Far This Year. (2016, January 13). CNBC.

Part II:

TV AND FILM

Chapter 10

Social Mood and James Bond Film Ratings

Mark Galasiewski and Chuck Thompson

April 10, 2007 (EWT) / October 31, 2012 / June 16, 2016 (TS)

"Popular Culture and the Stock Market" (1985) noted, "men are more 'masculine' during bull markets, and women more 'feminine.'" Social mood regulates these preferences simultaneously with overall stock prices. Icons of past positive mood periods include John Wayne and Marilyn Monroe in the 1950s and Arnold Schwarzenegger and Madonna in the 1980s. In negative mood periods, such stereotypes fall from favor as society embraces a greater variety of gender roles and identities. The fluctuating popularity of the longest-running film franchise to feature a traditionally masculine male figure bears out this observation.

Ian Fleming introduced the character of heroic secret agent James Bond in 1952, three years into a 17-year trend toward more positive social mood, and chronicled his exploits through a series of novels. Bond debuted on screen in 1954 in a U.S. television adaptation of Fleming's first novel, *Casino Royale*. He debuted in film in *Dr. No* in the U.K. in 1962 and in the U.S. in 1963. There have been 22 films in the James Bond series, and their quality and success have waxed and waned with social mood.

Public sentiment regarding the quality of James Bond films is recorded on the Internet Movie Database (IMDb), where tens of thousands of viewers rate films on a scale from 1 to 10. Figure 1 plots this measure of the popularity of Bond films against our benchmark sociometer, the PPI-adjusted Dow Jones Industrial Average.

The films' popularity first peaked with *Goldfinger* in 1964 as social mood approached a positive extreme. The ensuing negative mood trend of 1966-1982 brought some tough times for Bond films. As Prechter observed, negative mood impacted filmmakers, making them "introspective, doubting and cynical."[1] In 1967, that attitude manifested in a spoof of the series, also

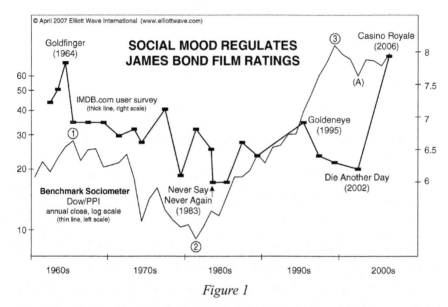

Figure 1

titled *Casino Royale*. The franchise continued to suffer as the bear market wore on. Its ratings bottomed with *Never Say Never Again* (1983), released shortly after social mood registered a negative extreme in 1982.

A trend toward positive mood in the 1980s and 1990s helped the character return to popularity. Low ratings for two Bond movies in the late 1990s were anomalous, although ratings bottomed again with the stock market in 2002. In 2006, the rating for a new version of *Casino Royale* registered an all-time high in tandem with all-time highs in both the Dow and global real estate prices, indicating highly elevated social mood.

The lofty rating for the latest Bond film coincides with a late stage in the Dow's current B-wave advance, a time when optimism often exceeds that seen at the end of the preceding five-wave advance. As long as social mood continues to wax positive, wave (B) will stay in force and reviews of any new James Bond movies should be relatively favorable. But once social mood turns negative in wave (C), we expect both shares and the series to fall from favor again. In the next Grand-Supercycle-degree bear market, new tales based on this hero will probably cease entirely.

2012 Update: For James Bond, Success Is a Matter of Mood (CT)

In a speech to a gathering of futurists in Boston in 2010, Robert Prechter reiterated his observation that during positive social mood trends people tend to be attracted to films with positive themes and those that have heroes and villains with distinct, white-vs.-black moral codes. During negative social mood trends, people tend to be attracted to films with negative themes and protagonists who have ambiguous moral qualities.

This observation has proved true over the past five decades with respect to the popularity of a white-hat hero, James Bond, a masculine secret agent flanked by beautiful women. The highest-rated releases of the James Bond film franchise have occurred during years when social mood was strongly positive. Prechter noted that through the early 1960s, "filmmakers did a good job making black-and-white hero movies. As a result, people rate those James Bond movies very high on the scale. As the trend went down, filmmakers put less of their heart into it, and they made worse movies."[2]

This link to social mood has continued, and the latest James Bond film rating bears out our prediction from 2007. Two years after the IMDb rated 2006's *Casino Royale* at 7.9, a new negative mood was driving stocks downward in wave (C) and producing a "Great Recession." It also sank the ratings for *Quantum of Solace* (2008), which received an IMDb rating of only 6.8.

After the stock market turned up again, *Skyfall* premiered in 2012. IMDb rates it above *Quantum of Solace* but below *Casino Royale*, thereby matching the relative position of the stock market at the time. As people felt their mood recovering from its depths, ticket sales were robust. *Skyfall* had the largest-ever U.S. box office opening for a Bond film.[3] At the premiere on October 23, Daniel Craig, who plays James Bond in the film, told the BBC, "This is my third premiere, and this is the biggest and the best." Geoffrey McNab, with *The Independent*, called the film "one of the best Bonds in recent memory."[4] Prince Charles and his wife Camilla, Duchess of Cornwall, attended the premiere along with a number of past Bond girls.[5,6] *Skyfall* opened on October 26 in 25 markets and "grossed a staggering $77.7 million, #1 everywhere," according to *Deadline Hollywood*. The publication reported,

> Smashing the all-time Saturday attendance record, this is the biggest opening of 2012 and the biggest 2D Friday-to-Sunday opening weekend in history there, and the 2nd biggest all-time Friday-to-Sunday opening weekend, behind just the 3D *Harry Potter and the Deathly Hallows Part 2*.[7]

2016 Update: Mood and Ratings Are Bonding Again (CT)

The latest James Bond film, *Spectre,* was released on November 6, 2015. It scored substantially lower than *Skyfall* in the IMDb ratings but not as low as *Quantum of Solace*. Socionomics accounts for this difference, too.

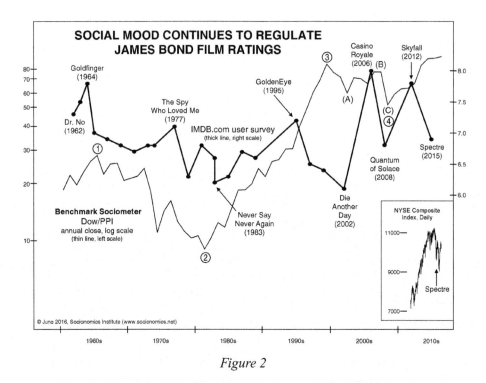

Figure 2

The Dow peaked at 18,312 in May 2015 and dove to 15,666 in late August. It rallied in late September but plunged again in January 2016, falling all the way to 15,660 by mid-February. The inset in Figure 2 displays the broader NYSE Composite Index, which most clearly recorded the negative mood trend in play at that time. This setback in stock prices was less severe than that of 2008, and so was IMDb's judgment of the associated Bond film.

James Bond is equipped with fast cars and impressive high-tech gadgets. He has a talent for outwitting the best criminal masterminds in the world. When it's time to pack a punch, he has the muscle to take down his opponents. But one thing he can't control is filmmakers' motivation and the public's appetite for the good guy/bad guy spy thrillers that the Bond franchise has served up for more than 50 years. For that, he needs a healthy dose of positive social mood.

*10: Social Mood and James Bond Film Ratings*125

NOTES AND REFERENCES

[1] Prechter, R. (1985, August). "Popular Culture and the Stock Market." *The Elliott Wave Theorist,* reprinted in *Pioneering Studies in Socionomics* (2003).

[2] Prechter, R. (2010, October). "Socionomics: A Better Model for Futurists, Part 2." *The Socionomist.*

[3] "Box Office History for James Bond Movies." *The Numbers.*

[4] Masters, T. (2012, October 24). "*Skyfall* Premiere is Biggest and Best—Daniel Craig." BBC.

[5] "*Skyfall* World Premiere: Prince Charles, Camilla Attend." (2012, October 24). ABC.

[6] Ruby, J. (2012, October 24). "The Spy Will Always Love Them: 007's Former Sidekicks Still Know How to Make an Impact on the Red Carpet at *Skyfall* Premiere." *The Daily Mail.*

[7] Finke, N., & Tartaglione, N. (2012, October 28). "*Skyfall* opens #1 in 25 Overseas Markets; Grosses $77.7 m and Smashes UK Records." *Deadline Hollywood.*

Chapter 11

Film Genres and Social Mood

Robert Prechter

August 17, 2012 (EWT)

One of our socionomic hypotheses is that trends toward negative social mood produce declines in the stock market and simultaneously dispose more people toward watching films with negative themes, such as horror, tragedy and misery. We have explored this idea in several articles.

We like testing socionomic hypotheses with other people's data sets, because doing so removes one potential for bias in data selection. I recently came across a useful list posted on The-Numbers.com that notes the highest grossing film released in the U.S. for each calendar year from 1920 to the present. Had we gathered these data, someone might ask, "Why choose only the highest grossing film?" "Why not limit the take to receipts only in the year of release or a certain number of months after release?" "Why use calendar years? Why not use a 12-month moving average?" And so on. But someone else considered this tally meaningful, so that's what we'll use.

The more I considered this particular list, the more it seemed suited for testing socionomic causality. The level of quality of each genre of entertainment fluctuates with the stock market, because waves of social mood regulate them both. Accordingly, this list of the highest grossing films takes into account not only immediate popularity, which according to socionomics should fluctuate with trends in the stock market, but also quality as judged by later viewers, because the more valued films live on and sell tickets in later years. The compilers' choice of listing films by total money earned over time removes arbitrary cutoff dates for each film's earnings. All films compete quite evenly with their contemporaries, because each one's earnings are pitted only against earnings of other films released at nearly the same time.

There is still some chance of an occasionally unfair result, since a film released in, say, December or January might not have appeared at the top of the list had it been released a month later or earlier, respectively. But any other choice of criteria would have similar, and probably worse, problems.

Most popular movies are sunny, fitting most people's general preference. The list of top-grossing films by year over a 92-year period, as you can see in Table 1, is packed almost exclusively with positively themed films.

But there are times when *more* filmmakers and viewers prefer *darker* movies. Socionomics proposes that such movies should become more popular, more numerous and generally of better quality during times when the trend in social mood is negative, as indicated by a falling stock market.

So, I posed two questions: Are there any times when the top-grossing film produced in a calendar year was a dark film? If so, how do those times match up with our benchmark sociometer, the stock market? Socionomics would predict that most, if not all, such films on the list should appear at times of negative social mood, which occur during and shortly following bear markets in stocks.

Most people would tag tragedies and horror movies as dark genres. I would include movies that do not have tragic endings but which otherwise are relentless tales of misery or fear. *Film noir*, with its gangsters and tales of betrayal, is on the milder side of dark. Most films within other genres—comedy, adventure, fairy-tale, fantasy, history, science fiction, drama, musical, war epic and western—are generally not at the dark end of the scale. There are exceptions in each of these categories, so each film needs to be judged individually.

Table 1 presents The-Numbers.com's list of the highest-grossing film released in each calendar year, not in chronological order but in alphabetical order. Please go through this list and mark the films that you would categorize as dark films. If you don't know the plots of some of them, you can look them up on Wikipedia, which provides plot summaries. After you categorize the films, you can turn to the next page to see how closely our answers match.

Mark what you consider to be negative-themed movies:

Table 1

101 Dalmatians	Kramer vs. Kramer
3 Men and a Baby	Lady and the Tramp
Aladdin	The Lion King
Alamo of the South Seas	The Longest Day
Avatar	The Lord of the Rings: The Return of the King
Back to the Future	Love Story
Bambi	Mary Poppins
Batman	Over the Hill to the Poorhouse
Beauty and the Beast	Peter Pan
The Bells of St. Mary's	Pinocchio
Ben-Hur	Pirates of the Caribbean: Dead Man's Chest
The Bible	Quo Vadis?
The Big Parade	Raiders of the Lost Ark
Billy Jack	Rain Man
Blazing Saddles	Robin Hood*
The Bridge on the River Kwai	Rocky
The Broadway Melody	Samson and Delilah
Butch Cassidy and the Sundance Kid	Saving Private Ryan
Cinderella	The Sea Hawk*
Cleopatra	Sergeant York
The Covered Wagon	Shanghai Express*
The Dark Knight	Shrek 2
ET: The Extra-Terrestrial	The Singing Fool
The Exorcist	The Snake Pit
Forever Amber	Snow White and the Seven Dwarfs
The Four Horsemen of the Apocalypse	Song of the South
Frankenstein	The Sound of Music
Funny Girl	South Pacific
Ghostbusters	Spider-Man
The Godfather	Spider-Man 3
Going My Way	Star Wars Ep. I: The Phantom Menace
Gone with the Wind	Star Wars Ep. III: Revenge of the Sith
Grease	Star Wars Ep. IV: A New Hope
The Greatest Show on Earth	Star Wars Ep. V: The Empire Strikes Back
Harry Potter and the Deathly Hallows: Part II	Star Wars Ep. VI: Return of the Jedi
Harry Potter and the Sorcerer's Stone	Swiss Family Robinson
Home Alone	The Ten Commandments
How the Grinch Stole Christmas	This is the Army
How to Become a Detective	Titanic
The Hunger Games	Tom Sawyer
Independence Day	Top Gun
It Happened One Night	Top Hat
Jaws	Toy Story
The Jazz Singer	Toy Story 3
The Jungle Book	White Christmas
Jurassic Park	You Can't Take it With You
King Kong	*Missing data; we inserted the top-grossing movie for these two years based on calendar year receipts.

If you are like me, you listed at least these eight titles as dark-themed movies:

The Exorcist
The Four Horsemen of the Apocalypse
Frankenstein
The Godfather
King Kong
Love Story
Samson and Delilah
The Snake Pit

as well as some of these:

Billy Jack
Jaws
Kramer vs. Kramer
Over the Hill to the Poorhouse

and possibly one or more of these:

Bambi
The Dark Knight
Jurassic Park
Star Wars V: The Empire Strikes Back

In all, this is 16 out of 92 movies, among which most people would have picked at least 8.

Table 2 shows the list again, printed in chronological order so you can see the years that these movies, highlighted in italics, appeared. Titles of the eight darkest movies (as I rate them) are ***bold and underlined***; those of moderately dark films are *underlined*; and those of mildly dark films are in *italics* alone.

The connection between the stock market and the issuance of top-grossing films with dark themes is striking. Figure 1 shows the timing of each of these films.

Over the Hill to the Poorhouse, a tale of misery redeemed by a happy ending, and *The Four Horsemen of the Apocalypse*, a tragedy in which the hero dies at the end, were the top-grossing films released in 1920 and 1921, the final years of a major bear market in stocks that started in 1905. Also, two acclaimed German horror films, *The Cabinet of Dr. Caligari* and *Nosferatu*, came out in 1920 and 1922, respectively.

The upturn in August 1921 kicked off the Roaring Twenties. For a ten-year period, no dark-themed movies made the list.

Table 2: Top-Grossing Film Released Each Calendar Year

Year	Title	$mil.	Year	Title	$mil.
1920	*Over the Hill to the Poorhouse*	3.0	1966	The Bible	34.9
1921	***The Four Horsemen of the Apocalypse***	9.2	1967	The Jungle Book	141.8
1922	Robin Hood*	2.0	1968	Funny Girl	58.5
1923	The Covered Wagon	3.8	1969	Butch Cassidy and the Sundance Kid	102.3
1924	The Sea Hawk*	0.0	1970	***Love Story***	106.4
1925	The Big Parade	11.0	1971	*Billy Jack*	98.0
1926	Alamo of the South Seas	3.0	1972	***The Godfather***	135.0
1927	The Jazz Singer	3.0	1973	***The Exorcist***	204.9
1928	The Singing Fool	10.0	1974	Blazing Saddles	119.5
1929	The Broadway Melody	2.8	1975	*Jaws*	260.0
1930	Tom Sawyer	11.0	1976	Rocky	117.2
1931	*Frankenstein*	12.0	1977	Star Wars Ep. IV: A New Hope	461.0
1932	Shanghai Express*	3.7	1978	Grease	181.8
1933	*King Kong*	10.0	1979	*Kramer vs. Kramer*	106.3
1934	It Happened One Night	2.5	1980	*Star Wars Ep. V: The Empire Strikes Back*	290.3
1935	Top Hat	1.8	1981	Raiders of the Lost Ark	245.0
1936	How to Become a Detective	6.0	1982	ET: The Extra-Terrestrial	435.1
1937	Snow White and the Seven Dwarfs	184.9	1983	Star Wars Ep. VI: Return of the Jedi	309.2
1938	You Can't Take it With You	4.0	1984	Ghostbusters	238.6
1939	Gone with the Wind	198.7	1985	Back to the Future	210.6
1940	Pinocchio	84.3	1986	Top Gun	176.8
1941	Sergeant York	16.4	1987	3 Men and a Baby	167.8
1942	*Bambi*	102.8	1988	Rain Man	172.8
1943	This is the Army	19.5	1989	Batman	251.2
1944	Going My Way	16.3	1990	Home Alone	285.8
1945	The Bells of St. Mary's	21.3	1991	Beauty and the Beast	218.7
1946	Song of the South	65.0	1992	Aladdin	217.4
1947	Forever Amber	16.0	1993	*Jurassic Park*	357.1
1948	***The Snake Pit***	10.0	1994	The Lion King	422.8
1949	***Samson and Delilah***	28.8	1995	Toy Story	191.8
1950	Cinderella	85.0	1996	Independence Day	306.2
1951	Quo Vadis?	30.0	1997	Titanic	600.8
1952	The Greatest Show on Earth	36.0	1998	Saving Private Ryan	216.3
1953	Peter Pan	87.4	1999	Star Wars Ep. I: The Phantom Menace	474.4
1954	White Christmas	30.0	2000	How the Grinch Stole Christmas	260.0
1955	Lady and the Tramp	93.6	2001	Harry Potter and the Sorcerer's Stone	317.6
1956	The Ten Commandments	80.0	2002	Spider-Man	403.7
1957	The Bridge on the River Kwai	33.3	2003	The Lord of the Rings: The Return of the King	377.8
1958	South Pacific	36.8	2004	Shrek 2	441.2
1959	Ben-Hur	73.0	2005	Star Wars Ep. III: Revenge of the Sith	380.3
1960	Swiss Family Robinson	40.4	2006	Pirates of the Caribbean: Dead Man's Chest	423.3
1961	101 Dalmatians	153.0	2007	Spider-Man 3	336.5
1962	The Longest Day	39.1	2008	*The Dark Knight*	533.3
1963	Cleopatra	48.0	2009	Avatar	760.5
1964	Mary Poppins	102.3	2010	Toy Story 3	415.0
1965	The Sound of Music	163.2	2011	Harry Potter and the Deathly Hallows: Part II	381.0
			2012	The Hunger Games (to date)	253.0

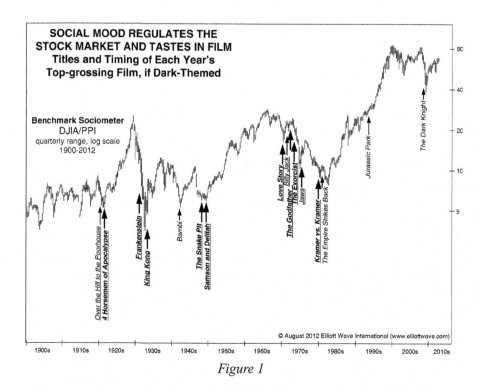

Figure 1

A bear market of even larger degree occurred from 1929 to 1932, and its economic consequence, the Great Depression, bottomed in 1933. *Frankenstein* was and still is the highest-grossing film released in 1931, the biggest down year of that bear market. *Dracula* also came out that year. Although the highest grossing film made in 1932 is a drama, the horror movie *Dr. Jekyll and Mr. Hyde*, which ranked third in gross earnings, garnered an Oscar (for lead actor), and 1932 remains the one and only year—so far—that a horror movie has won an Oscar. *King Kong* is the highest-grossing film produced in 1933, the year of the bottom in the Great Depression. These were precisely the years of negatively trending social mood, as indicated by a crashing Dow and a troughing economic contraction. Thereafter, horror movies stayed out of the highest-grossing category for *forty years*.

The sociometer used in Figure 1 is the PPI-adjusted Dow. The sideways bear-market pattern in that index lasted until 1949.

Bambi is a Disney animated feature released in 1942, the year of a major bear market bottom. While this movie barely qualifies as tragic, it is arguably the darkest Disney cartoon film, as Bambi's mother is shot and fire destroys the animals' forest home. The monster of the film is Man. Perhaps the second-most-tragic of the Disney animated films is *Dumbo*, released the previous year, in 1941; humans are the antagonists in that film, too.

As the 20-year sideways bear market pattern from 1929 to 1949 in the Dow/PPI reached its end, *The Snake Pit*, a tale of misery in an insane asylum, was the top-grossing film released in 1948. It is not a tragedy, as the incarcerated woman in the story survives intact. The final low in the Dow/PPI, however, was enough to draw the public to see *Samson and Delilah*, a relentless tragedy and the top-grossing film of 1949.

The upturn in 1949 kicked off a period of positive social mood and a multi-year advance in the Dow/PPI. Not one dark-themed movie made the list for the entire period of the 1950s and the 1960s.

Another negative mood period of high degree took place from 1966 to 1982. *Butch Cassidy and the Sundance Kid* was the top-earning film of 1969. It has a tragic ending, fitting a bear market, but the overall tone of the movie hardly seems to qualify as dark, so I did not pick it for the list. In 1970—the year of the Kent State shooting, the Beatles' breakup, a stock market low and an economic recession—*Love Story*, a tragedy, headed the list of the highest-earning films. In 1971, the violent and anti-establishment *Billy Jack* was the top earner. As the bear market wore on, things started getting serious. In 1972, a gangster epic, *The Godfather,* topped the list. In 1973, a horror film—*The Exorcist*—topped the list for the first time since 1933. In 1975, the year the associated recession ended, *Jaws*, a mild monster movie, became the highest-earning film released that year.

During the negative mood period of 1968-1982, a flood of ground-breaking horror films was released, led by *Night of the Living Dead, The Last House on the Left, The Shining, Alien, Halloween, Friday the 13th* and *The Evil Dead*, most of which are rated highly by critics. In 1979, the year of the Iran-hostage crisis and the final full year of decline in the Dow/gold ratio, *Kramer vs. Kramer*, a tale of misery but without a tragic ending, topped the earnings list. In 1980, during the associated recession, *Star Wars V—The Empire Strikes Back*, in which the bad guys triumph (temporarily for the series), was the top-earning film. The Dow/PPI finally bottomed in 1982.

There are *almost* no dark-themed movies on the top-earners' list for the entire rise in stock values during the bull market of the 1980s and 1990s. On the heels of a the bear market interruption of 1987-1990 (visible most readily in the Value Line indexes; see Figure 2 of Chapter 22) and its associated recession into 1991, the dark film *Silence of the Lambs*, though not the top-grossing movie of 1991, won five Oscars. In 1993, another mild monster movie, *Jurassic Park*, topped the revenue list. Unlike *Jaws*, this film drew viewers for reasons other than shock; it was the first major film featuring realistic computer-animated dinosaurs, and many pre-teen boys dragged their families to the theater to see them in action. Uncharacteristically, it came two years after the 1990 low in stocks and the recession that ended in 1991, but the official figures understate economic conditions of the time, as mass layoffs continued through 1993 and pessimism toward stocks maintained until 1994 [as recorded in Figure 1 of Chapter 12]. Fitting the mixed social mood, it is the mildest monster movie on the list.

Many horror films—including a new genre of torture movies—have come out since the sociometer's peak in 2000. Only one mildly dark-themed movie tops the earning list during this period: *The Dark Knight*, which was released in 2008, right in the middle of the biggest decline for stock prices since the early 1930s. Although not a horror film or tragedy, it was described at the time as the "darkest superhero film yet," and it broke box-office records. At the end, the hero destroys his reputation by publicly taking responsibility for the misdeeds of the film's evil antagonist.

We may attempt a statistical analysis along these lines someday. But for now, Figure 1 should serve to demonstrate yet again the value of the socionomic insight in elucidating when filmmakers and the public tend to become more willing both to craft and to patronize darkly themed films. When the next big bear market arrives, signaling a shift toward negative social mood, we will see new explorations of negative themes in films, awards for some of them and the eventual appearance of one or more of them on this list.

Chapter 12

The Timing of Quality Changes in Negative-Mood-Themed Films

Mark Galasiewski

January 17, 2007 (EWT)

The period from 1987 to early 1995 featured times of severe pessimism among stock market investors. It accompanied a Primary-degree correction in stock prices followed by a sequence of first and second waves, where pessimism often persists against the backdrop of a net rise in stock prices. As *Elliott Wave Principle* (pp. 79-80) pointed out, the one-sidedness of investor sentiment at the end of a second wave often exceeds that at the beginning of the preceding first wave.

Three graphs in Figure 1 show the high degrees of pessimism recorded during this period. Mutual fund managers on average held as much as 12.9% of their portfolios in cash by 1990. Short positions in S&P 500 futures contracts held by small traders ballooned through 1994. Bearish advisors polled by Investors Intelligence far exceeded bullish advisors through most of 1988, 1990 and 1994-95. The following socionomic study evidences another negative mood manifestation during the 1987-95 period.

Negative-Mood-Themed Films

Prechter's 1985 essay, "Popular Culture and the Stock Market," iden-tified horror films as manifestations of negative mood, which is why they tend to be most popular during and shortly after bear markets in stocks. Anecdotal evidence has suggested that other film genres rise and fall with the social mood, but until now no data were available that could capture the quantity, quality and popularity of various movie themes. Filmsite.org recently generated lists of the "greatest" English-language films in each genre, including the negatively themed styles of Horror, Crime/Gangster,

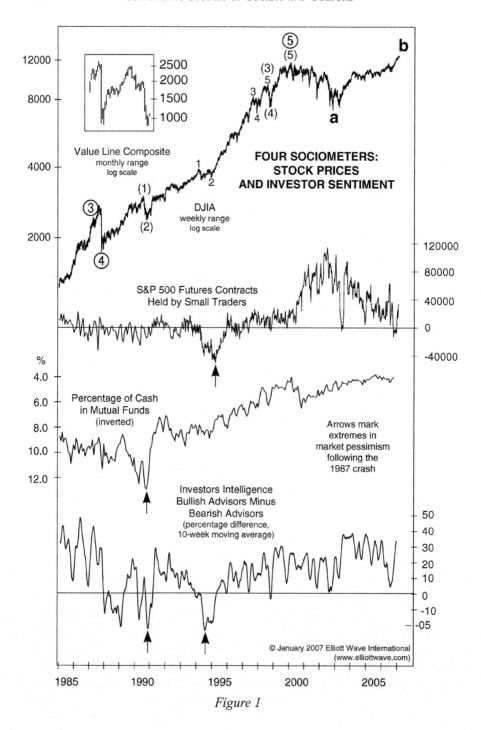

Figure 1

Disaster and "Noir" (classic *film noir* and its modern "post- (or neo-) noir" and "tech noir" derivatives). The site acknowledges that any list of "greatest" films is inherently subjective but asserts that the critics made their selections consistently. As data are hard to come by, we'll take what we can get.

Figure 2 shows that the annual number of highly regarded negatively themed films tends to peak in significant bear market years and trough near significant bull market tops. It is quite striking that the lowest readings on the chart occur in 1926, 1929, 1966 and 2005. The first of these years saw a major top in real estate prices and a stock market peak of Primary degree. The second and third of these years saw major tops in the Dow/PPI, and in the fourth year U.S. real estate prices were in their final full year of advance prior to their biggest decline on record while the Dow was approaching an all-time high within a corrective formation.

The years around 1932, at the bottom of the 1929-1932 crash, saw the release of not only such seminal horror films as *Dracula* (1931), *Frankenstein* (1931), *Dr. Jekyll and Mr. Hyde* (1932), *The Mummy* (1932), *The Invisible Man* (1933), and *King Kong* (1933), but also envelope-pushing Crime/Gangster films such as *Public Enemy* (1931), *I Am a Fugitive from a Chain Gang* (1932) and *Scarface* (1932), which the website describes as "one of the boldest, most potent, raw and violently brutal gangster-crime films ever made."

As the bear market formation of 1929-1949 in the Dow/PPI wore on, film noir replaced horror as the crowd favorite. Filmsite.org says that the genre is characterized by themes of "fear, mistrust, bleakness, loss of innocence, despair and paranoia"—clearly bear-market fare. The mid-to-late 1940s produced the famous noir films (some also categorized as Crime/Gangster) *Double Indemnity* (1944), *The Big Sleep* (1946), *Notorious* (1946), *The Postman Always Rings Twice* (1946), *Out of the Past* (1947), *The Third Man* (1949) and *Sunset Boulevard* (1950). After 1948, the popularity and quality of negative-mood films receded until 1966, the year of a major stock market top.

As a bear market held sway in the DJIA from 1966 to 1974, interest in negative-mood films began to revive. The late 1960s saw the release of such titles as *Bonnie and Clyde* (1967), *Cool Hand Luke* (1967), *In the Heat of the Night* (1967) and *Night of the Living Dead* (1968). *The Exorcist* (1973), which remains one of the few horror films ever nominated for Best Picture, and *Jaws* (1975) were among the first blockbuster fright films. *The Godfather* (1972), *Serpico* (1973), *Badlands* (1973), *The Godfather, Part II* (1974), *Death Wish* (1974) and the Dirty Harry "series" (1971-76) were

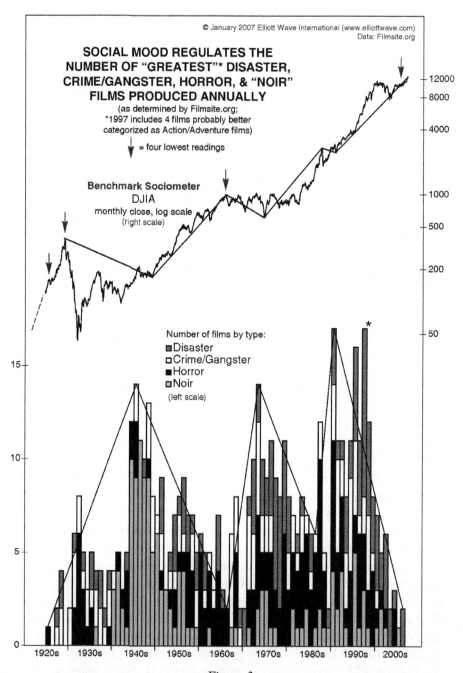

Figure 2

popular Crime/Gangster films of the period. "Post (or Neo)-Noir" films include *Chinatown* (1974) and *The Conversation* (1974). The Disaster films *Poseidon Adventure* (1972), *The Towering Inferno* (1974), *Earthquake* (1974) and *The Hindenburg* (1975) satisfied the public's need to experience, vicariously, misfortune on a massive scale. After 1979, negative-mood films receded sharply in popularity. The Dow/gold ratio bottomed in January 1980, and the bull market of the 1980s took off as positive mood returned. The lowest popularity of the decade for negativity themed films occurred in 1989, the year the Berlin Wall came down and the Soviet Union pulled out of Afghanistan.

Negative themes at the box office did a good job of expressing the trend toward negative social mood during the 1987-1990 corrective period and its aftermath (see Figure 1). The year of the initial crash (1987) saw an explosion in fright films, including *Hellraiser, Dead of Winter, The Lost Boys* and *Fatal Attraction*. The negative mood that produced a stock market decline, the 1990-1991 recession and the Gulf War also brought *Arachnophobia* (1990), *Jacob's Ladder* (1990) and *Misery* (1990). They were followed over the next several years by *Silence of the Lambs* (1991), *Bram Stoker's Dracula* (1992), *Interview with the Vampire* (1994) and *Seven* (1995). Crime/Gangster films of the period included (after a 16-year hiatus for the series) *The Godfather, Part III* (1990), *Goodfellas* (1990), *Reservoir Dogs* (1992), *A Bronx Tale* (1993), *Carlito's Way* (1993), *Natural Born Killers* (1994) and *Pulp Fiction* (1994). Neo-noir examples during the period include *Basic Instinct* (1992), *Devil in A Blue Dress* (1994) and *Fargo* (1996).

It may seem anomalous that in 1997 Filmsite.org rated highly a large number of Disaster releases (such as *Dante's Peak, Volcano, Titanic, Air Force One, Con Air, The Jackal* and *Speed 2: Cruise Control*), when the stock market mania was well under way. We would argue, however, that the last four films in that list should be categorized as Action/Adventure films, and *Titanic* as a Romance, which are staples of bull markets. Again, the subjectivity of those data can be a source of error.

[Technical note: Plotting numbers of highly regarded films per year indicated in Figure 2 as a percentage of the total number of films released per year would likely reveal the importance of negatively themed films in the 1930s and 1940s as being commensurate with the large (Supercycle) degree of that era's bear market.—Ed.]

Chapter 13

Fourth-Wave Foreshadowing— Case in Point: Torture Themes

Robert Prechter

October 15, 2004; expanded 2005 (EWT)

Even the most dedicated socionomist can't predict everything relating to social behavior. Back in 2000, I discreetly mentioned in an interview for *Prechter's Perspective* that entertainment during the upcoming bear market would probably feature human torture. It was an uncomfortable thing to say, but the signs were there. That prediction derived from the observation that the social characteristics of fourth waves foreshadow more severe manifestations in the next trend toward negative mood of larger degree. For example, at the wave IV low for stocks in 1921, *Nosferatu* presaged a series of vampire films in the larger negative mood trend of the 1930s. Likewise, at the wave ④ low in 1960, *Psycho* presaged a series of slasher films near the end of the larger trend toward negative social mood in the 1970s and early 1980s. A caption in a book on movies said that slasher films had broken "The Final Taboo." There is no such thing, as bear markets must continue to shock people with new horrors.

The appearance of the book *American Psycho* in 1991 (and to a lesser extent the film *Misery* in 1990), released just after the end of Primary wave ④, signaled that a major theme of the next bear market would be torture. (In a socionomic anomaly, a movie version of *American Psycho* was released in September 2000, near a major market top, although it was, as Wikipedia put it, a "dark, *comic* adaptation.") I said that in the next bear market the torture theme would show up in the movies, which it has, in films such as *Saw* and *Hostel*. But as specific as this expectation was, I was unprepared for many surprising nuances of its manifestation. For example:

(1) Who would have guessed that torture scenes would appear first not in films but on a prime time TV show? The 2002-2003 season of *24* opened

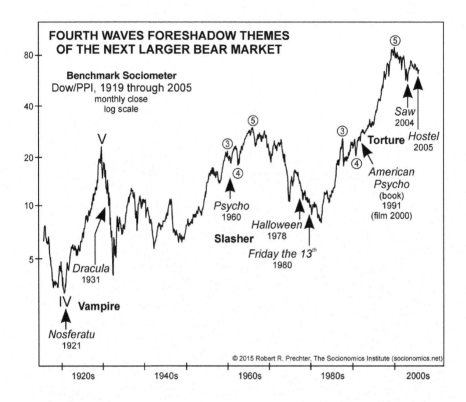

with a graphic scene of torture (administered by the good guys, no less) and featured half a dozen incidents of torture thereafter. In one episode, the hero died from torture and was then revived with electric shocks.

(2) Who would have guessed that the most graphic mainstream torture film of all time would be promoted from the pulpit and prompt conservative, religious Americans to bring their children to the film as a family outing? That is what attended *The Passion of the Christ* (2004).

(3) While we certainly would have anticipated incidents of actual torture during a major trend toward negative social mood, who would have guessed that U.S. government personnel would have been the focus of a torture scandal? Who would have guessed that administration officials would have issued memos condoning it?

Socionomists can predict what we call the "tenor" and "character" of social events but not often the specifics, which depend upon individual motivation and circumstances. Still, fourth waves give us a reliable preview of themes that will take stronger hold in coming bear markets.

Chapter 14

Social Mood Affects
Television Programming

Euan Wilson

October 2, 2009 (TS)

"Popular Culture and the Stock Market" (1985) and *The Wave Principle of Human Social Behavior* (1999) suggested that television is a sensitive enough medium to reflect Primary-degree trends in social mood. Prechter argued that television audiences prefer fun and simple adventures in positive mood trends but darker, more complex shows in negative mood trends.

Happy, fun and simple programs reflected the positive trend in social mood of the 1950s and early 1960s. Shows such as *I Love Lucy*, *Leave it to Beaver* and *Lassie* capture that era of irony-free humor, clear-cut morals and old-fashioned adventure.

In the negative mood of the early 1970s, shows became darker and more reflective. Top-rated programs such as *All in the Family* and *M.A.S.H.* displayed a social conscience and explored cynical themes.

In the positive mood trend of the 1980s and 1990s, the most successful television shows were once again safe and conventional. Comedies were light, fun, positive and family oriented. *Family Matters*, *Friends*, *Full House*, *The Cosby Show*, *The Fresh Prince of Bel-Air* and *Ally McBeal* all had warm appeal that reflected the mood of the day. Dramas were adventurous and had clearly delineated good guys and bad guys. Shows such as *Law and Order* took sides against criminals; *Baywatch* celebrated fun, adventure and beach life; *Dr. Quinn* and *ER* battled disease and the hardships of life. Even the fanciful *The X-Files* had a "good guys at work" theme.

During negative mood trends, the top-rated shows tend to be controversial, and they frequently break new ground, as *All in the Family* did in the 1970s. Since the 2000 top in stock prices, programming has been sliding into grey territory. Comedies are black and ironic; families are dysfunctional. *Breaking Bad* and *Weeds* both feature desperate parents who decide to deal drugs to solve problems of family economics. The critically acclaimed *Arrested Development* featured a broken yet hilarious family. *It's Always Sunny in Philadelphia* is described as "four friends who own Paddy's Pub in Philadelphia [who are] flat-out horrible people, but their reprehensible, selfish actions form the foundations for some twisted, hilarious comedy." "Flat out horrible people" as a focus for comedy can work when mood is negative.

Negative mood periods remain "us versus them," but "them" could be anyone—your best friend, spouse, trusted coworker, even yourself. The world's most popular show on television in 2008, *House*, is about a narcissistic, miserable, drug-addicted yet brilliant physician. (Tolerance of and even appreciation for drug addiction is a feature of negative mood periods [see Chapter 72 of *Socionomic Causality in Politics*].) *Damages* features characters who are completely capable professionally yet utterly despicable and hopeless everywhere else. The groundbreaking series *The Sopranos* was an exercise in the complexities of morality, family, good, evil and everything in between.

Socionomics Can Help Networks Choose Their Programs

We analyzed the viewership of the premium subscription channels, HBO and Showtime, from 2004 to 2009. The two channels have nearly identical churn rates approaching 65% per year, qualifying them for a comparative study

HBO's subscribership has been flat since 2007. Showtime, however, has made impressive annual gains, particularly since 2007, when social mood turned decisively negative. Normalizing Showtime's 2004 numbers to HBO's and charting them (see Figure 1) reveals Showtime's relative success over the past five years, 2004-2009.

Why the difference? We contend that Showtime has been more committed than HBO to expressing the negative mood.

HBO & Showtime Subscriptions
(in millions)

	2004	2005	2006	2007	2008	2009	% growth for 2004-2009
HBO	27.200	28.500	29.000	29.000	29.000	29.000	6.61%
Showtime	12.223	13.278	13.783	14.153	15.463	16.466	34.71%
Showtime 'Normalized' to HBO in 2004	27.200	29.548	30.671	31.495	34.410	36.642	34.71%

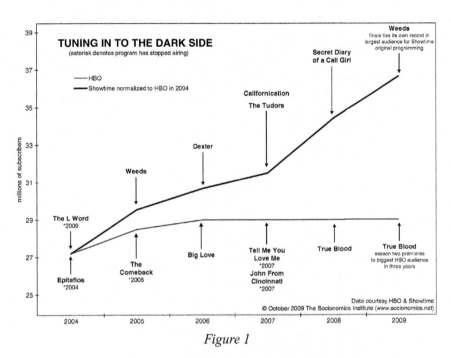

Figure 1

Since 2005, HBO has replaced its negatively themed *The Sopranos* and *The Wire* with positive-mood fare. *John from Cincinnati* was about a family that owned a beachside surf shop. *The Comeback* was a comedy about a past-her-prime star (*Friends* actress Lisa Kudrow) who tries to reach the same heights of success she had in the 1990s. Neither program was renewed for a second season. *Big Love*, a family show that just happens to involve polygamy, its only complex angle, has remained above water but has not been a ratings smash. Other shows have been ambivalent at best in their reflection of the new, darker mood.

Meanwhile, Showtime's programs have been dark, to the great appreciation of its subscribers. Its two flagship programs, *Dexter* and *Weeds*, offer moral ambiguity. The first is a drama about a serial killer who murders criminals. Only during a period of negative mood can a serial murderer be a hero. *Weeds* is similarly morally ambiguous. The show stars a suburban housewife whose husband suddenly drops dead. She turns to dealing marijuana to make ends meet and keep up appearances. As the show develops, she gets steadily more involved with violent gangs, corrupt law enforcement, Mexican mobsters and crooked politicians. Audiences love it. The family sticks together throughout, but all of the characters (the children, especially) openly acknowledge how screwed up their lives at home really are.

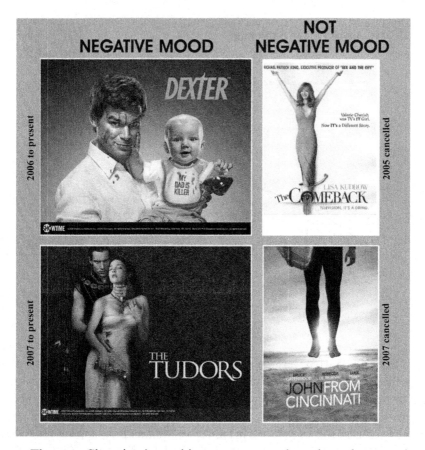

These are Showtime's two biggest programs, but others also appeal to the dark public mood. *The Tudors* details the debauchery and decadence in the court of King Henry VIII of England. *The L Word* is the second successful Showtime series based around predominantly homosexual characters. *Californication* features a depressed, alcoholic, sex-addicted writer. *Nurse Jackie* features *Sopranos* star Edie Falco playing a painkiller-addicted misanthropic nurse who cheats on her husband and loathes her coworkers and her patients; but at her core beats a heart of gold.

Moral ambiguity, decadence, expanded sexual boundaries, addiction, drug dealing, violence, vigilante murders and the dysfunctional-yet-surviving family: Showtime's top five shows include one or more of these negative-mood themes. Showtime's drubbing of HBO in the subscriber market is explicable socionomically given that its fare has been better suited to the trend toward negative social mood of recent years.

Chapter 15

This Christmas,
Socionomics is All Around You

Alan Hall

December 20, 2010 (TS)

Socionomics is not always about data and charts. If you pay attention, you can see it, hear it and feel it. Consider four recent films, which break disturbing new ground in the genre of dark Christmas movies.

Don't expect to see sugarplum fairies in *Nutcracker in 3D*, the latest retelling of Tchaikovsky's classic Christmas story. One reviewer writes, "Hide your children from this nightmare":

A movie for children in which robot dogs prowl alleys and razor-fanged vermin threaten little ones with torture? And which turns into a hardly subtle parable of Nazism, with storm troopers, promises of a "thousand-year" rule and dolls burned in ovens until the skies turn black?[1]

The Rat King and his Army
in "Nutcracker in 3D"

Another movie, *Rare Exports: A Christmas Tale*, portrays St. Nick as "a savage troll…as black as anything the Brothers Grimm could have dreamed up…a sinister old codger who chews off ears and whose demon minion kidnaps innocent children," says *The New York Times*. Soon after this satanic Santa is unearthed in Northern Finland, "children from a nearby village begin to disappear, and a group of reindeer hunters finds its annual crop slaughtered in the snow."[2]

If demons in the chimney, eviscerated Rudolphs and chewed off ears aren't evidence enough of negative mood, in December, a UK theatre company revived and brought to New York City Hans Christian Andersen's gruesome morality tale from 1845, published in the middle of a 24-year period of negative social mood. In *The Red Shoes*, a vain young girl—condemned to dance non-stop for all eternity—desperately asks an executioner to chop off her feet. The story inspired a movie released in 1948, the final year of a 20-year bear market in the Dow/PPI, in which the dancer jumps in front of a train. It also inspired a Broadway musical performed in December 1993, toward the end of a multi-year period of financial pessimism (see Figure 1 in Chapter 12); that story also ended in suicide. *The New York Times* reviewed the play:

Amputating the Red Shoes

> No little girl...will leave with sweet dreams of becoming a ballet dancer. [The play] is more likely to inspire nightmares involving severed body parts, public humiliation and concentration camps. You'll find it hard...to shake off many of the images conjured here from a darkness that feels like a swampy collective unconscious.[3]

Deadly Santa Encaged

"Rare Exports": Dasher, Dancer, Donner, Blitzen...Rudolph—*Dead*

The theme continues in *Black Swan*, an angst-laden quasi-horror flick about "ballet's dark side." The story comes complete with a nervous breakdown, psychosis, "ballet-themed stigmata," a Tchaikovsky soundtrack that "like a malevolent dance partner" provides "a hypnotic dirge," and camerawork that "finds infinite levels of dark menace." *The Seattle Times* says the director is "not at all interested in celebrating the art [of ballet]. Instead, he finds grotesqueries in it."[4]

The wildly popular Harry Potter books and movies have also reflected the darkening trend of social mood over the past decade. The first two movies were the lightest; each subsequent release has trended darker, with mounting danger and murder. The latest film, *Deathly Hallows*, uses negative-mood themes reminiscent of xenophobia and ethnic cleansing:

> The wizarding world quickly plunges into darkness as Voldemort's new regime takes action against muggle-born wizards (muggles are non-magical people), who they deem to be less valuable. It begins to resemble the Crusades, complete with an inquisition and accusations of heresy.[5]

You don't need a chart to understand the social mood behind Christmas movies that feature a demonic Santa, Nazi oppression of children, chopped-off limbs and ethnic cleansing.

[As shown in Figure 1, updated to the present, the Christmas season of 2010 turned out to be the last one within the time of the bear market in Dow/gold that took place from 1999 to 2011.]

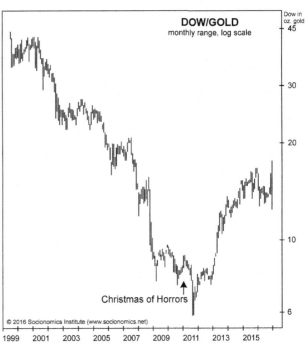

Figure 1

NOTES AND REFERENCES

[1] Whitty, S. (2010, December 3). 'Nutcracker in 3D': Hide Your Children From This Nightmare. *Newark Star Ledger*.

[2] Catsoulis, J. (2010, December 2). Discovering a Sinister Santa in Finland. *The New York Times*.

[3] Brantley, B. (2010, November 23). Dance-struck Little Girls: Run! Run in Horror!. *The New York Times*.

[4] Macdonald, M. (2010, December 9). 'Black Swan': Unlike Any Ballet Movie You've Ever Seen. *Seattle Times*.

[5] Cheung, A. (2010, November 21). Seventh Time's the Charm "Deathly Hallows" Shines as Best Potter Film Yet. *The News Record*.

Chapter 16

Negative-Mood Movies of 2012

Chuck Thompson and Clifford Smith

June 28, 2012 / October 2, 2012 (TS)

In June 1999, at the peak of a multi-year trend toward positive social mood, movie releases included *Austin Powers: The Spy Who Shagged Me, Tarzan, Big Daddy* and *Wild Wild West*, all of which were decidedly positive, light-hearted and sunny. A decade later, the year of the 2009 low in the DJIA saw the release of what critics agree is one of the most disgusting films ever made, *The Human Centipede*. Here in June 2012, Hollywood's line-up reflects the still-lingering negative mood as recorded in the dozen-year decline in the Dow/gold ratio and a new low this year in real estate prices.

Horror and Gore

Tinseltown's June 2012 releases include *Snow White and the Huntsman*, which casts the usually demure and affable heroine as a sword-wielding combatant trained in the art of war. *The New York Times* commented, "the movie tries to recapture some of the menace of the stories that used to be told to scare children rather than console them. Its mythic-medieval landscapes are heavily shadowed and austere."[1]

This month also brings *Prometheus*, the prequel to the 1979 horror classic, *Alien*. It tells the story of a team of space explorers who become stranded on a distant planet where they must fight in an attempt to save not only themselves but also the entire human race. Like 1979's *Alien*, the film is "filled with horror, gore and blood."[2] During a showing of the movie in New South Wales, Australia, a 15-year-old boy suffered a seizure after watching a "graphic surgery scene."[3]

Source: The Movie Guys

Space Terror: Prometheus *is full of horror, blood and gore.*

Abraham Lincoln: Vampire Hunter brings more flying body fluids to the June lineup. The film review website, Rotten Tomatoes, says that *Vampire Hunter* presents vampires "as they were meant to be experienced—as fierce, visceral, intense and bloodthirsty."[4] As

Lethal Politics: The 16th president axes opponents in *Abraham Lincoln: Vampire Hunter.*

the axe-swinging Lincoln disposes of his foes, there are "levels of heinous gruesome violence and some moments of sheer beauty," according to lead actor Benjamin Walker.[5]

The plot of *Piranha 3DD* begins with a marine biology student returning home for the summer to find that her dad has reopened her deceased mother's water park with "buxom lifeguards and former strippers" and an "'adults only' swimming pool full of mostly naked women."[6] It isn't long before the killer fish crash the party. The result? According to Straight.com, the film is void of any art-house moments and is "chock full of raunchy gore."[7]

End-of-the-World Films (CS)

Nicolas Cage's *Knowing* (2009), in which a solar flare tears through Earth's damaged ozone layer and incinerates the planet, defined the sci-fi apocalypse genre. In the past three years, things have ratcheted up a notch, with brilliant directors at the helm and A-list stars on the screen.

As the Dow/gold ratio recorded a major low in 2011, director Abel Ferrara's *444: Last Day on Earth* and Kirsten Dunst's *Melancholia* were released. As real estate prices recorded a new low in 2012, *El Fin* and *Seeking a Friend for the End of the World* came out. These movies differ from past end-of-the-worlders in a profound and fundamental way: No one on Earth

Facing the End: In *444: Last Day on Earth,* a hole in the atmosphere is set to cause humanity's extension at 4:44 am the following morning.

survives. That's right. Everyone dies, including the protagonists. These films embody part of the observation in *The Wave Principle of Human Social Behavior* (1999) that an extreme in negative mood opens the door for a popular philosophy to the effect that "hate and destruction will give the world what it deserves."

A Real-Life Space Program Based on the Same Fears

The planet-obliterating culprits in the four aforementioned films are, respectively, climate change, an Earth "twin" that suddenly emerges from the other side of the sun, a huge meteorite and an asteroid. Hollywood isn't alone in obsessing over Earth-shattering bodies. Today, the fear of an actual killer asteroid is so great that real-life activists hope to raise funds for an asteroid-detection satellite known as the Sentinel Space Telescope. The newly formed B612 Foundation, chaired by former NASA astronaut Ed Lu, aims to locate and map asteroids and other heavenly bodies that could endanger Earth. Scientists have long been aware of thousands of such "planet-killers," and there are potentially many more such bodies that need to be detected and watched, according to the group.[8] No doubt tracking them is a good idea, but socionomic causality seems to account for the timing of the heightened concern that prompted this group to form and to act.

NOTES AND REFERENCES

[1] Scott, A.O. (2012, May 31). The Darker Side of the Story. *The New York Times*.

[2] Bat, J. (2012, June 12). Movie review: 'Prometheus'. Woodlands Online.

[3] Zurko, R. (2012, June 11). 'Prometheus': Boy has Seizure During Graphic Movie Scene. *The Examiner*.

[4] Abraham Lincoln: Vampire Hunter (2012). Rotten Tomatoes.

[5] Weintraub, S. (2012, June 13). Benjamin Walker talks research, balancing history with the supernatural, playing different ages and more on the set of Abraham Lincoln: Vampire Hunter. Collider.com.

[6] Lowe, J. (2012, June 1). Piranha 3DD: Film Review. *The Hollywood Reporter*.

[7] Harris, M. (2012, May 31). Piranha 3DD is chock full of raunchy gore. Straight.com.

[8] Boyle, A. (2012, June 28). Asteroid Activists Launch Fund-raising Campaign for Space Telescope. MSNBC.

Chapter 17

Fortunes of **Alien** *and Its Tough Female Character Fluctuate with Social Mood*

Rosen Ivanov

June 13, 2013 (TS)

Popular Culture and the Stock Market (1985) opined that symbols of sexuality become less stereotypical in bear markets. That is, the lines become blurred as men become more feminine and women become more masculine. The classic 1979 film *Alien*—in which a vicious parasitic creature hunts and kills a spaceship's crew—found a welcome mat laid out by the negative mood trend of 1966-1982. Protagonist Ellen Ripley the buff gunslinger was right for those deeply negative-mood times, as was the movie's horror motif.

Prechter further noted in 2012 in *The Elliott Wave Theorist* [see Chapter 11],

> There are times when *more* filmmakers and viewers prefer *darker* movies. Socionomics proposes that such movies should become more popular, more numerous and generally of better quality during times when the trend in social mood is negative, as indicated by a falling stock market.

As such, the timing of the release of *Alien* in 1979, seven years into an eight-year trend toward negative social mood, was nearly perfect. But as social mood moved toward a positive extreme over the next two decades, the three *Alien* follow-up films were progressively less well received. Let's review each of those movies.

Alien—1979

To establish the lead character's baddest-babe-in-the-universe image, the first *Alien* film concludes with Ripley (portrayed by Sigourney Weaver) destroying the slimy-mouthed, acid-blooded creature that had killed fellow

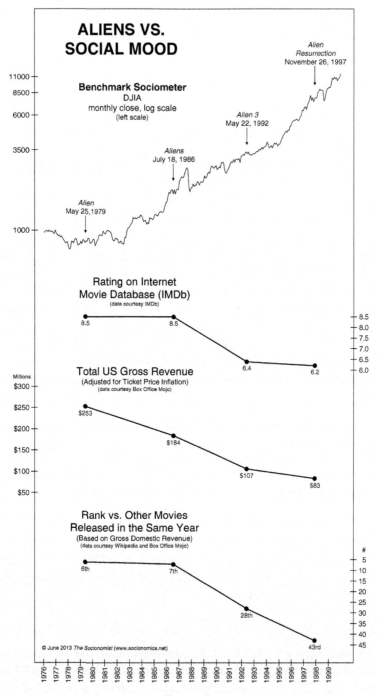

Figure 1

crew members on the spaceship Nostromo. *Premiere Magazine* ranked Ripley 8th on its list of 100 Greatest Movie Characters of All Time. The magazine listed her "defining moment" as her "nervy refusal to open the ship's hatch so that Kane (John Hurt) could be admitted—with a thing attached to his face."[1]

The film triumphed at the box office. It pulled in domestic earnings of $79 million—$253 million in today's dollars (see Figure 1). It was the #1 box office hit for 19 weeks and finished as 1979's sixth-best-grossing U.S. film. *Alien* has a quality rating of 8.5 on the popular Internet Movie Database (IMDb) and is 46th on IMDb's list of Top 250 titles.

Adjusted for ticket-price inflation, none of the subsequent films in the series exceeded *Alien's* gross domestic revenue. Rather, in line with socionomic causality, the franchise's take grew progressively less as the mood became progressively more positive.

Aliens—1986

A strong positive mood trend was underway by 1986 when the first sequel, *Aliens*, was released. The environment was not as welcoming, but the franchise got lucky with the arrival of director James Cameron, who made changes that were in tune with the mood of the time. Cameron steered *Aliens* away from the first film's dark horror motif and toward an action-adventure theme. In addition, he surrounded Ripley with macho male co-heroes, a team of marines. Together they use high-powered guns and flamethrowers to dispatch the monsters before destroying the colony with a nuclear blast—that is, standard fare for a typical audience in a positive mood environment.

The New York Times called *Aliens* a "flaming, flashing, crashing, crackling blow-'em-up show that keeps you popping from your seat."[2] The Ripley persona earned another 8th-place award, this one among heroes on the American Film Institute's list of 100 Heroes & Villains.[3] Cameron's action-adventure theme also brought other benefits to the franchise. *Aliens* was #1 at the box office for four weeks and made IMDb's list of Top 250 titles, coming in at #60. Total gross revenue for the film, however, lagged that of 1979's *Alien*.

Alien 3—1992

Alien 3, directed by David Fincher, was released on May 22, 1992, one month after the Dow topped 3,300 for the first time. There was some residual pessimism immediately following the bear-market years of 1987-1990, but the film went too far in the negative direction. It is exceptionally dark, as all characters from *Aliens'* 1986 cast are killed—including a ten-year-old girl and Ripley herself, who commits suicide. These depictions might have resonated in the year of a major extreme in negative social mood, such as 1932 or 1980, but not when the Dow was making new all-time highs. Cameron viewed the death of the girl as a slap in the face to fans who fell in love with the character.[4] Dean Foster, who wrote the novelizations of *Alien* and *Aliens*, called it "an obscenity."[5] In a review of *Alien 3*, Hal Hinson of *The Washington Post* called this version of Ripley "just another girl with a gun."[6] The film never made it to #1 and received no Top 250 accolades. It finished 28th among films released in 1992.

Alien Resurrection—1997

Even worse times lay ahead for the next installment in the franchise. Four months before its release on November 26, 1997, the Dow topped 8,000 for the first time during a full-on investment mania in a climate of extremely positive social mood. *Alien Resurrection*, directed by Jean-Pierre Jeunet, features two strong female characters: a cloned, superhuman Ripley and a female android. Their gender would have been better suited for a negative social mood backdrop.

Alien Ups and Downs: *The first film's horror theme (top photo) worked in 1979, as did the second film's action-adventure theme in 1986 (center photo). But the cloned, part-alien superwoman version of Ripley in the fourth film (bottom photo) was out of sync with the times in the feel-good 1990s, and it bombed at the box office. (Photos courtesy of IMDb.)*

The film floundered. In a review of *Alien Resurrection*, critic Roger Ebert said, "there is not a single shot in the movie to fill one with wonder—nothing like the abandoned planetary station in *Aliens*. Even the standard shots of vast spaceships, moving against a backdrop of stars, are murky here, and perfunctory."[7]

Like its immediate predecessor, *Alien Resurrection* never made it to #1 and received no Top 250 accolades. It finished a dismal 43rd among films released in 1997.

Conclusion

Both the popularity and quality ratings for the *Alien* franchise films declined as mood became more positive. The horror themes of the third and fourth films and their focus on strong female characters limited the franchise's success in the booming 1990s.

In a July 2011 Moviefone interview, actress Weaver said she believes Ripley's story is "unfinished." She hopes to see a film that takes audiences "back to the planet, where Ripley's history is resolved."[8]

If such a film becomes a reality, theme and timing will play key roles in its success. The producers of any future Ripley film already have a strong female character and riveting horror theme that audiences loved and will love again during times of negative social mood. A strong negative mood trend will give the *Alien* franchise its best chance of winning the affections of fans like those who gave the series its successful launch in 1979.

[In June 2012, shortly after the bottom in real estate prices, *Prometheus*, a gory prequel to *Alien*, was released. (See Chapter 16.) Fitting the negative mood, it garnered mostly positive reviews and became the 15th-highest-grossing film of 2012.—Ed.]

Rosen Ivanov was born in Bulgaria and earned a master's degree in finance from Denmark's Aarhus University in 2010. He currently lives in Aarhus, where he operates an education consulting business. His interests include financial markets, trading and understanding social causality. He became a certified Elliott Wave analyst (CEWA) in May.

NOTES AND REFERENCES

[1] *Premiere Magazine*. 100 greatest movie characters of all time. AMC Filmsite.

[2] Goodman, W. (1986, July 18). Film: Sigourney Weaver in 'Aliens.' *The New York Times*.

[3] 100 heroes and villains. American Film Institute.

[4] Kirk, J. (2012, June 14). 36 Things We Learned From the 'Aliens' Commentary. Film School Rejects.

[5] Interview: Alan Dean Foster (2006, March 9). AvP Galaxy.

[6] Hinson, H. (1992, May 22). 'Alien 3.' *The Washington Post*.

[7] Ebert, R. (1997, November 26). Alien Resurrection. RogerEbert.com.

[8] Larnick, E. (2011, July 17). Signourney Weaver on the legacy of 'Aliens' & her sequel that Hollywood won't make. Moviefone.

Chapter 18

A Student Observes Teen Fiction
Through the Lens of Socionomics

Lynda Edwards

October 2, 2012 (TS)

University of Delaware sophomore Laura Snyder has reviewed four decades of young adult fiction to see how teenagers express social mood through their reading tastes. She began with *The Outsiders* (1967) and ended with *The Hunger Games* (2008).

Snyder discerned a shift of tone for the genre in the 1980s. The first novel in the *Sweet Valley High* series debuted in 1983, just after the end of a 16-year bear market for U.S. stocks. In that environment of negative social mood, teens relished *Sweet Valley's* bitter undertones, such as cheating boyfriends and a drunken party girl transformed into a heroine by a terrible accident. Snyder noted that as mood waxed increasingly positive, girls abandoned such dark fare and in 1986 embraced the bouncy *Babysitters Club* series. These books asserted that teens can conquer daunting problems with intelligence, determination and good will.

Snyder also examined the mood arc in the *Harry Potter* series. The first volume hit stores in 1997, when mood was ebullient. Fans loved the book's glittering, magical universe featuring faithful, idealistic friends. As social mood soured, producing the bear market of 2000-2009, the books' magic turned lethal and the friendships were harshly tested. The final novel in the series, *Harry Potter and the Deathly Hallows* (2007), killed off several beloved characters. In 2008, the global mood was so dark, she observed, that teenagers turned to the bleak and ruthless *Hunger Games.*

Teen Fiction: *Laura Snyder's essay plumbed themes in teen literature.*

We are happy to see university students such as Snyder investigating the socionomic case.

Chapter 19

A Student Looks at Song Traits and Social Mood

Chuck Thompson
August 27, 2013 (TS)

Two months ago, our institute received a letter from SI member Bill Thomas, who noted that his family had "just entered its second-generation exposure" to socionomic theory. His 19-year-old daughter, Morgan Thomas, recently began her second semester at the University of Delaware, where she participated in a freshman honors seminar taught by Peter Atwater, an instructor of business administration and Socionomics Summit presenter [and a contributor to this book; see Chapter 26].

Thomas wrote an essay for the class titled "Moods and Music," which looked at the tempos, keys and complexity of popular songs during the stock market cycles of 1955-1974 and 1990-2011. She concentrated on the top five songs for each year on Billboard's Hot 100 list and compared her data to trends in the Dow Jones Industrial Average.

Thomas found no discernible relationship between major vs. minor keys and trends in the stock market, but she did find one with respect to tempo. Specifically, her data revealed that during times of positively trending mood, the most popular songs averaged 27 more beats per minute than they did in times of negative mood. "This lends a whole new meaning to the phrase 'feeling upbeat,'" she wrote.

Socionomics of Sound: *Morgan Thomas' essay looked at tempos, keys and complexity in popular music.*

"The third aspect of my study, complexity, was less quantifiable than tempo and key," Thomas wrote. "I considered a few aspects of musical complexity, including vocal harmony, timbre of vocals, and instrumentation." Thomas' analysis, while qualitative, suggested a correspondence between the complexity of music and social mood. For example, she found that when mood became negative, "new sounds and levels of complexity that broke away from the traditional forms began to pick up in popularity."

Thomas says further socionomic research on these topics should be helpful to music industry professionals, as it would aid their efforts to produce songs that resonate with the public.

Chapter 20

How a Negative-Mood Carol Morphed with the Times

Lynda Edwards

December 26, 2012 (TS)

There are years when the national mood is simply too negative for candy-coated Christmas carols. In 1943, the year after the U.S. stock market recorded its lowest price/earnings ratio of the century, Judy Garland needed a Christmas song for a scene in which she comforts her heartbroken baby sister in the movie, *Meet Me in St. Louis*. Songwriter Hugh Martin penned lyrics that included "(this Christmas) may be your last / Next year we may all be living in the past." The classic 'Have Yourself a Merry Little Christmas' was born.

Garland told Martin, however, that if she sang those lines to a sobbing child, "the audience will hate me like I'm a monster."[1] He responded with revamped lyrics that were fatalistic yet consoling for anyone enduring loneliness during the holiday. Martin's rewrite gave us these now famous lyrics: "Let your heart be light/ Next year all our troubles will be out of sight." He also crafted the resigned ending that made the song a bittersweet classic: "Someday soon, we all may be together/ If the fates allow/ Until then we'll have to muddle through somehow/ And have yourself a merry little Christmas now."

In 1957, social mood was becoming increasingly positive—a stark contrast to 1943. The DJIA was trading near its all-time highs, and the chirpy Christmas staple 'Jingle Bell Rock' had just been recorded. That's when Hugh Martin's song went through another transformation. In line with the new mood, Frank Sinatra decided that even Martin's revamped lines were too depressing for his upcoming album, *A Jolly Christmas*. Sinatra asked Martin to make the song "happy and swinging." Martin changed the encouraging "let your heart be light" to the more robust "make the yuletide gay" and ended with the eternal promise that "from now on our troubles will be miles away." "The fates" and "muddle through" were also cut in favor of "hang a shining star upon the highest bough."

This story is yet another example of how an era's popular music suits its social mood trend and, consequently, what society prefers to hear.

NOTES AND REFERENCES

[1] National Public Radio interview with Hugh Martin, Nov. 19, 2010.

Chapter 21

On Breaking Bad:
How Social Mood Helped It Become the
"Best Ever" Program

Robert Prechter

October 17, 2013 / December 2016 (TS)

In recent weeks, commentary from multiple sources has celebrated the now completed five-season run of TV's *Breaking Bad*. Articles have called the show "[maybe] TV's best series ever" (*USA Today*, 9/27), "perhaps the best drama of all time" (*Celebrity Report*, 10/1) and "perhaps the best show that's ever been on television" (*USA Today*, 10/3).

Certain times in the progress of social mood support peak artistic achievements in many fields, including the field of popular entertainment. The final episode of *Breaking Bad* aired on September 29, 2013, right in the middle of a period when major stock indexes were registering all-time highs. On AMC's post-show celebration, "Talking Bad," host Chris Hardwick said to the series' creator Vince Gilligan, "Thank you…for having a show that never dipped and ended on top." One could say nearly the same thing about the stock market of the preceding 4½ years.

There have been many thoughtful, artistic and widely celebrated TV series on the air in recent years. They include *Justified, The Closer, Slings and Arrows, Homeland, The Americans, Mad Men, The Walking Dead, Dexter, Weeds, Downton Abbey, Game of Thrones, The Wire, Being Erica, Arrested Development, Modern Family* and *House of Cards*. This cornucopia is reminiscent of the late 1930s in film and the late 1960s in pop music. In all three of these periods, stock prices by some measure were heading into and falling away from a B-wave top of large degree. According to long-standing Elliott wave labeling, the years 1939 and 1968 marked B-wave tops. The rally from 2012 is another B wave in terms of the real-money Dow (see Figure 1). Times of major B-wave advances, which are mixtures of bull and

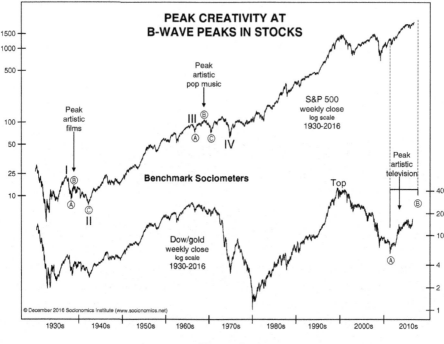

Figure 1

bear markets, seem to foster special creativity. Lauds for *Breaking Bad* are reminiscent of timeless praise for two artful, blockbuster films of 1939 (*The Wizard of Oz* and *Gone with the Wind*) and a comment about popular music from a major newspaper years ago: "Rock peaked in 1969." These times of peaks in the artistry of popular entertainment are marked in Figure 1.

Wave Ⓑ from October 1966 to December 1968 even fostered a brief blaze of artistry in television, which peaked with Patrick McGoohan's *The Prisoner*. In a nearly perfect ride along with wave Ⓑ, that acclaimed show began filming in September 1966, premiered in various markets beginning in September 1967 and completed its U.S. run in September 1968.

When people talk about the possibility that a season is the "best ever" for a popular artistic medium, chances are it will come near a B-wave top in social mood and stock prices. Apparently the mix of a return toward peak positive mood during the larger transition to more negative mood produces an ideal emotional state for stimulating artistic creativity.

Chapter 22

Memorable Film Quotes Appear
More Often in Negative Mood Periods

Robert Prechter

December 18, 2015 (TS)

The American Film Institute posted a list of the 100 most memorable movie quotations of all time. Its list is based on ballots returned from a selected group of over 1,500 directors, screenwriters, actors, editors, cinematographers, critics and historians. Selected quotations cover the period from 1927 through 2002.

A socionomist [see Chapter 21] might have guessed that major rising "B" waves in the stock market, in which society experiences a complex set of emotions, would score well in this tally. As it happens, the second- and third-largest number of annual quotes—those of 1939 and 1967—are in B waves, and quotes issued during other types of bear market rallies also score highly.

But the most impressive fact associated with these data is that a majority of quotes were crafted during periods in which the social mood trend was negative. The quote tally is a lagging socionomic indicator, because it takes time—about a year—to complete a movie. So, film scripts adopted during a positive or negative mood period turn into a completed film about a year later. This is the same shift we used in 1999 when comparing stock prices to conception rates using birth data [see Chapter 63].[1]

The periods of negative social mood—which are marked by the five declining lines on our sociometer in Figure 1—took place at the following times: 1929-1932, 1937-1942, 1946-1949, 1966-1982 and 2000-2002. The periods when memorable quotations distinctly cluster are almost precisely the same but shifted forward one year. The single largest number of annual quotes comes from the year 1942. Of the entire period of the data, from 1926 until now, this is the year of the lowest volume in the stock market,

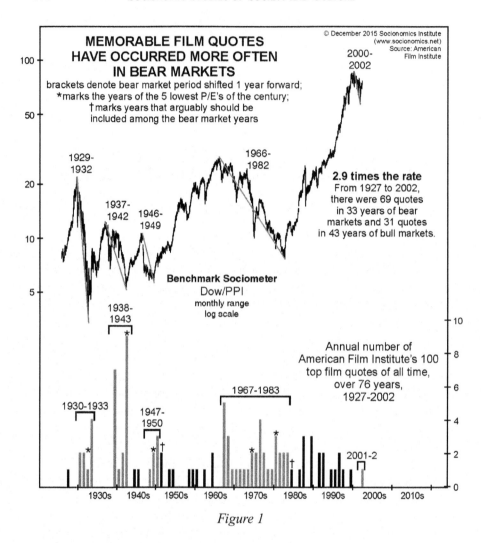

Figure 1

the lowest level for the Dow Jones Utility Average and the lowest overall value for stocks relative to GDP, all indicating extreme pessimism borne of a severely negative social mood.

Out of the 76 years when films produced these memorable quotes, 31 quotes appeared in the 43 bull market years and 69 quotes appeared in the 33 bear market years. The average annual rate for memorable quotes in bear markets is a substantial 2.9 times that for bull markets.

It is probably no coincidence that the years 1951 and 1984—in each case a year immediately following a period linked to a bear market—accounted for three of the memorable quotes. It is quite clear from the clustering of bars in Figure 1 that each of those years ended the set of memorable quotes produced during the preceding negative mood period. Nevertheless, we score them in the positive-mood column.

A chart of the Value Line Composite index (see Figure 2) indicates clearly that the years 1987-1990 suffered a bear market of Primary degree. Four of the five biggest annual tallies of film quotes for the entire two-decade period of mostly positive mood from 1981 to 2001 occurred in 1987, 1989, 1991 and 1992, i.e. during and for two years following that bear market, as investors stayed pessimistic toward the stock market (see Figure 1 in Chapter 12). In our coarsely designed study, all ten quotes ascribed to these years are counted in the positive-mood tally, representing a full third of its score.

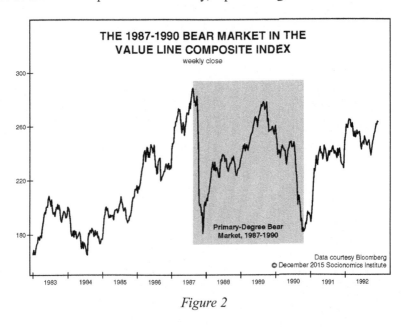

Figure 2

These observations reveal that 13 of the 31 quotes in the positive-mood column could be attributed to negative mood. Thus, the true rate at which negative mood encourages memorable film quotes is probably higher than our conservative statistic indicates.

Among the quotations on the original list of 400 from which the voters were allowed to choose, the most represented years are 1939 with 20 quotes, 1942 with 16 quotes and 1980 with 12 quotes. All three of these spikes occur within major bear markets, and the latter two years precisely mark important lows: 1942 (discussed above) and 1980, the very year of the bottom in the Dow priced in real money (the Dow/gold ratio).

Why memorable film quotes occur more often in times of negative social mood is debatable. It seemed plausible that such environments would foster humans' appetite for irony, which makes for a memorable quote. The #1 quote, "Frankly my dear, I don't give a damn," is an ironic twist following Rhett's long-time pursuit of Scarlett. The #2 quote, "I'm gonna make him an offer he can't refuse," is likewise ironic; it's not an "offer" at all. But the majority of the quotes on the list do not fall into this category, and a number of them are not even particularly clever; they just stick in people's minds, sometimes by embodying an emotion the movie elicited and sometimes by summarizing the feeling of the entire film in a single snippet.

The list of selected quotes is posted at http://www.afi.com/100years/quotes.aspx. The original list from which voters chose is posted at http://www.afi.com/Docs/100Years/quotes400.pdf. Maybe you can add to our observations.

NOTES

[1] Prechter, R. (2003). A Socionomic View of Demographic Trends or Stocks and Sex. *Pioneering Studies in Socionomics* (pp. 66-75). Gainesville, GA: New Classics Library.

Chapter 23

Of Mice and Mood:
Animation's History through
a Socionomic Lens

Euan Wilson

August 24, 2010 / February 4, 2011 (TS)

When Ted Turner pitched the idea for an all-cartoon network to in-vestors in 1991, he made a key point: People love cartoons. In fact, Turner showed, all kinds of people love them, with nearly half of cartoon viewers being kids' parents.[1]

The assertion piqued our curiosity: Since a broad swath of society enjoys cartoons, might social mood drive the sort of cartoons that studios produce and viewers watch?

Positive-Mood vs. Negative-Mood Cartoons

We found that cartoon styles have shifted dramati-cally with social mood as registered in our benchmark sociometer, the stock market. Cartoons made in times of positive mood are fun and wacky, whereas cartoons made in times of negative mood are more apt to be tragic, sexual or surreal. Positive-mood ani-mation is safe for the family, whereas many negative-mood cartoons contain themes of sexuality, drugs and racism.

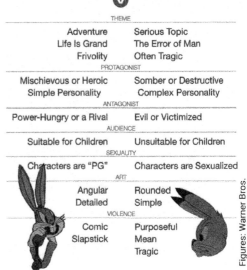

How Mood Rules Popular Cartoons

THEME	
Adventure	Serious Topic
Life Is Grand	The Error of Man
Frivolity	Often Tragic
PROTAGONIST	
Mischievous or Heroic	Somber or Destructive
Simple Personality	Complex Personality
ANTAGONIST	
Power-Hungry or a Rival	Evil or Victimized
AUDIENCE	
Suitable for Children	Unsuitable for Children
SEXUALITY	
Characters are "PG"	Characters are Sexualized
ART	
Angular	Rounded
Detailed	Simple
VIOLENCE	
Comic	Purposeful
Slapstick	Mean
	Tragic

Figures: Warner Bros.

Figure 1

Figure 1 summarizes the key differences in films appearing during times of positive vs. negative trends in social mood. See how many of the characteristics you can spot as we review the most popular cartoons of the past 90 years.

Positive Mood in the 1920s—The First Animated Stars

Felix the Cat and Mickey Mouse

The 1920s launched the age of plot and characterization for cartoons. Most historians consider Felix the Cat, that decade's most popular cartoon star, to be the first cartoon character with a distinct personality. Cartoon critic Maurice Horn called him "the high water mark of silent animation."[2] Felix is creative, adventurous, fun-loving, hard-working and intelligent—a positive-mood hero all the way. In the 1926 classic, *Two-Lip Time*, Felix courts a Dutch girl. Rather than fight a rival suitor, Felix inflates the man's pants with a tire pump and watches him float away into the clouds. It was an apt metaphor for both markets and cat; success came easily, and Felix's popularity soared through the decade.

The Right Hero at the Right Time: Felix the Cat (1925)

Figure 2

A Mouse Transformed: Pre-1929 Mickey gets into mischief; post-1932 Mickey accepts his destiny as hero.

Figure 3

Social mood reached a positive extreme along with stock prices at the end of the 1920s. This climate set the stage for Felix's impish new rival, Mickey Mouse. Viewers today hardly recognize the early incarnation of Walt Disney's creation. In *Steamboat Willie* (1928), Mickey is a prank-playing riverboat hand who throttles a cat that looks quite like Felix (Figure 3). Ebullient audiences loved the carefree, rascally mouse.

Negative Mood in the Early 1930s—Sex, Drugs and Menace

Mickey's New Direction; Felix's Demise

Mischievous Mickey's run screeched to a halt with the stock market crash of 1929-1932. Suddenly, Mickey was out of step with the times, and audiences let Disney know it. In 1931, Terry Ramsaye of *Motion Picture Herald* wrote, "Papas and mamas, especially mamas, have spoken vigorously…about [the] devilish, naughty little mouse…. Mickey has been spanked."[3]

Afterward, Mickey no longer caused mischief. The 1933 short, *The Mad Doctor*, was released in the depths of the Great Depression. Fitting the deeply negative mood, it left all frivolity behind. The story—seemingly inspired by 1931's *Frankenstein*—opens with wind, thunder, a dark stranger and Pluto's abduction. A doctor plans a gruesome experiment: He aims to replace Pluto's body with a chicken's to see whether the new creature will "bark, crow or cackle." The antics and songs are gone, while the doctor's menace and his castle are frightening. Mickey dodges traps and undead skeletons until the doctor's snares finally catch him. In the climax, Mickey eludes a buzz saw, only to wake up in bed and realize that the whole ordeal was a nightmare.

With the subsequent shift toward positive mood in the mid-1930s, Mickey took on yet another role: that of the heroic leading man. The transformation mirrored America's shift toward optimism, and this triumphant version of Mickey endures today.

Meanwhile, Mickey's predecessor, Felix, failed to adapt to the negative mood of the 1930s. Despite the breakthrough of sound, the cat clung to his muteness, and his popularity plummeted. Four times since, producers have tried to revive Felix—in 1936, 1958, 1991 and 1995, always in positive mood periods. The most successful attempt was Felix's run in the 1950s during a major trend toward positive mood, when he starred in 260 new shorts and regained much of his former zest. Each revival, though, faded when social mood again turned negative.

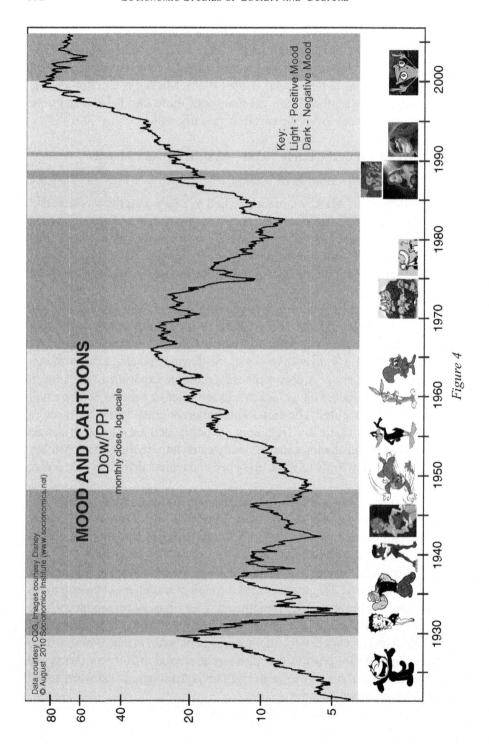

Figure 4

Betty Boop, Vamp

The Max Fleischer studio struggled to create a star to rival Mickey and Felix. It finally struck gold after mood turned negative in the early 1930s. Their star: vampish Betty Boop. Boop routinely sported a skimpy top, and her skirt was forever riding up. Betty was so risqué that one 1933 short, *Boilesk*, proved too much even for negative-mood tastes and was banned in Philadelphia.

Betty Boop tackled both coerced sex and drug use. In *Chess-Nuts* (1932), the Black Knight nearly deflowers Betty before Bimbo the dog comes to her rescue. In *Boop-Oop-A-Doop* (1932), Betty is a high wire performer in a circus as the villainous ringmaster lusts for her from below. After the performance, the ringmaster fol-

Negative-Mood Sex Symbol: Her torso covered by just a lei, Betty dances a hula (1933)

Figure 5

lows Betty to her tent, where he caresses her legs and threatens her job if she refuses to submit—a sore topic at the time, with a quarter of the U.S. unemployed. Koko the clown rushes in and knocks the ringmaster unconscious with a test-your-strength mallet. When Koko asks if Betty is OK, she answers in song, "He couldn't take my boop-oop-a-doop away!"

In another episode, *Ha! Ha! Ha!* (1934), Betty tries to ease Koko's toothache. She administers nitrous oxide but drops the mask and accidentally exposes the entire town to gas. What follows is downright trippy as townsfolk, plants, cars and bridges all collapse into convulsive laughter.

Positive Mood from 1932 to 1937—A Hero Emerges

The reign of sexy, druggy cartoons was short-lived. As social mood became more positive in the mid-1930s, Betty's creators fashioned a more modest wardrobe, but Betty couldn't make the transition. Her boop-oop-a-doop fizzled.

Betty's successor at Fleischer studios, Popeye the Sailor, debuted in 1933. His scruffy appearance and can-do spirit mirrored the mood that fueled the 1932-1937 bull market.

Popeye's nemesis, Bluto, underwent a fascinating metamorphosis. Paramount and Fleischer first billed him as "Bluto the Terrible! Lower than bilge scum, meaner than Satan, and strong as an ox!"[4] But as mood continued its positive trend, Bluto's personality softened from serious threat to mere rival. As Prechter

Kings Features syndicate

Tough, Purposeful: Popeye confronts problems with positive-mood gusto (1933).

Figure 6

stated in "Popular Culture and the Stock Market," when social mood is trending positively, society celebrates heroes in "good-guy-versus-bad-guy" conflicts; by the time mood reaches a positive extreme, "Everybody's a good guy."[5]

The specials *Popeye the Sailor Meets Sinbad the Sailor* (1936) and *Popeye Meets Ali Baba and His 40 Thieves* (1937) were positive-mood cartoons containing exotic settings, rollicking adventure and a hero's triumph. The shorts were so popular that some theaters billed them ahead of the feature films for which they opened.

Snow White and the Seven Dwarfs, released in 1937, also took full advantage of the multi-year extreme in positive social mood. Triumph over evil, hard work and adorable woodland creatures in the film all reflect the positive mood. The film's wicked witch is a pure villain, and Prince Charming is a one-dimensional, heroic savior. The film was a hit. Disney spent $1.4 million on *Snow White*. In the film's first theater run, he recouped that amount six times over.

Negative Mood from 1937 to 1942—Racism, War and the Fall of Man

Pinocchio and Fantasia Struggle to Find the Era's Theme

The Dow Jones Industrial Average fell 52% from 1937 to 1942, and the negatively trending social mood became manifest in worldwide expressions of anger and fear. But animation studios somehow missed the memo. Some of their films contained dark elements, but for the most part, their themes were sunnier than the times, and it affected their popularity.

Pinocchio is a good example. The mostly upbeat film premiered in 1940. It contains many negative themes, including imprisonment, drinking, fighting and gambling. But the delinquency is overshadowed by the film's positive theme of family love. *Fantasia* also premiered in 1940 and featured magic, demonic gargoyles and racial stereotypes. Disney's hero, Mickey, abuses sorcery and gets in way over his head. But like *Pinocchio*, *Fantasia's* overall tone—communicated through exciting visuals, beautiful music and Mickey being mischievous—was too positive, and audiences of the day mostly yawned, with both films taking more than a decade to break even.

A Censored Centaur: Sunflower, far left, *Fantasia's* black centaur. Because of subsequent censorship, it is difficult to locate a color image that contains the character. *Trouble Brewing:* Right, the film's positive-mood hero leaves negative-mood audiences unfulfilled (1940).

Figure 7

Peace on Earth's Morbid Message

MGM more fully captured the negative mood with *Peace on Earth* (1939). In the short, tools of war litter the world. A grandfather squirrel describes now-extinct Man to his progeny. After the final two living men kill one another, the squirrel and his fellow woodland friends dance among Man's remains. This story would be a difficult sell in a time of positive mood. But in a time of negative mood, audiences were open to a children's cartoon that suggested utopia can be born of humans' extinction.

Anti-Man: In Peace on Earth, cuddly creatures delight in humanity's end (1939).

Figure 8

Bambi Gets It Right

Just before the stock market low of 1942, Disney finally tapped into the negative mood with its landmark film, *Bambi*. Ostensibly a children's story about happy forest creatures, *Bambi* actually mirrors deep fear and misanthropy. Though never seen, Man's menace pervades the film. The murder of Bambi's mother remains one of animation's most memorable sequences. The scene continues to traumatize children 70 years after its release. According to boxofficemojo.com, the film made $3 million in its first release, a remarkable feat given that the occupying German military blocked its screening throughout most of Europe.

Coal Black and de Sebben Dwarfs

Amidst the deeply negative mood, the Warner Bros. studio produced cartoons that offend viewers today. The best example is 1943's *Coal Black and de Sebben Dwarfs*. In his 1983 book *Of Mice and Magic*, critic Leonard Maltin wrote,

> The stereotyped characters and 1940s-style enthusiasm for sex leave modern viewers aghast. The dialogue is strictly jive talk, and the pulsating music bounces the action along as the evil queen calls Murder Inc. to 'black out So White' and keep her from Prince Chawmin'.[6]

Lucky Sebben: So White and her entourage (1943).
Figure 9

Warner Bros. drew both Prince Chawmin' and the dwarfs with stereotypically expanded features, and So White (named Coal Black in the title) is an exaggerated, Betty-Boop-style sex symbol. Critic Steve Bailey commented in 2003:

> [The dwarfs] are little more than thick-lipped comic relief. The racial aspect is merely a smokescreen for what this cartoon is really about: sex. ...[The Wicked Queen's first words] are "Magic mirror on the wall, send me a prince about six feet tall." So White, far from Disney's virginal image, wears a low-cut blouse and thigh-high shorts, and sends blazes of erotic ecstasy through every male she meets.[7]

Wolfie and Red Celebrate Life's Baser Pleasures

In the same year, MGM tapped into the mixed social mood with Tex Avery's Wolfie and Red cartoons. *Red Hot Riding Hood* (1943) casts Red as a nightclub dancer and the wolf as a lustful cad. The short was a hit with soldiers and civilians alike, and Avery released three more in the series, to thunderous acclaim.

Maurice Horn noted, "Avery has been hailed as one of the most gifted and imaginative cartoon directors, a 'Walt Disney that read Franz Kafka.'"[8] Yet Avery's real genius was his timing. Such raunchy cartoons work best in the period from late in a bear market to early in a bull market. Cartoons would not openly address sex again for another 25 years.

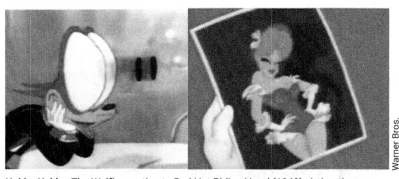

Hubba Hubba: The Wolf's reaction to Red Hot Riding Hood (1943). Animation aficionados will note the similarities between Red and another starlet from a mixed-mood era, Jessica Rabbit (1988).

Figure 10

Positive Mood from 1942 to 1966—Slapstick and Family Fun

As Prechter and Hall pointed out in the August 2009 *Socionomist*, the first halves of big third waves do not reflect rising optimism so much as declining pessimism.[9] Thus, popular cartoons in the early 1940s are fun, wacky works that, at the same time, sport wisps of negative-mood themes. Later in the trend, the cartoons became far sunnier, in tune with the positive mood behind the bull market.

Slapstick Hilarity

MGM gave violence a positive-mood spin with its Tom and Jerry series. Wrote Horn, "Their whimsical atmosphere, frenetic motion and choreographed violence were more in tune with the times than Disney's shorts."[10] The cat-and-mouse team engaged in slapstick antics with no harmful consequences. Characters might lose a tooth, get electrocuted or be driven into the ground by a telephone pole, but they always remained safe and whole to play-fight another day. The sunny mood showed through the characters, story, animation and gags in nearly every Tom and Jerry short, typified in *The Cat Concerto* (1946), released the year of a stock market top. Tom is an esteemed pianist and Jerry the unwitting resident inside Tom's piano. Hijinks ensue at Tom's recital, with Jerry taking credit for the performance. It was the right cartoon for the times, and Tom and Jerry won seven Academy Awards from 1943-53.

As mood became more positive, Warner Bros.' cartoon characters—Daffy Duck, Porky Pig, Bugs Bunny, Sylvester the Cat, Tweety Bird, Foghorn Leghorn, Yosemite Sam and others—developed distinct personalities, and the gags became layered. The worst that ever befell any of these characters was a spinning beak or singed whiskers. Plots lacked scary villains; violence was caricatured and derived mostly from zany rivalries along the lines of Tom and Jerry's.

Warner Bros.' beloved Wile E. Coyote and Roadrunner series (1948-1966) centered entirely on a humorous rivalry. The shorts aired during a roaring bull market, and in an extreme expression of inclusionism, both rivals managed to win empathy. Audiences wanted Wile E.'s elaborate inventions to succeed, yet they also delighted when the same inventions backfired. Viewers knew the spectacular failures would result in a long, whistling fall punctuated by a puff of dust. Positive mood engenders an appreciation for muted, humorous violence; successful cartoons deliver it.

From 1959 to 1964, Jay Ward Productions joined in the fun with *Rocky and Bullwinkle*, a cartoon series with wordplay, convoluted plots, twisted histories, "fractured" fairy tales and lovable characters. Nestled within this period was *King Leonardo and His Short Subjects* (1960-1963), with tales of hero Odie Cologne thwarting a pair of bumbling villains.

In the late 1950s and early 1960s, Hanna-Barbera provided new cartoon characters, including Huckleberry Hound, Yogi Bear, Ruff and Reddy, Quick Draw McGraw and The Jetsons. In our sociometer's final upward wave, one cartoon series in particular became family fare: *The Flintstones*, which aired evenings in prime time from September 30, 1960 to April 1, 1966, a run that ended less than two months after the Dow/PPI peaked in February of that year.

Woody Woodpecker: A (Nut-) Case Study

Woody Woodpecker, from his birth near the start of the 1942-1966 bull market until his demise just after its peak, offers a microcosm of our socionomic theme. The early Woody of 1941 was grotesque, insane and mean, a good example of the kind of characters produced in times of negative social mood. By 1945, the nascent positive mood trend had removed the psychosis from his eyes and mitigated his madness (see Figure 11).

In the early 1950s, amidst the bull market's powerful third wave, Woody was lean, determined, and blessed with clever scripts and fun villains upon whom to exact his heroics. Critics agree that this was the era of Woody's best cartoons, including *Termites from Mars* and *Socko in Morocco*.

During the 1960s, his antics became increasingly benign. By the late 1960s, Woody was cute incarnate and, to most critics, utterly boring. An anti-violence social morality crystallizing late in the positive mood trend led to heavy censorship, which took any remaining edge off Woody.

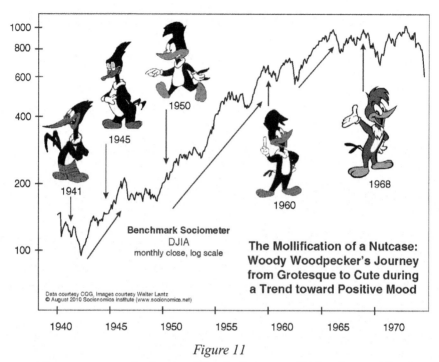

Figure 11

The move toward a benign Woody frustrated Walter Lantz, Woody's creator. Critic Leonard Maltin noted,

> For [Woody's] most recent Saturday morning program on the NBC network, [Lantz] had to remove every sequence in which a character fired a gun or hit someone on the head with a hammer. Is it any wonder that Woody and his cohorts became blander as the years rolled on?[11]

Initially, Woody Woodpecker successfully adapted to positive-mood tastes, but after reaching his comic peak early in the third wave, the anti-violence movement ground away what had made the character so funny. By the end of his run, he had become so sweet that he could not return to his former self when he needed to.

Negative Mood from 1966 to 1982—Sex, Violence and Nihilism

Since its inception in 1922, the Motion Picture Association of America has imposed an X rating on animated films only seven times. *Six* of those seven films premiered during the trend toward negative social mood that took place from 1966 to 1982.

The most famous of the adults-only animated films was also the first: *Fritz the Cat*. Ralph Bakshi created the film in 1972. Its adult rating was

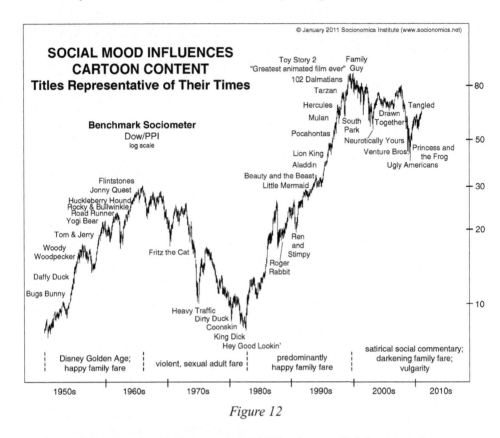

Figure 12

heavily promoted, with slogans such as "90 minutes of violence, excitement, and SEX" and "He's X-rated and animated!" The movie won instant critical acclaim. The public loved it, too; the film grossed over $100 million at the box office and paid for itself 100 times over. Said critic Leonard Maltin, "The film is a vibrant, personal statement about life in the 1960s, the sexual and political revolution, and hypocritical attitudes regarding 'good taste.'" The movie advocates free love and satirizes political correctness and party politics. Fritz engages in group sex in a bathtub, has a party broken up by police animated as pigs, shoots a toilet with a shotgun, floods his apartment and watches a synagogue congregation cheer when the U.S. sends weapons to Israel. And that's just in Act One.

In Act Two, characters smoke marijuana and shoot heroin. Prostitutes and car thieves work the street. Fritz witnesses a friend's murder and joins a domestic terrorist group. But despite all Fritz has witnessed, he remains unmoved and unchanged, experiencing no character growth whatsoever.

Eventually he abandons his terrorist cohorts and returns to his simple life of hedonism, embracing meaninglessness.

Bakshi wrote and directed several more taboo-tackling films, each of which did well at the box office. For example, *Heavy Traffic* (1973) opens with a pimp paying off corrupt cops who then bludgeon a homeless drunk into a bloody mess. *Coonskin* (1975) involves three African-American friends—a rabbit, fox and bear—who become leaders of Harlem's organized crime scene. Amid nearly continuous bloodshed, the trio engages corrupt law enforcement, the Mafia, racism and rival con artists. Critics called 1974's *Dirty Duck*, a rival studio release, even filthier than *Fritz*. 1982's *King Dick*, an Italian film from director Gioacchino Libratti that was translated into English, stars a dwarf on the run from a witch named Nymphomania who requires 69 orgasms to restore her beauty. Another 1982 animated film, *Hey, Good Lookin'*, focuses on Brooklyn's gang culture in the 1950s and includes episodes of reckless violence, spur-of-the-moment sex and hallucinations of giant nude women and garbage-can monsters. In a visual expression of negative mood, all of these films are darkly tinted.

There was every reason for the typical futurist, using linear extrapolation, to project the wave of negatively themed animations into the future. But after the stock market's low of 1982 (see Figure 12), a wave of positive social mood ushered in a near-total reversal in the appearance of culturally extreme animated films.

Cool Cats: Positive-mood Felix, the hero (left), acknowledges the applause; negative-mood Fritz, the slob (right), grabs what he can.

Figure 13

Positive Mood from 1982 to 2000—Heroes and Heroines

The positive social mood behind the bull market of 1982-2000 seemed determined to undo every bit of ugliness that the preceding negative mood trend had produced. Animated films became fun and brightly colored and featured richly detailed storylines with positive themes. The new look and feel was popular with both critics and audiences.

In *The Wave Principle of Human Social Behavior* (1999), Prechter noted that Disney's cartoon films succeed best in periods of positive social mood. The well-known Disney Renaissance, the ten-year period from 1989 to 1999 when Disney Animation Studios reverted to classic fairy tales and stories, returned the company to its glory days of the 1950s. The Renaissance produced such classics as *The Little Mermaid* (1989), *Aladdin* (1992), *The Lion King* (1994), *Pocahontas* (1995) and *Mulan* (1998). The first animated film to receive an Academy Award nomination for Best Picture, *Beauty and the Beast* (1991), was also produced during this time.

Everything is Magical: The Little Mermaid, Aladdin, The Lion King and Mulan all typify the positive mood of the 1990s bull market.

Figure 14

Negative mood returned during the Primary-degree bear market of 1987-1990 and lingered into the early 1990s, as evidenced by a dampened economy and investor pessimism as measured by stock market sentiment indicators (see Figure 1 of Chapter 12). A number of mixed-mood animations were produced during this period, including *Who Framed Roger Rabbit* (1988), with its sultry heroine Jessica Rabbit, and the grotesque *Ren and Stimpy* (1991), a children's show on Nickelodeon starring a scarcely recognizable dog and cat. The physical differences between this pair and the iconic positive-mood tandem Tom and Jerry (see Figure 15) are stark. Positive mood ended *Ren and Stimpy's* run in 1994.

Stark Dog/Cat Differences: Animated tandems in positive (Tom and Jerry, left) and negative (Ren and Stimpy, right) mood environments..

Figure 15

Pixar's *Toy Story 2* premiered in 1999. It was the perfect capstone to a two-decade-long trend toward positive social mood. A poll at the review aggregation site Rottentomatoes.com christened *Toy Story 2* with a rare 100% rating. Other accolades go further: By virtue of it having garnered the *most* reviews of all 100%-rated movies, many critics consider *Toy Story 2* to be *the best movie ever—animated or not*. We find it fitting that a film so rated was released precisely at the most significant stock market peak in recorded history, as indicated by an all-time high for the Dow priced in terms of real money (gold), which still stands today, and in terms of the Dow's dividend yield, which was the lowest ever recorded: 1.4%.

Negative Mood from 2000 to 2009—TV Gets Potty-Mouthed

Little of the negative mood trend of this period found its way into animated fare in cinemas, as evidenced by positive-mood hits from Disney-Pixar and Dreamworks. We attribute this condition to the "flat" form of the correction (in which wave B makes a new high), during most of which time optimism remained historically high as recorded by numerous measures.

Television, however, did provide some negative-mood fare. Comedy Central's *South Park*, which debuted in 1997 and has remained in production, is the most obvious example. It uses sharp satire and nasty language to skewer authority figures and the establishment, echoing even *Fritz the Cat* in terms of its political and social commentary. NPR correspondent Julie Rovner noted that *South Park* character Eric Cartman is "by far the most famous of the four foul-mouthed grade-schoolers who inhabit the cardboard-cutout town of South Park."[12] Cartman's antics, according to Rovner, include "giving his best friend HIV" and then urging him to stay optimistic. He also "ground up a rival's recently deceased parents and served them to him in a bowl of chili." Cartman's creators, Trey

Positive Mood and Negative Mood Nine-Year-Olds: Boy Genius (left, Elroy of The Jetsons, 1962-63 and 1985-87) and Evil Genius (right, Eric Cartman of South Park, 1997 to present).

Figure 16

Parker and Matt Stone, have called him a "Little Archie Bunker." (Bunker was the bigoted, sardonic star of the popular show *All in the Family* in the negative-mood decade of the 1970s.)

Drawn Together, another animated program on Comedy Central, featured caricatures of classic cartoon-movie character types, including "Disney Princess," "Marvel Superhero" and even "Betty Boop," all living together reality-TV-style. Also, 2010 saw the premiere of *Ugly Americans*, an alternate-reality parody of modern-day New York City, populated with monsters, zombies and demons.

Positive-Mood and Negative-Mood Princesses: *Cinderella, 1950 (left) and Belle of* **Beauty and the Beast,** *1991 (center) reflect the "G" rated fare of positive-mood trends. Note the risque, negative-mood allusions to these heroines in* **Drawn Together,** *2004-2007 (right).*

Figure 17

The Effects of Social Mood on "Adventure" Families:
The positive-mood Quests (left) versus the negative-mood Ventures (right). Note the grotesque features of many of the Venture characters.

Figure 18

The negative mood of this period encouraged the tradition of mocking former positive-mood icons. The critically acclaimed series, *The Venture Bros.* (2003-present), spoofs Jonny Quest, a cartoon hero of the 1960s and the mid-1990s, and the rest of the *Quest* cast, recreating them as failures. Even the villains are hopelessly incompetent, with names like Baron Underbeit, Phantom Limb and The Monarch—a butterfly-like supervillain riddled with more insecurities than a Wall Street mogul in October 2008.

In the meantime, the Internet is providing cartoonists an alternate, censor-free venue, much as the movie theatre did for Bakshi in the 1970s. *Neurotically Yours*, a webtoon, features Foamy the Squirrel—a frustrated little monster prone to outbursts of anger. Foamy has a low tolerance for any kind of stupidity and mercilessly shreds any character who doesn't meet his standard. Contrast Foamy to the happy-go-lucky squirrel, Rocky of *Rocky and Bullwinkle* fame, who thrived during the positive mood period of the 1950s and 1960s. Foamy's sharp-tongued impatience for typical modern life hearkens back to *Fritz the Cat*.

Two Completely Different Squirrels:
Rocky (left, 1960s) typifies positive mood; Foamy (right, 2003-present) displays a negative mood style.

Figure 19

There is a hint of a shift in the wind: The spy spoof *Get Smart* ran on television during the stock market's topping period of the late 1960s. Debuting in January 2010, the animated spy spoof *Archer* debuted on FX, fitting an element of positive social mood that has returned since the March 2009 low in stocks.

[Post-production insert: Reports from June 2017 confirm that Warner Brothers—in tune with positive mood—is developing an animated feature film on the Jetsons while also shopping the idea of a live-action, sitcom version of *The Jetsons* for television.]

Conclusion

It is clear that from animation's inception, waves of social mood have simultaneously driven the positive or negative tone of themes and styles in cartoons as well as trends in the stock market.

NOTES AND REFERENCES

[1] Turner, T. (Producer). (1991). Cartoon Network 1991 presentation reel. [Web].

[2] Horn, Maurice. (1980). Felix the Cat. *The World Encyclopedia of Cartoons*. New York City: Chelsea House Publishers, 271.

[3] Maltin, Leonard. (1980). *Of Mice and Magic: A History of American Animated Cartoons*. New York City: Penguin Books, 37.

[4] *Ibid*, 110.

[5] Prechter, Robert. (1985). "Popular Culture and the Stock Market," *The Elliott Wave Theorist*. Reprinted in *Pioneering Studies in Socionomics*, Gainesville, GA: New Classics Library.

[6] Maltin, Leonard. (1980). *Of Mice and Magic: A History of American Animated Cartoons*. New York City: Penguin Books, 250-251.

[7] Bailey, Steve. (2003, April 4). Internet Movie Database user reviews for *Coal Black and de Sebben Dwarfs*. IMDB.com.

[8] Horn, Maurice. (1980). Tex Avery. *The World Encyclopedia of Cartoons*. New York City: Chelsea House Publishers, 103.

[9] Hall, A., & Prechter, R.R. (2009, August). The Wave Principle Delineates Phases of Social Caution and Ebullience. *The Socionomist*, 1(3), 3.

[10] Horn, Maurice. (1980). Tex Avery. *The World Encyclopedia of Cartoons*. New York City: Chelsea House Publishers, 683.

[11] Maltin, Leonard. (1980). *Of Mice and Magic: A History of American Animated Cartoons*. New York City: Penguin Books, 186.

[12] Rovner, Julie. (2008, April 5). *Eric Cartman: America's Favorite Little $@#&*%*. NPR.org.

Chapter 24

Cinderella Shines

Chuck Thompson

March 26, 2015 (TS)

Disney's live-action remake of the classic animated fairy tale *Cinderella* earned more than $250 million in worldwide box office revenues in less than two weeks.[1] According to Box Office Mojo,[2] its nearly $70 million debut in the U.S. exceeded the weekend box office receipts of all other films playing in American theaters combined.

The film opened after an extended positive mood trend had carried the Dow Jones Industrial Average and the S&P Composite Index to new highs and elevated the NASDAQ index above 5,000 for the first time in 15 years. Such times have historically been good for Disney. As Robert Prechter noted in 1999, Disney cartoons are "bull market movies, reflecting the shared mood of both their creators and their viewers."[3]

Positively trending social mood from 1989 to 1999 drove the Disney Renaissance,[4] a time when Walt Disney Animation Studios produced classic fairy tales reminiscent of their glory days. After the most severe bout of negative mood in eight decades, Disney announced in 2010 that it was getting out of the fairy tale business.[5] The hiatus was short-lived.

As it has done throughout its history, Disney's animated films have succeeded during a time of strongly positive mood. The studio produced a huge hit with *Frozen* in 2013—the fifth-highest-grossing film of all time.[6] [As of the end of 2016, four more positive-mood films took top spots, pushing *Frozen* to ninth.] Disney's production president, Sean Bailey, said that his company once again views fairy tales as viable fare. Disney will follow *Cinderella* with more live-action remakes of its animated classics—*The Jungle Book* and *Alice in Wonderland*,[7] due out next year [and *Beauty and the Beast*, due out in 2017]. The company has also announced a sequel to *Frozen*. It is an extraordinary move, because it is rare for Walt

Disney Animation Studios to produce a theatrically released follow-up to one of its movies.[8]

Though the critical reception of *Cinderella* has been largely positive,[9] the film has its detractors. A March 17 *Vanity Fair* article asked, "In the age of Katniss, Hermoine, Maleficent and Elsa, what room is there for a princess whose quiet goodness is her best quality?" The article cites children's book author Jane Yolen, who called Cinderella a "sorry excuse for a heroine, pitiable and useless."[10] Amidst a positive mood trend, these critiques have amounted to little more than grumblings. The next time mood becomes unequivocally negative, critics and audiences en masse are likely to adopt such cynical attitudes with respect to the studio's sparkly, fairy-tale fare. In the meantime, prospects for these projects remain promising as long as social mood stays positive. Should a major negative mood trend develop, it would be wise for Disney to curtail its release of new fairy-tale films.

NOTES AND REFERENCES

[1] Lang, B. (2015, March 22). "Insurgent" Tops Foreign Box Office, "Cinderella" Passes $250 Million Globally. *Variety*.

[2] Subers, R. (2015, March 15). Weekend Report: "Cinderella" Shines, "Run" Stumbles. Box Office Mojo.

[3] Prechter, R. (1999). *The Wave Principle of Human Social Behavior*. Gainesville, GA: New Classics Library.

[4] Puig, Claudia (March 26, 2010). "Waking Sleeping Beauty" Documentary Takes Animated Look at Disney Renaissance. *USA Today*.

[5] Chmielewski, D.C. and Eller, C. (2010, November 21). Disney Animation is Closing the Book on Fairy Tales. *Los Angeles Times*.

[6] All-time Box Office: Worldwide Grosses, 1-100. Box Office Mojo.

[7] Fritz, B. (2015, March 10). With "Cinderella," Disney Recycles Fairy Tales, Minus the Cartoons. *The Wall Street Journal*.

[8] Miller, D., & Keegan, R. (2015, March 16). Big-screen "Frozen 2" to Defy Disney Tradition. *Atlanta-Journal Constitution*.

[9] Agar, C. (2015, March 15). Weekend Box Office Wrap up: March 15, 2015. Screen Rant.

[10] Jarvis, E. (2015, March 17). When Did Cinderella Get So Nice? *Vanity Fair*.

Part III:

CONSTRUCTION PROJECTS

Chapter 25

A Socionomic History of Skyscrapers

Peter Kendall

March 18, 2016 / April 8, 2016 (EWT)

Two years after the great stock market peak of 1929, the July 1931 issue of *The New Republic* hit upon the social significance of the Chrysler Building and the Empire State Building: "The material embodiment of the late bull market remains in our metropolitan structures of towering heights. They soar boldly above a surrounding mesa of roofs, very much as the spire-like graph of 1929 equity prices. The same causes explain both pinnacles."

In his 1947 book, *Cycles: The Science of Prediction*, Edward R. Dewey expanded upon the "skyscraper indicator," which proposes that tall buildings are built at the end of economic booms. He wrote,

> There has been an obvious explanation offered for the building of so many of our skyscrapers at peak prices in time of peak activity. That is the time when they can ordinarily be most easily financed. But why investors and bankers should be so eager to risk their money at the very time the risk becomes unduly heightened is a mystery our statistics do not explain.

Thanks to the discovery of socionomic causality, that mystery has been solved. *The Wave Principle of Human Social Behavior and the New Science of Socionomics* (1999), summarizing earlier essays in *The Elliott Wave Theorist*, explained that a trend toward more positive social mood unconsciously encourages borrowing, lending, investment and "construc-tiveness" in society irrespective of risk. (For more on the socionomic view of risk-taking, see Chapter 19 of *Socionomic Theory of Finance*.) "At social mood peaks," wrote Prechter, "the impulse to build shows up in the con-struction of record-breaking buildings."

By 1947, all-time highs for stocks and stories had accompanied one another so regularly that Dewey observed, "The pattern of our recurrent

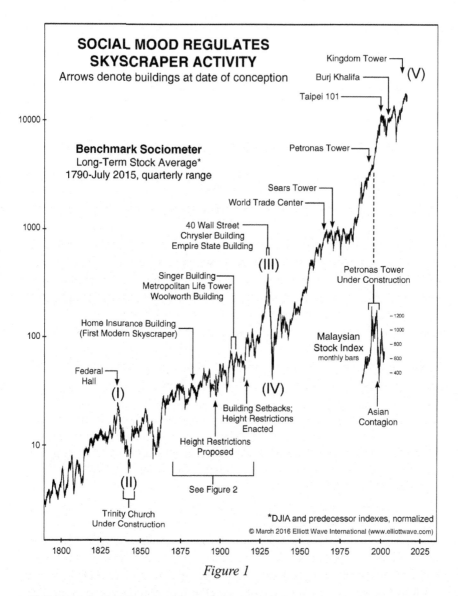

Figure 1

building booms has been so similar for many years that its repetition seems almost routine." In 1996, when Malaysia's Petronas Towers rose to challenge the Sears Building's quarter-century reign as the World's Tallest building with a new record height of 452 meters, the mainstream media took notice. "Buildings that are not merely high but awesomely high are assertions of power, demands to be noticed," stated *The New York Times*. The article added, "there is a particular moment in the life cycle of a rising culture when those impulses are irresistible."[1] In *Skyscrapers, A Social History of Very Tall Buildings* (1996), author George Douglas described the feelings behind the impulse to go higher and higher: "We take some joy in tall buildings; they give us a lift; they do something for the spirit." Douglas concluded, "Skyscrapers are largely the product of dreams and aspirations. Perhaps they respond to certain needs and moods of the people."

After the Petronas Towers were completed in March 1996, the September 1996 EWT turned retrospective observations into a forecasting tool:

> Of all the cultural relationships we consider here, the link between stock prices and the tallest buildings is one of the most fascinating because it is literally etched in stone. It's so obvious that even the media will make the connection, albeit a few years after it might help an investor. In contrast, *The Elliott Wave Theorist* is relating the significance of the widespread skyscraper-building impulse now, in time to benefit from the knowledge.

Within six months, Malaysian stocks had fallen more than 75% from a February 1997 peak (see inset on Figure 1), as the Asian Contagion hit global currency and stock markets in July 1997.

Given *The New York Times'* earlier contemplation of the "symbolic power of skyscrapers," one would think that some investors would have been prepared for the sharp change in trend. But investors expressed near total surprise at the reversal. It can be no other way, as social mood repeatedly makes humans experience euphoria and despair at the wrong times. Social mood is endogenously regulated, unconscious and non-rational, rendering most investors and builders powerless to resist it. No matter how towering the sell signals or how devastating the ensuing crashes, builders and investors in the aggregate never change their behavior. Since the Petronas Towers sell signal, there have been two even more successful skyscraper sell signals. Yet outside of a few obscure studies, the indicator garners virtually no credence or attention on Wall Street, let alone Main Street.[2]

Once again, it is time to heed a warning from the skyscraper indicator prospectively. The latest wave of extremely tall buildings marks the current occasion as another important, if not the most critical, time in the history of the indicator. To understand the strength of the signal, we will first look back at more than 200 years of construction history. Our focus will be primarily on for-profit structures because, in anticipating financial gain, they express the unbridled optimism of mature trends toward positive social mood, which invariably transforms city skylines near the ends of major bull markets in stocks. As investors begin using margin to chase after stocks for an anticipated big score, builders chase after the World's Tallest designation to score a personal monument.

While height is the most pronounced trait of a skyscraper, the purpose, style, width and location of a building are all critical elements that will help us establish the trends in social mood from times past to the present. Our journey begins 50 years after the start of the two-century trend toward more positive mood that began in 1784.

Wave (I)

Federal Hall (conceived 1835/completed 1842)

As material embodiments of positive social mood, tall buildings are far less transitory than stock prices. Some important structures testify for centuries to the positive mood that created them. Other structures are long gone, but, as we will see, the sites where they once stood continue to reverberate with the influence of subsequent social mood extremes.

The four corners of Wall and Broad streets in Lower Manhattan offer a prime example of a location that builders have continually re-shaped at key turning points in social mood. In 1789, when the bull market and the United States of America were in their opening decade, the first U.S. Congress convened on the northeast corner of this intersection. On this site, the first capital building of the U.S. housed the first secretaries of State, Treasury and Defense as well as the first President of the United States, George Washington. A civilian statue of Washington stands on the steps of the current Federal Hall, marking the spot of his inauguration. A few months later, the Bill of Rights was ratified here. So, this is one of the most important sites in the formation of the United States.

As impressive as they are, real estate development and stock market gains today are tame compared to what took place in the wake of wave (I), which peaked in 1835. According to Pulitzer Prize-winning New York

Federal Hall

historians Edwin G. Burrows and Mike Wallace, in just one year, from 1835 to 1836, the total value of Manhattan real estate rose more than 75%, from $143 million to $233 million,[3] with "many lots and buildings quickly resold." As usual, easy money played a role: "The surge was stoked by a tremendous expansion in the availability of credit." According to the New York City Landmarks Preservation Committee, the First Ward district of lower Manhattan went from 43 new buildings in 1834 to 100 in 1835 to 600 in 1836. Following a major fire in late 1835, the increasing height of new buildings and the revised use of the damaged buildings showed the influence of a multi-decade extreme in positive social mood. According to the Preservation Committee, structures erected in 1834 were mostly two and three-story homes. In 1836, "following the fire, a large proportion were four- and five-story brick 'stores.'"[4] Due partly to humans' stair-climbing limits but more importantly to the intervention of a period of negative social mood that lasted until 1859 and ushered in the Civil War, the maximum height of buildings rose just one floor over the next quarter century.

The positive social mood at the peak of wave (I) attained stone form with the erection of the monumental Federal Hall, which still stands diagonally across from the New York Stock Exchange at Wall and Broad streets, on the same corner that served as the first seat of the U.S. government in 1789. Construction commenced with the peak in stocks in 1835 and finished at the bear market low of 1842. It was one of the many Greek Revival buildings that went up at the end of wave (I). "All along Wall Street, banks and insurance companies began demolishing their former residences and erecting stone-front, porticoed Doric temples. Within a few years, the street boasted perhaps the greatest concentration of classical columns since the fall of Rome," wrote Burrows and Wallace. Another Greek Revival building, the Astor House, was built at this time by John Jacob Astor. It was New York's first luxury hotel.

Wave (III)

Elisha Otis invented the safety elevator in 1852, but it was not until stock prices surged in the 1860s that elevator sales took off. Office buildings, in line with rising stocks, "went vertical, climbing to unprecedented heights," wrote Burrows and Wallace. "'Our business men are building up to the clouds,' one newsman exclaimed." As stocks crested temporarily in 1870, the Equitable Life Insurance Co. installed the first steam-powered passenger elevator in its new headquarters on Broadway in downtown Manhattan. Equitable's directors were skeptical of the venture's merit, but they were soon reassured by the quick leasing of what was then a new standard for office buildings. "Multitudes came to ride the building's elevator to see the panoramic view afforded by this first example of what in time would be called a skyscraper."

That now-famous designation officially came with another important technological breakthrough in 1883. According to the *Guinness Book of Records*, the 10-story Home Insurance Company Building in Chicago rates as the first skyscraper because its designer, William Jenney, used a

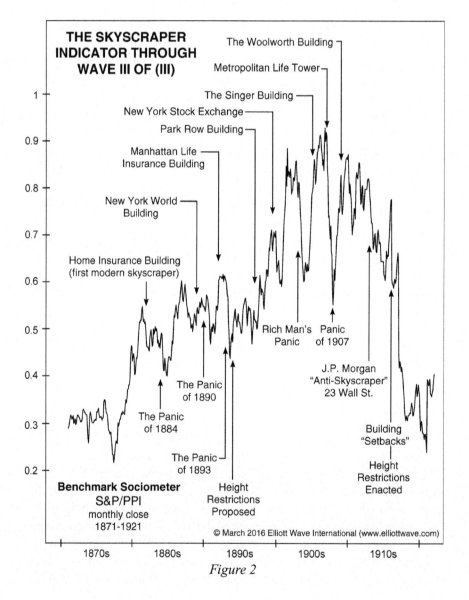

Figure 2

steel frame to support the walls as well as the weight of the building. In typical timing, the Home Insurance Building was under construction when the stock market turned down; it was completed after the Panic of 1884 gripped Wall Street.

PLATFORM IMAGE AND ELISHA OTIS PORTRAIT: COURTESY OF OTIS ELEVATOR CO.

The World Building (1889/1890)

Before 1889, the world's tallest structures were primarily churches and shrines such as the Washington Monument. The diagram of the Principle High Buildings in the mid-1880s (Figure 3) shows the many tombs and steeples that the 170-meter memorial surpassed when it was finished in 1885.

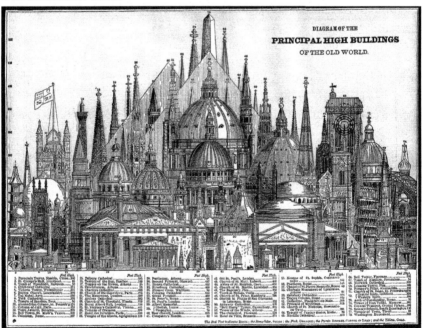

Figure 3

Our succession of World's Tallest skyscrapers begins with the World Building in 1889, because it was the first to surpass the height of Trinity Church in New York City. The World Building marked a key moment in the history of the World's Tallest buildings, because it signaled a pivotal shift from honoring the past to celebrating the future. This change meshes well

with the wave structure of the bull market, since it occurred after the pivot point [see Chapter 8 of *The Socionomic Theory of Finance*] of wave (III) in the stock market, when investors shift from a net fear of falling prices to a net expectation of rising prices.

The World Building

Construction on the World Building at the far end of Park Row in downtown Manhattan began on October 10, 1889, at a peak in the stock market. Reaching 94 meters, Joseph Pulitzer's office was the first to look down on the Trinity Church steeple (86.5 meters). He finally moved into the rotunda at the top of the World Building in December 1890, a month after that year's financial panic had run its course. After the building's completion, architect Harvey Wiley Corbett recalled, "Architects said nothing could be higher; city planners said nothing should be higher, and owners said nothing higher would pay."

The Manhattan Life Insurance Building (1892/1894)

Planning for the Manhattan Life Building began in 1892, when the company held a competition for the

Manhattan Life

design of its new headquarters. Stocks peaked the following year, and once again a giant building was going up as selling overtook Wall Street, in this case the Panic of 1893. When it was finished in 1894, the Manhattan Life Insurance Building was the World's Tallest.

The Curious Case of 100 Broadway

The American Surety Company's construction of its headquarters at 100 Broadway began in 1894. According to *The New York Times*, the building rose to 95 meters, just a few centimeters shy of the Manhattan Life Building's record. Why did American Surety stop short of the record? It seems like an odd decision, but there is a socionomic explanation. When the trend of social mood turned negative in the mid-1890s, society's aspirational impulse for one-upmanship slipped away, and a collective fear of heights replaced it. A 1996 *New York Times* story on 100 Broadway's designation as a city landmark confirms that the American Surety Building went up at a time when a new crop of tall buildings "was shocking New Yorkers. In 1894, the *Real Estate Record & Guide* said the incipient generation of 20-story buildings 'evokes only one feeling, that of horror.'" The New York Chamber of Commerce proposed restrictions on tall buildings, and most architects agreed with a bill introduced in the state legislature to restrict heights. "By 1895, anti-skyscraper sentiment had spread beyond the professions." Objec-

tions included the shutting off of light and air to adjacent buildings as well as "adding of damp dark places" that "encourage the spread of typhoid fever and tuberculosis."[5] The "Act to Limit the Height of Buildings In New York City" was presented to the New York state senate in February 1896. In July 1896, stocks fell to a multi-year low amidst a deep economic contraction.

The Park Row Building, (1896/1899)

As the trend toward positive mood resumed in the last years of the 19th century, new skyscrapers resumed their assault on New York City's skyline. The Park Row Building epitomized the quick, popular re-embrace of the skyscraper. "Early in 1896 the Chamber of Commerce announced its opposition to skyscrapers,"

Park Row

records *The New York Times*. "But later that year construction began at 15 Park Row, which was to be the tallest building yet." Stretching to a height of 119 meters, 15 Park Row became the World's Tallest when it opened on July 20, 1899, a few days before the Dow made an interim peak that was not materially exceeded for another six years. The building also marked the beginning of the skyscraper as mega-project, as it took almost three years to complete. The *Real Estate Record and Guide* called it "one of the largest operations ever undertaken." Still, an undercurrent of anti-skyscraper sentiment remained. One writer derisively referred to the Park Row as a "horned monster."

The New York Stock Exchange (1901/1903)

    Elliott Wave Principle calls a "third of a third" wave "the powerful middle section of an impulse wave." Wave III of wave (III) within the two-century uptrend ended with a triple top in the first decade of the 1900s.

New York Stock Exchange

    As the triple top commenced, the New York Stock Exchange knocked down its original building, which was diagonally across the street from Federal Hall. Work on the modern New York Stock Exchange building started in May 1901, two months ahead of the initial peak in the topping process that spanned the first decade of the 20th century. Upon completion in 1903, the building, in the words of architectural writer Joseph Korom, "became the embodiment of the nation's growth and prosperity." The NYSE was completed a few months ahead of the Rich Man's Panic.

    At each of the next major stock market peaks in real-money terms (see Dow/gold inset in Figure 4) in 1966 and 2000, respectively, the New York Stock Exchange decided to build a new headquarters. In both cases, however, immediate reversals toward negative social mood scuttled the proposals. The plan at the positive mood extreme in 2000 was particularly dazzling. The project grew to a value of $1.4 billion and was finalized in October 2000, one

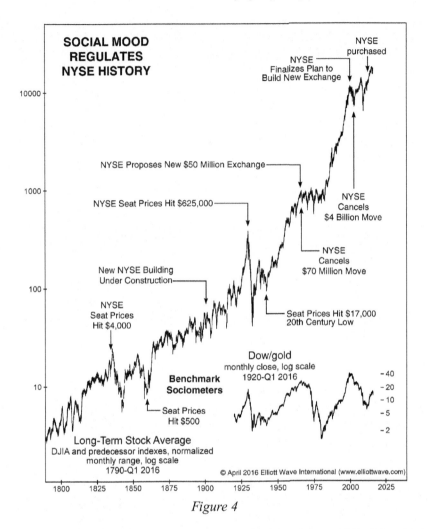

SOCIAL MOOD REGULATES NYSE HISTORY

NYSE purchased

NYSE Finalizes Plan to Build New Exchange

NYSE Proposes New $50 Million Exchange

NYSE Seat Prices Hit $625,000

NYSE Cancels $4 Billion Move

New NYSE Building Under Construction

NYSE Cancels $70 Million Move

NYSE Seat Prices Hit $4,000

Seat Prices Hit $17,000 20th Century Low

Dow/gold
monthly close, log scale
1920-Q1 2016

Benchmark Sociometers

Seat Prices Hit $500

Long-Term Stock Average
DJIA and predecessor indexes, normalized
monthly range, log scale
1790-Q1 2016

© April 2016 Elliott Wave International (www.elliottwave.com)

Figure 4

month after the NYSE Composite index peaked for the year. If builders had carried out the plan, the J.P. Morgan Building across the street would have been the NYSE's visitor center. The exchange itself would have been housed in a 2 million-square-foot office tower next door. The project was cancelled in 2002, the year of a bear market bottom. The NYSE itself ceased to exist as an independent entity when the Intercontinental Exchange purchased it in December 2012, the year after the Dow/gold ratio bottomed and the year that U.S. real estate prices bottomed after their biggest fall on record. Figure 4 shows how closely the NYSE's fortunes have tracked our sociometers.

The Singer Building (1902/1908)

The Singer Building was originally supposed to rise just 35 stories, but "the Singer Sewing Machine Company decided to double that height" with a tower of 186.5 meters. After a long delay, the company finally marshalled the resources to commence building in September 1906, just months after the Dow's January 1906 peak and the ensuing Panic of 1907. The Singer was part of a skyscraper boom that turned much of lower Manhattan into a construction zone through the first decade of the 20th century. "Although significantly taller than previous skyscrapers, the Singer Tower held the title for only a year, when it was surpassed by the Metropolitan Life Tower."

Singer Building

Metropolitan Life Tower (1905/1909)

Like the Singer Building, the Metropolitan Life Tower reached record heights with the construction of a relatively slender tower. It was actually a 50-floor addition to Met Life's headquarters, an 11-story building that occupied a block at Madison Avenue and 23rd Street. When it was complete, postcard companies flooded "the market with views of and from the tower, as part of an outpouring of skyscraper ephemera."[6]

(In 1929, Metropolitan Life decided to retake the World's Tallest crown with a 100-story "giant skyscraper" across the street from the Met Life Tower. With the onset of the Great Depression, however, the company abandoned its plans.)

Met Life Tower

The Woolworth Building (1907/1913)

As this postcard photo reveals, the scale of the Woolworth Building was much more expansive than the slender World's Tallest towers that preceded it. At 983,000 square feet, its total floor space exceeded that of every prior office building.

The Woolworth Building was dubbed "The Cathedral of Commerce" because of its worshipful attitude toward business as expressed through various frescos and ornaments such as the caduceus, the staff of Mercury (at right). The messenger of the gods is also protector of merchants—as well as gamblers, liars and thieves.

The building also demonstrates finance's emerging dominance; it was built because it secured an anchor tenant, the Irving Bank. According to historian Gail Fenske, author of *The Skyscraper and the City*, development of the Woolworth Building evolved from discussions between Frank Woolworth and the Irving Bank's president, Lewis Pierson, "around 1907." It took the bank's prestige as a financial firm to make the project viable. The bank occupied the building's elegant entryway plus several floors at the base of the building. This corbel of Pierson holding up the building while eyeing his ticker tape appears in the entryway. The Woolworth Company occupied just a floor and a half, because Frank Woolworth, the founder of the 5- and 10-cent retail chain, was determined to maximize profits.

Woolworth Building

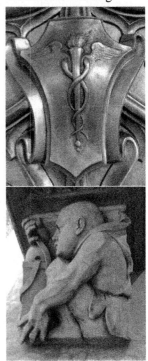

The Bankers Trust Building (1909/1912)

In 1909, as the retrospectively constituted S&P Composite index recorded an all-time high that would stand for fifteen years, Bankers Trust chose the architects that would design the "world's tallest financial building" on "the world's most expensive" piece of ground, valued at $825 per square foot, on the southwest corner of the intersection directly across from the Federal Building. As wave (III) completed its middle wave, finance displaced religion even more definitively than it had with the World Building in 1889. The January 1922 issue of *American Magazine* labeled the building "a thirty-five story cathedral of finance."

Due to the success of the Bankers Trust Building, the same architect was selected in 1913 to design the new J.P. Morgan & Co. building, which replaced the existing headquarters diagonally across the street. By this time, the bear market was well established. In response to the now squarely negative trend in social mood, Trowbridge & Livingston replaced the five-story J.P. Morgan building at 23 Wall Street with an even more diminutive three-story structure.

Banker's Trust

Due to the dramatic contrast with the skyward thrust that had preceded its construction, Morgan's new headquarters was dubbed Wall Street's "anti-skyscraper." It was finished in 1914, coincident with a nadir in social mood that marked a multi-year stock market low and prompted the outbreak of World War I.

The Bank of Manhattan Building and the Chrysler Building (1928/1930)

By 1928, New York's building boom had roared back to life as a positive trend in social mood supported a real estate boom and a mania for stocks. In 1929, two Art Deco giants found themselves pitted against one another for the title of the World's Tallest. One was the Bank of Manhattan Building at 40 Wall Street, and the other was the Chrysler Building. In order to stay ahead, the architects of 40 Wall raised their announced height from 256 meters to 282.5 meters, making it 60 centimeters taller than the

Chrysler Building

Bank of Manhattan Building (background)

Chrysler Building. But on October 23, 1929, one day before Black Thursday, the Chrysler Building surprised its rival by raising its seven-story spire, perhaps the most iconic peak in the New York City skyline. At 318 meters, it became the new World's Tallest when it was finished in May 1930.

Because it was completed first, the Bank of Manhattan Building was the World's Tallest for two months. So, for a shining moment in the immediate aftermath of wave (III), a building dedicated solely to finance held the title. The picture at right shows the steeple of Trinity Church in front of the Halicarnassus-inspired pinnacle of the Bankers Trust Building, topped yet again by the pinnacle of the Bank of Manhattan building, displaying the full range of architectural peaks in wave (III).

The Empire State Building (1929/1931)

The Chrysler Building's reign was also brief, as eleven months later an even more stupendous tower, the Empire State Building, reached a record height of 381 meters, a fitting tribute to the matching feat by the Dow Jones Industrial Average, which peaked in 1929 at 381 points. Securing the title of the World's Tallest building was clearly the aim of the Empire State's developers, but Paul Starrett, the project's foreman, clarified that the building's height was set by "the limit of efficient and economical operation. The height and beauty of the Empire State Building rose out of strictly practical considerations." From its conception within days of September 1929's wave (III) peak to completion, the Empire State building took just 19 months to erect. This pace remains a record for a project of its scale.

From 1929 to 1939, per-square-foot sales prices in Manhattan fell from $6.91 to $2.29, a 62% decline. Due to the Great Depression, the Empire State Building did not become profitable until 1950, when the Dow Jones Industrial Average was finally heading back to new all-time highs in wave III of wave (V). In 2013, the Empire State's owners issued an Initial Public Offering.

Wave (V)

The World Trade Center (1968, 1973)

The wave (IV) bear market of 1929-1932 lasted just three years in nominal terms, but in PPI terms it lingered on until 1949. This period of negative social mood had such a powerfully dampening effect on the constructiveness engendered by the positive social mood behind the pre-ceding bull market that it was a full 35 years before the next World's-Tallest project got underway, once again at a positive extreme in social mood. Wave III finished with a triple top in 1966, 1968 and 1973, and it was marked by a triplet of World's Tallests. The first two such buildings were the Twin Towers of the World Trade Center, which were dedicated in 1973.

Empire State Building

The World Trade Center

The influence of social mood is readily apparent through the on-again/off-again series of plans for a world trade center that spanned almost the entirety of wave III and beyond. The concept first appeared at the 1939 World's Fair, where a "world trade center" pavilion was dedicated to "world peace through trade." Movement in this direction was promptly extinguished by World War II, which persisted through the stock market's wave II bottom in 1942 and ended three years into wave III. In 1946, at the end of wave ①, "New York lawmakers conceived of the idea of an international, world trade center" (see Figure 5). During the ensuing decline for wave ② into 1949, however, the "idea was scrapped." In January 1960, the very month that marked the end of wave ③, planners adopted the idea of a five-million square foot world trade center on the east side of Manhattan. In January 1962, near another stock market peak, the project was shifted to the west side of Manhattan and doubled in size. Later that year, as stocks completed wave ④ down, local businessmen launched a series of legal and political

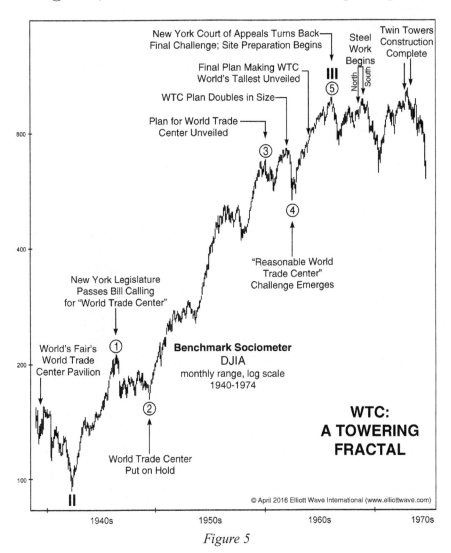

Figure 5

challenges to the project. These protests lasted four years. The "Committee for a Reasonable World Trade Center" demanded that the project be scaled down. But in January 1964 the stock market ascended to new all-time highs once again, and a completed design was finally announced. The World Trade Center would be the new World's Tallest.

In March 1966, the month after wave III's end, the New York State Court of Appeals turned back the final legal challenge to the World Trade Center, and site preparation began. In August 1968, steel work started on the north tower. The south tower headed skyward in January 1969. Wave III's speculative peak came in December 1968, right between these two dates. In January 1973, the Dow briefly surpassed 1000. One World Trade Center was completed ahead of that peak, while Two World Trade Center was completed right after it. At the Twin Towers' dedication in 1973, World Trade Center architect Minoru Yamasaki expressed sentiments compatible with positive mood when he called the World Trade Center a "representation of man's belief in humanity, his belief in the cooperation of men and, through cooperation, his ability to find greatness."

On September 11, 2001, both towers were attacked and destroyed. The attack took place just ten days before that year's stock market low. This key event reflected the start of a multi-decade trend toward negative social mood as measured by the Dow/gold ratio. The ensuing "war on terror" continues to this day.

The Sears Tower, (1969/1973)

Later in 1973, the Sears Tower in Chicago surpassed the height of the World Trade Center. That building remained the World's Tallest until 1998, when Malaysia's Petronas Towers officially reached their record height.

Petronas Towers (1992/1996)

Ground-breaking for Malaysia's Petronas Towers took place in 1992. Initially, the towers were not designed to be record-breakers. In the mid-1990s, as Malaysian stocks soared to all-time highs, the architectural design grew

Sears Tower

to its final height. In a departure from preceding World's-Tallest skyscrapers, the towers were a government-sponsored project. They were named for the state-run oil company that occupies one of the buildings. As noted earlier, the Malaysian stock market experienced a major plunge immediately after the towers were built.

A Chinese challenger to the Petronas Towers' record height was proposed at the same time. It was postponed, however, after the Asian Contagion hit in 1997.

Taipei 101 (1999/2004)

Construction of Taipei 101, the next World's Tallest building, started in 1999 and carried through the global extreme in positive social mood that arrived in the first quarter of 2000. The building is owned by Taipei Financial Center and houses various financial firms as well as the Taiwan Stock Exchange. So, for a brief period at the end of the bull market, financiers once again resolved to tower over the world.

Petronas Towers

Burj Khalifa (2004/2008)

After stock-market lows in late 2002 and early 2003, the worldwide mania for stocks resumed, and so did builders' race to the sky. The Burj Dubai—as it was initially named—was conceived in 2004 and built through the global stock market peak of 2007. In the same way that the Empire State Building soared over its nearest rival by almost 40%, the Burj set out to "beat all records on a scale that will be a dramatic testament to Dubai's faith in the future." To

Taipei 101

keep competitors at bay, the building's eventual height was a closely guarded secret. Eventually, the Burj topped out at 830 meters, a stunning 39% higher than Taipei 101. Once again, social mood changed course long before the Burj could reach its ultimate height, as Dubai stocks crashed almost immediately after construction commenced. Instead of retreating or postponing the project, the Burj's builders kept right on building. As global stocks bottomed in 2009, the project had to be bailed out by the government. The building's name was changed to the Burj Khalifa, in honor of the project's savior, Khalifa Bin Zayed, president of the United Arab Emirates.

Burj Kalifa

Kingdom Tower (2010/2019)

Today, there is a new World's Tallest building on the rise. The Kingdom Tower (a.k.a. Jeddah Tower) is taking neo-futuristic form in Jeddah, Saudi Arabia, where it is expected to rise to a record height when completed in 2019. Beneath the surface, however, the project betrays subtle signs of a tiring trend in positive social mood. Unlike plans for the Singer Building, the Woolworth Building, 40 Wall Street, the World Trade Center and the Petronas Towers, which grew taller as their respective social-mood peaks approached, Kindgom Tower's prospects are shrinking. The initial plan called for it to be more than double the height of the Burj and reach upward a full mile. But "the building has been scaled down from its initial 1.6 km proposal" to one kilometer. Like the

Kingdom Tower

Burj Khalifa, in which residential units and hotel rooms occupy more than half of the floors, the primary purpose of the Kingdom Tower will be luxurious accommodation for guests and residents. This ultimate lap of luxury swiftly experienced financial difficulty. On April 4, 2016, following a multi-month setback in the Dow and amidst a renewed "sliding oil price and growing tensions with its regional oil-exporting rival Iran," Saudi Arabia announced plans to "ramp up its austerity program and avert the threat of national bankruptcy." In another meaningful departure from history, the architect of the Kingdom Tower declared that his building is not designed to make money. He noted that "the Burj has had trouble filling its floors" and explained that the real motivation behind the building is the ego of its owners, saying, "Supertall towers generally aren't built for financial reasons. Someone says, 'I just want to build it, and I am rich enough.' It is for bragging rights." The buildings' not-necessarily-for-profit status is burnished by the fact that it is partially owned by the government of Saudi Arabia.

A Slew of Regional Tallest Buildings

The unfolding Grand Supercycle peaking process in global stock prices has coincided with more than just a string of World's Tallest buildings. Many regions and countries have unveiled their tallest *local* commercial structures. New record-high buildings are rising or are already in place in Spain (2008), Hong Kong (2010), Kuwait (2011), Great Britain (2012), Austria (2014), Japan (2014), Kuala Lumpur (2014), Brazil (2014), Chile and South America (2014), the U.S. (2014), Peru (2015), Russia and Europe (2015).

One World Trade (2005/2014)

One World Trade is the tallest building in the United States as well as in the Western Hemisphere. In addition to signaling the approach of a major peak in positive social mood and therefore the stock market, the story of the building's progress and regress demonstrates yet again how strongly social mood influences building plans.

Shortly after the Twin Towers fell in 2001, the invocation at Ground Zero was "Never Forget." A few feet from the new building, tourists still pour into various attractions paying tribute to those that perished there. While people remember the most shocking social *events* of their lifetimes, the prevailing social *mood* that prompted those events is unremembered. Back in 2001, with social mood in the midst of a strongly negative trend, scholars became "convinced that the age of skyscrapers is at an end."[7] They also predicted that "no new megatowers will be built, and existing

ones are destined to be dismantled."
These "predictions" were nothing but
expressions of the negative mood of
the time. Re-development of the World
Trade Center site started in 2002. With
the bear market still in place, the devel-
oper, Silverstein Properties, refused to
go any higher than 82 stories. Concerns
"that higher floors would be a liability
in the event of a future terrorist attack"
carried the day.

By 2005, as social mood trended
back toward the positive, such worries
simply melted away. A plan for a building that would be even taller than the
original World Trade Center emerged.
But it takes more than just a dream
to create a modern-day "supertall."
One World Trade is a great example
of how incredibly difficult it is to get
these complex, legally and politically
challengeable structures built, and the

One World Trade

bout of negative mood in 2007-2009 did not help matters. But positive
mood returned and finally triumphed. As stocks recovered, the building
was erected, and in November 2014 tenants started to move in. *The New
York Times* recorded that the occasion marked the "culmination of thirteen
years of unusually public squabbles over architects and designs; of political jockeying and bureaucratic bickering; and of complicated construction
work." "Even if you set aside all of the extraordinary considerations of this
particular site," concurred *Architectural Digest*, "Just consider Hudson River
politics: imagine trying to get the respective governors of New York and New
Jersey to agree on wallpaper, much less the Western Hemisphere's largest
office building which is connected to many of the city's subway lines." The
socionomic explanation for their eventual cooperation is the swell of good
feelings, ambition and cooperation produced by a march toward historically
positive social mood. From the 1,776-foot-high tip of its antenna tower to
the PATH station platform 80 feet below the street, One World Trade testifies
to the manner in which obstacles slip away and grand plans come together
at extremes of positive social mood.

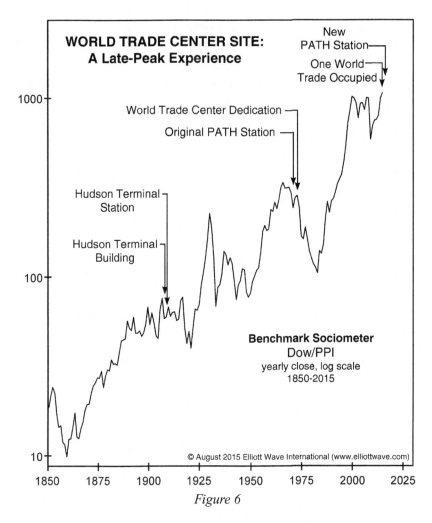

Figure 6

In 1973, the Twin Towers added 10 million square feet of space to the downtown office market. To put that amount in perspective, the reigning World's Tallest up until that time, the Empire State Building, has 2.3 million square feet of office space. One World Trade has just 3.5 million square feet of space. So, the breadth of skyscrapers, as measured in square feet of space in downtown Manhattan's tallest building, is diminishing. One World Trade does own one world record: the most expensive. At $3.9 billion, it's the costliest building ever built, by a long shot. The next closest is the London Shard at $1.9 billion. Like the Kingdom Tower, One World Trade will struggle to turn a profit. Despite state subsidies, owners don't expect rent to pay the bills. Toward the end of a more than two-century trend toward more positive social mood, "they are counting on millions of tourists looking for a view."

The Latest and Greatest Frenzy of Construction

The larger the degree of a positive mood peak, the taller the skyscrapers become and the more numerous they are. At Supercycle-degree peaks, construction activity is particularly robust, as evidenced by the row upon row of "doric temples" and new stores that shot up in 1836 and then the flurry of World's Tallest buildings that were conceived almost simultaneously in 1929. History is also resoundingly clear about the corresponding severity of the crashes that follow such sentiments. Each of the stock market setbacks in 1837-1842 and 1929-1932 was the largest in U.S. history at the time of its occurrence, as were the deflationary depressions that accompanied them.

The larger Grand Supercycle degree of the approaching extreme in positive mood is apparent in comparisons to the peak of 2000. Since then, the total number of skyscrapers (defined as buildings over 200 meters) has risen 350%,[8] while the number of "supertall" skyscrapers (defined now as buildings over 300 meters) is up 536%. To account for a new class of towers that will rise more than 600 meters, the Council of Tall Buildings added a "megatall" designation in 2011. At the time, the Burj Khalifa was the lone member of this group. Since its completion in 2010, two more megatalls have gone up, four more are under construction, and rumored blueprints call for several more. The Council's commentary on the World's Tallest buildings reveals that the ongoing surge in the number of tall buildings emerged with the dawn of the most torrid phase of the Mania Era:

> It was only in the mid-1990s that it became common for more than one supertall to be added to the lists annually, with 1995 being the last year when no supertalls were completed. Now, less than two decades later, the number of supertalls completed annually has entered

Lineup of Tallest Buildings

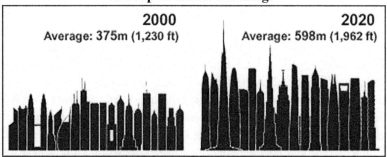

2000
Average: 375m (1,230 ft)

2020
Average: 598m (1,962 ft)

Source: Council of Tall Buildings

double digits, and is set to continue to rise. Meanwhile, the number of megatalls set to complete in the upcoming decade [by 2020] is similar to the number of supertalls completed in the 90s. In terms of height, therefore, 600 meters seems to be the new 300 meters.[9]

A Peak of Grandeur in China

Half of the 50 tallest buildings either already built or planned through 2020 are located in China. The country's last two highest towers were built in the Shanghai financial district—the Shanghai World Financial Center in 2007 and the Shanghai Tower in 2015. The completion of these towers shortly followed the last two major peaks in the Shanghai Composite Index. Figure 7 shows these stock market peaks and China's respective tallest buildings.

In a resounding echo of prior building-boom peaks in 1906, 1929 and 1966 in New York, China's boom includes construction of a "replica of Manhattan," which now stands in the port city of Tianjin. When the $50 billion project started in 2009, it was billed as "the world's largest financial district in the making." It includes knock-offs of Rockefeller Center and the Twin Towers. Even though it is close to completion, it is "missing one key element"—people. Chinese authorities continue to insist that the ghost town will become a bustling financial district, but the already well-developed skyscraper shape of the Shanghai Composite argues against it, at least within the next few decades. We believe that the greatest building boom in recorded history—China's—is coming to an end. It should give way to a bust of comparable scope.

The Chinese government's prominence in the latest building boom supports this forecast. Tianjin's Manhattan project is all part of a years-long stimulus effort through which the Chinese government has attempted to build its way out of economic contraction. The June 2015 issue of *The Elliott Wave Financial Forecast* demonstrated the usefulness of this observation. As Chinese stocks were still rising strongly, EWFF noted that the Chinese government had begun encouraging state-run firms to issue shares to pay down egregious debt loads. We stated, "Government always gets on board the biggest trends when they are about to end or are already over." As noted in Figure 7, Chinese stocks topped that very month. Three of the last four World's Tallest buildings—Petronas Towers, Burj Khalifa and Jeddah Tower—have been enabled by government money, so the same conclusion can be drawn with respect to the global skyscraper boom overall.

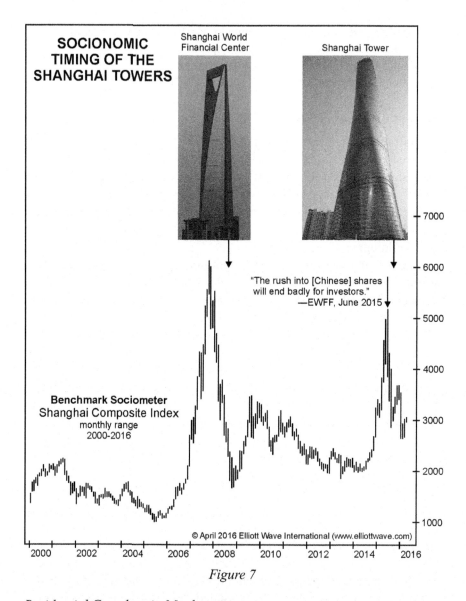

Figure 7

Residential Grandeur in Manhattan

The recent boom in luxury residential construction on the island of Manhattan is entirely consistent with what happens at the end of every peak in positive social mood. A plaque (see below) affixed to a Rasario Candela building on 80th Street commemorates 1929's "Unprecedented Wave of Luxury Apartment House Construction in New York City." In 1929,

133 EAST 80TH STREET

DESIGNED BY ROSARIO CANDELA IN 1929, 133 EAST 80TH STREET
EMBODIES THE ARCHITECT'S SIGNATURE ACHIEVEMENTS DURING
AN UNPRECEDENTED WAVE OF LUXURY APARTMENT HOUSE
CONSTRUCTION IN NEW YORK CITY LEADING UP TO THE GREAT
DEPRESSION. EMPOWERED BY ZONING THAT PERMITTED TALLER
BUILDINGS THROUGH A SERIES OF TERRACED SETBACKS, CANDELA
TRANSFORMED THESE AERIES USING STYLISTIC ORNAMENTATION
THAT REDEFINED THE CITY'S SKYLINE WITH FANCIFUL PENTHOUSES
AND WATER TOWER ENCLOSURES. THE BUILDING'S DESIGN
INCORPORATES A BLEND OF FRENCH GOTHIC AND TUDOR REVIVAL
ELEMENTS THAT ARE RESTRAINED ON THE LOWER STORIES AND
ROMANTICALLY PICTURESQUE ON THE UPPER STORIES.

LISTED ON THE NATIONAL AND NEW YORK
STATE REGISTERS OF HISTORIC PLACES

2010

architect Fred French unveiled plans for a record-high, 57-story apartment tower. Even though—and from a socionomic perspective, because—French famously insisted it was impossible to overbuild in Manhattan, the project was cancelled soon after the crash.

The crest of the current wave (V) extends residential luxury much higher and more broadly. Since 2010, when the plaque was installed, at least seven residential towers that dramatically exceed French's ambition have been either completed or announced. These towers are already reshaping the New York City skyline. 30 Park Place, for instance, which recently went up across the street from the Woolworth Building, now rises 25 stories higher than the Woolworth. When complete, it will be the tallest residential building downtown—at least for a short while. An even taller tower will rise to 414 meters—33 meters higher than the Empire State Building—at 125 Greenwich Street. On a lot that is about the size of a large house, the 77-floor building will have just 128 residential units. Meanwhile, the top 30 floors of the Woolworth building are currently being converted into 34 luxury condominiums, including a 9,000 square-foot penthouse that will occupy the building's observation deck. It is still available for $110 million.

Many modern structures are nothing if not dramatic. This picture of the 76-story apartment building at 8 Spruce Street in Manhattan is one of the many residential towers now needling their way into the New York City skyline. The "undulating stainless facade is designed to provoke a "feeling of graceful movement." It was completed in 2011.

8 Spruce Street

Then there's 2 World Trade Center, which is currently under construction in the shadow of One World Trade. As this next picture illustrates, the planned building, appropriately in our view, appears ready to fall over. Like a teetering stack of boxes, it leans so dramatically that walking under it will seem like a precarious endeavor. Once again, a Wall-Street-area building boom should mark a major peak in positive social mood, just as it did in the immediate aftermath of wave (I) in 1835 and at the end of wave (III) in 1929.

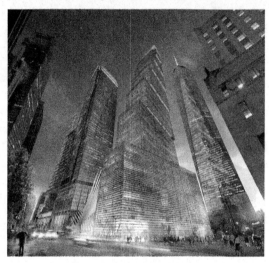

2 World Trade Center

According to *National Geographic*, New York City's skyscraper (700 feet or taller) count is up 45% over the last twelve years. With fifteen new skyscrapers under construction and nineteen proposed, the number will soon double again from the 2004 total of 28—that is if everything goes according to plan. In our view, this outcome is very unlikely, as the next turn toward negative social mood will prompt the rapid scrapping of numerous building plans.

Signs of Slackening in the Boom

The latest additions to the Manhattan skyline constitute an extremely bearish divergence. Besides falling well short of the world-record heights that resided here through the most powerful phases of the two-century bull market, most of the city's new buildings are uncommonly thin. "What's most striking about these towers is their shape," noted one news article. "The Twin Towers had a ratio of base width to height of 1-to-7 (209 feet-to-1,368 feet); an apartment house about to begin construction on 57th Street will be a feathery 1-to-23."

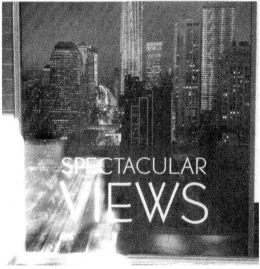

NYC apartment poster promotion, September 2015

A real-estate broker told CNBC that many brand new units go "unoccupied much of the time by nouveau riche, transnational owners." Some of the newest Manhattan condo towers are owned almost entirely by foreigners. Various articles refer to this demand as "haven investment." This observation fits right in with our forecast for a major peak in property investment. As our publications have previously noted, foreign investors possess a historically abominable timing record. High foreign commitments to west-coast U.S. real estate in 1989 and to U.S. stocks in September 2000, for instance, contributed to our successful forecasts for important setbacks in both markets. Our observation is especially applicable to real estate, where locals' feel for the history of their own property market gives them a huge home field advantage.

What are the locals up to lately? Here's a recent synopsis from Bloomberg:

Manhattan Property Owners Are Cashing Out

With New York real estate values and rents surging, owners of commercial properties acquired as recently as a year ago are already seeking buyers. Institutions from around the world are using Manhattan real estate as an investment haven. Demand "seems to be insatiable," from new investors, and some developers are seizing on the opportunity to profit now rather than moving ahead with construction plans. The wave of cash flooding Manhattan real estate shows no signs of abating.

That article appeared on August 20, 2015. *The Olshan Report*, which tracks high-end NYC home sales, records that since then prices for properties going for $4 million and up are in retreat. By the end of last year, properties on average were taking two months longer to sell than at year-end 2014. Meanwhile sales of homes listed for $10 million or more dropped 16% from 2014. A December Bloomberg headline confirms the trend: "Manhattan Luxury-Home Price in a Slide" as landlord concessions and vacancy rates rise from lows established earlier in 2015. In mid-January, *The New York Times* confirmed the weakness at the top end of the market: "Prices Drop for Luxury New York Real Estate."

The *Times* nevertheless reassured readers that the overall market is locked in an uptrend. "Industry experts say the market remains strong." "Developers are undeterred," says another *Times* offering from early February. Of course, confidence is exactly what we should expect the experts to exude near an extreme in positive social mood.

For more than two centuries, Manhattan property prices have led the way down as well as up. In 1929, the initial crack lower also started at the high end of the market. According to economists Tom Nicholas and Anna Scherbina, Manhattan real estate prices fell 67% from the third quarter of 1929 to the end of 1932, and the "value of high-end properties strongly co-moved with the stock market over this span."[10] The ultimate financial damage was worse, however, as "real estate was much slower to rebound than the stock market. A typical property bought in 1920 would have retained only 56% of its initial value in nominal terms two decades later."

The 2006-2012 Housing Crisis Was Just the Opening Act

Conquer the Crash (2002) observed, "overwhelming evidence of a major stock market decline is enough by itself to portend a tumble in real estate prices." Today, just about every major global stock index exhibits a long term Elliott wave termination pattern. All by itself, the one-kilometer-high building going up in Saudi Arabia gives us a high level of confidence that the next bear market will be sizeable. The global breadth of skyscraper development confirms the Elliott wave message from global stock markets, indicating that the emerging decline will be of an even higher degree than that of the 1930s. It should cover the globe and go much deeper than any preceding real estate decline over the past two centuries in most, if not all, major markets. Many of the projects that are currently on the drawing board will be reduced in stature, postponed or canceled.

From War Zone to Construction Zone and Back

A recent project hints at the coming major change in both mood and markets from ascension to stalling to reversal. The rendering placed on Figure 9 shows the latest World's Tallest proposal. In late November, 2015, the Bride, a development named for Basra, an Iraqi city at the northern edge of the Persian Gulf, was slated to reach a record height of 1,152 meters, 150 meters higher than the Jeddah Tower. At that time, a slew of headlines announced its imminent construction "on land that is believed to be the exact location of the Garden of Eden!"

By December 19, however, Basra's master plan was driven out of the Garden. A director with the architectural firm that designed the complex told Arabianbusiness.com that it "had to be put on hold because of the oil price." Thus, the constructiveness fostered by an extended trend toward

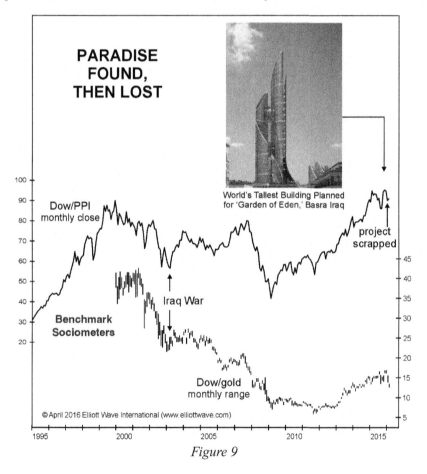

Figure 9

positive mood is in a pitched battle with its negative-mood counterpart, destructiveness.

Today's spectacle of record-breaking skyscraper activity will lead to its opposite. "At troughs, few buildings are built, and many of those already in place may be burned or bombed out of existence," said *The Wave Principle of Human Social Behavior* in 1999. That's what happened to the Twin Towers in 2001, and extremely tall buildings are once again likely to become targets of violence. It won't be a pretty picture, as broad areas of social life will be impacted. Much as the World's Tallest buildings are planned and started near the peaks of positive mood trends but are invariably completed in the depths of the ensuing negative mood trends, wars tend to begin near the bottoms of bear markets and are completed in bull markets. Figure 10 illustrates the relationship between three great American building booms and the three biggest military conflicts in U.S. history: the Civil War, World War I and World War II. The negative social mood behind the upcoming bear market should ultimately lead to a war of greater scope.

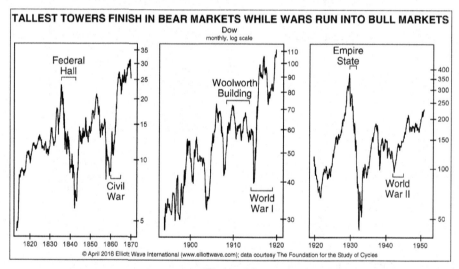

Figure 10

NOTES AND REFERENCES

[1] Goldberger, Paul, "Why Cities Set Their Sights So High," *The New York Times*, August 4, 1996.

[2] Referring to the Skyscraper Indicator as the "Skyscraper Index," Wikipedia calls it "a whimsical concept put forward" by a property analyst at Dresdner Kleinwort Wasserstein *in January 1999*. As revealed by our opening quotation, that date is off by at least 68 years.

The latest skyscraper boom has not gone completely unnoticed. Recent coverage on extremely tall buildings and their meaning includes "The New New York Skyline," by Pete Hamill, *National Geographic*, November 15, 2015, and "Skyscrapers and Boom-Bust Cycles," by Mark Thornton, *Daily Reckoning*, January 16, 2016. Thornton covers the media's mostly tepid response to the indicator and its effectiveness in recent years. A larger version originally appeared in the *Quarterly Journal of Austrian Economics*, Spring 2005.

[3] Edwin G. Burrows and Mike Wallace, *Gotham, A History of New York City to 1898,* 1999.

[4] *Stone Street Historic District Designation Report*, New York City Landmarks Preservation Committee, 1996. The Stone Street Historic District is a two-block section of lower Manhattan that was originally constructed during the building boom of 1836. In June 1996, NYC designated the neighborhood a landmark. At that point, parts of the district constituted a borderline slum with graffiti covering many of the metal safety doors. Over the course of the peaking process, however, it's been refurbished into a thriving restaurant district. As *The Elliott Wave Theorist* noted in 1996, positive mood leads to buzzing restaurants. "When people feel good, they like to get out, be seen, eat well and drink socially." Every day at lunch time and into the late-night hours, a feeding frenzy of positive-mood activity overtakes the buildings on Stone Street, recalling the mood that attended their construction in the mid-1830s.

[5] Sarah Bradford Landau and Carl W. Condit, *Rise of the New York Skyscraper: 1895-1913,* 1996.

[6] Roberta Moudry, *The American Skyscraper: Cultural Histories,* 2005.

[7] James Howard Kunstler and Nikos A. Salingaros, "The End Of Tall Buildings," Planetizen.com, September 17, 2001.

[8] "The Skyscraper Curse," Clearproperty.com, April 23, 2015.

[9] "The Tallest 20 in 2020: Entering the Era of the Megtall," September 19-21, 2012, Council of Tall Buildings.

[10] Tom Nicholas and Anna Scherbina, "Real Estate Prices During the Roaring Twenties and the Great Depression," Real Estate Economics, Summer 2013.

Chapter 26

The Socionomic Timing of
Construction Projects at a Major University

Peter Atwater

(adapted from a chapter in *Moods and Markets,* 2013)

As a parent of a soon-to-be-graduating high school student, I have had several opportunities recently to tour college campuses. In the process, I observed numerous concrete expressions of peak positive mood in the architecture of several bastions of higher education.

On the heels of this experience, I decided to investigate the timing of construction projects at my alma mater, the College of William and Mary. Figure 1 shows how the timing of such projects relates to a benchmark sociometer, the Dow Jones Industrial Average, since 1900. With few exceptions, the college built new facilities on campus at major stock market peaks, namely those of the late 1920s, the late 1960s-early 1970s, 2000 and 2007.

In the two earlier booms, new academic buildings were followed quickly by the construction of enhancements such as more spacious dormitories and improved athletic facilities. William and Mary opened its "Sorority Court" in September 1929, the month of that era's all-time high in the Dow.

Near the peaks of booms over the past 20 years, William and Mary—and judging by my own visits, other colleges, too—have gone well beyond creating facilities for the core undergraduate academic program. Recent building activity supports graduate studies, student activities, athletics and the arts. This is what we saw at the extremes of prior positive mood trends except that today it is on a bigger scale.

That colleges are adding high-cost, nice-to-have facilities implies an extreme level of self-assurance about their financial future, which makes me pessimistic about the long term prospects for the higher education industry. If the stock market makes another all-time high, more building will probably

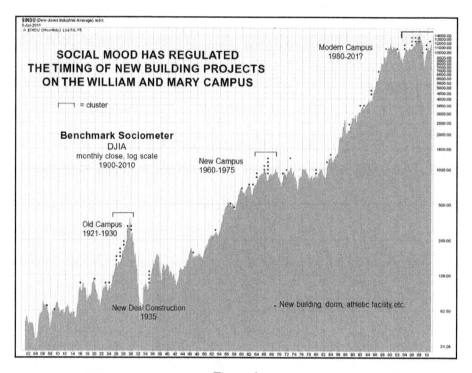

Figure 1

ensue. But the next time the stock market falls a long way, the American university system could experience a devastating one-two punch in which a business contraction brought on by negative social mood coincides with a revolutionary change in education technology under which centralized brick-and-mortar facilities become less necessary. The setup is akin to that for the newspaper and recording industries circa 2000.

Regardless of higher education's future, the lesson in Figure 1 remains: Those who run universities are usually conservative in their construction plans, but they repeatedly express their wealth, optimism and confidence at times of positive social-mood extremes by erecting new buildings and expanding the quality of students' living facilities. Each time they do so, stocks soon fall and the economy contracts.

Chapter 27

High School Classrooms:
Built on Positive Social Mood

Euan Wilson on a study by Marah Boyesen

June 20, 2013 (TS)

Marah Boyesen teaches personal finance to high school seniors in Bryn Athyn, Pennsylvania. For the past several years, she has integrated socionomics into her curriculum. By showing students how socionomics is relevant to them, Boyesen has drawn even distracted teens into this exciting new subject.

Socionomists have observed that huge construction projects are often planned and begun near extremes in positive social mood, though the most ambitious projects often are not completed until one or more years later. This relationship may be relevant to financiers who invest in buildings, but what does it mean for a high school student? When Boyesen showed them how social mood has affected their own campus—the very buildings in which they reside, learn and play—the observation hit home.

Taking cues from Peter Atwater's study of construction projects at the College of William and Mary, Boyesen discovered that her school, too, initiated every major building project on campus at or very near a stock market peak. Twice there was a 30-year hiatus on building that lasted until the next positive extreme in social mood. At the most recent peak in 2007, the school, *for the first time ever*, went into debt to the tune of tens of millions of dollars to finance a building project. Many individual homebuyers were doing exactly the same thing. Her students got the point: Social mood affects everyone.

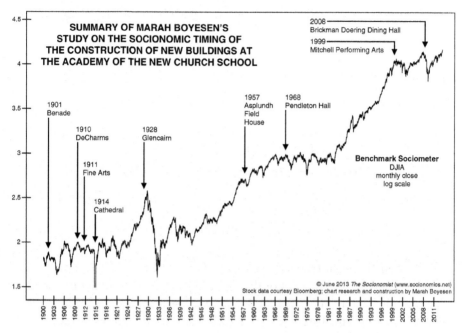

Figure 1

Chapter 28

Social Mood and Roller Coasters

Peter Kendall

July 31, 2015 (EWFF)

People love to ride roller coasters when social mood is trending positively. When social mood is trending toward the negative, people lose interest in roller coasters.

The recurrent infatuation with coasters stretches all the way back to 1873, when the first roller coaster ride was built from a converted coal delivery track in the mountains of Pennsylvania. The Mauch Chunk Switchback Railway's opening run coincided with the completion of a 16-year, 340% advance in U.S. stock prices. The Panic of 1873 hit shortly thereafter. The Mauch Chunk survived the Panic and remained popular through the end of the 70-year bull market dating from 1859. In an expression of historically elevated social mood, a newly formed Mauch Chunk Switchback Railway Company bought the attraction from the Central New Jersey Railroad on May 24, 1929. Within three short years, the amusement "fell victim to the Great Depression." In 1932, as the Dow Jones Industrial Average hit its post-crash low, the Mauch Chunk's rails were sold as scrap. Socionomic causality explains the entire cycle: People in a positive mood wanted thrills, and the ride provided them. At the peak, investors wanted in on the action. When the mood shifted sharply toward the negative, the appeal of the ride melted away, and so did investors' money.

The first roller coaster originally designed as an amusement was constructed in 1883 at Coney Island. Its name, the Switchback Railway, honored its inspiration. A coaster historian described the success of the ride as "nothing short of amazing," yet it was short-lived. The ride was built in a time of positive social mood, but it was completed only a few months ahead of the Panic of 1884 and did not survive the economic downturn that followed. "Inside the Apple," a New York City history site, estimates that the Coney Island ride lasted just three years. A decade later, in 1897, Steeplechase Park, the first major American amusement park, opened at Coney Island one year after a major bottom in the Dow. Roller coasters flourished on Coney Island and elsewhere from that year forward.

Figure 1 shows the initial burst of enthusiasm for roller coasters that occurred at the beginning of the 20th century. It peaked in 1905, one year ahead of a top in stocks that led to a nine-year bear market. After the stock market low of 1914, coasters' popularity came roaring back. Most roller-coaster histories refer to the 1920s as "The Golden Age of Roller Coasters." The most famous was Coney Island's Cyclone, which debuted in June

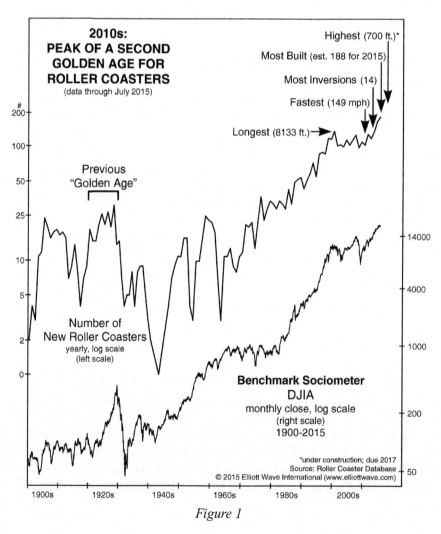

Figure 1

1927, in the sixth year of the great bull market of the Roaring Twenties. The following year, 1928, saw a record 31 new roller-coaster openings nationwide. That was the last full year of the Roaring Twenties. The rides' fortunes changed dramatically with the shift toward negative social mood in 1929. "The Great Depression marked the end of the first golden age, and theme parks in general went into decline." (Wikipedia) In 1943, the year following the 1942 bottom in stocks and the century's lowest stock market value as a percentage of GDP—an indicator of exceptionally depressed social mood—the number of new coasters built fell to zero.

Like the Dow, the amusement park industry did not recover until the 1950s. It took until 1976—when the Dow made a peak that held for over six years—for builders to surpass 1928's record with 37 new roller coasters. After running sideways through the early part of the 1980s in concert with the Dow, the number of new roller coasters built annually finally began moving steadily higher along with our benchmark sociometers. In the second half of the 1990s, as the mania for stocks reached fever pitch, coaster construction simultaneously boomed.

In May 2001, U.S. theme parks were predicting another record summer. *The Elliott Wave Financial Forecast* made the following forecast:

> Contrary to the opinion of amusement industry experts, roller coasters are not on an ever-upward path. The business should experience a deep depression. If you own an amusement park or amusement park shares, sell this year.

This prediction, based entirely on our perception of a major shift in social mood, turned out to be accurate. The leading amusement park stock, Six Flags, Inc., fell for the next eight years until the company filed for bankruptcy in June 2009, the exact month that the 2007-2009 recession ended.

Social mood reversed toward a positive trend in 2009, and both the stock market and Six Flags rose from the ashes. By 2010, Six Flags Entertainment was back on the stock exchange and, as Figure 2 shows, its new shares climbed virtually step by step with the Dow Jones Industrial Average. Figure 1 confirms that the total number of new coasters built annually has continued to reach new highs along with the U.S. stock averages. Positive social mood is behind both of these trends.

With 188 openings scheduled for 2015, this year will see a record number of new coasters. In addition to the new ones, many older coasters have returned to vogue due to the addition of new twists and turns that

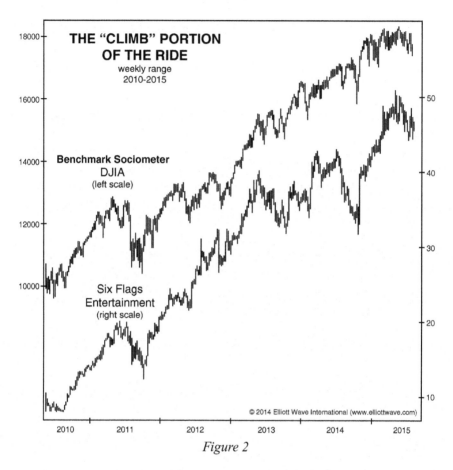

Figure 2

provide bigger thrills. After years of neglecting its rides, last year Coney Island added a new coaster, the Thunderbolt.

Notes on Figure 1 describe how over the course of the ongoing peaking process in stock prices the coaster industry has pushed limits in every possible direction. The longest coaster (at 8133 feet), the Steel Dragon in Nagashima, Japan, went up in 2000. The fastest coaster (reaching 149 mph), the Formula Rossa in Abu Dhabi, opened in 2010. The cork-screwiest (with 14 inversions), the Smiler in Staffordshire, England, was launched in May 2013. The tallest (at 700 feet), from U.S. Thrill Rides, is now under construction in Orlando, Florida. It will also include more "loops, dives, spirals and inversions than riders have ever before experienced." In a fitting gesture, developers named this record-breaking coaster the Skyscraper.

We have observed [see Chapter 25] that at the greatest extremes in positive social mood, blueprints for the World's Tallest buildings tend to grow higher as the peak in stock prices arrives. The same phenomenon is happening to plans for this roller coaster. Originally slated to rise 535 feet, the Skyscraper's newly planned 700-foot rise is 53% higher than the current world's-tallest coaster. Its track will be a mile long. If the Skyscraper coaster is completed, its projected 2017 debut will probably turn out to be one of the last great feats of the latest golden age of roller coasters. [Note: The debut has since been re-scheduled for 2018.—Ed.]

The only reversal from positive to negative social mood of a degree remotely comparable to the impending one is that of 1929. In 2015, Coney Island's coaster season got off to an ominous start when the Cyclone's first run ended at the top of its first drop. As *The New York Daily News* described the scene, "Shaken-up riders had to walk back down the incline the coaster had just climbed." We envision something like this happening to the coaster industry as a whole in the upcoming bear market.

Part IV:

TRANSPORTATION

Chapter 29

Social Mood and Automobile Styling

Mark Galasiewski

July 16, 2006 / October 2, 2006 (EWT)

At some time in your life, you'll be on a car lot, shopping for new wheels. While you're motivated by price and features, styling also matters. But what determines that styling, the shapes, the colors?

In 1985, Robert Prechter's "Popular Culture and the Stock Market"[1] noted correlations between major movements in the stock market and cultural trends in music, movies, fashion, politics and automobile styling. The cause of changes in the tone of all these phenomena, the essay proposed, was the same: a shared, unconscious mood that swings naturally between positive and negative poles. These swings register in the stock market, creating a "meter" of social mood. The idea that the cycles of history are neither random nor controllable was controversial at the time and remains so today.

This study expands upon one idea in the essay—car styling—and shows that changes in it are consistent with those in social mood as evidenced by trends in the stock market. Figure 1 depicts an idealized social mood cycle and its associated style manifestations.

Socionomics cannot predict the nature and timing of every aspect of automobile styling, but it offers an excellent perspective from which to begin. Just as the Wave Principle manifests clearly in overall market indexes, socionomics is concerned with human behavior *in the aggregate*. As social mood begins shifting toward the positive—signaled by the stock market's advance from a significant low—fashions become more colorful, and structure and tradition dominate popular art. By the time social mood peaks, bright colors and flamboyance dominate fashion, and wild colors and vitality rule popular art. As "Popular Culture and the Stock Market" observed, "bright colors are associated with market tops and dull, dark colors with market bottoms." Alternatively, when social mood begins turning negative, colors become muted, and "anti-fashion" expressions begin to appear. When social mood reaches its nadir, drab colors and conservative styles dominate fashion, and pop art is deliberately ugly, heavy and dead-looking. These same impulses influence automobile styling.

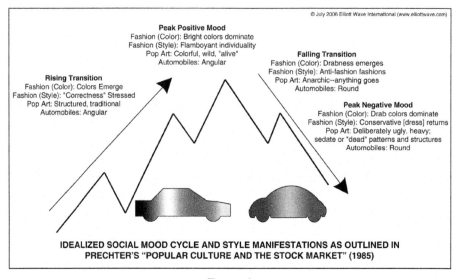

© July 2006 Elliott Wave International (www.elliottwave.com)

Peak Positive Mood
Fashion (Color): Bright colors dominate
Fashion (Style): Flamboyant individuality
Pop Art: Colorful, wild, "alive"
Automobiles: Angular

Falling Transition
Fashion (Color): Drabness emerges
Fashion (Style): Anti-fashion fashions
Pop Art: Anarchic--anything goes
Automobiles: Round

Rising Transition
Fashion (Color): Colors Emerge
Fashion (Style): "Correctness" Stressed
Pop Art: Structured, traditional
Automobiles: Angular

Peak Negative Mood
Fashion (Color): Drab colors dominate
Fashion (Style): Conservative [dress] returns
Pop Art: Deliberately ugly, heavy;
sedate or "dead" patterns and structures
Automobiles: Round

IDEALIZED SOCIAL MOOD CYCLE AND STYLE MANIFESTATIONS AS OUTLINED IN PRECHTER'S "POPULAR CULTURE AND THE STOCK MARKET" (1985)

Figure 1

Tenors of mental orientation are deep and broad, and they express themselves in many ways. Regarding automobile styling in particular, Prechter's essay made claims congruent with the observation that a positive trend in social mood generates feelings of definiteness in moral judgment whereas a negative trend in mood generates feelings of moral ambiguity. This general definiteness and indefiniteness also seem to show up in aspects of art and product design. Public sculptures, for example, are often angular when social mood is positive and "blobby" when social mood is negative. So it is with automobile design. In 1985, Prechter noted social mood's influence on "the angularity versus roundness of automobile styling," and Chapter 15 of *The Wave Principle of Human Social Behavior* added, "angular styles sell well in bull markets, while rounded lines sell better in bear markets."

When the trend of social mood is positive, automobile frames become boxier. Hoods, roofs, sides and trunks become more rectangular. Straight, parallel lines and sharp angles have a definiteness that appeals to people when they are in the mood to solve problems and improve their lives. As positive mood reaches an extreme, consumers also demand more room, bigger engines and more sophisticated styling, prompting designers to push the limits of an automobile's length, width, height and power. Other positive-mood characteristics include hood ornaments and chrome embellishments, which express individuality and flamboyance. Wider windows offer greater visibility for those looking either in or out. Convertible rooftops, the miniskirts of the automotive world, signal friskiness and fun. Motorcycles become popular, as they increase visibility and fun to the max.

When the trend of mood is negative, car frames become more rounded; bodies and roofs become bulbous; hoods and trunks become curved or snub as buyers seek consolation in softer forms. Simpler styling and smaller capacities decrease total surface areas. Consumers and manufacturers also seek to increase efficiencies as protectionist mentality waxes (which is also expressed politically). Car bodies are more enclosed, and windows are smaller and narrower as people seek to reveal and express less of themselves. Chrome disappears. By the end of the transition, convertibles are out of favor and only delinquents ride motorcycles.

To explore these ideas, we surveyed the past 85 years of automotive history, covering almost three complete cycles in social mood as reflected by the PPI-adjusted Dow Jones Industrial Average. These cycles took place in 1921-1949, 1949-1982 and 1982-present. The representative automobiles discussed below either sold well or stand out in the collective memory of the culture as characteristic of their times. We divide our discussion of car styling into three sections: *body form*, *roof type* and *color*.

Body Form

Our survey begins with the first complete social mood cycle in the era of the automobile. The positive portion prompted the bull market of the Roaring Twenties, and the negative portion fostered the bear-market-dominated period of the 1930s and 1940s.

1921-1929 (Positive Mood)

As trend toward positive mood began in the 1920s, mass-market automobiles expressed aesthetic values compatible with correctness, structure and tradition. By the end of the period, the peak positive mood resulted in styles that were flamboyant and colorful. Positive-mood themes remained constant throughout the period. Roofs and bodies were rectangular, and hood ornaments and other chrome embellishments were common. Among the cars of the period, a few stood out for their popularity or extravagance:

- Henry Ford first produced the **Ford Model T** (Figure 2) in 1908. The ensuing decade-long, negative mood period eventually dampened sales. But when the social mood turned positive in 1921, the car resurged in popularity, and production exceeded 1 million cars for the first time. The narrow and angular "Tin Lizzie" sold well for several more years until Ford replaced it with a redesign of the 1903-1905 Model A.

- Introduced in 1927, the new **Ford Model A** (Figure 2) retained the boxy features of the Model T. But unlike the all-black[2] Model Ts of the early 1920s, the new Model As were also available in four bright colors. This is a classic example of a company responding to consumer demands for flashier styles in the middle and late stages of a positive mood trend. The new Model A immediately became the company's second great success, with sales hitting 1.3 million in 1929. But its heyday was short-lived. Social mood turned deeply toward the negative in 1929-1932, and Ford terminated Model A production in 1931.

- Ever wonder where the admiring phrase "It's a doozy!" came from? The **Duesenberg J** (Figure 2) was the prince of the American auto world when it was unveiled at the New York Car Show in 1928. Its rectangular body was custom-designed and comparable in quality and luxury to a Rolls Royce. Its engine derived from those used in

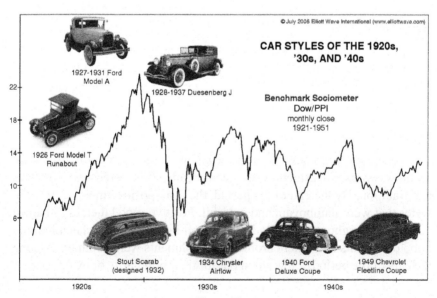

Figure 2

American fighter planes during World War I. Earlier in the 1920s, the Duesenberg brothers had made a name for themselves after a prototype of the Duesenberg Model A became the first American car to win a European Grand Prix race in 1921 (and, incidentally, would remain the only American car to do so until the 1960s). Duesenberg cars also won the Indianapolis 500 in 1924, 1925 and 1927. The brothers had initially failed in their attempt to market their high-performance cars to the non-racing public, and their company went bankrupt in 1922, a year after a major low in stock prices. But two years after Errett Lobban Cord added the brothers and their company's assets to his expanding automotive empire in 1926, the Model J was born. In the flamboyant atmosphere of the late 1920s, it quickly became the darling of well-heeled gangsters and Hollywood celebrities. In 1932, at the nadir of social mood, Cord produced a supercharged ("SJ") version of the car with 320 horsepower and a top speed of 135 MPH that attracted such notable owners as Clark Gable and the Duke of Windsor. But by then the market for large, boxy, high-performance or luxury automobiles had dried up. Dash and flash no longer sold. The new mood engendered attitudes of modesty and practicality.

1929-1949 (Negative Mood)

Designers in the early 1930s rediscovered simplicity and economy. They began designing cars in wind tunnels and using monocoque (unibody) structures to increase efficiencies. As negative mood dampened stock prices throughout the 1930s and 1940s, automobiles of all types—from coupes to pickups to hot rods—took on bulky, rounded or "helmeted" appearances like that of the 1940 **Ford Deluxe Coupe** (Figure 2). Hood ornaments and other ritzy chrome embellishments found on cars of the 1920s disappeared. Protruding headlamps got tucked into the body of the car and became headlights. Defensive, protective fenders grew, wrapping around the front and even over the sides of wheels. By the end of the period, windows were smaller all around, as seen in the 1949 **Chevrolet Fleetline Coupe** (Figure 2). Some automotive creations took negative-mood design to an extreme:

- The 1934 **Chrysler** (also **DeSoto**) **Airflow** (Figure 2) was the first mass-produced American car to be designed in a wind tunnel and to utilize unibody construction. Although its unorthodox features initially steered consumers away, the model set a precedent for negative-mood car designs with its pug nose, curved lines and bulbous frame.

- The **Stout Scarab** (Figure 2 and next photo) was the brainchild of William B. Stout, an automotive and aircraft engineer who had worked for the Packard Motor Car Company during World War I. Stout is most famous as the designer of the Tri-Motor airplane, which Ford acquired when it purchased Stout's aircraft manufacturing company, the Stout Metal Plane Company, in 1924. After a dispute with Ford over the plane, Stout left the company in 1932. That year he produced a prototype of the Scarab, and his new venture, the Stout Motor Car Company, began limited production of it in 1935. With a long wheelbase and removable seats, and without a driveshaft, the Scarab was very spacious—a Volkswagen bus or a modern minivan before its time. Although Stout made only nine Scarabs, the design attracted such high-profile customers as industrial magnates Harvey Firestone, Philip Wrigley and Willard Dow. General Eisenhower even used one as a mobile office in North Africa during World War II; he later presented it as a gift to France's General De Gaulle. The car's expensive price tag of $5,000 helped ensure limited production. Nonetheless, the Scarab's style expressed in the extreme the classic formal manifestations of negative social mood: enclosed, rounded bodies, snub noses and small windows. These same traits would characterize later negative-mood cars as well.

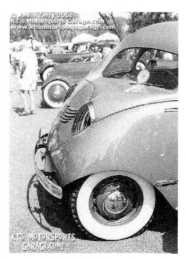

1935 Stout Scarab

- Pontoon fenders, a wraparound "coffin nose" grille, and hidden pop-up headlights helped the **Auburn Cord** 810/812 (photos below) become the darling of auto shows in New York, Chicago and Los Angeles in 1935. It attracted 7,639 requests for more information. It also represented the Cord Corporation's dying breath. In the 1930s, unable to sell the super-luxury cars that had made him famous in the 1920s, E.L. Cord had come to rely on profits from the corporation's kitchen cabinet division to subsidize its automotive divisions. The model 810, the company's first visible nod to the realities of the new mood, looked at first to be the company's salvation. Instead, it was too

1935 Auburn Cord

little too late. Cord closed the Auburn division in August 1937 and liquidated his corporation's remaining assets several months later.

- As the stock market's 20-year corrective process neared its end in 1949, the soft amorphousness that attends bear market designs reached an extreme in the 1948 **Studebaker Starlight Coupe** (photos below). The rear of the car, which had four windshield-like curved windows and a large bulge in the center of the trunk that looked like it might have housed an engine, appeared so much like the face of an automobile that people said they "couldn't tell if it was coming or going." In that sense, the car's form was a fitting metaphor for the end of a sideways correction in the Dow/PPI, which was still down by two thirds after 20 years.

1949-1966 (Positive Mood)

It is no coincidence that the Classic Car Club of America pinpoints 1948 as the end of its namesake automobile era. In 1949, the multi-decade trend in social mood reversed, and car styles changed as a new bull market lifted off. Gone were the subdued curves and rounded body parts fitting a negative-mood era. The new cars reflected society's desire for clarity, structure and speed. Lines were clearly defined with rectangular front grilles, flat-plane sides, and square hoods, roofs and trunks. Flamboyant individuality returned via chrome, tailfins and convertible roofs. As the bull market progressed, Detroit issued a number of representative cars:

- The "Classic" **Ford Thunderbird** (Figure 3) featured chrome "bullets" on the grille, exhaust pipes that emerged from the rear bumper, and pointed headlight covers that appeared to extend in a straight line back to the tailfins (which tilted outward on the '57 model in Figure 3). Ford introduced the T-Bird in 1955, in the middle of the fastest change toward positive mood as evidenced by the steepest rise of stocks' bull market. The second generation of the car, introduced in 1958, was so sharply angular, and its sides hung so low, that it became known as the "Square Bird." That year, the new Thunderbird won the first of the three *Motor Trend* "Car of the Year" awards that it would eventually collect, and its sales success prompted designers to duplicate its rectangular features across all Ford lines. The 1962 Thunderbird Sports Roadster attracted several prominent owners, including Elvis Presley.

- The **Chevrolet Impala** (Figure 3) was similar to the Ford Thunderbird in its rectangular form. Introduced in 1958, it became the best-selling automobile in the United States in 1960 and maintained that rank through the end of the decade. In 1965, just prior to the peak of the Dow/PPI the following year, Chevrolet sold one million Impalas, an industry record for the period for a single model in a year.

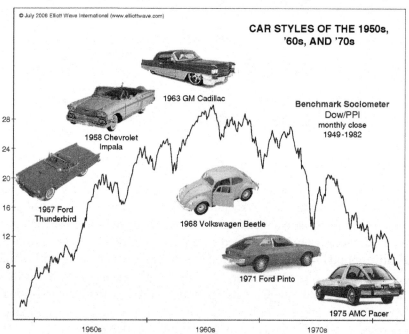

Figure 3

- The **General Motors Cadillac** (Figure 3) of the 1950s and early 1960s featured broad sides, sharp corners and an ostentatious front grille. Leading the automotive avant-garde, GM styling chief Harley J. Earl placed conical, artillery-shell-inspired "Dagmar" bumpers on the Cadillac as early as 1946. Then, inspired by the twin rudders on the Lockheed P-38 Lightning aircraft, Earl added angular tailfins in 1948. In later years, other manufacturers would add these speed symbols to their models. Tailfins reached their peak expression in the 1959 Cadillac Eldorado (next photo) smack in the middle of the upward trend in stocks. In 1964, the Cadillac sealed its image as an automotive icon of the positive mood period when a black limousine "Caddie" pulled up in front of New York City's Madison Square Garden to deliver the Beatles to thousands of screaming fans.

1959 Cadillac Eldorado

- By the time the Dow peaked in PPI-adjusted terms in 1966, society's preference for angularity in car styling had reached such an extreme that on its **Mercury Monterey**, **Parklane** and **Breezeway** models, Ford offered a rear window that cut *inward* (see photo at right), coming up with yet another angle in producing angles.

1965 Mercury Monterey

1966-1982 (Negative Mood)

In 1966, at the top of a 17-year bull market in stocks, the U.S. automobile manufacturing industry was the envy of the world. By the end of the subsequent 16-year bear market in the Dow/PPI, U.S. car makers had ceded considerable ground to overseas competitors, and one of the "big three" manufacturers (Chrysler) was on the brink of bankruptcy, finally to be bailed out by government-guaranteed loans in 1981, the final full year of the Dow/PPI's bear market. Car designs over that period had negative-mood features, although they were not as pronounced as those of the larger-degree period of negative mood in the 1930s-1940s. Key representatives include the following:

- The **Volkswagen Beetle** (Figure 3) was small, rounded and lowly powered, which are classic negative-mood car features. The vehicle began production as Adolph Hitler's "people's car" in the negative-mood year of 1938. A design that Dr. Ferdinand Porsche had envisioned at the extreme in negative mood in 1932 served as its model. The Beetle then migrated to the United States in 1949, the final year of the negative mood period. Following the Dow/PPI's peak in 1966, the Beetle—along with its minivan sister, the VW Bus—became a popular canvas on which counterculture hippies and flower children painted symbols of peace and love. In the bear market rally year of 1968, the car was the centerpiece of a popular film, *The Love Bug*. In the bear market rally year of 1972, the Beetle displaced the Ford Model T as most produced car in history when lifetime production exceeded 15 million units. As the trend toward negative mood wore on, however, the car's happy-hippie image went out of fashion. Volkswagen stopped selling the model in the United States in 1978, as the negative trend in social mood neared its end.

- Along with the Chevrolet Vega and the AMC Gremlin, the **Ford Pinto** (also **Mercury Bobcat**) (Figure 3) represented the U.S. automobile industry's contribution to the rising popularity of small cars during the early 1970s. The basic hatchback or coupe model had a wide, sloping rear end, giving the back of the automobile a football-like shape. A wagon version of the vehicle, called the Ford Pinto Cruising Wagon, even sported a small, round "bubble window" in place of rear side windows (see next photo), a feature also popular on many conversion vans of the period. In the midst of its production run from 1971 to 1980, which marked the year of the bottom in the Dow priced in real money (gold), the Pinto became the subject of a scandal. Internal documents showed that Ford executives had decided to ignore a design flaw that made the gas tank susceptible to explosion upon rear impact. Their reasoning was that settling lawsuits would be cheaper than spending $11 per car to fix the problem—a classic example of negative-mood thinking. In another testament to the power of negative mood to produce

memorable failures, the Vega, Pinto and Gremlin respectively rank second, third and fourth on the popular radio show *Car Talk*'s listener-determined list of the "Worst Cars of the Millennium." First place goes to the Yugo GV, which was designed in 1981, the final full year of the negative mood period as measured by the Dow/PPI. The 1970s were also the worst decade for the quality of Jaguars, about which owners quipped, "make sure to store a mechanic in the trunk." In "Popular Culture and the Stock Market," Prechter wrote, "1970s pop art, produced during the bear market, generally consisted of massive hunks of dark iron or stone sculpture, much of which was detested for its ugliness and later removed." The same can be said of many 1970s automobiles.

- The American Motors Corporation's chief stylist, Richard A. Teague, originally envisioned the AMC Pacer (Figure 3) as a futuristic bubble-like vehicle, as shown in his 1971 sketch of the concept, reproduced at right. The final version of the car had a more traditional small-car front but came close to retaining the rounded backside that Teague had intended for it. He achieved this aspect of his design by using rounded rear  glass window panels—an innovation not seen since the Studebaker Starlight Coupe in 1948. Its spherical appearance was so striking that when it was introduced in February 1975, reviewers called it a "fishbowl on wheels" and a "jellybean in suspenders." The Pacer sold 145,528 units in its first year, about half of its total six-year production run, which spanned most of the second half of the bear market in the Dow/PPI.

1982-2000 (Positive Mood)

The positive social mood that emerged from the ashes of the early 1980s prompted changes in the design of automobiles. The automobile industry began producing cars that expressed the increasingly optimistic society's rediscovery of scientific achievement and boldness.

- Introduced in January 1981, a year before the end of the 16-year bear market, the **De Lorean DMC-12** (Figure 4) was a car ahead of its time—but only by a few years. It featured Giorgetto Giugiaro's angular "folded paper" design, stainless steel paneling, and mechanical, gull-wing doors. Such Space-Shuttle-age styling oozed scientific

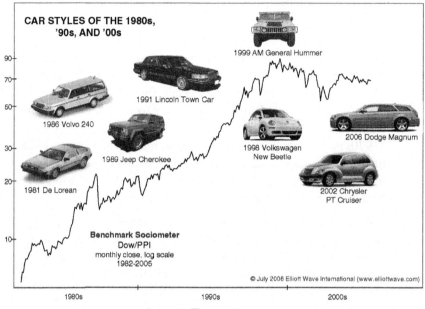

Figure 4

precision—a theme last seen in the "rocket ship" tailfins and "nose cone" protuberances of stylish 1950s automobiles. But people in a negative mood were not ready for such flair. John De Lorean produced only about 8,600 units of his dream car before his company went bankrupt in 1983. Just two years later, the car reemerged in popular culture in a blockbuster film, *Back to the Future*. In the movie, a scientist converts a De Lorean into a time machine in which a young man travels back in time to the year 1955. The choices of destination and vehicle were appropriate. The social mood in both 1985 and 1955 was early in a positive transition. The De Lorean in the film served as a symbol of the hopes and ambitions of many people as the trend toward positive mood of 1982-2000 got underway.

- The **Jeep Cherokee** (Figure 4) was the earliest beneficiary of the craze for "offroad" Sport Utility Vehicles (SUVs)—a fitting mode of transportation for the positive mood period that lay ahead. It was introduced for model-year 1974, just as the DJIA rose to barely miss making a new all-time high in October 1973. Never mind that the most difficult terrain most owners challenged it on was the gravel road down to a suburban athletic field. The Cherokee, like all SUVs after it, announced through its rugged, rectilinear form, "I'm a risk-taker, and I'm ready to tackle the mountains of life!" As the bull market got going in earnest in the 1980s, the exceptionally angular Cherokee became chic and popular.

- The **Volvo 200 Series** (Figure 4), born in the autumn of 1974, was popular with large middle class families until the company replaced it in 1993. Its boxy design fit the emerging positive mood.

- The **Lincoln Town Car** (Figure 4) was introduced for model-year 1981. It benefited greatly from the ensuing positive trend in social mood and became Ford's best-selling luxury car. The Town Car was one of the longest cars produced in the United States, and its side trims and hood ornament suggested establishment, tradition and class. The popularity of the original design was so enduring that designers modified the car only once (for model-year 1990, making only minor cosmetic changes) before a decidedly negative-mood version of the automobile appeared for model-year 1998 (see discussion below).

- The **AM General Hummer** (Figure 4), a civilian version of the U.S. military's M998 High Mobility Multipurpose Wheeled Vehicle (HMMWV or "Hum-vee"), was the archetype of late 20th-century consumer extravagance. Its heavy weight, high cost and poor fuel efficiency epitomized excess. Its military pedigree, tank-like paneling, and complex grille projected muscularity and vigor, and its boxy angularity exuded manly decisiveness. The 1992 Hummer quickly attracted the attention of such positive-mood icons as the CEO of Coca-Cola (who purchased the first fifteen) and Arnold Schwarzenegger (who reportedly purchased the first two Limited Edition versions and now owns eight Hummers in all). General Motors, attracted by the Hummer's $20,000 per-vehicle profit margin, purchased the brand in late 1999—just in time for social mood to turn negative.

- Production of the largest SUV ever, the **Ford Excursion** (photo at right), began in 2000. The 2000 peak in stock prices marked the start of a negative trend in social mood as well as a temporary end of the SUV expansion era. In  2005, Ford eliminated the Excursion, and last month (June 2006) GM joined the downsizing trend by ceasing production of the largest of the Hummer models, the Hummer H1.

2000-Present (Negative Mood Trend in Progress)

Car designers lately seem to be looking back to car styles of the 1930s-1940s and the 1970s for inspiration. Retro-inspired, negative-mood models are appearing in quantity. Rounded edges and bodies, blunt noses and smaller windows are back. Socionomists not only understand these changes but also predicted them. Although the bear market likely has more to go, the influence of negative social mood is already evident in the following models:

- Initially shown as a concept car at the North American International Auto Show in the pessimistic environment of 1994 (see Figure 1 in Chapter 12), the **Volkswagen New Beetle** (Figure 4) entered production in 1998, just months after that era's high in the Value Line Composite index. That year the DJIA dipped 20%, and VW's reincarnated icon gave a preview of the coming trend in automobile styling. The New Beetle was *Motor Trend*'s Import Car of the Year for 1999, and it continued to sell briskly throughout the 2000-2002 decline in stock prices.

- In model-year 1998, ahead of the downturn in stock prices, the **Lincoln Town Car** (at right) went under the knife for its first  major cosmetic change, reappearing with its edges softened considerably and its hood ornament removed.

- The blunt-nosed grille of the 1934-Airflow-inspired **Chrysler PT Cruiser** (Figure 4) has been a common sight on city streets since the company introduced the model in 2000 for model-year 2001. In the negative-mood year of 2001, the car won the "North American Car of the Year" award. In 2003, as the stock market recovered, demand dropped off considerably. In an attempt to spur sales, Chrysler wisely introduced a convertible version for model-year 2005. But as the current stock market rally has progressed, the popularity of the PT Cruiser has fallen off accordingly.

- The **Dodge Magnum** (Figure 4) was based on a concept car introduced shortly after the global stock market low of 2003. Its blunt nose gives it a tough, truck-like look, and its narrow windows recall car models from the 1930s and 1940s. Unlike traditional station wagons, its roof slopes downward toward the rear, giving its backside a rounded appearance. In 2004, *Road & Track* Design Director Richard Baron predicted, "a lot of sport-utility-vehicle owners probably would look favorably upon the Magnum and climb down from their oversize trucks."[3] We shall see.

- Like water hitting a stone, negative mood continues to smooth the edges in auto designs, even those of the most established  bullish icons. Would you ever have guessed that the ancestors of the car pictured here were once nicknamed "bricks"? Fans know this car as a **Volvo 2006 S60 5T**.

Roof Type: Convertible Roofs vs. Hardtops

In the early years of the automobile industry, all cars were open cars, reflecting their evolution from buggies and bicycles. But after Edward Budd introduced of the all-steel body in 1914, enclosed cars increasingly became the standard. Closed-body vehicles outsold open vehicles for the first time in 1925. In 1927, nine manufacturers (Buick, Cadillac, Chrysler, duPont, LaSalle, Lincoln, Stearns, Whippet and Willys) introduced the first "convertible" roofs. The innovation was a response to the demand for adventure and flash that accompanied the positive social mood of the late 1920s. 1929, the year the stock market peaked, saw the release of the most luxurious convertibles ever—including those made by Auburn, Cadillac, Chrysler, Cord, Duesenberg, Marmon and Packard.

Demand for convertibles declined during the negative-mood years of the 1930s and 1940s but re-emerged with the positive trend in mood in the 1950s and 1960s. Convertibles claimed about 5% of the market in 1957 and peaked at around 6% at the top of the Dow/PPI in 1966. The subsequent trend toward negative social mood devastated convertible sales, which plummeted to about 1% by 1970. In 1976, Cadillac advertised its Eldorado as "the last convertible in America." Car analysts give many rational-response reasons for the decline of the convertible in the 1970s, but as one observer pointed out, most of their claims were bogus:

> There were several reasons cited for the demise of the North American convertible in the '70s. Some claimed it was due to impending roll-over legislation, which never came. And sun/moon roofs offered a type of open air motoring without the convertible's disadvantages. It was even said that the three-point seatbelt wouldn't function in them, which we now know is not true. What really happened was that American manufacturers quit building convertibles because the public stopped buying them. They were merely heeding what the market told them.[4]

Yet only a socionomist knows *why* the public stopped buying these cars.

In 1982, the negative social mood responsible for Americans' waning interest in convertibles came to an end, signaled by the termination in August of a 16-year bear market in the Dow/PPI. That year, Chrysler sold 23,000 convertible LeBarons, an unexpected sales success that prompted other manufacturers to begin making convertibles again. By the late 1990s, convertible sales had recovered to account for about 3% of U.S. new car registrations. That this percentage falls short of the 1966 high is consistent with the personality of fifth waves identified by Frost and Prechter's observation (*Elliott Wave Principle*, p. 80) that stock market advances become weaker and narrower in their late stages.

Car Colors[5]

The influence of social mood on automobile color preferences was evident early in the 20th century. In the years around 1909, social mood was positive. The stock market (as registered by the reconstructed S&P 500, not shown) had been advancing for 13 years; President Teddy Roosevelt was at the peak of his popularity; the tallest buildings in the country, the Singer and Metropolitan Life Buildings, had just opened in New York City; and consumers were in the mood for colors, which Henry Ford was then offering on his Model T. As social mood passed through a negative phase early in the century's second decade, the stock market's decline accelerated, the war in Europe intensified, and in 1915 Ford eliminated the color option. For the next eleven years, consumers could buy Model Ts only in black. Color consultant Leatrice Eiseman says that an owner of a black car is "empowered, not easily manipulated, loves elegance, appreciates classics"—traits characteristic of early positive mood trends.

In the 1920s, positive mood brought brighter and more varied colors back to mass-market cars. In 1923, DuPont developed fast-drying color lacquers for automobiles. Henry Ford adopted the new paint technology in 1926, in the middle of the boom. Ford's decision to continue offering only black cars during the late 'teens and early 1920s was a wise choice economically (the "Japan" or Brunswick" black lacquer he used cost less and cured up to 7 times faster than color variants), and his decision to offer colors in 1926 was well-timed socionomically. The records of DuPont Automotive, which began tracking the popularity of automobile colors in 1953, reveal that consumers tend to favor black until just past the middle of a positive-mood trend, which was precisely the position of mood in 1926, as depicted in Figure 2.

Another automotive entrepreneur sensitive to the power of color was the flamboyant E.L. Cord, whose career during the 1920s and 1930s practically served as a meter of social mood all by itself. Cord was already a successful car salesman when he joined the troubled Auburn Automobile Company in 1924. He quickly sold off 500 unsold cars after repainting them in bright colors—a feat that convinced Auburn management to hand him control of the company. But bright colors worked against Cord during the 1930s, when the social mood brought about a preference for earth tones. Eiseman says that deep brown implies an owner who is "down-to-earth, no-nonsense"; taupe/light brown expresses "timeless, basic and simple tastes"; neutral gray suggests "sober, corporate, practical, and pragmatic"; and dark green

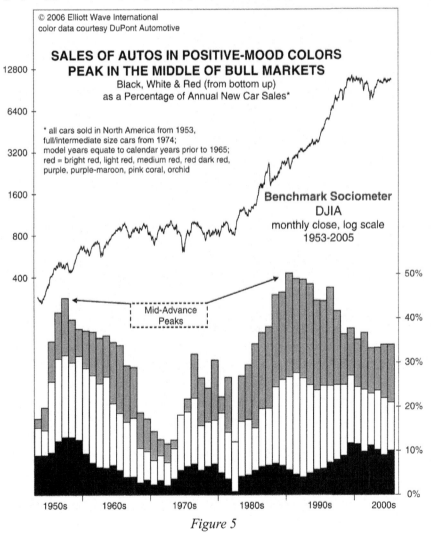

Figure 5

implies "traditional, trustworthy, and well-balanced." Such values were the antithesis of those represented by the land yachts in Cord showrooms during the Depression years, which were painted lemon, chartreuse and Chinese red.

As the positive mood trend gathered steam in the late 1950s, consumers abandoned the dark shades that dominated automobile colors during the prior two decades in favor of more vibrant hues. The energetic new mood fostered demand for angular forms and richer colors. Recognizing a relationship between color and form, N.J. Mooney, DuPont's color advisor at the time, wrote in 1955,

> In the early Thirties, it was possible to produce many equally bright colors. However, the bulky models of that era were not conducive to the use of brilliant colors, and it was only with the introduction of the elongated lines of the hard top models that colors of this type effectively complemented the automobiles.... The trend toward colors of high intensities became widespread late in 1954 with the introduction of the 1955 models, and today the public is offered the widest selection of color in the history of the industry.[6]

Figure 5 shows that white and red have a similar profile to black. The color white, which Eiseman says indicates "fastidiousness"—a positive mood trait, as opposed to sloppiness, a negative mood trait—dominated the top spot for 11 years from 1955 to 1965, followed by blue, turquoise and black. The technical difficulties of preserving the quality of red in automobile paints restrained use of the color until chemists solved the problem in 1963. Until then, red, which Eiseman says is "sexy, speedy, high-energy, and dynamic," made its mark through its other shades, such as purple-maroon, orchid and coral-pink. The surge of coral-pink into the top three shades sold in 1957 marked the high point for the three "mainstream" positive-mood hues at a market share of approximately 50% (see Figure 5). Their subsequent divergence from the stock market's trend signaled that the 1949-1966 bull market was entering its final stages.

The only time from 1957 to 1966 that a negative-mood color entered the top three was 1961-1962, years that witnessed a violent stock market plunge, the Bay of Pigs incident and the Cuban Missile Crisis. An earthy shade—medium brown-gold—took second place in both years.

In 1966, negative-mood colors began an 8-year ascendancy that would eventually gain them a 66% market share (see Figure 6). By no mere coincidence, that same year saw the start of an 8-year bear market in stock prices; the United States stepped up its fighting in Vietnam; China imploded in the Cultural Revolution; and negative social mood in the United States nourished anger to such an extent that it forced the resignation of President Richard Nixon in 1974.

The shift was gradual at first. Starting in 1968, when hand-painted, floral-print Volkswagen Beetles and Buses became a sign of the times, what we observe to be a distinctively "post-peak" color—yellow—first showed its influence. DuPont calls yellow (along with its more popular sibling, red) a "notice me" color. According to Eiseman, sunshine yellow represents a "sunny disposition, joyful and young at heart," and bright

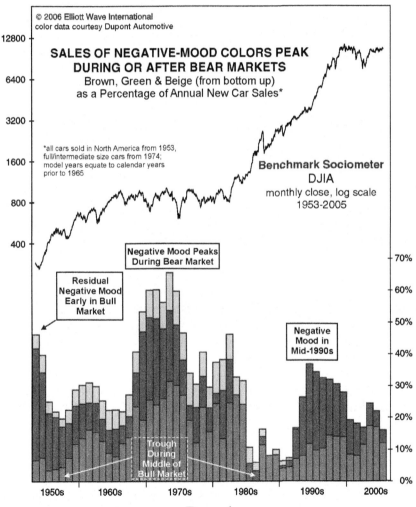

Figure 6

yellow-gold is "intelligent, warm, loves comfort and will pay for it." During the bear-market-rally years of 1967 and 1972, yellow-gold surged to 7.8% and 9.9% of sales, respectively, the best performance of any individual yellow shade on record. In 1971, midway through the 8-year bear market, two yellow-influenced, "mixed-mood" colors—yellow-green and copper-bronze—appeared for the first time in the top three. But by 1974, the year the nominal stock averages bottomed, yellow shades had completely relinquished their top rankings to the negative-mood hues of maroon, beige and darker shades of green. That year, red in all its shades (except maroon, which we classify as a brown) disappeared completely as a color option for intermediate and full-sized cars. The only other year on record that lighter shades of red disappeared completely for the category was 1982, the year of the bottom in the Dow/PPI. In that year, manufacturers offered only light and dark red-brown (which we have also classified as browns). You can see the complete absence of red in 1974 and 1982 in the color bars of Figure 5.

After the negative mood trend ended in the early 1980s, brightness returned to automobile colors, highlighted by an explosion in the popularity of red in the middle of the trend toward positive mood of 1982-2000. In 1983, Prince released the song 'Little Red Corvette', and in 1984 Bruce Springsteen sang about a lighter shade of red in 'Pink Cadillac'. In 1985, dark red became a top-three color, replaced by medium red in 1986. In 1988, the industry offered a color called "bright red." By 1989, *USA Today* found the trend toward brighter automobile colors—and its similarity to that of the last bull market period—newsworthy:

> Cruising Main Street in a turquoise ragtop or metallic-purple muscle car may be a faded memory, but get ready: *American Graffiti*-style colors are back. Automakers plan a '50s revival for 1990 and '91. Hot colors: bright reds, yellows; pearly whites, creams, metallic greens, taupes and teal…. Buyers in '88 chose white, red and gray over darker shades of the early '80s.[7]

In 1990, the "mainstream" positive-mood colors collectively topped out—recalling their 1957 peak in the middle of the 1942-1966 bull market, again signaling that the advance was about half over. The positive mood at larger degree kept the popularity of these colors elevated, but a phase of negative mood, similar to the one that appeared during the stock market correction of 1961-1962, interrupted the trend. Followers of investor sentiment have long recognized that the period of pessimism following the 1987 crash ended in 1994 (see Figure 1 in Chapter 12). The pessimism of the early and middle 1990s cloaked itself in greens and browns, which together took a 37% market share by 1994, up from 6% in 1990.

Since 1998, the biggest story in automobile colors has been the rise and then the absolute dominance of silver (see Figure 7). Silver entered the top three in 1999, displacing white as the most popular color in Europe and North America in 2000, and became the #1 color globally in 2001. The color has less precedence than others as a meter of social mood, having first emerged as an automobile finishing in 1974. But its history since then suggests that, like yellow, silver is a "post-peak" color that precedes deeper expressions of negative mood in the future. Eiseman says that the owner of a silver car is "elegant, loves futuristic looks, cool"—a perfect description of post-peak complacency, in our opinion. At the risk of overanalyzing a limited data series, we note that the popularity of silver has a habit of peaking some years after major stock market tops and some years before final bottoms. Silver was first popular during the rally in stocks from 1974-76, and its popularity peaked a few years later, in 1979. After disappearing as a category altogether following the bear market low in 1982, the color returned as an option leading up to the stock market top in 1987, and its popularity again peaked a few years later, in 1991. Halved in stature by the pessimistic mood of the early to mid 1990s, the popularity of silver then began a meteoric rise in 1998. By the time it peaked in 2002, two years after the stock market top in 2000, the color covered approximately 28.1% of all new cars. In the past, colors have peaked in popularity when they achieved a market share of about 20%. Silver's six-year run above that level—like the topping investment mania it has mirrored—is unprecedented. With the color still holding a 21% market share in 2005, we would definitely short-sell silver as a car color right here.

[As stocks subsequently plunged in 2007-2009 and recovered thereafter, the popularity of silver as a car color has fallen persistently, fulfilling the author's prediction. In 2016, an industry publication reported, "At 11%, silver has not been at or below this level since 1998."[8]—Ed.]

During the 2000-2002 decline, yellow again played its subtle but meaningful post-peak role after many years of neglect. In its 2001 color report, DuPont recognized the flashback to the earlier era that yellow represented:

> An ongoing retro-trend also is apparent with the rise of yellow as a top-12 color over the past two years, with continued gains predicted for 2002. It is seen in pale shades and soft golden metallics for sport luxury vehicles with stronger hues adding punch to sporty cars and light trucks. The last time yellow experienced this level of popularity was when bright sun-colored VW Beetles tooled down the road to

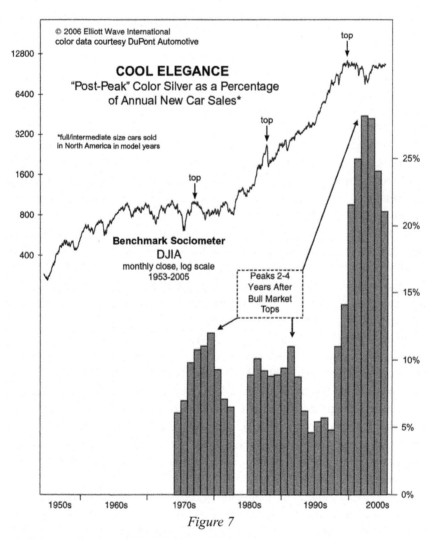

Figure 7

the tune of the Beatles' "Yellow Submarine." ...The move to a "heritage look" through classic colors such as yellow may be driven by consumers' need to connect with comfortable traditions while still embracing a bit of optimism.[9]

DuPont's color popularity report of 2004 pointed out that yellow joined the ranks of the top ten colors in 1992, another post-peak period. When the company releases the 2006 model year figures, we will not be surprised if yellow shades again play a prominent minor role as the current rally peaks. [In line with that forecast, the popularity of yellow peaked in 2006-7 at 3% and fell in 2008 and 2009 to 2% and 2.3%, respectively.—Ed.]

Since 2002, brighter colors have returned to select categories of automobiles and in muted combinations, reflecting a "positive-but-less-than-optimal" social mood during the current bear market rally. As DuPont noted in its 2005 year-end summary,

> While silver continues its six-year reign as the number one color choice, it continues to decline in popularity in favor of a fuller palette of true, high-chroma colors. Silver is also giving way to its sister neutral color—medium dark gray. Significant 5% gains were seen in 2005 color trends for gray in complex formulations that show color infusions of various color hues.[10]

Sales of grey and blue automobiles seem to have no consistent pattern of correlation to the stock market and therefore no directional implications with respect to social mood. But the recent use of grey to dilute the brightness of other colors suggests that the negative mood trend is beginning to reassert itself. [The real estate market had peaked just a few months earlier and plunged for the next six years, within which time stocks fell the most since 1929-1932.—Ed.]

The Chrysler "Woody" Indicator

One of the odder and more endearing styles is the real or faux wood-sided "woody" automobile. Our studies show that the style mainly shows up during negative mood periods. One manufacturer in particular—Chrysler—has timed its reintroduction of the style with periods of low stock prices so consistently that we consider it to be a bottoming indicator for the stock market.

The use of wood in automobiles had been in decline since Edward G. Budd and the Dodge Brothers introduced the all-steel car body to the mass market in 1914. Wood all but disappeared from automobile bodies by the late 1930s. So when Chrysler offered real wood paneling on its Town & Country series in 1941 and 1942 at the end of a five-year trend toward negative mood, and then again during the negative-mood years of 1946 to 1949, the public welcomed it as a novelty. The company eliminated the option in 1950 as a 17-year trend toward positive mood began.

A year and a half after the Dow/PPI's peak of 1966, Chrysler revisited the woody theme by offering "simulated wood panel design applications" on its station wagons for model-year 1968. (This is the one time that the "Chrysler woody indicator" did not coincide with a stock market bottom, since it arrived early in the negative mood period.) For the 1983 model year, introduced the very quarter that the 16-year correction came to a close,

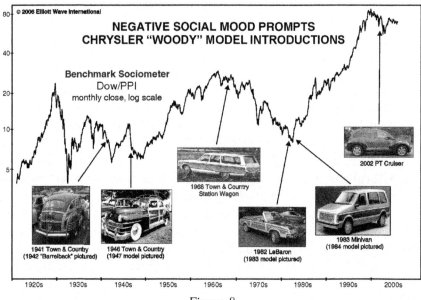

Figure 8

Chrysler offered faux wood siding on its new minivans. For model-year 2002, as the stock market was nearing the end of a 2½-year decline, Chrysler offered a "woody" option on its negative-mood flagship, the PT Cruiser, proving once again the company's uncanny ability to identify periods when society most desires to slow down and "get back to nature," expressing that sentiment with earth tones and wood.

Conclusion

Our research suggests that correlations between trends in car styles and in the stock market are neither random nor planned. We propose that both sets of trends are powered simultaneously by waves of unconscious social mood—a mood shared by all kinds of people, including stock market investors as well as designers and consumers of automobiles.

The automobile industry could benefit greatly by adopting a socionomic perspective. Automobile manufacturers make the same forecasting mistakes that economists and investors do when they rely on the persistence of past trends.

Future trends in social mood will affect automobile styling, just as they have in the past. The next positive mood trend will accompany a trend toward larger and more angular car bodies, larger windows, more convertibles, and positive-mood colors. The next negative mood trend will foster desires for smoother and smaller car bodies, smaller windows, fewer convertibles, and negative-mood colors. But it will also lead to hard times for, and the consolidation of, much of the global auto industry—and certainly to the demise of companies that fail to lead in design changes that could save them.

NOTES AND REFERENCES

[1] Reproduced as Chapter 2 in *Pioneering Studies in Socionomics* (2003).

[2] Henry Ford may once have said, "the customer can have a car painted any color he wants as long as it's black," but such was not always his policy. Actually, Ford offered Model Ts in several colors from 1908 to 1914 and from 1926 to 1927 (its final year of production). Both were periods of very positive social mood.

[3] See endnote 1.

[4] Vance, Bill. *The History of the Convertible*, CanadianDriver.com.

[5] The July-August 2008 issue of *Radar* magazine reported on this portion of Galasiewski's study, and DuPont referenced it in its 2006 Automotive *Color Popularity Report.*

[6] Mooney, N.J. (1955). *Automotive Color Popularity 1954*, E.I. DuPont de Nemours & Co., Detroit, MI.

[7] Hoffman, Kathy Barks (1989, July 20). "Car Colors Take 50's Tone," *USA Today.*

[8] Axalta Coating Systems. (December 8, 2016). *Global Automotive 2016 Color Popularity Report.*

[9] DuPont Automotive. (2002, January 2). *Color Popularity 2001*, E.I. DuPont de Nemours & Co., Detroit, MI.

[10] DuPont Automotive (2005, November 29). *Color Popularity 2005*, E.I. DuPont de Nemours & Co., Detroit, MI.

Chapter 30

When Cars are Stars—
Social Mood and Automobile Performance

Mark Galasiewski

April 10, 2007 (EWT)

NASCAR-related revenues are hitting all-time highs. Two car-racing films—*Cars* and *Talladega Nights*, in which Ricky Bobby expresses the prevailing sentiment by exclaiming, "I wanna go fast!"—smashed box-office records last year. Auto manufacturers are offering consumers far more performance capability than most of them will ever use. What can these conditions tell us about the future of the U.S. stock market?

Prechter's 1985 essay, "Popular Culture and the Stock Market," showed that the tone of human activities generally mirrors trends in social mood, as recorded by fluctuations in stock indexes. As social mood becomes more positive, the tempo of everything from car engines to dance halls to stock trading picks up. When it trends toward the negative, tempos slow.

Based on these empirical observations, we hypothesized that automobile manufacturers, responding to mood-driven fluctuations in consumer demand, would tend to increase the power and speed capacities of production cars throughout positive trends in social mood and reduce them throughout negative trends, as recorded in stock indexes.

Comprehensive historical data on horsepower are hard to come by, but our friend John Carder of Topline Investment Graphics came up with a novel proxy: the highest Chevrolet Corvette engine power offered annually. As it turns out, these data are an excellent meter of social mood as confirmed by a plot of the PPI-adjusted Dow Jones Industrial Average (see Figure 1). Technical note: Since 1965, model years have begun several months in advance of the calendar year, so in Figures 1 & 3 we have placed the bars representing model years so that they properly straddle the year-end dates.

The Corvette, introduced in 1953, was a product of the wave of positive social mood that had begun lifting the stock market higher after the

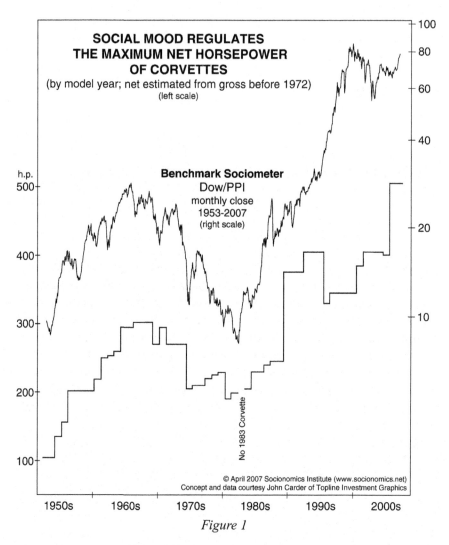

SOCIAL MOOD REGULATES
THE MAXIMUM NET HORSEPOWER
OF CORVETTES
(by model year; net estimated from gross before 1972)
(left scale)

Benchmark Sociometer
Dow/PPI
monthly close
1953-2007
(right scale)

h.p.

No 1983 Corvette

© April 2007 Socionomics Institute (www.socionomics.net)
Concept and data courtesy John Carder of Topline Investment Graphics

Figure 1

low of 1949. In the early 1950s, society was interested in having fun, but flamboyance was still out of fashion among manufacturers and consumers as the negative mood of the 1929-1949 correction still lingered. Reflecting this residual mood, conflict re-erupted internationally (in Korea), and political witch-hunts festered domestically in the form of McCarthyism. As the October 2006 issue of *The Elliott Wave Theorist* noted, "traditional" green colors took a higher percentage of total U.S. new car sales in 1953 than at any other time in the history of DuPont's records, while "sexy" red shades hardly registered. Sales of the 1953 Corvette were lukewarm, and in 1954 sales actually declined.

The demand for more "sportiness" in vehicles rose in 1955 as the stock market experienced its fastest-rising wave within the 1949-1966 bull market. That year, the Corvette's horsepower surged by 30%, and Ford joined the trend with the introduction of the Thunderbird. In 1956, construction of the Interstate Highway System began in earnest. By 1963, when the Beach Boys released *Little Deuce Coupe*, an album devoted almost entirely to celebrating cars, the sports car trend had gone mainstream.

As the U.S. stock market roared to a top in the mid-1960s, manufacturers pulled out all stops in an effort to satisfy performance fever. In 1964, General Motors' Pontiac division chief John De Lorean violated a GM ban on placing large engines in smaller cars and thereby introduced the first "muscle car," the Pontiac GTO. Chrysler immediately countered with the first "pony" car, the Plymouth Barracuda. Later that year, Ford followed with the Mustang, shocking the world by selling 1,000,000 units of the car in its first 18 months. For the 1966 model year, General Motors added the Chevy Camaro and the Pontiac Firebird to its lineup, and Chevrolet introduced its largest engine, the "427" (named for the number of cubic inches in its cylinder volume). In 1966, the year of that era's peak in the Dow/PPI, Ford became the first American manufacturer to field winning cars in Europe's 24 Hours of Le Mans endurance race. Corvette engine power peaked the following year, when GM offered twenty cars with the "L88" version of the engine, which produced 430 (gross) hp officially and 550 (gross) hp by unofficial estimates. Horsepower in U.S. cars overall peaked with the introduction of the 450 (gross) hp Chevrolet Chevelle Super Sport 454 in the model year 1970, which came into production a year after the Value Line Composite index topped for that era.

Following the industry trend, the Corvette's maximum horsepower, which had been flat since 1966, began to decline in 1970 in concert with the stock market. As with respect to the decline in sales of convertibles [profiled in Chapter 29], conventional wisdom is that external events caused the change. One hypothesis holds that high performance died out in the 1970s due to the imposition (or the threat) of government regulation. In 1970, Congress passed the Clean Air Act and established the Environmental Protection Agency and the National Highway Traffic Safety Administration. The U.S. auto industry feared regulation; "safety does not sell" was an oft-heard phrase. But adherents of that view miss the big picture. A more accurate explanation is that the decline in stock prices, the imposition of government intervention and the decline in automobile horsepower were all products of the negative social mood of the time.

Astute auto industry observers knew that the performance craze was exhausted, and some noted it at the time. As *Car Life* wrote in its review of the 1970 Chevelle, "Without even raising the specters of insurance and social justice, it's fair to say that the Supercar as we know it may have gone as far as it's going."

Well after consumers' preferences turned toward safety and economy, fuel prices rose in late 1973, and in 1974 the federal government imposed a national 55 mph speed limit. Fun was no longer popular, either, so Chevrolet eliminated the convertible Corvette in model-year 1975, which came to market near the bottom in stock prices of Q4 1974. Maximum horsepower for the car continued to decline into 1981, one year after the price of oil peaked and a year before the bottom in PPI-adjusted stock prices. For model year 1983, which began at that era's low in the Dow/PPI, Chevrolet did not even offer a new Corvette due to production problems and a surplus of 1982 models.

The need for speed returned in the 1980s along with the positive social mood that fueled a new rise in stock prices. By 1983, when Prince compared the object of his affection to a "little red Corvette" in a song by the same name, both maximum and average horsepower began creeping up again. In 1987 and 1988, Congress permitted states to raise speed limits on rural highways and roads. Positive mood reached fever pitch during the 1990 model year, in the middle of the 1982-2000 bull market. Communism and the Berlin Wall crumbled, South Africa freed Nelson Mandela, and—recalling the mid-trend leap of 1955—the Corvette's horsepower surged 53%, the largest annual increase on record. A premium 1990 Corvette model, the ZR-1, set seven international and three world speed records, which remain unbeaten by any Corvette model since. In 1995, U.S. states began raising speed limits after Congress repealed the 55 mph maximum.

In 1996, Corvette horsepower dropped steeply due to compliance with emissions-related regulations that California had initiated in 1994, a year marked by severe pessimism according to surveys of investment advisors (see Figure 1 in Chapter 12). But technological advances propelled by social mood eventually overcame those challenges, and maximum horsepower broke out to new all time highs along with stocks in the 2006 model year.

From a low of 97 hp in at the nadir of social mood in 1982, the average horsepower of new passenger cars in the U.S. has steadily risen to almost double that figure, with maximums climbing far higher. The 2007 Corvette's 505-hp V8 remains among the most powerful engines ever offered by major manufacturers. Yet it is dwarfed by the Bugatti's Veyron's 1000-hp turbocharged V-16, which at top speed gets 2.3 miles per gallon and burns through its 22 gallon tank of gas in just 12 minutes. An Italian development team, Project 1221, is reportedly developing a turbine-powered production car that it hopes will achieve 270 mph, beating the Veyron's top speed record of 253 mph. Its planned power rating is 1500 bhp. (Bhp is "brake horsepower," a raw measure that does not factor in power losses that result when the engine is integrated into the car.)

Peak horsepower and top speed always earn bragging rights. But there are other measures of performance—acceleration, for example. Drag racing exploded in popularity in the 1960s, and automakers happily indulged that market with ever-larger engine blocks. In 1968, the year Mattel introduced its wildly popular Hot Wheels brand of die-cast toy cars (see Figure 2, showing an ad for a Drag Race Set from 1970), the number of production car models manufactured for the North American market that were able to accelerate one quarter mile in 14 seconds or less boomed (see Figure 3).

Figure 2

The result was some monstrous engines. In 1968, the year of the high in the Value Line Composite index, Chrysler introduced the Plymouth Hemi Super Stock Barracuda (and its sister, the Dodge Super Stock Hemi Dart) for the 1969 model year. The car was so quick that among production cars street-drivable in the United States and tested by major car magazines, no car was able to beat its 10.5-second time for a quarter mile until 2006, when the Bugatti Veyron bettered it by three tenths of a second.

Why did it take 38 years for a production car to exceed an acceleration record? Undoubtedly it took time to overcome the technical restrictions imposed on street-legal vehicles in the United States after 1970 as well as the weight added to automobiles during the 1980s and 1990s. But the timing of the second boom suggests a more important reason: Society was waiting for another era of peak positive mood, which did not arrive until the late 1990s and mid-2000s. Offerings of fast-accelerating car models peaked at 23 in the 1969 model year, concurrently with that era's high in the Value Line Composite index. Today's extremely positive mood as indicated by record highs in real estate prices and the nominal Dow appears to have produced a new-high total of 27 such models.

Another performance measure that has become increasingly popular is the 0-100-0 mph time, which requires not only acceleration but also braking.

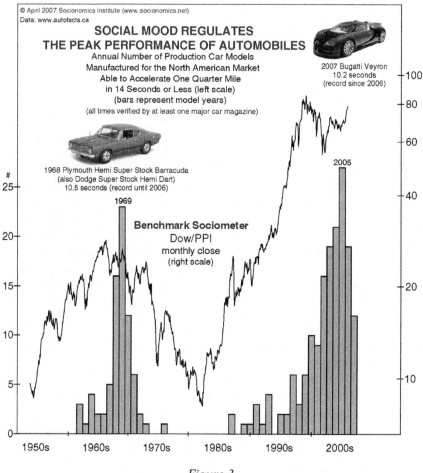

Figure 3

Since acceleration is mainly a function of a vehicle's power-to-weight ratio (horsepower divided by total vehicle weight), and deceleration is much easier with lower mass, this measure allows lower-horsepower cars to compete. The best-performing racing cars of the 1960s, such as the Shelby AC Cobra 289, which reportedly achieved 0-100-0 times of less than 14 seconds, sported ratios approaching 0.2 hp/lb. Due to its high horsepower, the heavyweight Bugatti Veyron boasts 0.24 hp/lb. and completes the 0-100-0 in 9.9 seconds. In 2006, a British design team with a racing pedigree unveiled the Caparo T1, an ultralight carbon composite two-seater that claims a ratio of 0.46 and a 0-100-0 time of only 8.5 seconds.

Post-Peak Extremes

Based on the history of car-performance manias, we hypothesize that the capabilities of production automobiles tend to reach an extreme shortly following peaks in positive social mood as indicated by tops in stock market indexes. The lag effect is due partly to the amount of time required to implement plans initiated near peaks and partly to a spirit of excess that attends the initial rebound in sociometers following the peak.

The earliest example of performance going "over the top after the top" is the 1932 Duesenberg SJ, which boasted 320 hp and a top speed of 135 mph at a time when even the most powerful cars rarely exceeded 100 mph. Its maker soon went bankrupt. Following the 1949-1966 bull market, engine performance reached a crescendo after the secondary peak in the Dow of December 1968.

The most recent extremes in automobile performance appear to be occurring as the stock market approaches a secondary peak with respect to the top of 2000. During this rebound, U.S. car manufacturers have introduced a host of high-performance vehicles inspired by cars from the late 1960s. For model-year 2005, Ford offered a "New" Mustang based on the '67-'68 model and began production of the GT, a car inspired by the Le-Mans-winning GT-40 of the late 1960s. For model-year 2007, the Mustang line expanded with the Shelby GT500, which this year is available with "an upgrade racing pack that boosts output close to 540 horsepower." For model-year 2005, Chrysler introduced two new cars with decidedly muscular features, the Dodge Magnum and the Chrysler 300. For model-year 2005, Dodge unveiled an update of the 1970 Challenger that will begin production in 2008, and Chevrolet announced a "retro" Camaro for 2009. Manufacturers, it seems, are revisiting the late 1960s in more ways than one.

Whether the car-performance craze for this cycle has passed remains to be seen. Topline's John Carder noted that at the end of last year, the most commonly sold vehicle on eBay Motors was a Ford Mustang (particularly the 1966 model), with one going every 26 minutes. He says a Corvette changed hands every 46 minutes. Veteran market analyst Doug Casey reports that some months ago he watched a 1970 Plymouth Hemi Barracuda go for $2 million on a televised car auction. Such anecdotes certainly fit the profile of an extreme in positive social mood and therefore the stock market and auto performance.

Hinting at a subtle change since the peak in 2000, U.S. federal, state and city governments are increasingly providing tax and other incentives for purchasers of environmentally friendly vehicles. This month, the U.S.

Supreme Court ruled that the Environmental Protection Agency has the authority to regulate carbon dioxide from automobile emissions and scolded it for not doing so. Reflecting the ongoing bear market in the Euro Stoxx 50 index [not shown; see Figure 1 of Chapter 46 in *Socionomic Causality in Politics*], the European Commission has proposed stricter emissions and speed limits. The German government is proposing an emissions-based car tax. After an E.U. minister called for speed limits on the autobahn recently, a poll showed that a majority of Germans favor such limits. One London borough plans to levy parking permit charges according to engine size. An increase in negative mood will make people even more critical of excess.

On the consumer side, interest in racing appears to be waning. The two publicly traded NASCAR companies, International Speedway Corporation of America (ISCA) and Speedway Motorsports (TRK), reported record annual revenue in 2006, largely as a result of existing broadcast, advertising and sponsorship deals. Yet event attendance and TV ratings have languished, and their stocks remain well off their 2000 highs (see Figure 4). These companies went public during the early portion of the stock market mania of the 1990s and have generally tracked the broad indexes since. Like the major indexes, their prices will soon complete "B"-wave bear market rallies.

On the producer side, resources of the traditional developers of high-performance production cars in the U.S. and Europe are strained. Ford's stock price is 80% off its all-time high, and General Motors' is down

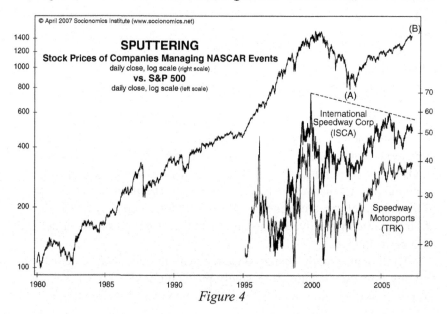

Figure 4

two thirds, to as low as it was in 1963. The optimistic mergers of the late 1990s appear to be unwinding as well. Daimler is divorcing Chrysler. In 2005, BMW dumped MG Rover into receivership. Ford is selling sports-car maker Aston-Martin. It may be only a matter of time before Fiat sells Ferrari and Volkswagen gives up Bugatti, Lamborghini or Bentley. In January, *Automobile* magazine reported that at a Volkswagen board meeting one influential member, referring to the Bugatti Veyron, said it was time for "these costly sandbox exercises to end." The article added that the car "probably won't achieve its 300-unit sales target, which now seems optimistic." As in past cycles, the industry again appears to have placed its chips on premium models. The power and speed of the coming stock market decline will end production of many, if not most, of these "boy toys." Nevertheless, in a future major trend toward positive mood—as long as the automobile remains the primary mode of personal transportation—auto makers will surely exceed today's horsepower and performance records.

Chapter 31

Negative-Mood Automobiles

Euan Wilson

September 11, 2009 (TS)

Engine Power

Mark Galasiewski's April 2007 report, "When Cars are Stars—Social Mood and Automobile Performance" [Chapter 30], found a positive correlation between trends in the maximum horsepower of the Corvette and trends in the PPI-adjusted Dow Jones Industrial Average. The current study includes EPA data for the average horsepower of all American vehicles from 1975 to date. Figure 1 presents these data along with normalized data for the Corvette's maximum horsepower before 1975.

Our graph shows that as the stock market rose along with a positive trend in social mood, so did the horsepower of the typical American car. Conversely, engine power fell along with the negative mood that fueled bear markets. A low in average horsepower per car occurred in 1981, the last full year of the 1966-1982 bear market in the Dow/PPI. After 1982, horsepower rose with the stock market in a trend that carried into the 2000s. Along with the sharply negative mood trend of October 2007 to March 2009, the appetite for high engine power has waned.

American automakers made a series of flawed assumptions over the past decade, which led them to continue issuing positive-mood cars. GM's colossal Hummer brand is gone just seven years after launch. Hummer sales fell from more than 33,000 in 2005 to just above 6,000 in 2008. Pontiac, GM's famous muscle car brand, will close after 82 years of operation. Chrysler, the paragon of American can-do that once made rocket engines for NASA, filed for bankruptcy. Chrysler obeyed the mantra of "big, heavy and powerful" far too long. The company's biggest losses stemmed from monster vehicles such as the Dodge Nitro, Ram, Jeep Commander and 300C. When social mood turns toward the negative, bigger is no longer considered better.

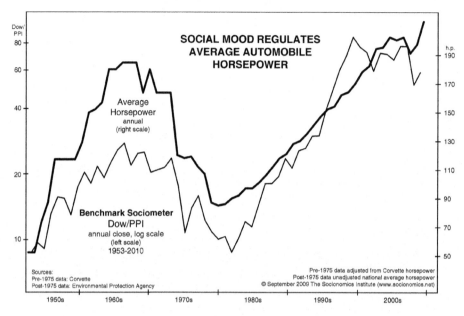

Figure 1

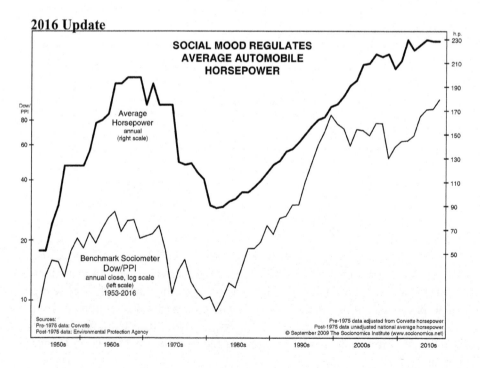

Figure 2

The Big Three auto makers now survive only with government life support. Ford and GM required bailouts; Chrysler agreed to a shotgun marriage with European-based Fiat. For the bailouts and mergers to work in the long term, U.S. automakers must figure out how to produce cars that Americans will buy. The shortest route to that knowledge is to understand the socionomic implications of social mood trends.

2016 Update: Figure 2 updates our study through model-year 2016. As you can see, socionomic causality remains fully evident, as the average horsepower for U.S. automobiles bottomed in 2009 along with the stock market and has surged in tandem with stocks to a new all-time high. These are dual products of the latest trend toward positive social mood.

Fuel Efficiency

In times when social mood is in a negative trend, cars shed weight and power in order to gain fuel efficiency. Such changes reflect the public's newfound disdain for big engines and a desire to save money on gasoline. EPA data tell us that from 1975 (the first year data are available) to 1982, average miles per gallon increased from 13 mpg to 21 mpg. The low in the Dow/PPI occurred in 1982, which was also the final year of a steep rise in efficient-engine technology. Twenty-four years later, in 2006, the national average remained 21 mpg. Thus, the average fuel efficiency of U.S. car engines stood in place for two and a half decades, whereas the previous seven years (1975-1982), the final years of a 16-year bear market, had seen a huge increase. Fuel efficiency became less important during the positive mood trend as the desire for horsepower trumped other concerns.

Auto Styling

In 2007, Galasiewski described consumers' auto preferences during times when social mood trends negatively. One newly popular automobile reflects preferences in all four areas he identified—power, efficiency, weight and body—in negative-mood fashion. The Smart Car is

one of only two vehicles in the U.S. that actually increased year-to-year sales (up 83%) in 2009. The Smart Car has rounded styling, and its small, 3-cylinder, 70-horsepower engine gets 41 miles per gallon on the highway. It also scores well in the negative-mood priority of safety, getting top marks in eight out of eleven categories. The car sells in an average of 28 days, while the industry average is 95 days. Everything about the Smart Car design satisfies the desires of people experiencing negative social mood, and customers have responded with gusto: Its sales, for now, are the fastest growing in the country. Smart Car sales should continue to wax and wane inversely to fluctuations in social mood as registered in the stock market.

Chapter 32

Big Recovery Leads to Burning Rubber

Euan Wilson

May 2, 2011 / July 30, 2012 (TS)

Mark Galasiewski's April 2007 report [Chapter 30] linked people's attitudes toward the power and speed capacities of production cars to trends in social mood. It was no surprise that shortly after the March 2009 low in stock prices, GreenMuze.com published an article by a University of Victoria Ph.D. candidate in engineering titled "The Muscle Car is Dead."[1] His fundamental reasoning: Chrysler was bankrupt, gasoline prices were at all-time highs the year before, and the public had begun to ridicule vehicles with massive engines. A quick Google search for "muscle cars dead" turns up dozens of articles forecasting the style's demise. Most of them ran in the first half of 2009, when both the stock market and the Great Recession were bottoming out.

A socionomist recognizes that such journalistic assertions are mood-inspired and based on linear extrapolation. Society at that time was experiencing a significant extreme in negative social mood, and futurists concluded, as usual, that resulting social conditions would remain as they were.

Two years later, after the fastest doubling of the S&P Composite Index in history, the three headliners at the 2011 Chicago Auto Show left no doubt that the muscle car was back (see photos).

Go Ahead and Squeal: 2012 models, (from left to right) the Chevrolet Camaro ZL1, the Dodge Charger SRT8 and the Shelby GT350 Convertible.

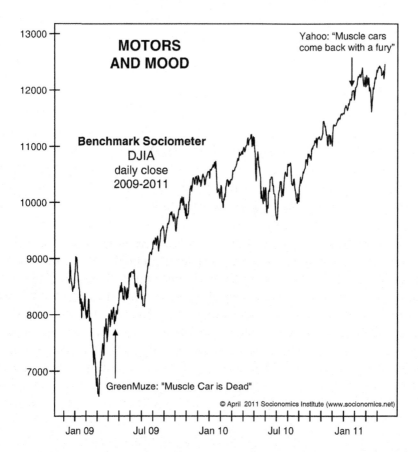

Note the style of each vehicle's front bumper: square faced and aggressive. Even more aggressive are the engines. The Charger's engine has 465 horsepower, the Camaro tops out at 560 hp, and the Shelby has an option that allows for as much as 624 hp. As Galasiewski pointed out in his study, positive social mood makes people shout, "I wanna go fast!"

The return of these muscle cars reflects two years of a positive trend in social mood. While attending the Chicago Auto Show, Jim Resnick of Yahoo! Autos noted that the event's top ten cars averaged 450 hp. In the climate of one-upmanship, it was go big or stay home.

In the next negative mood trend, cars and their engines will shrink. But until that day comes, muscle cars will continue to roar.

2012 Update: 1,000 Horses in One Car

Our research has shown that during times of elevated social mood, automakers typically build, and auto aficionados embrace, engines with ground-breaking power. Such vehicles embody the zest for life that positive social mood engenders.

In the 1950s and 1960s, muscle cars sporting as much as 450 hp ruled America's "car culture." In line with the socionomic perspective, the trend toward positive social mood since March 2009 has inspired even bigger and more powerful auto engines. A headline in the April 12 *Motor Trend* magazine reported word of another super car: "We hear: Ferrari Enzo replacement will pack 920 HP, debut in early 2013." DigitalTrends.com recently reported that Shelby and Ford will raise the bar on automobile horsepower even further:

Ford decided to give the newest version of its Shelby GT500 Mustang 650 horsepower, 100 more than last year's model. That's enough, Ford claims, to propel the GT500 to a 200 mph top speed. Why stop there, though? Shelby American will unveil a Mustang with 1,000 horsepower at April's New York Auto Show.

Raising the Bar: Shelby's 1,000-hp Mustang will arrive after a four-year upward run in the stock market.

For the uninitiated, a 1,000-horsepower engine has *six times* the strength of a standard Toyota Camry with its pedestrian 178-hp motor.

The Shelby is not the first commercially available car to unleash 1,000 horses. In 2005, during the previous trend toward positive social mood, the Bugatti Veyron offered 1,001 hp. The engine's size held steady through the stock market decline of 2007-2009, finally increasing to 1,183 hp after a two-year advance in the stock market into 2011. This year, as the stock market kept climbing, it jumped up to a record 1,200 hp. The Bugatti, however, is accessible only to the super rich, as it sports a $2.4 million price tag.

NOTES AND REFERENCES

[1] Williams, T. (2009, May 4). The Muscle Car is Dead. Greenmuze.com.

Chapter 33

New Car Fever: Americans Want More, Faster, Bigger...on Credit

Chuck Thompson and Robert Prechter

August 31, 2015 (TS) / December 2015 / Q1 2017

This year the stock market reached a new all-time high, indicating a strongly positive social mood. When social mood is trending positively, people want higher levels of horsepower and speed, and automakers respond. Today, that trend is evident in super-fast cars with ever-larger engines.

A *USA Today* article dated August 9 proclaims, "The golden age of the muscle car is now." Today's offerings include the Dodge Challenger and Charger, which can be purchased with 707-horsepower Hellcat engines. Chevrolet's Corvette ZO6 packs 650 horsepower, and Ford will soon offer a 526-horsepower Shelby GT 350 Mustang. Demand for the vehicles is high. Dodge's 2015 Hellcats sold out early, and factories are doubling its production for 2016. The 2015 edition of the Shelby GT 350 Mustang sold out before the first vehicle rolled off the assembly line.[1]

It's not just powerful cars that are flying off dealers' lots. Other popular items are large, gas-guzzling sport utility vehicles (SUVs) and trucks. Positive social mood is driving up demand for such vehicles despite their low gas mileage and hefty price tags. General Motors is responding to demand for large vehicles by boosting production. It plans to manufacture an additional 48,000 to 60,000 large SUVs and trucks for the 2016 model year.[2]

The increasing optimism and confidence that positive mood inspires have simultaneously facilitated a rise in car-buyers' debt. In the second quarter, auto loans were up $92 billion compared to the same period last year. It was the largest increase since 2006, the year before the stock market last topped out. U.S. auto loans now total $932 billion.[3] In addition, auto loan companies are loosening lending standards so they can finance more vehicles. The February 2015 issue of *The Elliott Wave Financial Forecast* reported that term lengths on some loans now stretch out as far as eight years and that credit standards have "slipped markedly."[4] Lenders and borrowers alike will rue these deals the next time the trend of social mood turns negative.

December 2015 Update: In concert with the stock market's new all-time high in 2015 and its continued nearness to that peak, the year 2016 promises to bring about yet another record in automobile power, this time from Bugatti:

> The French automaker has now confirmed that the new car will be called the Bugatti Chiron and will make its official debut at the 2016 Geneva Motor Show in March next year. ...Bugatti is already making stout claims about the car, saying it will be the "world's most powerful, fastest, most luxurious and most exclusive production super sports car." That means the Chiron will make more power than the 1,500-horsepower Koenigsegg Regera and will run from zero to 60 mph faster than 2.7 seconds, with early rumors suggesting the Chiron will make the sprint in 2.3 seconds. Powering the Bugatti Chiron will be a quad-turbocharged 8.0-liter W16 with torque output said to be somewhere around 1,106 lb.-ft. The car will carry a price tag of around $2.5 million to start. ...Even though customers can't drive the car yet, Bugatti says that it has already taken 100 orders for the new car.[5]

Post-Production Update: In Q1 2017, as the U.S. stock averages are breaking all previous price records, auto manufacturers are accordingly issuing cars that break half a dozen power and speed records. Six days into 2017, Bentley announced its most powerful vehicle ever. The new Continental Supersports automobile generates 700 horsepower and reaches a top speed of 209 miles per hour, which made it the world's fastest four-seater production car. Further fitting positive-mood imperatives, "The car also received some unique styling cues to give it a sportier appearance...."[6] In the first week of March, the Huracan Performante with 640 hp became "the most powerful V10 Lamborghini ever." Its engine propels the car from 0 to 60 mph in less than 2.9 seconds, and its speed "set a new record on the Nurburgring track in Germany, beating the previous production car holder... by five seconds."[7] Pagani's "new Italian supercar,"[8] the hand-built Huayra Roadster convertible, sports a 12-cylinder, 764-hp engine and goes from 0 to 60 in less than 3 seconds. It sells for $2.4 million. The 812 Superfast, with a 12-cylinder, 800 hp engine that drives the car from 0 to 60 mph in less than 3 seconds and reaches a top speed of 210 mph, is "Ferrari's most powerful production model ever...the speediest production car in its history."[9] The car is in such demand that it has already sold out for the year.

Makers of driverless cars are on the same bandwagon. NIO's prototype EP9 is a "sleek...candy-colored vehicle [that] recently set an autonomous-car speed record at the nearby Circuit of the Americas, lapping the Formula One circuit at a driverless top speed of 160 mph."[10] Extremely positive social mood has even affected Europe's popular family station wagons, among which the Porsche delivers 550 hp, the Mercedes goes from 0 to 62 mph in 3.5 seconds, and the BMW "looks like a sports car from the front."[11]

At the April 2017 New York Auto Show, Fiat Chrysler introduced the 2018 Dodge Challenger SRT Demon, a 6.2-liter, 840-hp racer, which "has set off a frenzy. Potential buyers have flooded dealerships to get on waiting lists."[12] The vehicle breaks production-car records in reaching 60 mph in 2.3 seconds and 140 mph in 9.65 seconds. It has also set the record for the longest wheelie from a still start, at nearly 3 feet, its 770 pounds of torque producing "the highest g-force ever recorded at launch in a production car."[13] It requires 100-octane fuel, and its body colors include "Octane Red" and "Yellow Jacket." At the same show, Trans Am displayed its "455 Super Duty" car with a 1,000-hp, supercharged, 7.4-liter (455 cubic-inch) V8 engine.

In June, Jaguar announced a new XE SV Project 8 sedan that employs 592 horsepower, reaches a speed of 200 mph and goes from 0 to 60 mph in 3.3 seconds. The new Ford GT squeezes 647 horsepower out of a twin-turbo V6 engine, which propels the car to 60 mph in 3 seconds and from there to a top speed of 216 mph, all for only $450,000. Its styling is aggressive, and promotional photos show the vehicle painted yellow-gold. At the pinnacle of performance, however, is Bugatti's Chiron [see Chapter 32], which in the same month achieved a new milestone in automobile engine muscle: 1,500 horsepower. Its 16-cylinder engine propels the car to 60 mph in 2.5 seconds and to a top speed of 261 mph. This so-called "hypercar," says *USA Today*, "is the physical manifestation of stock market and real estate booms that have left the 0.01% crowd flush with cash to manifest their wealth."[14] All four expressions—stock market booms, real estate booms and new all-time records in automobile power and speed—we contend, are products of the same thing: historically positive social mood. Speaking of new records, the DJIA and the S&P Composite index have reached new all-time highs this summer, providing compatible evidence of elevated social mood.

In a superficially different but socionomically related event, Royal Caribbean has announced that its next cruise ship—Symphony of the Seas—will be "the biggest of all time"[15] at 1,188 feet in length, 215 feet in width and 230,000 gross tonnage. Its production is scheduled to be completed in April 2018. As Hall and Wilson said in [Chapter 45], during positive mood trends, "bigger is better."

NOTES AND REFERENCES

[1] Phelan, M. (2015, August 9). Golden Age of Muscle Cars is Now. *USA Today*.

[2] Woodall, B. (2015, August 13). Exclusive: GM Boosting Production of Big SUVs and Trucks—Sources. Reuters.

[3] LeBeau, P. (2015, August 12). Auto Loans Hit Nearly $1 Trillion. CNBC.

[4] Hochberg, S., & Kendall, P. (2015, February). Autos Are Subprimed for a Fall. *The Elliott Wave Financial Forecast*.

[5] Elmer, Stephen, "Bugatti Chiron Promises to be the World's Fastest, Most Powerful Car," AutoGuide.com, November 30, 2015.

[6] Quick, Darren, "209-mph Bentley Continental Supersports Becomes World's Fastest Production Four-seater," New Atlas, Internet, January 6, 2017.

[7] Elliott, Hannah, "New Huracan Performante Is the Most Powerful V10 Lamborghini Ever," Bloomberg, March 6, 2017.

[8] Elliott, Hannah, "This $2.4 Million Convertible Is Among the Most Outrageous Cars Today," Bloomberg, March 8, 2017.

[9] Ebhart, Tommaso and Matthew Miller, "Ferrari Unleashes 'Superfast' Flagship to Bolster Volume Push," Bloomberg, March 7, 2017.

[10] della Cava, Marco, "NIO Unveils 2 Unusual, Sleek Electric Cars," *USA Today*, March 13, 2017.

[11] McHugh, David, "Faster Is a Thing, Once Again," AP, March 8, 2017.

[12] "A Demon of Ungodly Speed," *USA Today*, April 12, 2017.

[13] "Dodge//SRT Demon : 840hp Supercharged 6.2L HEMI V8 Fastest 0-60mph," *DesignMoteur*, April 11, 2017.

[14] della Cava, Marco, "$3M Bugatti Thumbs Its Nose at Your Ride," *USA Today*, June 28, 2017.

[15] Kim, Soo, "Royal Caribbean's Next Cruise Ship Will be the Biggest of All Time," *The Telegraph*, March 8, 2017.

Chapter 34

Beyond the Redline—
A Socionomic Relationship Between
Motorcycle Speed and Markets

Murray Gunn
HSBC Macro Technical Analysis
June 22, 2015
(reprinted with permission)

The internal combustion engine is one of history's greatest inventions. Developed by various pioneers, it came to the fore in the late 19th century as motorized transport was taking off. In the 4-stroke variety, popular in motorcycles, the engine process works with an intake of air which is compressed, ignited and then expelled through an exhaust. Put more simply: suck, squeeze, bang, blow. This simple process has been at the heart of power development over the past century and has enabled faster and faster speeds, with fluctuations in speed enhancement socionomically mirroring trends in the stock market. The latest motorcycle missile to come into production could be yet another warning sign of peak positive mood. Suck, squeeze, bang, blow could well turn out to be an appropriate metaphor for the stock market.

A Socionomic Relationship

Robert Prechter's socionomic theory postulates that social mood drives trends in the economy, politics and culture, and further that social mood is patterned according to the Elliott Wave Principle. Socionomics contends that developments in societies are shaped endogenously by mass crowd psychology rather than, as orthodox thinking suggests, driven exogenously by crowds reacting to events.

Socionomics turns orthodox thinking on its head by switching the causality of economic, political and cultural developments. For example, orthodox thinking would be that recessions make business people cautious, but a socionomist would contend that it is cautious business people who make recessions. Or, rather than war making people angry, it is angry people who make war. It is not stock markets going up that make people optimistic; it is optimistic people that drive stock markets upward. And so on.

Whereas bear markets in stocks are driven by negative social mood and its associated emotions of pessimism and timidity, bull markets in stocks are driven by positive social mood and its associated emotions of optimism and confidence. It should not be surprising, therefore, that these swings in social mood are manifest in cultural preferences, too. One such manifestation is changes in motor vehicle power and aggressiveness.

In July and October 2006, *The Elliott Wave Theorist* featured articles by Mark Galasiewski in which he noted a mood-regulated relationship between automobile styling and the stock market: Aggressive styling coincides with bull markets and more passive styling coincides with periods of retrenchment. He followed this up with an April 2007 article showing a similar positive relationship between the performance of production car models and the stock market, with engine power increasing during bull markets and declining during bear markets. According to socionomic theory, waves of social mood regulate both sets of changes.

Get Your Motor Running

Positive social mood prompts people to feel the need for speed. As anyone who has ridden a motorcycle will tell you, the rush of acceleration on the senses is more acute on two wheels than on four. So, if a relationship exists between the power of motor cars and the stock market, we should see a similar relationship between the speed of motorcycles and the stock market.

The black line in Figure 1 shows the top speed of each year's fastest production motorcycle from the 1890s onward. The grey line is the Dow Jones Industrial Average.

The first and most important point to make is that socionomic relationships are *not* trading systems. Although a relationship appears to exist, trying to construct buy and sell signals from such data sets is daunting.

The point of the graph is to show that positive mood coincides generally with a desire for more motorcycle power, and that negative mood coincides with a pause in that desire. To gain some context, let's take a brief ride through the history of motorcycle production as it relates to trends in social mood, as reflected in the stock market.

The world's first production motorcycle was produced in Munich in 1894. The Hildebrand & Wolfmüller Motorrad had 2.5 brake horsepower

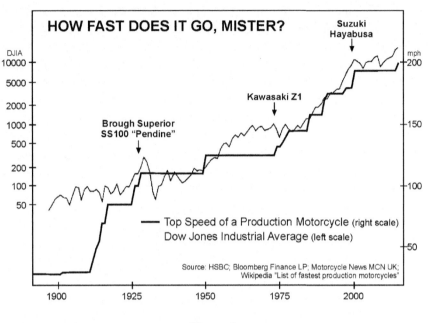

Figure 1

(bhp) and a top speed of 28 miles per hour (mph). That top speed was beaten in 1901 by the New Werner, which had a top speed of 30 mph. A decade later, the FN Four produced 40 mph, and a year later, in 1912, the Scott Two Speed set a new record of 50 mph. In 1913, the Williamson Flat Twin made it to 55 mph. This progress is reflected in the stock market during that time, which was choppy but slowly rising.

Then things started to get serious. Up to that point, motorcycles had a power of between 2 and 4 bhp, but in 1914 the Pope Model L arrived with 12 bhp. This was a dramatic increase in power, and the top speed surged to 70 mph.

The Dow Jones Industrial Average made a low in December 1914 and then began a run that would take it to the dizzying heights of the late 1920s. This period also witnessed a strengthening desire for more motorcycle speed.

In 1916, the Cyclone V-Twin more than doubled the Pope Model L's bhp to 25 and gave a record top speed of 85 mph. That record was broken in 1925 by the iconic Brough Superior SS100, which had the power of 45 horses (bhp) and a nice round 100 mph top speed. T.E. Lawrence (aka Lawrence of Arabia) was one of the first owners of the SS100, and it was on an SS100 that, a decade later, he would have his fatal crash. (As an interesting aside, Lawrence wasn't wearing a helmet when he crashed. Research by the neurosurgeon that treated him, Hugh Cairns, would ultimately lead to the use of crash helmets by military and civilian motorcyclists.)

George Brough beat his own record two years later in 1927 with the production of the Pendine model of the SS100, which had a top speed of 110 mph. It proved to be a climactic moment for motorcycle speed, as that record held for two decades. Compatibly with socionomic theory, the Dow Jones Industrial Average (as with many other indexes) topped out two years later, in 1929, and it took over two and a half decades for the DJIA to exceed that year's historic high.

Vintage motorcycle circa 1938
Source: Shutterstock

At this point, there is a divergence in the relationship between motorcycle speed and the stock market. In 1949, the year of a stock market low, the Vincent Black Shadow came into production, creating a new top speed record of 125 mph, utilizing 55 bhp. The speed record then stayed still for another two decades whilst the Dow Industrials forged ahead.

In the 1950s and 1960s, however, the focus of motorcycle production started to shift to Japan, which was rebuilding its society after the Second World War. From 1950 until January 1973, the Tokyo Stock Exchange's Tokyo Price Index (TOPIX) rose by 4,098%. Clearly, this period in Japan featured increasingly positive social mood. This positive mood was reflected by the production, in 1973, of the Kawasaki Z1 motorcycle, which, by producing 132 mph from 82 bhp, broke the previous record set in 1949. In line with that new record, the TOPIX topped out in January 1973 and fell by 35% into a November 1974 low. The Dow topped out at the same time and fell 45% over the subsequent two years.

In 1974, a bull market began in both the TOPIX and the Dow that would see them undergo spectacular rises into year-end 1989 and 1999, respectively. In this period, motorcycle speed advanced consistently, with records being set by, amongst others, the Ducati 900SS at 135 mph in 1975, the MV Agusta Monza at 145 mph in 1977, the Kawasaki GPZ900R Ninja at 158 mph in 1984, and the iconic Honda CBR1100XX Super Blackbird at 180 mph (162 bhp) in 1996. In 1999 came the Suzuki Hayabusa. At a top speed of 194 mph from 173 bhp, the "Busa" was considered to be the pinnacle of production-motorcycle speed.

So positive was social mood at this time that, after the shock of the Hayabusa beating the Blackbird's record, a "gentlemen's agreement" was reached between the motorcycle manufacturers to limit the speed of their production bikes to 300 km/h (186 mph). This harmonious sentiment fit a hypothesis within Prechter's socionomic theory, which is that peace tends to break out after a period of positively trending social mood.

The Dow Jones Industrial Average topped out in 2000 and fell 38% into the 2002 low. The Dow then rallied into October 2007. At that time, there was a break away from the motorcycle agreement. MV Agusta produced its F4 R 312, which, as the name suggests, was capable of a 312 km/h (194 mph) top speed from an eye-popping 190 bhp.

The Dow crashed 54% from 2007 into 2009. It has rallied since then and currently stands some 25% above the previous 2007 high. This brings us to 2015 and the Kawasaki Ninja H2.

Kawasaki is producing two versions of its new motorcycle, which gains extra power via a supercharger. At the time of this writing, official testing was still going on, but the "street legal" version H2 has 200 bhp and a top speed of around…well, the speedometer is set to stop at the "official" limit of 186 mph. An H2R version is deemed to be for use "on track" only. It claims an incredible (wait for it) 300 bhp and an estimated top speed of around 260 mph. A recent test from *Motorcycle News* in the UK produced statistics of 249 bhp and a top speed of 205 mph, but experts anticipate higher numbers with some gearing changes.

The fairing on the bike has a wing design. This detail is appropriate, because the power of the motorcycle is over four times that of the Continental A-65 engine used in Piper J-3 Cub aircraft.

Scream if You Want to Go Faster
Source: Shutterstock

The motorcycle press describes the H2 as a "game changer" in the evolution of motorcycle production. In years to come, it may well be seen as such.

For socionomists, the emergence of this supercharged missile after a long period of positively trending social mood is right on track. It should also be a warning that long term positive trends in social mood and the stock market are maturing.

As test rider Adam Child wrote after his 205 mph test ride on the Kawasaki H2R, *"That was epic; pure and brilliant insanity."* When it comes to recent trends towards debt and the U.S. stock market in particular, we couldn't agree more.

Part V:

COMMERCIAL AND INDUSTRIAL SAFETY

Chapter 35

Social Mood and Aircraft Accidents

Mark Galasiewski

January 17, 2007 (EWT)

Famed investor Carl Icahn once said, "The fastest way to become a millionaire is to invest in the airline industry as a billionaire." Henry Hardevelt, an analyst at Forrester Research, added, "The U.S. airline industry makes NHL hockey matches look like fifth-grade recess. It's brutal and bloody. The sad truth is an investor could get a better return starting a Subway sandwich shop than an airline." They were talking about the financial side of the business. We're going to look at the physical side.

The economic contractions that take place during trends toward negative social mood are particularly hard on the people who fly, maintain and guide airplanes. They must make do with less time and fewer resources in an already highly competitive industry. We postulated that a negative mood—held by passengers, crew, managers, maintenance workers and pilots alike—would tend to increase the probability of aircraft accidents and that a positive mood would tend to decrease it.

Such did turn out to be the case. Figure 1 shows an inverted graph of the annual number of U.S. general aviation accidents per 100,000 flight hours along with the Dow Jones Industrial Average for the past 30 years. It shows that when social mood trends positively, aircraft safety has generally increased, while accidents have occurred late in periods when social mood has trended negatively. The correlation (r) of the accident data to the log of annual closes in the DJIA is -91, with a p-value of 10^{-12}, meaning that the result is highly statistically significant. When using detrended data, we find no correlation (r = 0.047, p = 0.98).

There are no comprehensive data available prior to 1975, so this series may be too short to allow us to draw a firm conclusion. But the surges in the number of accidents leading up to 1982 and 1994 are conspicuous, since they confirm the extremes registered by stock market sentiment indicators

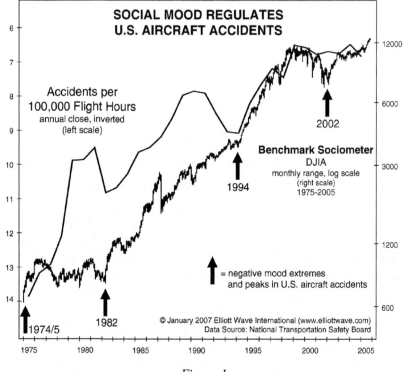

Figure 1

in those years. [See Figure 1 in Chapter 12.] If the negative social mood at those times is responsible for spikes in the number of aircraft accidents, then similar spikes should occur near the ends of future bear markets. We will return to this study at a future date.

Chapter 36

Commercial and Industrial Fatalities

Mark Galasiewski

November 16, 2007 (EWT)

In August, news of coal mining accidents in Utah that killed six miners and three rescue workers gripped the nation. The news seemed surprising, because mining fatalities in the United States are relatively rare nowadays. Annual mining fatalities reached a peak of about 600 a century ago, when the worst mining accident in the nation's history killed about 362 people in Monongah, West Virginia in 1907. Since then, such events have become substantially fewer.

The Utah accident piqued our interest. Social mood is less positive than it was in 2000. Is it possible that there is a relationship between shifts in social mood and industrial fatalities? Perhaps there is something about negative mood that causes a lapse of judgment on the part of company managers and employees, potentially producing dangerous situations. Or perhaps the economic contractions that develop during times of negative mood force companies to attempt to do more with fewer resources, potentially raising the risks to employees.

The Utah incident seems to be a case in point. Immediately afterward, the owner of the mine claimed that an earthquake had caused the collapse. But a representative of the University of Utah Seismograph Stations challenged that claim, saying that they had recorded not an earthquake but "the collapse of the mine."[1] Later, a retired inspector and former worker at the mine said that the company had ignored several warning signs, including reports of weakening support structures. "In my opinion," he said, "there were bad mining practices."[2] In particular, the company appeared to have been using a dangerous technique called retreat mining (in which support pillars are removed while retreating back toward the mine entrance). The mine owners had planned to close the mine in 2008.

The case is still open, but we decided to investigate our hypothesis that social mood might be a determining factor in the frequency of commercial and industrial fatalities. We surveyed data on all the annual sea, rail, fire,

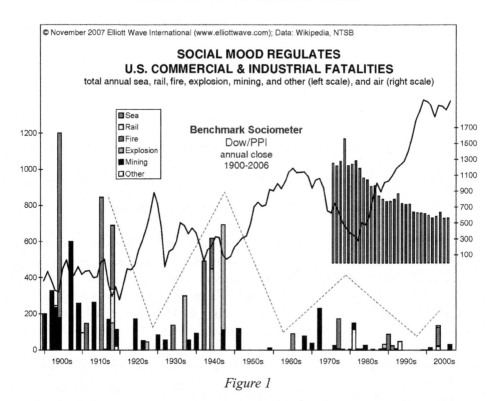

Figure 1

explosion, mining and other fatalities in the United States compiled in Wikipedia's lists on those topics, as well as data on air fatalities in the United States compiled from 1974 by the National Transportation Safety Board. The large number of passengers per flight amplifies the effect of a single human error to a degree uncommon in other industries, so we placed them on a scale separate from the others. Figure 1 shows the stunning results of the study.

It does appear that commercial and industrial fatalities have tended to rise during negative mood trends and recede during positive mood trends, and they have decreased overall as the stock market has risen over the past century. This result is particularly noteworthy given that air travel always expands when the economy does, yet fatalities nevertheless decrease during such times.

We postulate that negative social mood leads to lapses in judgment. On that basis, we predict that commercial and industrial accidents will take more lives in the future whenever trends toward negative social mood bring the stock market substantially lower.

NOTES AND REFERENCES

[1] O'Driscoll, Patrick and Andrea Stone. (2007, August 7). "Rescuers Race to Save Utah Miners." *USA Today*.

[2] Frosch, Dan and Jennifer Lee. (2007, August 17). "Rescue Halted at Mine After 3 Deaths and 6 Injuries." *The New York Times*.

Chapter 37

Negative Mood Leads to
Industrial Fatalities in Bangladesh

Mark Galasiewski

May 3, 2013 (APFF)

The Dhaka Stock Exchange General Index advanced in five waves from 2009 to a high in early December 2010. The next issue of *The Asian-Pacific Financial Forecast*, published on December 31, presented the following chart and forecast:

As published in December 2010

Figure 1

The Dhaka General Index of Bangladesh gained 269% since its April 2009 low. It completed five waves up in early December and has since fallen below its uptrend line—probably a sign that a correction has begun in Bangladesh.

Since then, the Bangladesh stock market has fallen in five waves and is now approaching the end of its decline.

Negative Mood Prompts Lapses of Judgment

The November 2007 issue of *The Elliott Wave Theorist* [Chapter 36] observed that commercial and industrial fatalities have tended to increase during negative mood trends and recede during positive mood trends. A pair of industrial disasters in Bangladesh in recent months has demonstrated that idea all too well.

In November 2012, the deadliest factory fire in the nation's history killed 117 people at a garment factory in Dhaka. Last week, the nation's worst industrial disaster ever occurred when the Rana Plaza, an eight story commercial building in Dhaka housing five garment factories, collapsed. More than 500 people died, and more bodies are being found as we go to press.

The negative social mood impelling the decline in Bangladesh's stock market since 2010—its largest setback in over a decade—appears to share responsibility for Bangladesh's recent industrial fatalities.

The November 2012 disaster, which occurred near a stock market low (see Figure 2), supposedly started because of an electrical short circuit. Such industrial mishaps can result from managerial neglect or technical oversight. But government officials suspect arson, citing evidence from fires at other factories, including one where a security camera filmed workers attempting to set fire to piles of cotton.

Last week's disaster occurred after a 60% decline in the Dhaka General Index. Police have charged the owners of the building and the factories with criminal negligence, which potentially carries the death penalty. Why? The day before the collapse, inspectors discovered cracks in the building and called for its evacuation and closure. Shops and a bank on the first floor immediately closed, yet the garment factory's owners told thousands of employees to go into the building and work. "They were under tremendous pressure to meet shipment deadlines," a former president of the Bangladesh garment manufacturers' association told the *Guardian*.

"The Dhaka General…completed five waves up…and has since fallen below its uptrend line—probably a sign that a correction has begun."
—GMP/APFF, Dec. 31, 2010

BEAR MARKETS BREED INDUSTRIAL FATALITIES

Benchmark Sociometer
Dhaka SE General Index
daily close, log scale
2009-2013

Bangladesh's deadliest factory fire kills 117 people

Bangladesh building collapses one day after inspector's warnings are ignored, killing more than 500 in nation's largest industrial disaster.

© May 2013 Elliott Wave International
(www.elliottwave.com); data courtesy Bloomberg, CQG

Figure 2

Negative social mood fosters careless attitudes. Secondarily, it brings on stock market declines and economic contractions, which in turn breed social pressures that lead to risk-taking and negligence. Administrative authorities in Bangladesh and abroad may be able to reduce the scope and/or the severity of tragedies in Bangladesh's garment factories in the future, but they cannot alter the tendency for some companies and individuals to engage in reckless, risky and negligent behavior during periods of negative social mood.

October 2016 Update: Just days after the collapse of the Rana Plaza, we concluded that Bangladesh's stock market was near the end of the decline from 2010, as indicated by label "5" in Figure 2. Last week, 34 people died

Figure 3

in a factory fire, which was the nation's worst disaster since the Rana Plaza collapse. We believe this event follows on the heels of the final low within a triangle formation for wave ④.

Investigators are trying to determine what caused the September 2016 fire. We think it will turn out to be the same thing that investigators found in earlier disasters: criminal negligence. Investigators and prosecutors are well aware of the errors of judgment that owners and managers can make under deadline and cost pressures. Such pressures tend to be substantial when social mood is at a negative extreme, as indicated by the ends of major bear-market formations in our benchmark sociometer, the stock market.

Chapter 38

Disasters with Mass Fatalities Often Occur Near the End of Negative Mood Periods

Mark Galasiewski

May 2, 2014 (APFF)

Our study from November 2007 [Chapter 36] surveyed a century of business-related disasters in the United States. It concluded that commercial and industrial fatalities tend to fluctuate with social mood, since they have increased during bear markets in stocks and receded during bull markets.

If there is a relationship between major accidents and stock prices, perhaps investors can use this relationship to their advantage. Excluding natural disasters, many social disasters that make front-page news—such as major outbreaks of infectious disease and high-profile corporate bankruptcies—occur after social mood has been trending negatively for some time. The same is true of highly lethal commercial and industrial disasters, which tend to occur along with bear market bottoms near negative mood extremes. Such events can even be immediate buy signals for the overall stock market.

To test our hypothesis, we looked at all commercial and industrial disasters since World War II that resulted in more than 500 deaths in countries for which stock market data are available on Bloomberg. Those criteria turned up 16 incidents, which we have graphed in Figures 1A and 1B.

Two points about the data:

1. The study uses Wikipedia data as its primary source. Because such open-source lists rely on volunteers rather than specialists, some significant incidents may have been omitted. But to our knowledge Wikipedia's compilation of "Accidents and disasters by death toll" is the most comprehensive list publicly available. It thus serves as the best source we know of for a study focused on only the most lethal commercial and industrial incidents in modern times.

Figure 1 depicts in chronological order all Post-WWII commercial and industrial disasters resulting in more than 500 deaths in markets where stock market data are available on Bloomberg (source: Wikipedia)

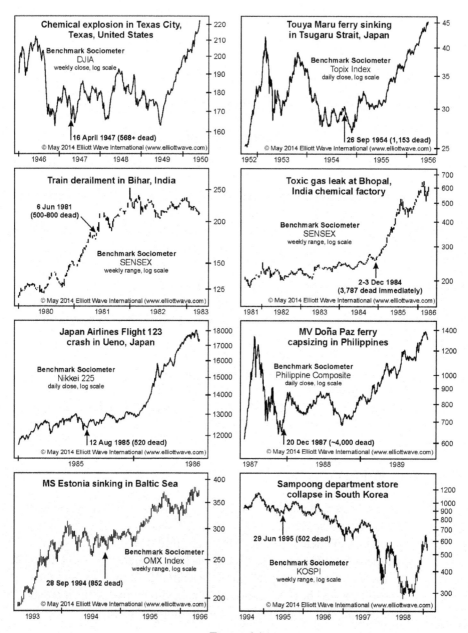

Figure 1A

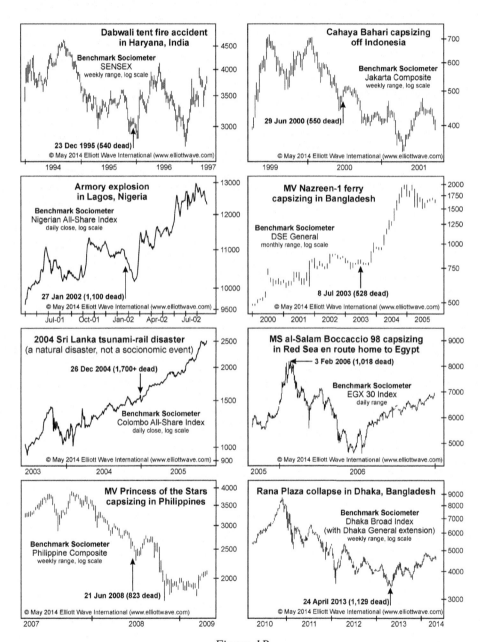

Figure 1B

2. The rail disaster in Sri Lanka occurred in the middle of a bull market when a tsunami that followed the 2004 Indian Ocean earthquake overwhelmed the train. No human factor appears to have contributed to the disaster, so it appears to be a natural disaster, not a socionomic event. We have nevertheless included it in our study because it is on Wikipedia's list.

Results of the Lethal Disasters Study

Of the 16 incidents, 13 occurred during bear markets, two in the middle of bull markets, and one at a major high. Three of the incidents failed as stock-market buy signals because their associated stock indexes almost immediately resumed larger bear market declines. But the remaining 13 incidents—81% of them—proved to be good intermediate-term buy signals, with a maximum drawdown of just 12%.

Nine of the incidents proved to be immediate buy signals, occurring within days of significant lows with minimal drawdowns. We believe these coincidences are not random; rather, stock market declines and laxity with respect to safety standards are both products of negative trends in social mood.

Our 2007 study covered commercial and industrial disasters in the United States. Most of the 16 disasters cited in the current study occurred in Asia. That our observations hold for different areas of the world provides more evidence that attributes of basic human nature, not cultural factors, account for socionomic outcomes.

Chapter 39

Roads and Recessions:
A Socionomic Analysis of Driving Risk

Euan Wilson

September 11, 2009 (TS)

Might social mood regulate driving safety? This question led us to an answer that surprised us: Traffic deaths actually *decrease* quite reliably during trends toward negative social mood as indicated by falling prices for stocks.

That feelings of anger increase in periods of negative social mood would seem to suggest that traffic deaths should be higher at such times, yet the facts show otherwise. Total miles driven, total auto deaths and deaths per mile driven all fall when the trend of social mood is negative. The reason seems to be that negative social mood leads to layoffs and decreased business activity, which in turn lead to lower traffic density, which increases driving safety. A 10% drop in miles driven translates into about 10% fewer cars on the road on average. Another reason might be less adventuresome drivers.

For the past 90 years, major declines in traffic fatalities have consistently corresponded with periods of negatively trending social mood (see Figure 1). Even the boom decades of the 1950s and 1960s saw small drops in traffic deaths during pullbacks in the DJIA. These drops occurred within a larger overall trend that accompanied the biggest rise in traffic fatalities since the 1920s. The negative mood of the early to mid-1970s saw the largest drop in auto deaths since the 1940s. The depressed mood of 1987 through 1991, interrupting the 1980s and 1990s bull market, accompanied another big decline in auto deaths. Traffic deaths and total miles driven per capita have fallen dramatically once again since 2005, the last full year of rising real estate prices. The sharp drop in fatalities in 2008 mirrored the drop in the stock and property markets. Annual auto fatalities since 2005 have slid a substantial 14%, following our sociometers downward.

Interpreting the data after the 1970s becomes complicated due to technologies that made driving safer. A trend toward positive social mood in the 1980s and 1990s did herald a rise in traffic-related deaths but not as dramatically as in the 1920s or 1950s. The advent of seat-belt and airbag technology is the primary reason for the overall downward drift in fatalities from 1970 forward.

A better test for our hypothesis would be to analyze auto *accidents* per year. But data on accidents from the U.S. Bureau of Transportation Statistics date only from 1990, which is too little time to observe long term patterns.

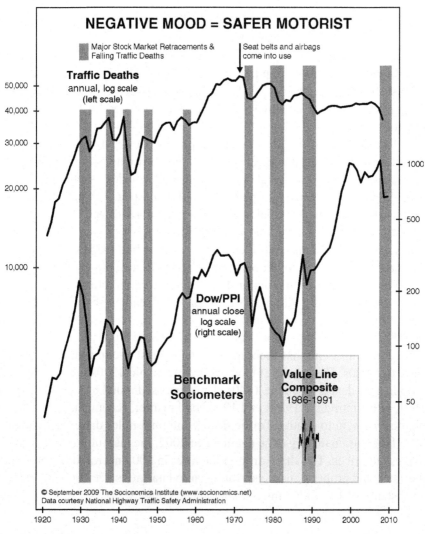

Figure 1

Speed Limits and Social Mood

Governments tend to be more reactive than proactive, including when they regulate speed limits. In positive mood periods, they tend to relax speed limits, whereas in times of negative mood they crack down on speeding with regulation and fines. These changes generally come years after trends in fatalities change, so we know that legislation is not the reason for fluctuations in road safety.

Today, four years after the high in traffic deaths in 2005 and two years after the stock market top of 2007, states, right on cue, are once again acting to restrict the positive-mood habit of speeding. *USA Today* recently reported that Georgia "now adds an extra $200 fine to the tickets of 'super speeders' – defined as drivers caught traveling more than 75 mph on two-lane roads or 85 mph on any highway." Kansas made it illegal to drive in the farthest-left lane of multilane highways except when passing or turning left. Alabama, Mississippi, Florida, Tennessee and Georgia joined forces in July to "Take Back our Highways" in a weeklong dragnet targeting dangerous drivers. Florida is pushing hardest by requiring all drivers at fault for at least three crashes in three years to attend driving school in order to keep their license.

The arrival of these new regulations following the deepest bear market in over seven decades is no accident. Increased enforcement and control are merely expressions of negative social mood. Initiated after four straight years of falling traffic deaths, they are particularly—and typically—ironic.

Part VI:

EXPANSION AND CONTRACTION OF BUSINESS AND TRADE

Chapter 40

Jobs in Atlanta

Robert Prechter

August 13, 2004 (EWT)

It pays to bet with socionomic implications. Six years ago, in April 1998, *South* magazine surveyed 100 prominent Atlantans about the future of the city. Atlanta had been a great bullish bet in 1975, when, as I pointed out, "Atlanta was in recession, the Braves were in the basement and property was in a deep slump."[1] It rose from the depths and in ensuing years hosted the Olympics and ran the busiest airport, and its baseball team won the World Series. It also became a financial center, and that was the crux of the problem. As I wrote for the magazine in 1998,

> Atlanta is a financial center. The lubricant of finance is speculation, confidence and expansion. Today, the stock and bond markets, which fuel our financial industry, are overvalued and leveraged to the hilt. According to one source, the most aggressive real estate speculation in the country is right here in Atlanta.
>
> In 1975, things looked bad, providing an excellent base upon which to build a huge expansion. In 1998, things look great, but the expansion is stretching to the limit.

That month marked the all-time high in the Value Line Composite stock index. Three months later, the stock price of the Atlanta-based Coca-Cola company topped out. Two years later, Coca-Cola announced the largest number of layoffs since the company was founded.

Something funny happened along the way toward economic contraction. All through 2003, newspapers reported that Atlanta was adding jobs at a brisk pace. Economists were duly celebrating the boom and explaining why Atlanta was different from other cities. After the end of the year, we

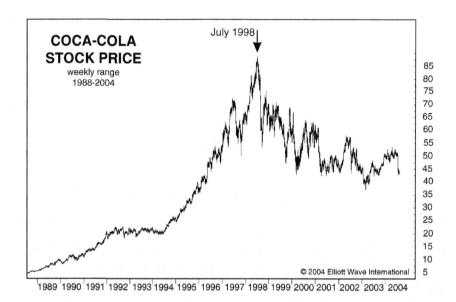

COCA-COLA
STOCK PRICE
weekly range
1988-2004

July 1998

© 2004 Elliott Wave International

were told that Atlanta had added 68,000 jobs, making it "a national leader in job creation"[2] It didn't make sense to me. It didn't fit the financial profile, and it didn't fit anecdotal evidence.

On March 11, 2004, the truth came out: Actually, Atlanta lost 85,000 jobs in 2003. What accounted for what *The Atlanta Journal-Constitution* called these "drastically different numbers"? Simple: "One reason for the huge swing is that *many companies that had gone out of business weren't counted in the initial survey*," a rather crucial oversight. In other words, what hid one aspect of the economic decline—a decrease in employment—was another aspect of the economic decline—an increase in bankruptcies. To sum up what happened, about 153,000 Atlantans were thrown out of work when their employers went under, and 68,000 of these workers—fewer than half—were re-hired by other companies. That's quite a different picture.

The importance of Coca-Cola's stock price to the affluence—and therefore to the employment situation—in Atlanta cannot be overstated. "Name an important local institution," says an article, "and there's likely to be Coke money or inspiration behind it."[3] Those institutions include the Centers for Disease Control, the Centennial Olympic Park, Emory University (a quarter of whose endowment comprises $1b. worth—formerly almost $2b. worth—of Coke stock) and foundations that donate heavily to social services, charities, colleges, wildlife preserves, museums, parks and the arts. Coca-Cola stock rose 1,000% just in the 1990s, which means the stock mania funded many of these financial and philanthropic expenditures.

Needless to say, the newspaper reports that despite a drop of 55% in Coca-Cola stock, "Stockholders Hope Dreams Can Return."[4] A top economist in the Atlanta area assures newspaper readers, "The big job losses are over."[5] The socionomic outlook does not agree. There was a moderate jobs recovery in the first half of 2004, but at a larger degree of trend, the trend toward job losses and economic contraction in Atlanta—and in the nation and much the world for that matter—has further to go. Anyone who took advantage of that warning from 1998 has avoided six years of misery and will be in great shape to scoop up some stock, business and property bargains when the next bottom arrives.

[Coca-Cola stock bottomed five years later at a price of $37.44/share. 3 months afterward, the Great Recession ended.]

NOTES AND REFERENCES

[1] Prechter, R. *View from the Top of the Grand Supercycle* (1996), p. 43.

[2] Kanell, Michael E. (2004, March 11.) "Atlanta Lost Jobs After All." *Atlanta Journal-Constitution*, p. A1.

[3] Saporta, Maria. (2004, May 9.) "Coke's Legacy in Atlanta." *Atlanta Journal-Constitution*, p. F1.

[4] Van Dusen, Christine. (2004, May 9.) "Coca-Cola Stockholders Hope Dreams Can Return," *Atlanta Journal-Constitution*, p. F7.

[5] Kanell, Michael E. (2004, March 11.) "Atlanta Lost Jobs After All." *Atlanta Journal-Constitution*, p. A1.

Chapter 41

Waves of Positive Mood Prompt Expansions of Rupert Murdoch's News Corporation

Mark Galasiewski

March 4, 2011 (APFF)

The story of Rupert Murdoch and the company he built, News Corporation, is the story of a man who turned a single Australian newspaper publisher into a media empire that ranks among the world's largest. He did it through persistent acquisitions over half a century. Was it all due to good foresight on his part? On the contrary, if you look at the major events in the company's history from a socionomic perspective, it is clear that the optimism of the moment repeatedly influenced the timing of Murdoch's acquisitions at least as much as any business logic did. The record shows that almost all of his major purchases have coincided with intermediate-term tops not only in News Corp.'s stock price but also in the Australian stock market.

When his father passed away in 1952, Murdoch inherited News Limited, which owned a newspaper in southern Australia called the *Adelaide News*. He spent the next several years buying suburban and provincial newspapers in Australia. At the pinnacle of all this activity in 1960, he purchased three newspaper companies in Sydney, Australia's largest city. Those purchases set a precedent for behavior that he has repeated consistently throughout his career. Positive extremes in social mood have prompted him to purchase major assets at high prices near the end of booms. Afterward, stock prices either have made no net progress for months or have fallen into major bear markets that have lasted years (see Figure 1).

Murdoch made his next acquisitions abroad, where his tendency to get caught up in the optimism of the times continued. In 1964, he took a stake in a New Zealand newspaper. As the stock market in Australia topped out in 1968-1969, News Limited—in a rare, well-timed move—offered shares on the Australian stock exchange and took stakes in Britain's *News of the*

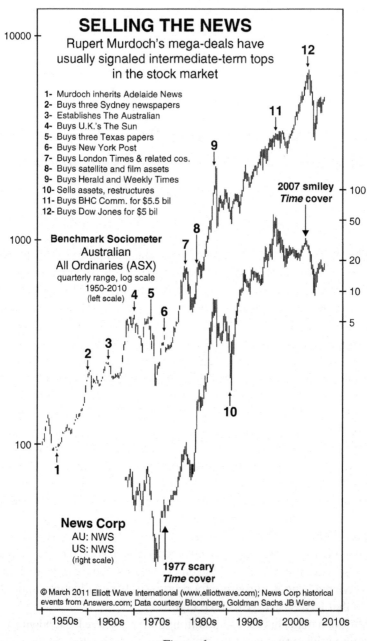

Figure 1

World and *The Sun*. As the stock market rolled over in 1973, News Corp. entered the United States by acquiring three Texas newspapers. By the October 1974 low, the ASX All Ordinaries had fallen by 55%, and News Limited's stock price had fallen by 89.5%.

As the saying goes, however, bull markets erase many investment mistakes. Persistence paid off for Murdoch as a new bull market took off globally. He continued buying so many more U.S. publications that, after he purchased *The New York Post* in 1976, a *Time* magazine cover from 1977 featured a caricature of Murdoch as King Kong with the headline "EXTRA!!! Aussie Press Lord Terrifies Gotham." That scary cover, reflecting negative social mood, marked the kickoff to a major advance in the stock price of News Limited, which was soon after reorganized as a holding company, News Corporation.

1977

In early 1987, Murdoch bought the Herald & Weekly Times group—a company his father once chaired—for A$2.3 billion, which was the largest single purchase of newspapers on record. The acquisition made News Corp. the largest English-language newspaper publisher in the world. It also foreshadowed a high in global stock prices and in the company's stock that would last for years.

By the end of 1990, as a recession took hold, creditors had become concerned about News Corp.'s debt load, and the company—under pressure from its earlier bad timing—began to sell off assets and to restructure. That ill-timed decision occurred just after the stock market bottom of October 1990 and just before the January 1991 low in News Corp.'s stock price and the start of the next wave up in News Corp.'s fortunes.

In 2000, News Corp. made its then-most-expensive acquisition by paying $5.5 billion for BHC Communications, an owner of ten U.S. television stations. The acquisition made News Corp. the largest television broadcaster in the United States. That event also marked both a significant high in global stock prices and the last chance to sell News Corp.'s stock at the end of its rise from the 1974 low.

In early 2007, another $5 billion mega-deal—in which News Corp. acquired Dow Jones, the publisher of *The Wall Street Journal*—followed

soon after the February 2007 high in News Corp.'s
stock price. Not long after that, the company
announced that it was launching a new cable
financial network called Fox Business Channel.
The March 2007 issue of *The Elliott Wave Financial Forecast* noted this action as a sell signal
for U.S. stocks and commented, "If Fox gets on
the air soon, it will be able to report some of
the most dramatic footage in stock market history." In July, *Time* magazine featured Murdoch
on its cover a second time. His smiling visage
appeared the very month of that era's high in the

2007

Dow Jones Composite Average and just before the start of the 2007-2009
global financial crisis—the perfect second bookend to the company's long
growth period. By the 2009 low, News Corp.'s stock price had fallen 84%
from its all-time high.

Since then, after a near doubling in the price of News Corp.'s stock,
Murdoch seems to be feeling optimistic again. His company is now
attempting its biggest acquisition ever—a deal worth $12.5 billion for the
remaining shares that it does not already own of BSkyB, Britain's dominant
satellite broadcaster.

2013 Update: The negative mood behind the global stock market
setback of mid-2011 undermined News Corporation's fortunes, as the
company became the focus of a series of scandals. On July 13, the company
withdrew its takeover bid for BSkyB. At the 2011 low in the S&P 500
and two months after the low of a 12-year plunge in the Dow/gold ratio,
Murdoch faced down "the worst investor revolt in News Corp history."[1] The
following year, on June 28, 2012, shortly after the worldwide low in real
estate prices, Murdoch announced that News Corporation's assets would
be split into two publicly traded companies. The split formally took place
on 28 June 2013, a lagging effect of the preceding negative mood extreme.

NOTES AND REFERENCES

[1] Rushe, Dominic and Sabbagh, Dan, "Murdoch Seeks to Face Down
Worst Investor Revolt in News Corp History," *The Irish Times*, October 22,
2011.

Chapter 42

Grameenphone IPO Signals an Approaching Top

Mark Galasiewski

December 4, 2009 (APFF)

In late November 1996, Bangladesh was in the throes of a financial mania. The Dhaka stock exchange had risen several hundred percent in just four years. As that advance was peaking, an upstart telecommunications consortium launched the nation's first cellular phone service. The company, called Grameenphone, was inspired by the microcredit concept pioneered by its business associate, the Grameen Bank. Grameenphone's Village Phone experiment later become famous for turning some rural Bangladeshi women into telecom entrepreneurs, much as Grameen Bank had allowed others to start dairy farming and other small businesses. The venture's start near the top of the mania (see Figure 1) suggests that the positive mood of the moment influenced its organizers' decision-making.

Over the next two and a half years, the Dhaka General Index collapsed 87% and the nation's economic growth rate slowed. Grameenphone was nevertheless able to leverage its early lead to grow its subscriber base, which expanded rapidly during the ensuing boom. By 2006, after the index completed a third-of-a-third wave advance, the company had a market share of about 65%, with 10 million subscribers. International observers lauded Grameen Bank and Grameenphone's Village Phone for empowering the poor, and Grameen Bank's founder, Muhammad Yunus, received the Nobel Peace Prize.

Fast-forward to three years later, and the Dhaka General has now advanced almost ten fold since its 1999 low, having gone parabolic in what could be a fifth wave in the decade-long bull market. On November 16, the index jumped 21.2% in what looks like a small third-of-a-third-wave

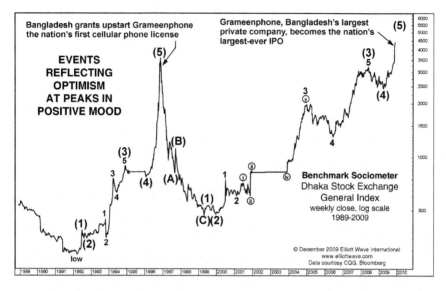

Figure 1

advance within wave (5). The big event that day? Grameenphone, which had grown to become the nation's largest private company, went public, closing up 153% from its offering price. "I think the debut has been fantastic," said the director of a brokerage firm in Dhaka. "This will give a huge boost to the stock market."

We agree that the stock market will continue rising for the time being, as wave (5) works out its final subdivisions. But longer term, Grameenphone's IPO is more likely to mark a major top, just as the receipt of its cellular license did 13 years ago almost to the day.

The next bear market will also likely lower the world's estimation of Professor Yunus, Grameen Bank and Grameenphone's Village Phone program. As early as 2001, *The Wall Street Journal*'s Daniel Pearl (who was beheaded by Al Qaeda in Pakistan in 2002) and Michel M. Phillips discovered that the bank had become plagued with debt repayment problems, which it was able to hide because it is its only regulator. Following Yunus' Nobel award in 2006, Jeffrey A. Tucker of the Ludwig von Mises Institute showed that the bank was not really an enterprise at all, having in fact always been dependent upon grants and cheap loans from international lenders and the Bangladeshi government. *The Economist* magazine has pointed out that the Village Phone model "may soon have had its day," as handsets proliferate and competition drives down margins for all players. Grameenphone also continues to lose market share, which is now down to 44%. It seems that, far from being a revolutionary practice, its program of lending and selling to the very poor will simply follow the same growth-and-decay pattern experienced by other temporarily trendy, subsidized technologies. The "Teflon coating" that positive mood affords social leaders and corporate heroes has swept such criticisms under the rug for now. But people in a negative mood are not so forgiving.

December 2016 Update: Bangladeshi stocks ended wave (5) up on December 3, 2010 and subsequently declined 60% to a low in 2013. [See real-time commentary and updated chart in Chapter 37.] Following the initial 30% plunge in the stock market, the Bangladeshi government on January 29, 2011 ordered a "wide-ranging inquiry into the microfinance institution [Yunus] founded 34 years ago, after a Norwegian documentary accused him of mishandling donors' money."[1] About a month later, with the market down 40%, the government fired Yunus from his position as managing director at Grameen Bank and began commenting unfavorably the very idea of microcredit.

Four years later, Bangladesh's National Bureau of Revenue (NBR) filed a court case against Yunus for allegedly failing to pay $1.5 million in tax. The case was subsequently stayed by the High Court, but negative social mood persisted, encouraging hostile political forces to break through the Nobel laureate's thinning Teflon coating. In December 2016, with Bangladeshi stocks still off 44%, the NBR launched a new investigation into the financial affairs of Yunus, his family and Grameen Bank.

NOTES AND REFERENCES

[1] Polgreen, Lydia, "Microcredit Pioneer Faces an Inquiry in Bangladesh," *The New York Times*, January 29, 2011.

Chapter 43

Social Mood Regulates the
Timing of Bank Failures

Mark Galasiewski

October 1, 2010 (APFF)

Bankruptcies and buyouts of failing institutions often reflect credit contractions brought on by negative social mood. Such events tend to occur near the end of stock market downtrends and therefore often serve as buy signals for stocks. For example, the Penn Central bankruptcy in June 1970

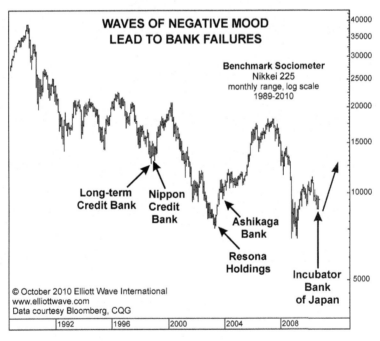

Figure 1

and the Chrysler bailouts of 1980 and 2009 marked lows in U.S. stocks, in all three cases to within a month (using the Dow/gold measure in 1980).

The same picture has emerged in Japan. Shortly after the 1998 low in the Nikkei 225 stock index, failed lenders Nippon Credit Bank and Long-Term Credit Bank of Japan were nationalized. Shortly after the 2003 low in the Nikkei, Ashikaga Bank required a government bailout and Resona Holdings filed for bankruptcy.

A recent event in the small-company sector may once again indicate psychological capitulation near the low in the Nikkei 225. In early September, Incubator Bank of Japan, Ltd., a small-business lender, declared bankruptcy, triggering the government's deposit insurance cap for the first time since its creation in 1971. The crisis at Incubator looks well placed to mark another low in Japanese stock prices.

Chapter 44

Sweet Correlations

Mark Galasiewski

January 17, 2007 (EWT)

Commentators mired in the mechanics paradigm of social change ask us, "Could the positive social mood that produced various financial manias be a product of the popularity of mood-elevating pharmaceutical drugs such as Prozac?" Those familiar with the socionomic hypothesis that social mood motivates social action can probably predict our response. As Prechter wrote in the October 2006 issue of *The Elliott Wave Theorist*, "using mood-elevating drugs is a symptom of social mood, not a cause." In particular, the increase in the public's use of mood elevators, stimulants and high-energy foods appears to be a phenomenon of the final, speculative stage of a decades-long trend toward positive social mood.

The September 1996 issue of EWT, after noting the large number of coffee shops that had sprung up in Manhattan, identified in real time the significance of the then-burgeoning phenomenon:

> Does EWT need to ruminate about the possible significance of the popularity of social gathering places for the ingestion of stimulants? Hardly. There is ample historical precedent in fifth waves of Cycle degree and higher. Readers of R.N. Elliott's biography in *R.N. Elliott's Masterworks* recall that the "tea room" was so ubiquitous in the 1920s that Elliott himself wrote an accounting column for a magazine devoted to that one industry. Little, Brown & Co., a major house, published his book on the subject in 1926. Can we go back further? You bet. In the book, *The South Sea Bubble*, John Carswell reveals that in the years leading up to the great speculative washout of 1720, "There was a new sociability, whose symptom was the coffee-house." If you could go back to Roman times at social mood peaks, you would see the same thing…. Our goal in studying social history is to identify the parallels that are just different enough

in their particulars that people can't see how obviously social behavior repeats at similar junctures in the social mood. Strictly from the evidence of today's coffee house popularity, we can write the following formula: 17-teens ≈ 1920s ≈ 1990s. That's the same formula indicated by the wave pattern in the stock market.

Eight years later, as the stock market was beginning to recover from its 2000-2002 hangover, the September 2004 issue of *The Elliott Wave Financial Forecast* noted the consequences for companies that had participated in the boom for stimulants and sweets:

> Another sign of slipping brand power is the recent fall-off in sales for a wide range of sugary products and caffeine-laced drinks that were refreshment mainstays during the long bull market. In August, Coke's largest bottler saw a 22 percent profit decline and warned of a "difficult" third quarter. Unilever, which sells Breyer's ice cream and Lipton tea, reported an unusual drop in ice cream and iced tea sales in Europe over the summer. Sunny Delight, an orange-flavored soft drink that is loaded with sweeteners, became a "phenomenon" after its launch in 1998. Since 2000, however, sales have fallen sharply as consumers have become "increasingly wary." Krispy Kreme, once a "sweet deal for investors" and doughnut [and coffee] lovers alike, has lost almost 75% of its value over the last year. In August, Krispy Kreme reported a 56% drop in quarterly profits. In a similar reversal, Starbucks shares fell sharply when sales came in way under expectations. The socionomic implications of this flight are clear: the sugar rush and caffeine buzz that kept consumers tuned in to the high energy and social imagery of the bull market are subsiding because they are incompatible with bear market psychology. Bear markets are anti-fitness, so this is not a health kick. People just don't want to feel jazzed up as much as they used to.

A plot of the per capita consumption of sweeteners and the S&P/PPI over the past half-century supports our hypothesis that social mood influences society's demand for quick-energy foods. The correlation (r) of the raw sweetener data to the log of annual closes in the S&P/PPI is 0.88, with a p-value of less than 10^{-6}. When using detrended data, we obtain r = 0.71 and $p < 10^{-6}$. These results are highly statistically significant. The consumption binge that paralleled the 1974 to 2000 bull market in the U.S. expressed itself not only in burgeoning trade deficits, declining savings rates and financial speculation but also in a craving for sweets.

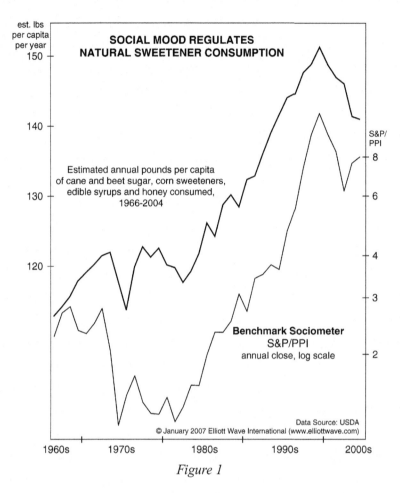

Figure 1

The positive mood trend of 1982-1999 engendered a "need for speed," inspiring people to adopt more active lifestyles in sports, fitness, travel, parties, amusement parks, etc., which burned up added calories from the extra sugar. But as activities in society slow down during a negative mood trend, high rates of sugar consumption are unsustainable. During the negative mood trends of 1973-1974, 1977-1982 and 2000-2002, natural sweetener consumption decreased considerably. When the data for 2005 and 2006 are released, we expect they will show that sweetener consumption rebounded somewhat along with the stock market. But after that, as the major bear market that began in 2000 resumes a downward trend, we expect to see the decline in sweetener consumption continue.

Chapter 45

How Sweet It Was

Alan Hall and Euan Wilson

April 7, 2011 (TS)

In the September 2004 issue of *The Elliott Wave Financial Forecast*, Peter Kendall observed slowing sales and declining stock prices for "a wide range of sugary products and caffeine-laced drinks that were refreshment mainstays during the long bull market." Mark Galasiewski expanded on Kendall's ideas in the January 2007 issue of *The Elliott Wave Theorist* [Chapter 44]. Galasiewski charted a positive correlation between stock prices and per-capita sugar consumption and forecasted, "we expect to see the decline in sweetener consumption continue." As our updated chart (Figure 1) shows, that is exactly what happened.

The peak in overall sugar consumption in 2000 is also evident in annual carbonated drink consumption (see Figure 2). It grew until 2004 and has fallen markedly since, especially after 2006, when home prices reversed to a downward trend after a historic extreme in positive social mood.

Trends in our sociometers also appear to correlate with the size of drink containers. Soda bottles' capacity quadrupled as the bull market raged in the 1980s and 1990s. "Bigger is better" is a common social theme in times of positive social mood, as illustrated by the erection of skyscrapers [see Chapter 25], larger roller coasters [see Chapter 28] and larger cruise ships [see Chapter 33] and by the popularity of SUVs [see Chapter 29] at such times.

In October 2009, seven months after a major low in stock prices and four months after the Great Recession ended, Coca-Cola for the first time announced a smaller can size option in the U.S. (see Figure 3). Considering the time it takes to develop and introduce new package designs, it is likely that the initiative for the mini can was launched when social mood was trending rapidly toward the negative a year earlier. Coca-Cola's press release, quoted below, contains subtle references to the real reason for the change (see underlined text):

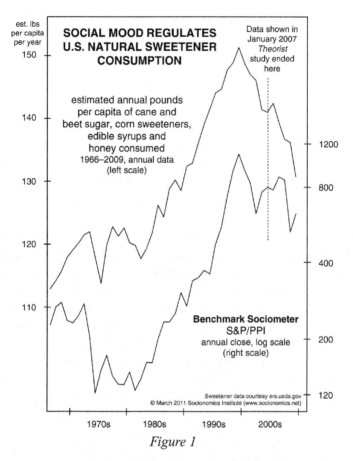

Figure 1

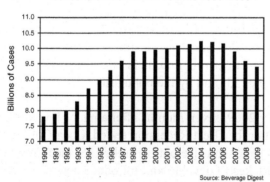

Figure 2

"The Coca-Cola mini can is a great option for <u>smaller thirst occasions</u>, and
for calorie-conscious consumers," said
Hendrik Steckhan, president and general
manager, Sparkling Beverages, Coca-Cola
North America. "Our new sleek mini can
<u>supports the idea of moderation</u> and of-
fers people yet another way to enjoy their
favorite Coca-Cola beverage."[1]

Figure 3

Since the announcement and during the
continuing advance in stock prices thereafter, there has been almost no advertising of
Coca-Cola's small-fry option.

Another example of producers catering to changing tastes resulting
from changes in social mood has appeared after a two-year rise in the stock
market. Starbucks, another big player in the drinks market, just announced
a new cup-size option for its iced drinks, many of which come loaded with
sugar. Dubbed the "Trenta," the cup (see Figure 4) is 55% larger than the
"Venti," Starbucks' previous largest size. The larger cup should be a success
as long as positive social mood continues to support higher stock prices.
During the next trend toward negative mood, the "Trenta" and all the sugar
that comes with it will likely be retired.

STARBUCKS INTRODUCING NEW SIZE
FOR ICED DRINKS

*The Trenta is 325 ml larger than Starbucks' "Venti" cup for iced
drinks, which currently is its largest size on offer.*

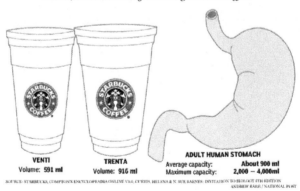

Figure 4

NOTES AND REFERENCES

[1] Garza-Ciarlante, Diana (October 14, 2009). *Coca-Cola Unveils Sleek, New 90-Calorie Mini Can.*

Chapter 46

A 200-Year Socionomic Study
of U.S. Sugar Consumption

Alan Hall

July 11, 2014 (TS)

The rate of sugar consumption appears to track large-degree trends in social mood. We can now extend our observation to a two-century relationship.

Figure 1 shows that trends in the PPI-adjusted Dow Jones Industrial Average and annual per-capita sugar consumption in the U.S. are similar, and the timing of most of the important turns is quite close. For example, both data series topped in 1854; following stocks' peak in late 1929, sugar consumption peaked in 1930; and both data series topped again near the positive social mood extreme at the beginning of the 21st century. Also, as the U.S. stock market has been tracing out five large Elliott waves since the 1700s, sugar consumption has roughly followed.

The two biggest lows in U.S. sugar consumption coincided with the two largest wars in the country's history. Proponents of mechanical causality may be inclined to presume that shortages caused the drop. But subsequent wars had no such result; sugar consumption continued to rise during World War I, and it reversed well before the outbreak of World War II. Prior to the Civil War, sugar consumption went sideways during the negative mood trend that generated the stock market decline of 1835-1842, rose with the subsequent rally, and slowed during the second decline before it began falling with the onset of the Civil War. The explanation that best fits all these chronologies is that the two biggest declines in sugar consumption and the two biggest wars of the past 200 years were both consequences of negative trends in social mood.

Social mood propelled stocks and sugar consumption net higher into the turn of the 20th century, but the higher-degree trend toward negative mood

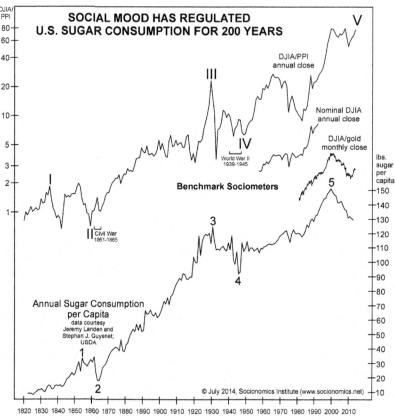

Figure 1

of the 1930s and 1940s halted the rise and eventually drove consumption back to 1918 levels. Consumption rose again during the positive mood period of the 1950s and 1960s.

Sugar consumption tracked the performance of the nominal DJIA from 1966 to 1982, as shown in the first inset. Late in this period, on May 25, 1977, *The New York Times* published an article titled "Sugar: Villain In Disguise?"[1] In 1982, social mood embarked on a major positive trend that took stock prices and sugar consumption to new all-time highs. The most persistent decline in sugar consumption is the drop since 1999, which fits EWI's identification of a major top in the Dow priced in real money (gold) in 1999, as shown in the second inset. The alignment between these data series suggests a common underlying motivation, which we propose is social mood.

Why Does Society Get a Sweet Tooth During Positive Mood Trends?

Socionomic theory explains why a trend toward positive social mood would induce people to consume more sugar and vice versa: People who have optimistic expectations for the future feel more energetic and are impelled to be more active. They want a source of more energy and are less fearful of the consequences of indulgence. People who have pessimistic expectations for the future feel indolent and are impelled to be less active. They do not crave a source of more energy and are more fearful of the consequences of indulgence.

Academic literature provides support for this hypothesis. In their 1993 book, *The World of Consumption*, University of London researchers Ben Fine and Ellen Leopold wrote,

> [It] is apparent that what is consumed is not obviously determined by physiological or biological needs. Psychological needs also play a role. Sweet foods, in particular, are well-known to be associated with the attempted satisfaction of psychological needs.[2]

Specifically, author Bernard Lyman reported,

> In a study carried out among a hundred American students, the effects of 22 moods on the choice of a number of foods and dishes have been determined. In boring mood, more diverse foods have been selected. Sweets have been chosen in joy and happiness.[3]

Other researchers have observed that a craving for sugar, which is a carbohydrate, may reflect the desire to achieve greater vitality, a positive mood inclination:

> The carbohydrate cravers were significantly less depressed after snacking, whereas non-cravers experienced fatigue and sleepiness. These findings suggest that carbohydrate cravers may eat snacks high in carbohydrates in order to restore flagging vitality.[4]

Evolution programmed early humans to seek sweet, energy-dense foods to enhance survival. For hunter-gatherers, scarcity regulated consumption. In today's sugar-rich environment, however, unconscious, non-rational social mood and its cultural consequences seem to regulate sugar consumption.

Utility-Maximizing, Economic Responses to Price Changes Fail to Explain the Shifts in Sugar Consumption

If people simply shifted their sugar consumption consciously and rationally in response to changes in price to maximize the utility of their

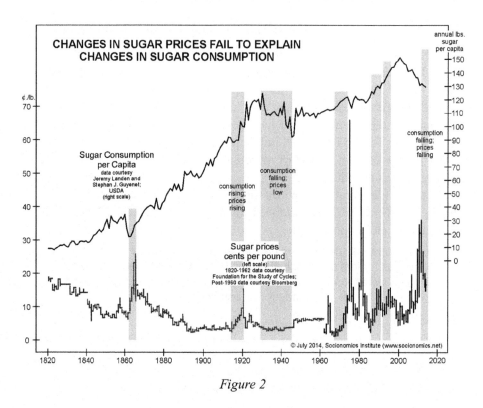

Figure 2

money, we would see higher sugar prices prompting lower consumption and vice versa, but that is not what the data show.

Figure 2 plots sugar consumption versus sugar prices. The shaded boxes identify some of the key periods when the two indexes moved contrarily to the way they would if the price of sugar governed consumption trends. Note especially the spike in prices in the 1860s, which happened *after* the plunge in consumption. Since 2000, several years have seen simultaneous declines in consumption and prices. Economic causality, then, does not seem to account for fluctuations in sugar consumption.

Positive Social Mood Coincides with Accelerated Sugar Production

Figure 3 plots social mood as reflected in PPI-adjusted stock prices versus the U.S. production of sugar from sugar cane. While the two indexes do not move in lockstep, the three largest increases in sugar production—as delineated by the shaded boxes—occurred during and especially toward the final years of trends toward positive social mood as indicated by rises in the Dow/PPI. The peaks of the surges in U.S. sugar production in 1938,

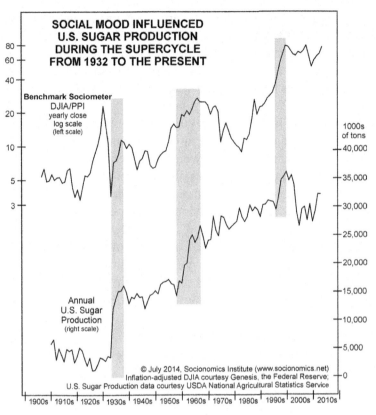

Figure 3

1967 and 2000 either lagged by one year or coincided exactly with positive extremes in social mood. Producers gave consumers what they wanted when they wanted it. During the large-degree trend toward negative social mood in the 2000s, sugar production and consumption fell sharply.

An International Perspective on Social Mood, Sugar Consumption, Industrial Production and Urbanization

Since sugar consumption increases when society is feeling energetic and productive, various individual societies' productive capacities should be associated with sweetener intake. Researchers have found exactly that relationship.

In their 2003 paper, "The Sweetening of the World's Diet," Barry M. Popkin and Samara Joy Nielsen studied more than 100 countries from 1962 to 2000. They found, "As GNP per capita of the country increases, all measures of caloric sweetener increase significantly...."[5]

Sociologists might be inclined to attribute increased sugar consumption to the ability to afford more sugar. Or, they might attribute greater productivity to increased sugar intake. Either formulation would be the usual default of A causing B. Socionomics once again proposes that a hidden variable, C—social mood—is behind parallel trends in both sugar consumption and disposable wealth. We believe our graphs better support the socionomic explanation. Notice in Figure 1 that sugar consumption in the U.S. peaked in 2000 and trended downward from that time along with the Dow/gold ratio even though many Americans were objectively becoming richer as the biggest real estate boom in U.S. history was underway, culminating in 2006. Both hypotheses would have accommodated a peak in sugar consumption in 2006, but only socionomics accommodates a peak in 2000.

Further evidence of social mood's influence on sugar intake and economic productivity comes in Figure 4, a scatterplot from a September 2013 study by Credit Suisse.[6] The chart reveals a positive correlation between countries' per capita consumption of sugary soft drinks and per-capita GDP. Soft drinks don't make economies hum. Social mood regulates productivity and cravings for sugar simultaneously.

Figure 8: Annual global soda consumption versus GDP per capita

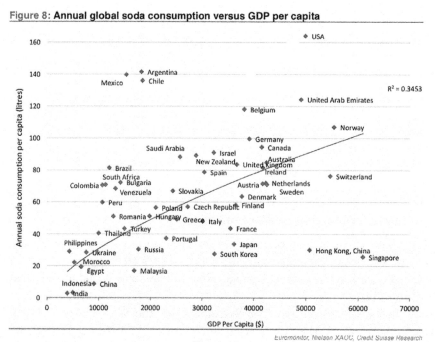

Figure 4

Lagging Consequences of the Historic Sugar Binge

A negative mood trend begins in the midst of lifestyle and public-health landscapes that were created during the preceding peak in positive social mood. When those landscapes are borne of extreme excess—the public health equivalent of irrational exuberance—they can set the stage for adverse health conditions during the subsequent downtrend.

Figure 5 plots U.S. sugar consumption versus the Dow/PPI along with the incidence of diabetes and obesity in the United States. Diabetes and obesity are lagging indicators of the old uptrend. High sugar intake increases the incidence and severity of both of these diseases, which can take years to develop.[7,8]

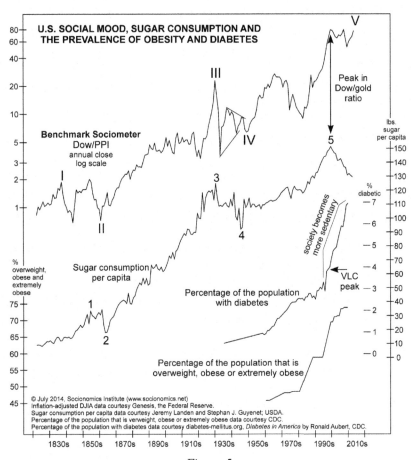

Figure 5

Obesity was rare for thousands of years. It became common only in the 20th century, reaching epidemic status as society approached the extreme of a multi-century trend toward positive social mood.[9] According to a study in *The Lancet*, "no nation has managed to significantly decrease its obesity rates" since the early 1980s, when the large-degree positive mood trend began. The study found that nearly 30% of the world's population is now overweight or obese.[10]

Sugar consumption remains at historically elevated levels even though it has declined substantially from its all-time high in 2000. People continue to gorge on 130 pounds of sugar per year, far above the two-century average of about 75 pounds. But due to the slackening of positive mood as indicated by the fall in the Dow/gold ratio (Figure 1), they aren't burning as many of the extra calories. As mood becomes less positive, people are becoming less energetic, less employed, less inclined to exercise, more sedentary and therefore at greater risk of developing obesity and diabetes. The upward spikes in obesity and diabetes after 2000 are consistent with socionomic theory, as was the increase in diabetes—even *without* an increase in obesity—during the negative mood period of 1966-1982.

Society Increasingly Seeks Reasons Not to Eat Sugar

The Elliott wave labels in Figure 1 imply that the rate of sugar consumption in the U.S. peaked in 2000, years ahead of the nominal DJIA but right in line with the Dow priced in real money (gold). As with the decline in smoking [see Chapter 80], shifts in aggregate behavior are conforming to—not causing—the new trend.

Socionomic theory holds that social mood is unconscious. Therefore, people undergoing a trend toward negative mood feel less optimistic, less energetic and ultimately less inclined to eat sugar, but they do not know why. So, they search for reasons to explain the way they feel. Too much sugar has always been bad for health, but society is paying attention to that fact now as never before. In 2009, in the wake of the largest trend toward negative social mood since the Great Depression, society's spokespeople are vilifying sugar. *Men's Health* asked President Obama about the idea of a national tax on soda and sugary drinks. Obama said, "I actually think it's an idea that we should be exploring."[11] Soon thereafter, the First Lady proposed a program to eliminate sugary drinks and food from vending machines in school cafeterias, and experts quoted in articles poured approbation on sugar:

Big Sugar's Sweet Little Lies
For nearly a decade [1966-1976], the sugar industry had been buffeted by crisis after crisis as the media and the public soured on sugar and scientists began to view it as a likely cause of obesity, diabetes, and heart disease. Industry ads claiming that eating sugar helped you lose weight had been called out by the Federal Trade Commission, and the Food and Drug Administration had launched a review of whether sugar was even safe to eat. Consumption had declined 12 percent in just two years....[12]

—*Mother Jones*, December 2012

Public Health: The Toxic Truth about Sugar
Added sweeteners pose dangers to health that justify controlling them like alcohol.... sucrose and HFCS [high fructose corn syrup] are addictive in much the same way as cigarettes and alcohol....[13]

—*Nature*, February 1, 2012

Sugar Can Make You Dumb, Scientists Warn
Too much sugar can eat away at your brainpower, according to scientists who studied how a steady diet of high fructose corn syrup sapped rats' memories.

— Agence France-Presse, May 15, 2012

Food for Thought: Eat Your Way to Dementia
The epidemic of type 2 diabetes, if it continues on its current trajectory, is likely to be followed by an epidemic of dementia.... That's going to be a huge challenge to the medical and care systems.

—*New Scientist*, September 3, 2012

Sugar is indeed toxic. It may not be the only problem with the Standard American Diet, but it's fast becoming clear that it's the major one.... obesity doesn't cause diabetes: sugar does.[14]

—*The New York Times*, February 27, 2013

Sugar, even at moderate levels, could be toxic to your health—or at least to your sex life, a new study says.[15]

—*The Washington Post*, August 13, 2013

Coca-Cola accused of "obscene" hypocrisy in £20 million "anti-obesity" drive.[16]

—*The Independent*, May 27, 2014

In September 2012, the New York City Board of Health "approved a ban on the sale of large sodas and other sugary drinks at restaurants, street carts and movie theaters, the first restriction of its kind in the country."[17] The sugary drink ban dissolved in the courts before it could be implemented, but it may foreshadow policies to come when the large-degree trend toward negative social mood resumes as indicated by the next decline in the Dow/gold ratio.

A recent news report observed that most Americans would have to drop their sugar intake by two thirds to meet new recommended dietary guidelines from the World Health Organization.[18] Such a decline could take place during the next major trend toward negative social mood.

As indicated by fourteen years of soft prices for the Euro Stoxx 50 index [not shown; see Figure 1 of Chapter 46 in *Socionomic Causality in Politics*], social mood turned negative in Europe in 2000. That trend has finally induced the UK to consider anti-sugar policies. The BBC reported on June 26 that the Scientific Advisory Committee on Nutrition, a group of independent experts that advises Public Health England, "reviewed 600 scientific studies on the evidence of carbohydrates—including sugar—on health" and thereafter halved its recommended sugar intake in order to "tackle the obesity crisis."[19] Public Health England now plans to investigate "measures to protect children from food advertising while online and whether a sugar tax would have any merit."

Seeking Socionomic Sweet Spots of Economic Utility

Food producers could position themselves advantageously if they would learn to act socionomically. Some of them have already made changes; for example, *The Wall Street Journal* recently reported,

> Longtime dietary labels like low fat and low sugar have been joined by 'low carb,' 'all-natural'.... Sales of products labeled free of high-fructose corn syrup have jumped 45% in the past four years.... Food corporations have figured out how to adapt their foods to become solutions to health problems....[20]

Sugar alternatives are becoming increasingly hot commodities. *The Independent* reported in June, "[The] quest to find an alternative—a product mimicking sugar's delicious taste, without the ruinous side effects—has become a multibillion-pound industry."[21] It may be worth keeping an eye on stevia as an alternative to sugar. Stevia, extracted from the plant *Stevia rebaudiana*, has up to 300 times the sweetness of sugar and a negligible effect on blood glucose levels. Established food and beverage giants Cargill and Coca-Cola have placed big bets on it.[22] There are also smaller players, some of whom have stock prices that trade in the pennies despite recent record harvests and new investors.[23] On June 25, the stock picking website, The Motley Fool, asked, "Can Stevia Give Coca-Cola New Life?" In 2013, Coca-Cola tested the Argentine market for the natural sweetener in its "Coke Life" beverage. This move "helped generate a 7% jump in beverage volumes, compared to a 2% drop in North America."[24] But Coke Life, which "comes in a green can, so you know it's healthy,"[25] still contains four teaspoons of sugar.

The two-century trend of habitual—and profitable—sugar consumption will be slow to reverse. The anti-sugar trend has a lot of room to run. Dietary dogmas are shifting from self-providence to self-deprivation and from carefree consumption to concerned abstinence. These new perspectives are manifestations of the larger shift toward negative social mood as indicated by the Euro Stoxx 50 and Dow/gold ratio, but they will not become really intense until the nominal Dow and the Dow/PPI also turn down.

NOTES AND REFERENCES

[1] Brody, J.E. (1977, May 25). Sugar: Villain in Disguise?; Personal Health. *The New York Times*.

[2] Fine, B., Leopold, E. (1993). *The World of Consumption*. p. 169. Routledge.

[3] Lyman, B. (1989). *A Psychology of Food*. pp. 45-53. Avi Books, New York.

[4] Wurtman, R.J., & Wurtman, J.J. (1989, January) Carbohydrates and Depression. *Scientific American*.

[5] Popkin, B.M., & Nielsen, S.J. (2003, November). The Sweetening of the World's Diet. *Obesity Research*, 11 (11), 1325-1332.

[6] Boesler, M. (2013, September 12). America Drinks So Much Soda, They Literally Had To Expand This Chart To Fit It In. *Business Insider*.

[7] Basu, S., Yoffe, P., Hills, N., & Lustig, R.H. (2013). The Relationship of Sugar to Population-level Diabetes Prevalence: An Econometric Analysis of Repeated Cross-sectional Data. PLoS ONE 8(2): e57873: doi:10.1371/journal.pone.0057873.

[8] Malik, V.S., Pan, A., Willett, W.C., & Hu, F.B. (2013). Sugar-sweetened Beverages and Weight Gain in Children and Adults: A Systematic Review and Meta-analysis. *The American Journal of Clinical Nutrition*.

[9] Haslam, D. (2007). Obesity: A Medical History. *Obesity Reviews*, 8(s1), 31-36.

[10] Duhaime-Ross, A. (2014, May 30). Nearly 30 Percent of Humans Are Overweight or Obese. *The Verge*.

[11] Kartch, J. (2009, September 8). Obama Floats Soda Tax. *The American Spectator*.

[12] Taubes, G., & Couzens, C.K. (2012, November/December). Big Sugar's Sweet Little Lies. *Mother Jones*.

[13] Lustig, R.H., Schmidt, L.A., & Brindis, C.D. (2012). Public Health: The Toxic Truth About Sugar. *Nature*, 482, 27-29.

[14] Bittman, M. (2013, February 27). It's The Sugar, Folks. *The New York Times*.

[15] Kim, M. (2013, August 13). Study: Sugar Even At Moderate Levels Toxic to Mice Health, Reproduction. *The Washington Post*.

[16] Payne, T. (2014, May 26). Coca-Cola Accused of 'Obscene' Hypocrisy in L20m 'Anti-obesity' Drive. *The Independent*.

[17] Grynbaum, M.M. (2012, September 13). Health Panel Approves Restriction On Sale of Large Sugary Drinks. *The New York Times*.

[18] WHO: 5 Percent of Calories Should Be From Sugar. (2014, March 5). *USA Today*.

[19] Gallagher, J. (2014, June 26). Call to Halve Target for Added Sugar. *BBC News Health*.

[20] Jargon, J. (2014, June 22). The Gluten-free Craze: Is It Healthy? *The Wall Street Journal*.

[21] Jarvis, A. (2014, June 12). Coca-Cola Life Will Contain a Natural Sweetener—But How Do Sugar Substitutes Measure Up? *The Independent*.

[22] Stevia—The Suppliers: From Cargill to PureCircle. (2012, March 30). *Just-Food*.

[23] Stevia Corp. Expands Production Base Following Record Harvest. (2014, May 21). *Yahoo! Finance*.

[24] Duprey, R. (2014, June 25). Can Stevia Give Coca-Cola New Life? *The Motley Fool*.

[25] Kral, G. (2014, June 18). Coca-Cola's Coke Life is Sweetened With Stevia. *AM New York*.

Chapter 47

Want That Sugary Drink? It'll Cost You

Chuck Thompson

June 16, 2016 (TS)

In the July 2014 issue of *The Socionomist* [Chapter 46], Alan Hall showed that social mood substantially regulates sugar consumption. He also found that positive mood periods induce experts and the public to accept sugar, whereas negative mood periods induce them to disapprove of sugar.

Since 2008, which witnessed the largest shift toward negative mood since the Great Depression, officials in 40 governments around the U.S. have made attempts to tax sugary drinks. The positively trending mood since 2009 has hindered their success, although Berkeley, California managed to pass a soda tax in 2014.[1]

Here in 2016, after a nine-month setback in U.S. stock averages, sugary drinks are being targeted by government officials around the country. One city is adding warning labels to the beverages. Other cities want to tax them.[2]

In June, by a vote of 13-4, the Philadelphia City Council approved a 1.5-cent-per-ounce tax on sugary drinks—including sodas, teas, sports drinks and energy drinks—making Philadelphia the second city to pass a soda tax. Mayor Jim Kenney wants to use proceeds from the tax to fund a pre-K school program. In April, Democratic presidential candidate Hillary Clinton voiced support for the program and for the tax, which the city plans to begin collecting on January 1, 2017. The American Beverage Association and a group called Philadelphians Against the Grocery Tax have vowed to fight the tax in the courts.[3]

Citizens of Oakland, California will vote in November on a proposal to add a one-cent-per-ounce tax to sweetened beverages. Supporters of a similar tax in Boulder, Colorado are making preparations for a vote in the fall. Beginning in July, San Francisco will require that ads for sugar-sweetened drinks carry warning labels.[4]

We expect to see more support for taxes on sugary drinks and impediments to their sale and/or consumption during upcoming negative mood trends. The two-century trend toward higher per-capita sugar consumption ended in 2000, a year after the Dow priced in real money (gold) made its all-time high. The anti-sugar movement should maintain for a number of years, until the bear market pattern in the Dow/gold ratio finally ends.

NOTES AND REFERENCES

[1] Terruso, J. (2016, May 9). Proposed Philly Soda Tax Gets Wide Attention. Philly.com.

[2] Malcolm, H. (2016, May 29). Cities Proposing Taxes on Sugary Soft Drinks. *USA Today*.

[3] Burke, M. (2016, June 16). Philadelphia Becomes First Major City to Pass Soda Tax. *USA Today*.

[4] Same as Endnote 2.

Chapter 48

Elliott Waves in U.S. Meat Consumption

Alan Hall

March 28, 2013 (TS)

Figure 1 displays a familiar five-waves-up pattern, signaling a larger-degree trend change. The rise in meat consumption from 1935 to a plateau in 2002-2007 and its subsequent fall through 2012 have closely paralleled the advances in stocks in real-money (gold) terms, which ended in 1999, and in real estate prices, which ended in 2006. It shows the classic form described in Chapter 2 of *Elliott Wave Principle* (1978): "Fifth waves in

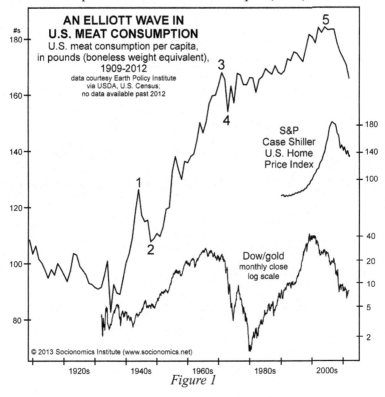

Figure 1

stocks are always less dynamic than third waves in terms of breadth. They usually display a slower maximum speed of price change as well."

Two recent examples of food fear illustrate the psychology behind the emerging downward trends in sugar and meat consumption. Reports in April 2012 of a New Zealand woman who allegedly died from her 2-gallon-a-day Coca-Cola habit and the 2013 European horsemeat hysteria both express food fears that, in socionomic terminology, translate to, "We are in a bear market for sugar and meat consumption."

The history of U.S. food legislation reflects fears that accompany trends toward negative social mood. In the midst of a bear market in stocks, the Food and Drug Act of 1906 prohibited the interstate transport of "adulterated" food or drugs. A broad wave of food fear emerged again in the deep bear market of the 1930s. In 1933, the Food and Drug Administration (FDA) recommended a complete revision of the 1906 Food and Drugs Act, launching a five-year legislative battle while the DJIA climbed to its 1937 peak. When it plunged sharply to a low in 1938, Congress finally passed the new Food, Drug, and Cosmetic Act, significantly increasing federal regulatory authority over food and drug safety. Three decades later, after the Dow/PPI peaked in 1966, Congress passed the Wholesome Meat Act in 1967 and the Wholesome Poultry Act in 1968, which requires states to maintain stringent meat and poultry inspection programs. More recently, one year after the 2009 low in stock prices and with the Dow/gold ratio still plummeting, the Food Safety Modernization Act of 2010 vastly broadened the power of the FDA to regulate any aspect of food production with the aim of providing a safer food supply. These are not solely rational reactions to conditions but also non-rational expressions of fear, with debatable effectiveness.

Chicken: The ideal (left) and the reality (right) in today's poultry industry. Expect to see increasing focus on the health risks of industrially produced meat.

Chapter 49

Alcohol Stocks: A Reliable Mood Indicator

Alan Hall on a study by Murray Gunn

June 13, 2013 (TS)

Socionomist Murray Gunn is the Head of Technical Analysis for HSBC. HSBC is part of HSBC Holdings, the world's largest bank in terms of assets. Gunn writes reports for the firm's global clients.

At the April 2013 Socionomics Summit, Gunn showed that comparing the relative price histories of stock market sectors can reveal subtle expressions of underlying social mood and give socionomically savvy investors an advantage in the markets. As he put it,

> There is a lot of information in relative relationships that is not immediately obvious when looking at...markets [that] follow the same general trend. By looking at the ratio of relative strength, we can easily see where mood preferences are being expressed.

In Figure 1, Gunn displayed an inverse relationship between social mood as reflected in the Dow/gold ratio and the relative strength of prices for stocks of alcoholic beverage companies. He explained,

> Society's attitude toward alcohol is a good gauge of social mood. If we compare the relative performance of booze shares to the stock market, we should be able to proxy that mood. The black line on this chart shows the inverted relative performance of the S&P Distillers and Vintners Index versus the overall stock market. The grey line is the Dow Jones Industrial Average in gold terms. So, as the black line is going up, booze shares are underperforming, and as the black line is going down, booze shares are outperforming. There certainly seems to be a relationship here. With alcohol being a depressant, we should probably expect booze to outperform as social mood becomes more negative.

Mood Indicator

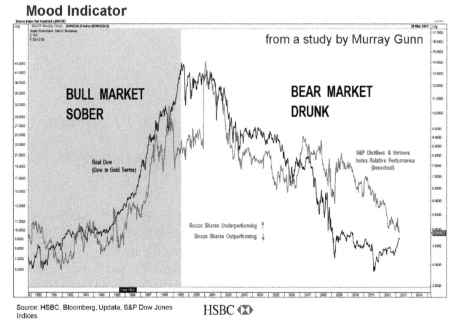

Figure 1

Gunn found the same relationship between the European Beverage Index and the Euro Stoxx/gold ratio (not shown) and concluded, "The trend of alcohol shares outperforming in the U.S. and Europe is consistent with the negative trend in social mood."

It is encouraging to see accomplished market technicians and socionomists such as Murray Gunn use the socionomic perspective to discover new indicators of social mood, especially ones with practical value for investors.

Chapter 50

Back to the School of Hard Knocks?
The Education Industry Faces
a Multi-Decade Peak

Alan Hall

March 8, 2011 (TS)

America's higher education business is in the late stages of a bubble, one that is credit-fueled, government-supported and widely popular. Nevertheless, a massive shift in society's attitudes toward education is beginning. During the next major trend toward negative social mood, educational institutions will encounter spectacular challenges to survival. If your income depends on higher education, get ready for a dramatic change of fortune.

Signs of Peak Psychology

Society's feelings about education shift in concert with social mood. A 1987 report, "Changing Public Attitudes Toward Higher Education," presented this chronology:

> In the late 1940s...people had no quarrel with colleges. They wanted more of them, they wanted more young people to go, and they admired professors. This approving public attitude...continued into and throughout the Golden Era of higher education (1955–1970).... The confidence of the general public in colleges and universities... diminished between 1965 and 1985, a period of time in which...the public and elected officials look[ed] critically at higher education.[1]

The shift in attitudes described in that passage occurred in almost perfect step with the Dow/PPI ratio [not shown; see Figure 3 in Chapter 46]. The positive-mood attitude during the sociometer's uptrend of 1942-1966 changed to a negative-mood attitude during the sociometer's downtrend of 1966-1982.

Public Agenda's report on education, titled "Great Expectations," recorded society's mindset toward higher education in 2000: "Higher education is perceived as extremely important, and for most people a college education has become the necessary admission ticket to good jobs and a middle-class lifestyle."[2] This attitude has continued to manifest in a record percentage of Americans in college, record tuition prices, record student-loan debt levels and several other telling indicators, all implying a positive trend in higher education that is stretched to the limit.

Record Popularity

Higher education is more popular than ever in America. Figure 1 shows U.S. per-capita college enrollment reaching an all-time high in 2008 (the latest data available). Note that the rapid growth of enrollment has slowed since 1969 and especially since the mid-1990s, generating a profile similar to that in meat consumption [as displayed in Figure 1 of Chapter 48].

In Figure 2, the top graph is a plot of U.S. PhDs granted per capita from 1900 to

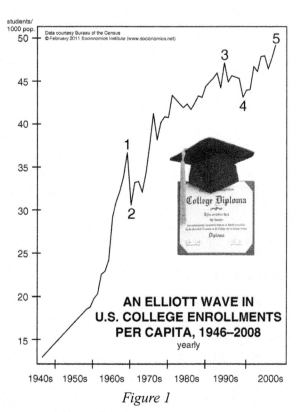

Figure 1

2008 (the latest data available), which has also reached a record high. The average U.S. PhD candidate requires 8.2 years to earn a doctorate,[3] so we backset the line by eight years to reflect the moment of decision to pursue the degree. Doing so reveals a general tendency for the annual totals of PhDs granted to fluctuate with the Dow Jones Industrial Average. The 1941 peak in PhDs and the 1945 low in PhDs lagged the 1937 high and the 1942 low in stocks by four and three years respectively. Our guess is that back then it took less time to earn a PhD, especially with a war on.

We predict that these lines will continue to track the stock market. By our wave labels in Figure 1, we predict a major reversal to the downside.

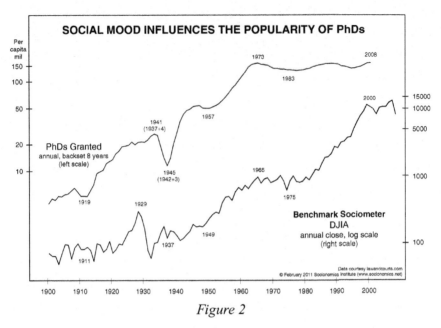

Figure 2

Record Prices

Yale and Harvard have the longest annual tuition price histories we could find among U.S. universities. They serve as our proxy for tuition prices in general, as other colleges have mirrored these tremendously rising costs. Collegeboard.org reports that average tuition and fees for public four-year colleges in 2010–2011 are 3.59 times what they were in 1980–1981, *after* adjusting for inflation via the Consumer Price Index.[4] Many non-Ivy-League universities' tuitions have approached and even exceeded those of the Ivies.[5] According to campusgrotto.com, seven of the eight Ivy League schools made their list of the top 100 most expensive schools in 2008–2009.[6] In 2010–2011, only five of them made the list. No Ivy League school reached higher than the 16th-most-expensive university in either year, and Harvard never appeared on the list.

Figure 3 shows Yale's tuition prices from 1701 to 2009, adjusted by the Producer Price Index. Advancing real prices over three centuries have traced out an Elliott wave. Harvard's tuition data for this period (not shown), while spottier, display the same five-wave sequence.

The implied five-wave structure since the 1600s[7] suggests that the most severe decline ever registered in the real cost of an Ivy League education is imminent. The range between the 1898 wave (III) high and the 1917 wave (IV) low is a reasonable and minimum target, per the retracement guideline

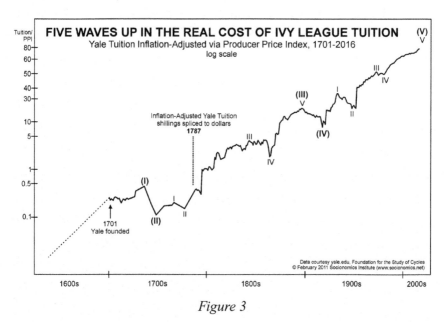

Figure 3

in Chapter 2 of *Elliott Wave Principle* (1978). [To review a practical
application of this guideline, see Figure 1 in Chapter 50 of *Socionomic
Causality in Politics.*—Ed.]

A Flood of EduCredit

Since 1997, the total value of student loans has ballooned over 800%,
from $92 billion to $833 billion. We compared that rate of growth to several
other measures of debt, including U.S. mortgages, government pensions,
gross public debt, consumer credit outstanding, credit card debt and credit
market borrowing, none of which come close to this multiple. Student loan
growth has also far outpaced a number of significant economic indexes,
including the Case Shiller Home Price Index, the Bureau of Labor Statistics'
Medical Care Cost Index and the Bureau of Labor's Prescription Drug Index.
In fact, we were unable to find any significant measure that grew faster than
student loans over this period. The total amount of U.S. education loans
outstanding today equals 93% of total annual U.S. defense spending. In June
2010, it surpassed total U.S. credit card debt for the first time.

The U.S. government continues to encourage people to borrow money
to finance an education and to make non-borrowers help pay for it. AP
reported on December 18 that Congress' new $858 billion tax package in-
cludes $22.1 billion in tax breaks, deductions and credits for students and
their families.[8] This is exactly what the government did for home buyers,
to disastrous result.

The For-Profit College Boom

The heart of today's education bubble rests in private, profit-seeking companies such as Capella University, DeVry University and the University of Phoenix. For-profit college enrollments are up more than 60% since 2004–2005.[9]

According to a PBS *Frontline* documentary titled "College Inc.," many for-profit colleges recruit at job fairs, encourage and arrange loans for students, deliver questionable educational value, sport high dropout rates and spend more on marketing than on teachers' salaries.[10] *The New York Times* wrote, "Education experts…say these schools have exploited the recession as a lucrative recruiting device while tapping a larger pool of federal student aid."[11] No wonder they are behaving that way; as *Frontline* put it, "The taxpayers are essentially funding this industry."[12]

A November 23 Pew Research Center study, "The Rise of College Student Borrowing," says more students than ever attend private, for-profit colleges and are more likely to be older, female, from minority and low-income groups and have dependent children and little parental support. The reason is that they don't need money to enroll; they just need instructions on how to fill out the government's loan forms. As a result, "For almost every field of study at every level, students at private for-profit schools are more likely to borrow and tend to borrow larger amounts than students at public and private not-for-profit schools."[13] In 2008, 97% of bachelor's-degree recipients at private, for-profit colleges borrowed money, compared to 62% at public colleges. Even as jobs generally disappeared amidst the largest overall credit contraction in history, the student-loan credit boom helped sell college educations to the broadest audience in history.

Supercycle-Degree Grade Inflation

Positive mood inflates academic grades, too. Writer and teacher Stuart Rojstaczer compared "grade inflation" to an asset bubble. In the January 28, 2003 edition of *The Washington Post*, he explained his perspective as a teacher:

> Parents and students want high grades. Given that students are consumers of an educational product for which they pay dearly, I am expected to cater to their desires…. So I don't give C's anymore, and neither do most of my colleagues…. University leaders, like stock market analysts talking about the Internet bubble not so long ago, sometimes come up with ridiculous reasons to explain grade inflation…. Many students and parents believe these explanations. They accept the false flattery as the real thing. Unlike high-tech stock prices, the grade inflation bubble, I'd guess, will not burst.[14]

Figure 4 is from Rojstaczer and Christopher Healy's March 2010 paper, "Grading in American Colleges and Universities,"[15] to which I have added Elliott wave labels indicating a clear five-wave rise in grades that began in the 1930s. We most emphatically believe this bubble, too, will burst.

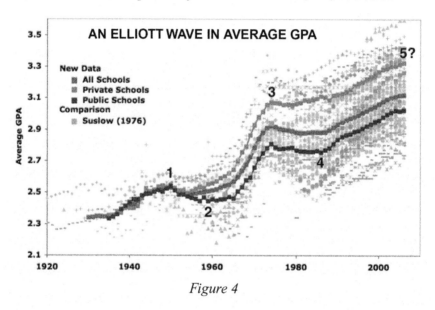

Figure 4

Chapter 14 of *The Wave Principle of Human Social Behavior* offered a possible explanation for this broad academic trend. It proposes that a positive trend in social mood generates increasing alignment, benevolence, convergence, liberality, supportiveness and a *tendency to praise.* A negative trend in social mood produces the opposite traits.

Social Mood Drives Academic Performance

We do not have student performance data for the Great Depression, but we do have some telling anecdotes. In *The Chosen: The Hidden History of Admission and Exclusion at Harvard, Yale, and Princeton,* Jerome Karabel reported that Princeton's social base became narrow and insular during 1929-1932, a time when a trend toward negative mood prevailed. He also noted that Carl Brigham, who created the Scholastic Aptitude Test (SAT) and served on Princeton's Committee on Admissions, "witnessed the unpleasant spectacle of the SAT scores of Princeton freshmen dropping to record lows in the early 1930s."

Figure 5 shows that academic performance improved following Princeton's record-low SAT scores. The chart shows high school seniors' scores on the Iowa Tests of Educational Development (ITED). It is from John H. Bishop's 1989 study in *The American Economic Review*, which asked, "Is the Test Score Decline Responsible for the Productivity Growth Decline?" The socionomic answer is no, and neither did the decline in productivity cause falling test scores. A trend toward negative social mood caused them both. Bishop's graph shows that scores climbed with positive social mood to a record high right at the peak of wave I in the Dow/PPI in 1966 (see Figure 6) and bottomed in the late 1970s along with stock values, then rose with stock prices thereafter.

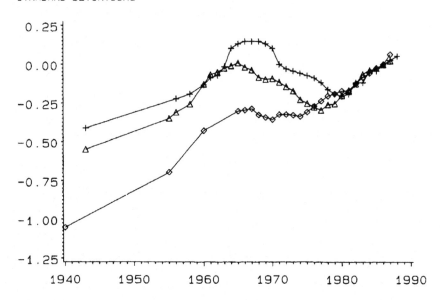

FIGURE 1. IOWA TEST SCORE TRENDS FOR IOWA STUDENTS. + = ITED, GRADE 12. △ = ITED, GRADE 9 AND ITBS, GRADE 8. ◇ = ITBS, GRADES 3 AND 4. ABSCISSA = STANDARD DEVIATION UNITS; ORDINATE = YEARS. ◇◇◇◇ = GRADES 3 AND 4. ⊟⊟⊟ = GRADES 8–9. ++++ = GRADE 12

Figure 5

Figure 6 extends the data by graphing SAT scores and the Dow/PPI from 1965 to 2009. A trend toward negative social mood simultaneously propelled the wave II bear market and carried SAT scores to lows in 1981. During the subsequent wave III advance, the rise in SAT scores was

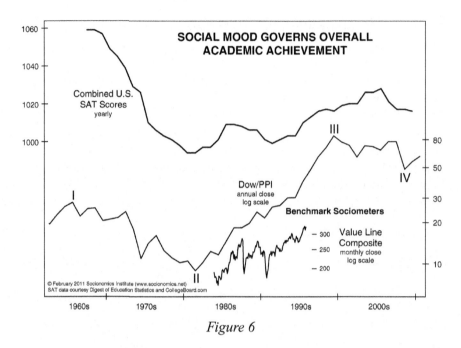

Figure 6

interrupted for several years by the 1987–1990 stock market correction (see inset). After bottoming in 1991, shortly after the 1990 low in stocks and the year its associated recession ended, SAT scores rose until 2005, the last full year of rise in real estate prices. From there, SAT scores have followed benchmark sociometers downward. It is evident to socionomists that social mood influences overall educational, business and asset-price performance.

A Multi-Decade Shift in Psychology

In financial markets, signs of trend exhaustion often precede a reversal. Higher education in the U.S. is giving similar signs. The weariness is apparent via rising dropout rates, declining international education rankings, waning student effort, anger about student debt, chronic government intervention, and rising grassroots doubt about the value of higher education. All of these items support the case for a looming reversal.

Dropouts, Laggards and Slackers

The October 2010 issue of *The Fiscal Times* addressed the dropout rate:

Millions of first-year college students and their families now paying for the most expensive postsecondary education in U.S. history face

a land mine: just 56 percent of those who enroll in a four-year college earn a bachelor's degree.... Over the past decade, the U.S. has
fallen from leader to 12th place in the ratio of young people with the
equivalent of a bachelor's degree, well behind Russia, Canada, Korea
and Japan.[16]

According to the Chronicle of Higher Education, a new book, *Academically Adrift: Limited Learning on College Campuses*, is a "damning
indictment of the American higher-education system." The authors charge
large numbers of U.S. college students with failing to develop "general
analytical competencies [and] higher-order cognitive skills."[17]

Forty-five percent of students in our sample did not demonstrate
any statistically significant improvement in Collegiate Learning Assessment [CLA] performance during the first two years of college.
[Further study has indicated that 36 percent of students did not show
any significant improvement over four years.][18]

Students have slacked off studying. *Academically Adrift* found that
35% of students reported studying five hours or less per week. According
to the February 2010 "University of California Undergraduate Experience
Survey," the number of hours per week that students spend on leisure and
socializing jumped from 25 in 2003 to 41 in 2008. "At every type of institution, in every major, every demographic group, there's been a longtime
increase in leisure time," said one of the researchers.[19]

Doubters

As noted above, the broader public's attitude toward education grows
more skeptical when social mood trends negatively. In 1972, during the
wave II bear market (see Figure 6), Carl Bereiter's essay, "Schools Without
Education," described rising disillusionment among public schoolchildren,
who think "that a great deal of school work is pointless, that grades don't
really tell how good you are, that school rituals are a subject for derision."[20]
A 1972 Gallup poll, "Public Attitudes Toward Education," suggested parents
shared these feelings.

Indebted parents and students as well as many economists are also
beginning to question the value of a college education. We have seen
numerous stories about this new attitude, such as "What's a Degree Really
Worth?" in *The Wall Street Journal* and "Academic Bankruptcy" in *The New
York Times*. A new book, *Higher Education? How Colleges Are Wasting
Our Money and Failing Our Kids*, accuses U.S. universities of "educational
malpractice." It says that schools in the U.S. are unique in doling out

crippling six-figure loans and that a $250,000 education from Harvard or Yale is a waste of money. One of the co-authors wrote,

> Undergraduate business classes...are just a charade; 19-year-olds play as if they are chief executives of General Electric. It is a waste of time and money.... Prices got to where they are because both universities and administrators spent like drunken sailors.[21]

A March 2011 CNBC article asked, "Is an Ivy League diploma really worth the money?" Some interviewers answered in the negative:

> "Businesses are giving less preference to Ivy League grads since the advent of specific program rankings," says Dr. Mel Schiavelli, president of Harrisburg University of Science and Technology in Pennsylvania. "Yale does not have an accounting program that equals the University of Maryland, and accounting firms recruit accordingly."[22]

High school valedictorian Erica Goldson captured society's shifting attitude toward education in her June 2010 graduation address, which went viral across the Internet.[23] She delivered a powerful and unexpected critique of the institutional educational system, described students forced to "yield to the authoritarian ideologies of instructors" and quoted John Taylor Gatto, a noted critic of compulsory schooling. Goldson also quoted another prominent critic of American life and culture, H.L. Mencken, from *The American Mercury* in April 1924:

> The aim of public education is not to spread enlightenment at all; it is simply to reduce as many individuals as possible to the same safe level, to breed and train a standardized citizenry, to put down dissent and originality. That is its aim in the United States, whatever pretensions of politicians, pedagogues other such mountebanks, and that is its aim everywhere else.

Doubts about education's cost/benefit ratio are arising even within mainstream culture. *The New York Times* reported,

> With no advertising and little news media attention, "Race to Nowhere" has become a must-see movie in communities where the kindergarten-to-Harvard steeplechase is most competitive. The movie looks at the downside of childhoods spent on résumé-building... portrays the pressures when schools pile on hours of homework... introduces boys who drop out of high school from the pressure, girls who suffer stress-induced insomnia and worse, and students for whom "cheating has become another course."[24]

One psychologist in the film says, "When success is defined by high grades, test scores, trophies, we know that we end up with unprepared, disengaged, exhausted and ultimately unhealthy kids." A movie on the same topic, *Waiting for Superman,* is the 20th most successful documentary film ever, according to Box Office Mojo.

Doubts about the value of formal education extend even to the very top degrees. *The Economist* reported,

> A PhD may offer no financial benefit over a master's degree. It can even reduce earnings.... Drop-out rates suggest that many students become dispirited.... Research at one American university found that those who finish [their PhDs] are no cleverer than those who do not....[25]

The Treadmill Image: As social mood grows more negative, the "education is futile" mindset grows increasingly popular.

The same article depicts "armies of low-paid researchers and postdocs" as "the ugly underbelly of academia" and says many PhD students "describe their work as 'slave labor'":

> The production of PhDs has far outstripped demand.... America produced more than 100,000 doctoral degrees between 2005 and 2009. In the same period there were just 16,000 new professorships.... Universities have discovered that PhD students are cheap, highly motivated and disposable labor.... In Canada 80% of postdocs earn $38,600 or less per year before tax—the average salary of a construction worker.[26]

The "education is futile" attitude extends to Europe. Italy's president recently complained of "the pervasive malaise among young people." A former Italian prime minister said, "[Student] protests [are] against a general situation in which the older generations have eaten the future of the younger ones." In Spain, "mileuristas"[27] (thousand-euro-ers) is the new term for a generation of college graduates facing low pay and terrible job prospects. In France, they are "the 'babylosers'—a term coined by sociologist Louis Chauvel to contrast them with 'babyboomers.'"[28] In the U.K., former Prime Minister Gordon Brown warned, "the world faces youth unemployment of 'epidemic proportions.'"[29]

Government "Reform"

The title of the aforementioned documentary, "Race to Nowhere," is a play on Barack Obama's "Race to the Top" fund, which provides grants to schools that implement teacher testing and other requirements. Diane Ravitch, an education historian and former United States Assistant Secretary of Education, criticized the strategy, saying it presupposes a "crusading confidence that data—derived from testing—can tell us all we need to know not just about what's wrong with failing schools, but how to fix them." Ravich depicted "a culture of test-prep that is inimical to real education." She wrote,

> No school or school district or state anywhere in the nation had ever proved the theory correct. Nowhere was there a real-life demonstration in which a district had identified a top quintile of teachers, assigned low-performing students to their classes, and improved the test-scores of low-performing students.[30]

Charter schools, another linchpin of education reform, aren't measuring up:

> [A] study by two Stanford economists...(staunch charter supporters), involved an enormous sample, 70 percent of all charter students. It found that an astonishing 83 percent of charter schools were either no better or actually worse than traditional public schools....[31]

While reform can help, no scheme will be able to counter the next trend toward negative social mood, which will sap students' energy, decrease overall educational performance, reduce the amount of disposable income available to pay for an education and induce a backlash against the idea of financing educations through debt.

Malaise and Mental Illness

As a consequence of the large-degree trend toward negative social mood since 1999 as implied by the deep setback in the Dow/gold ratio, U.S. college students' mental health has worsened over the past decade. According to *The New York Times*,

> National surveys show that nearly half of the students who visit counseling centers are coping with serious mental illness, more than double the rate a decade ago. More students take psychiatric medication, and there are more emergencies requiring immediate action.[32]

A recent survey by the American College Counseling Association found that "44 percent [of the students] in counseling have severe psychological disorders, up from 16 percent in 2000."

Education's Next Chapter

When social mood enters another negative trend, many long-term upward trends in education will reverse. If the attitude shift during the trend toward negative mood of 1966–1982 proves a valid guide, society will increasingly reject the popular view that a college degree is necessary to prosper.

For-Profit Scandal Potential

The desire to expose scandals and punish people heats up during negative mood trends. Social mood became so negative in 2009 that anger bore down on some of the more opportunistic for-profit schools. In August 2010, the U.S. Government Accountability Office released a report titled "Undercover Testing Finds Colleges Encouraged Fraud and Engaged in Deceptive and Questionable Marketing Practices." It "detailed undercover investigations into 15 for-profit schools that uncovered misconduct by school staff."[33] The SEC launched an insider trading investigation into Apollo Group—one of the largest for-profit education corporations—in October 2010. When social mood turns negative again, we may see academic versions of the Madoff scandal and the closing of many for-profit universities.

Tenured Scapegoats

Today there are early signs of social mood casting tenured professors in the role of scapegoat. For example, Christopher Shea's recent article, "The End of Tenure?" says,

> In tough economic times, it's easy to gin up anger against elites. The bashing of bankers is already...robust.... But in recent months, a more unlikely privileged group has found itself in the cross hairs: tenured professors.

Shea says numerous blogs and op-ed pages now portray tenure as an elite entitlement:

> ...guaranteed jobs for life, teach only a few hours a week, routinely get entire years off, dump grading duties onto graduate students.... Or maybe they stop doing research...dropping their workweek to a manageable dozen hours or so, all while making $100,000 or more a year. Tenured and tenure-track professors earn most of the money and benefits, but they're a minority at the top of a pyramid.[34]

More Walkaways

Student loan defaults are surging:

> The U.S. Education Department expects nearly half of the money
> lent to students attending for-profit colleges to enter default over a
> 20-year period [and] that 16 percent of the dollars lent to all college
> students who entered repayment in 2008 will go into default.[35]

Acquiescing to intensive lobbying, Congress made student borrowers with private loans equally liable to pay. "College Inc.," the PBS *Frontline* documentary mentioned previously, stated, "If you default on a federal student loan, you will be hounded for life." Yet, as more ex-students struggle with edu-debt and the public attitude swings against the higher education system, borrowers will find ways to escape payment, or the government may shift the load to taxpayers. Congress is already considering setting major precedents for debt forgiveness:

> Policy makers are working behind the scenes to come up with a way to
> let states declare bankruptcy and get out from under crushing debts,
> including the pensions they have promised to retired public workers.[36]

If such legislation passes, student-loan forgiveness could eventually follow. In the next bear market and economic contraction, the 50% default rate predicted by the education department will surely prove far too conservative.

Ballooning Risks Will Lead to Evaporating Endowments

Harvard lost 30% of the value of its endowment fund in the financial implosion of 2007–2009. With the subsequent return to positive social mood, Harvard Management Co. has reverted to full optimistic mode. *Barron's* reported on December 22, "Much of Harvard's portfolio is a 'who's who of emerging markets ETFs.'"[37] When social mood turns negative again, this investment approach will produce even more expensive losses for Harvard as well as other university endowment funds across the country.

Expect Fundamental Changes

Elliott wave analysis suggests that the next bear market will be larger than that of 1929–1932, implying huge structural changes in education. Traditional educational institutions may eventually lose control of the manufacture and distribution of educational services much as the music and publishing industries have lost their grip on the distribution of music and text. Negative mood and its results in bear markets and economic contractions topple dominant players and open the field to nimbler entrepreneurs,

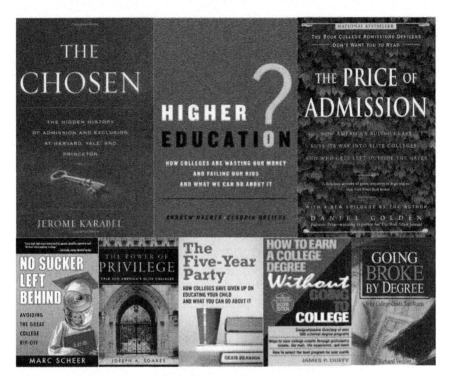

Bear-Market Baccalaureate Bashing: Booksellers may want to stock up on anti-Ivy-League and anti-college tomes, which should fly off shelves. And perhaps the DIY (Do It Yourself) book genre will yield to LIY (Learn It Yourself).

who will develop alternatives to institutional education. This process is already underway. For example, there are about 5400 educational apps for the iPad,[38] and in January Mashable.com posted a list of 100 impressive new online educational resources.[39] A generation of young people will find ways to bypass traditional secondary education; the majority may avoid it completely. Many institutional educators will not see the massive change coming.

Negative social mood favors social traits of polarization, avoidance of effort, exclusion, separatism and decentralization. These tendencies will increasingly burden institutional education. Although rocker Alice Cooper sang, "School's out for summer," school may be "out" for longer than that the next time negative social mood ushers in a period of severe retrenchment and reorganization.

NOTES AND REFERENCES

[1] "Changing Public Attitudes Toward Higher Education," *ASHE-ERIC Higher Education Report, 16*(6), September 1987.

[2] Immerwahr, J., & Foleno, T., "Great Expectations," *Public Agenda Report*, 2000.

[3] Berger, J., "Exploring Ways to Shorten the Ascent to a Ph.D.," *The New York Times*, October 3, 2007.

[4] "Trends in College Pricing," *Trends in Higher Education Series*, page 13, Figure 5, January 2010.

[5] *Highest Tuition 2010-2011: Top 100*, October 18, 2010.

[6] Top 100 Colleges by Highest Tuition, October 18, 2009. Campus-Grotto.com.

[7] Harvard University. (2003). *Dictionary of American History*. Our assumption that pre-1701 tuition prices were lower is based on the report that in 1636, when Harvard was founded, "Tutors[were] ill-paid... Harvard students, many of whose families paid their tuition with farm produce, consumed much 'beef, bread, and beer' and fathers frequently had to pay for broken windows."

[8] Associated Press, "Highlights of the Tax Package Before the Senate," *The Boston Globe*, December 15, 2010.

[9] Lederman, Doug, "3 Million and Counting," *Inside Higher Ed.*, August 26, 2010.

[10] Public Broadcasting System, College inc., 2010. [Web].

[11] Goodman, P., "In Hard Times, Lured into Trade School and Debt," *The New York Times*, March 13, 2010.

[12] See endnote 10.

[13] Hinze-Pifer, R., & Fry, R., "The Rise of College Student Borrowing," *Pew Research Center Social and Demographic Trends,* November 23, 2010.

[14] Rojstaczer, S., "Where All Grades are Above Average," *The Washington Post,* January 28, 2003.

[15] Rojstaczer, S., & Healy, C., "Grading in American Colleges and Universities," *Teachers College Record*, 2010.

[16] Lewis, K., "High College Dropout Rate Threatens U.S. Growth," *The Fiscal Times*, 2010.

[17] Glenn, D., "New Book Lays Failure to Learn on Colleges' Doorsteps," *The Chronicle of Higher Education*, January 18, 2011.

[18] Arum, R., & Roksa, J., "Are Undergraduates Actually Learning Anything?" *The Chronicle of Higher Education*, January 18, 2010.

[19] Epstein, Jennifer, "Anything but Studying," *Inside Higher Ed*, February 9, 2010.

[20] Bereiter, C., "Schools Without Education," *Harvard Educational Review*, 42(3), 1972.

[21] Egan, M., "Book Says Many U.S. Universities Are Waste of Money," Reuters, July 30, 2010.

[22] Koba, M., "Ivy League Diplomas Still Worth Price of Admission?" CNBC.com, March 7, 2011.

[23] "Valedictorian Speaks Out Against Schooling in Graduation Speech," Best of the Web, June 25, 2010.

[24] Gabriel, T., "Parents Embrace Documentary on Pressures of School," *The New York Times*, December 8, 2010.

[25] "The Disposable Academic," *The Economist*, December 16, 2010.

[26] *Ibid.*

[27] Donadio, R., "Europe's Young Grow Agitated Over Future Prospects," *The New York Times*, January 1, 2011.

[28] Burke, J, Keeley, G., & Kington, T., "After the Boomers, Meet the Children Dubbed 'Baby Losers'," *The Guardian*, May 11, 2008.

[29] Elliot, L., "Gordon Brown to Warn Against Global Youth Unemployment Epidemic," *The Guardian*, January 18, 2011.

[30] Mosle, S., "Facing Up to Our Ignorance," *Slate*, March 11, 2010.

[31] *Ibid.*

[32] Gabriel, T., "Mental Health Needs Seen Growing at Colleges," *The New York Times*, December 19, 2010.

[33] "For-profit Colleges: Undercover Testing Finds Colleges Encouraged Fraud in Deceptive and Questionable Marketing Practices," US Government Accountability Office, August 4, 2010.

[34] Shea, C., "The End of Tenure?" *The New York Times*, September 3, 2010.

[35] "Half of Money Lent to Students at For-profits Will End Up in Default, Government Predicts," *The Chronicle of Higher Education*, December 22, 2010.

[36] Walsh, M., "A Path is Sought for States to Escape Their Debt Burdens," *The New York Times*, January 20, 2011.

[37] Coleman, M., "Harvard's Endowment Includes Brazil, China ETFs," *Barron's*, December 22, 2010.

[38] Hu, W., "Math That Moves: Schools Embrace the Ipad," *The New York Times*, January 4, 2010.

[39] Lifshits, Y., "100+ Online Resources That Are Transforming Education," *Mashable*, January 8, 2011.

Chapter 51

A Developing Reversal in the Multi-Decade Trend Toward Globalization

Alan Hall

August 29, 2016 (TS)

Social mood affects our perceptions of other people and our willingness to cooperate with them. Stock indexes are our best meters of social mood. When mood trends positively at large degree, stock prices rise, and cooperation, inclusion and free trade grow stronger. When mood trends negatively at large degree, stock prices fall, and opposition, exclusion and protectionism grow stronger. The September 1992 issue of *The Elliott Wave Theorist* described this perennial fluctuation:

> Major bear markets are accompanied by a reduction in the size of people's unit of allegiance, the group that they consider to be like themselves. At the peak, there is a perceived brotherhood of men and nations.... In other words, at a peak, it's all "we"; everyone is a potential friend. At a bottom it's all "they"; everyone is a potential enemy. When times are good, tolerance is greater and boundaries weaker. When times are bad, intolerance for differences grows, and people build walls and fences to shut out those perceived to be different.[1]

A two-century trend toward positive social mood dating from the late 1700s ultimately impelled a widespread vision of the world as an integrated, inclusive, culturally tolerant marketplace. This "everyone is a potential friend"[2] attitude helped produce the greatest level of human interconnectedness and trading activity in history. The phenomenon earned its own name—globalization. Globalization may be history's grandest manifestation of positive social mood.

Elliott Wave International's long term Elliott wave analysis of the inflation-adjusted World Stock Index (see Figure 5) and the gold-adjusted Dow [see Figure 1 in Chapter 48] suggests that a large-degree transition from positive to negative social mood began globally in 1999-2000 and remains underway. Expressions of the emerging negative mood have included a smattering of closed borders, trade barriers and trade sanctions as well as increasing popularity for exclusion, isolation, nationalism and authoritarian leaders. The subtle long-term trend toward negative social mood is therefore darkening the formerly rosy view of, and vision for, globalization. Groups of all sizes increasingly find fault with the whole idea. Globalization is facing a large setback, which will take place when these two sociometers turn down again.

A 500-Year View of Globalization

Figure 1 is a 500-year chart assembled in 2016 by economists Mohamed Nagdy and Max Roser.[3] They used data from several sources to plot the sum of world exports and imports as a percentage of world GDP. In other words, the graph depicts world trade activity adjusted for total economic productivity, which is a good measure of globalization. The data series are plotted together, which makes for some gaps and overlaps, but the chart is instructive nonetheless.

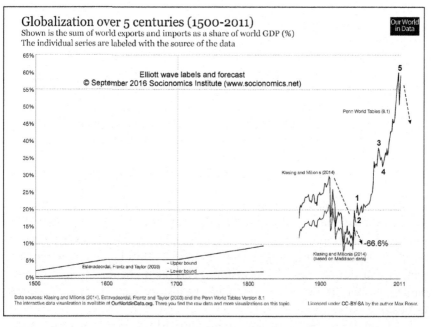

Figure 1

Nagdy and Roser described a long period of worldwide poverty and limited trade (see the left lines in Figure 1) that held sway prior to history's "first wave of globalization," which began some time before the start of their data in 1870:

> [G]lobally the sum of exports and imports never exceeded 10% before 1800. And trade grew only very slowly. This changed over the course of the 19th century: Technological advances, especially in the communication and transport sector, and political and economic liberalization gave rise to the international economy and the world entered the "first wave of globalization." Until 1913, worldwide trade grew by more than 3% annually. This first wave [at the top of which we have placed the label "I"] came to an end with the decline of liberalism and the rise of nationalism. Around the beginning of the First World War political powers chose protectionism over internationalism, and world trade slowed down [at the bottom of which we have placed the label "II"]. [P]rotectionism gave way to the second—and still ongoing—wave of globalization after the end of World War II [which we have labelled "III"]. Since then, world trade has been growing rapidly; and more and more countries have turned away from isolation and opened to liberalism and internationalism.[4]

Large-degree trends toward negative social mood produced the protectionism, isolationism and instances of the "decline of liberalism and the rise of nationalism" mentioned above. Large-degree trends toward positive mood produced the liberal trade policies and the expansive waves of globalization that followed.

According to our analysis, a major rising wave peaked in 1912 and a major setback lasted until 1946. The advance from that time may have peaked in 2008 or may do so in concert with another high in the U.S. stock market. Either way, the Elliott wave model implies that the biggest retrenchment since the early 1900s, which was 66.6%, will soon begin.

The Most Recent 150 Years of Social Mood and Globalization

Figure 2 zooms in on the data over the past 150 years. The top line is the nominal DJIA. The middle line is Nagdy and Roser's globalization metric. The bottom line overlays two data sets to create a nearly continuous measure of world exports. Elliott wave labels applied to this measure likewise suggest that a five-wave advance from 1932 is ending. Data during the two world wars are missing, but we have hypothesized a low for wave 2 based on major lows in European GDP in 1946 and U.S. GDP in 1947.[5]

The numbered turning points in the bottom graphs do not line up with those in the DJIA, indicating that waves of Cycle degree in overall social

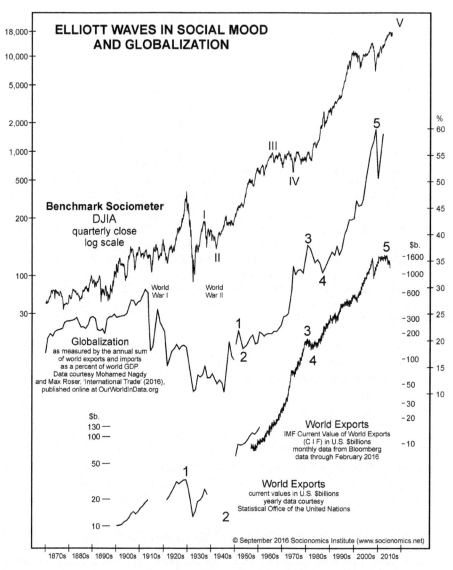

Figure 2

mood are not regulating the smaller ebbs and flows of globalization. Only the trends at Supercycle degree seem correlated. Nevertheless, all three series sport five waves up, implying a roughly contemporaneous upcoming reversal.

Positive Social Mood Impelled Globalization and Synchronized World Stock Markets

Socionomic theory proposes that positive social mood engenders a cooperative spirit, which spurs globalization, which increases the sharing of mood, which in turn increases the synchronization of stock market indexes. Because positive social mood encourages expansion in "the size of people's unit of allegiance,"[6] greater acceptance of differences and more porous international boundaries, it follows that a large-degree trend toward positive social mood would be shared increasingly widely, thereby coordinating many countries' stock indexes.

Figure 3 plots benchmark stock market indexes for the U.S., UK, France and Germany along with Nagdy and Roser's globalization metric. Notice that all these graphs have become more similar since the 1940s. Some countries' stock market indexes are exceptions to this tendency, such as Japan's Nikkei 225 stock market index, which topped in 1989. But in recent decades, trends among global stock markets and economies have become increasingly synchronized.

In 2006, Robert Prechter noted, "[All] investment markets had begun moving together, not contra-cyclically as they had in the past.... The flip side of markets going up together is that when the reversal comes they all go down together."[7] That is exactly what happened in 2008-2009, when stock markets and commodities plunged in tandem worldwide.

A paper from 2008 titled "A Century of Global Equity Market Correlations" confirmed the increased synchronization among international stock market indexes:

> Between many country indices, correlations are now relatively high (0.8 or above). Yet only a few decades ago, it was widely noted that correlations between stock markets were low.... We examine this pattern systematically for the last century and find it to be most pronounced in the recent past. [It is] much stronger today than...during the last era of globalization before 1914.[8]

Other researchers confirmed increasing synchronization among all kinds of financial markets.[9,10] A 2009 paper, "Impact of Globalization on Stock Market Synchronization: Some Empirical Evidence," included a warning for investors: "The growing international financial integration and the temporal linkage between financial markets [could] undermine the effectiveness of the age-old paradigm of international diversification."[11]

Figure 3

A Shift in the Popularity of Globalization

The top graph in Figure 4 plots the PPI-adjusted Dow Jones Industrial Average, a useful proxy for global social mood.[12] The middle graph plots the percentage of articles in *The New York Times* containing the term *globalization*. That line began rising in the early 1980s along with the Dow/ PPI. It peaked in 2000, made a low in 2003 and reached a lower low in 2010, closely following the stock market's trends.

The bottom graph shows the percentage of English-language books in the Google Books database that contain the term *globalization*.[13] As with the *Times* articles, the percentage of Google-scanned books mentioning globalization skyrocketed in the late 1990s, following the upward trend in our benchmark sociometers. The line peaked in 2006, coincident with the peak in U.S. housing prices and just before the 2007 top in stocks, and then fell with these measures into 2008, the last year for which we have data.

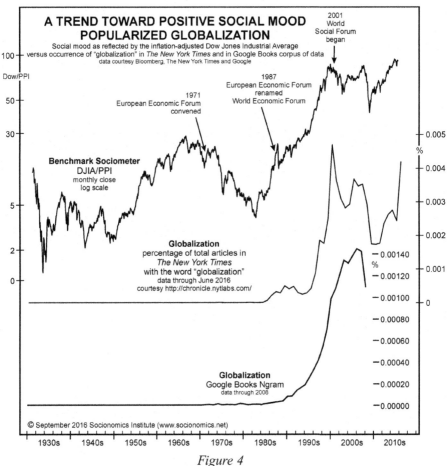

Figure 4

The current bull market in the Dow/PPI may lead to a new high in newspaper references to globalization. But there seems to have been a qualitative change in such references at the turn of the century in tandem with the downside reversal in the inflation-adjusted World Stock Index (see Figure 5), the Euro Stoxx 50 index [see Figure 1 in Chapter 46 of *Socionomic Causality in Politics*] and the real-money Dow (Dow/gold) [see Figure 1 in Chapter 78]. In the 1990s, the *Times* published many articles with titles such as "'Globalization' Does a World of Good"[14] and "For Coke, World Is Its Oyster."[15] Since 2000, typical titles are "A Global Boom, but Only for Some"[16] and "Perils of Globalization When Factories Close and Towns Struggle."[17]

Classic Yet Erroneous Linear Extrapolation

Most experts fail to anticipate changes within their own field because they linearly extrapolate current trends. A telling example is the abandonment of the A.T. Kearney/Foreign Policy Magazine Globalization Index (not shown) at a positive extreme in social mood. The proprietors' explanation for the decision reveals social mood at work:

> [In] 2007 the [A.T. Kearney Global Business Policy Council (GBPC)] discontinued publication of its annual Globalization Index, which for more than a decade had tracked the progress of increased financial, trade, and other types of global connectivity. Simply put, globalization had graduated from a carefully studied set of trends to an assumed constant—a relentless engine that was shrinking the world, with upside for businesses everywhere. The elimination of "globalization" from our business vocabulary was simply a testament to its incredible success.[18]

What was evident was globalization's incredible success *at a peak in positive social mood*; by no means was that condition to be construed as permanent. Nine years later, the GBPC did an about-face while expressing distress and uncertainty:

> Globalization appears to be on a hiatus.... The (GBPC) believes that what comes next is more uncertain than at any other time in the quarter-century in which we have been studying and analyzing the global operating environment.[19]

The August 2012 issue of *The Socionomist* [republished in edited form as Chapter 26 in *The Socionomic Theory of Finance*] explained the origin of feelings of uncertainty:

> The commonly held view is that negative events cause the future to be less certain. Our view is that the trend toward negative social mood both causes the events and impels people to view their future as uncertain.... When we observe widespread expressions of certainty or uncertainty, we can use them as indicators of public mood—and plan accordingly.[20]

In the current case, the feeling of uncertainty is due to an emerging global trend toward negative social mood, which has produced a new, negative trend in globalization, not to any objective measure of uncertainty with respect to prediction, as the GBPC's action of 2007 unequivocally proves.

Understanding socionomic causality is crucial for anticipating changes in social trends and for avoiding blunders borne of the linear extrapolation of trends at their extremities.[21] For a full discussion of this topic, see Chapter 21 in *The Socionomic Theory of Finance*.

A Breaking Wave of De-Globalization

The inflation-adjusted MSCI World Stock Index (see Figure 5) topped in the year 2000 and made a lower peak in 2007. During this period, anti-globalization activists began to gain traction with their claims that globalization and capitalism were wrecking the environment and impoverishing people. In 2001, the formerly open meetings of the World Economic Forum became private and surrounded by tight security.[22] There have been increases in protests,[23,24] anti-globalization movements,[25,26] activism[27] and academic critiques.[28] From 2005 to 2008, media pundits described proponents of globalization as racist and elitist,[29] a prominent rock star called Davos attendees "fat cats in the snow,"[30] and leading economic thinkers joined in the criticism.[31] In 2013, *The Economist* observed, "Ordinary folk trust Davos Man no more than they would a lobbyist for the Worldwide Federation of Weasels."[32] By 2015, the name "Davos Man" was "often an epithet, spoken with venom."[33] Both *Forbes* and *The Financial Times*

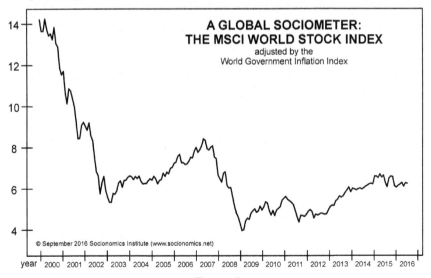

Figure 5

acknowledged a groundswell of anti-globalist sentiment.[34,35]

Today, old trade pacts signed when global social mood was trending positively are increasingly perceived as having created problems. New trade agreements struggle under darkening clouds of suspicion. The Trans-Pacific Partnership (TPP) has encountered so much opposition that it has been negotiated largely in secret. Opponents paint it as a detriment to the average person and a boon to corporations. Indeed, Apple, Google, Facebook, Uber, Amazon and other industry leaders recently issued an open letter urging the next U.S. president to support the agreement.[36]

In 1992, Ross Perot was the only American presidential candidate warning of a "giant sucking sound" of U.S. jobs supposedly vanishing due to the North American Free Trade Agreement. In contrast, all three of the leading candidates in the 2016 U.S. presidential race have voiced opposition to the TPP. Donald Trump called the scheme "a horrible deal"[37] and "an attack on America's business."[38] He said, "[We] are killing ourselves with trade pacts that are no good for us and no good for our workers."[39] Bernie Sanders said the TPP is a "disastrous trade agreement designed to protect the interests of the largest multi-national corporations at the expense of workers, consumers, the environment, and the foundations of American democracy."[40] On May 9, Hillary Clinton said she opposes the TPP in its current form and called for a new "Trade Prosecutor" to protect American markets and report directly to the president.[41]

Protectionist impulses are also showing up in China, which "faces its own version of Trumpism."[42] On July 5, the European Union put significant obstacles in the way of its pending free-trade accord with Canada,[43] including the possibility of veto by any one of the national parliaments in the 28-member bloc.[44]

Brexit was another event in the mood-driven trend toward de-globalization. The media used it to inundate readers with anti-globalization commentary. Headlines read, "Globalization Sucks,"[45] "Britain just killed globalization,"[46] "a rebellion against globalization,"[47] "A Warning Shot Against Globalization,"[48] "Tensions over Globalization,"[49] "Shun Globalization?"[50] "Has Globalization Been a Mistake?"[51] and "The End of Globalization?"[52]

The benefits and drawbacks of globalization are the same as they ever were; it is only perceptions of them that change. Positive social mood induces people to focus on benefits; negative social mood induces them to focus on disadvantages. Shifting social mood along with globalization's own waves are driving a newly energized battle between a desire for unity and a desire for division.

What to Expect During De-Globalization

Predicting specific expressions of social mood is tricky. Socionomists nevertheless have a leg up on other trend watchers. By studying history from a socionomic perspective, we can see how changes in social mood have affected the character of social expressions, helping us anticipate future changes. If de-globalization intensifies, we would expect to see:

- fear of foreigners increase;
- borders tighten;
- security and customs lines lengthen;
- international air travel suffer setbacks;
- free trade policies roll back;
- new tariffs and other impediments to trade introduced;
- international trade slow;
- international businesses experience supply-chain disruptions, shipping problems and shortages of raw materials;
- immigration policies tighten;
- many of the foreign workers in the U.S. lose their jobs;
- shortages of specific kinds of labor;
- international universities go under;
- students studying abroad sent home;
- international tourism decline;
- international stock markets and economies become less synchronized;
- cross-border capital flows slow;
- protection become a growth industry, much as airport security has;
- countries reduce international cooperation; and
- countries increase border conflicts.

In short, a large-degree change in social mood should coincide roughly with a large-degree reversal in the trend of globalization. If you want to anticipate changes in global openness, international trade and global economic activity, keep your eye on Elliott waves in globalization metrics along with those in the world's stock markets, humanity's early warning system for changes in social behavior.

NOTES AND REFERENCES

[1] Prechter, R. (1992, September). Cultural Trends. Exclusionism: The Next Major Trend. *The Elliott Wave Theorist.*

[2] *Ibid.*

[3] Nagdy, M., & Roser, M. (2016). International Trade. Our World in Data.

[4] *Ibid.*

[5] Maddison Project.

[6] See endnote 1.

[7] Prechter, R. (2006, June 16). We Appear to be the Only Advocates of a Deflation-Depression Scenario. *The Elliott Wave Theorist.*

[8] Quinn, D.P., & Voth, H.J. (2008). A Century of Global Equity Market Correlations. *American Economic Review*, 98(2), 535-40.

[9] Liu, X.F., & Tse, C.K. (2012). Dynamics of Network of Global Stock Markets. *Accounting and Finance Research*, 1(2).

[10] Walti, S. (2005). The Macroeconomic Determinants of Stock Market Synchronization. *ResearchGate.*

[11] Ansari, M. (2009). Impact of Globalization on Stock Market Synchronization: Some Empirical Evidence. *International Journal of Commerce and Management*, 19(3), pp. 208-221.

[12] Hall, A. (2007, November). Sizing Up a Superpower: A Socionomic Study of Russia. *The Socionomist.*

[13] Globalization. Google Books Ngram Viewer.

[14] Dale, R. (1996, March 22). 'Globalization' Does a World of Good. *The New York Times.*

[15] Cohen, R. (1991, November 21). Coke's World View—A Special Report.; For Coke, World Is Its Oyster. *The New York Times.*

[16] Porter, E. (2014, March 18). A Global Boom, But Only for Some. *The New York Times.*

[17], B. (2015, May 17). Perils of Globalization When Factories Close and Towns Struggle. *The New York Times.*

[18] Peterson, E.R., & Laudicina, P.A. (2016, January). From Globalization to Islandization. AT Kearney.

[19] *Ibid.*

[20] Hall, A. (2012, August). Social Mood Impels Feelings of Certainty and Uncertainty. *The Socionomist.*

[21] The Fallacies of Trend Extrapolation and Reliance Upon Exogenous Causality. (2009, September). *The Socionomist.*

[22] Oakley, R. (2001, January 25). Security Tight for World Forum. CNN World.

23 Webster, C. (2008, January 22). The Davos Buzz. *Forbes*.

24 Beating Up: Barrett Report on Police, Media and WEF Protests. (2000, November 15). AustralianPolitics.com.

25 UAWC Participates in the World Social Forum in Tunis. (March 26, 2015). *La Via Campesina*.

26 Evans, P. (2008). Is An Alternative Globalization Possible? *Politics & Society*, 36(2), pp. 271-305.

27 Da France Presse. (2001). José Bové, Militante Francês Antiglobal-ização, Chega a Porto Alegre. Folha de S.Paulo.

28 Sayer, A. (2015). Why We Can't Afford the Rich. Bristol, UK: Policy Press.

29 Ash, T.G. (2005, February 2). Davos Man's Death Wish. *The Guardian*.

30 Noon, C. (2006, January 26). Bono Teams Up With Amex, Gap for Product Red. *Forbes*.

31 Summers, L. (2008, April 27). America Needs to Make a New Case for Trade. *Financial Times*.

32 Davos Man and His Defects. (2013, January 26). *The Economist*.

33 Alcorn, S. (2015, January 21). The True Biography of 'Davos Man'. *Marketplace*.

34 Mourdoukoutas, P. (2015, January 21). Globalization's Biggest Threat—Slow World Economic Growth. *Forbes*.

35 Why Globalizers Still Retain the Upper Hand. (2015, December 30). *Financial Times*.

36 An Open Letter to Presidential Candidates. (2016, May 4). ITC.

37 Wolff, A. (2016, May 5). There's Only a Slim Chance TPP Will Be Ratified This Year. *Fortune*.

38 Petroff, A. (2015, April 23). Donald Trump Slams Pacific Free Trade Deal. CNN Money.

39 Donald Trump on Free Trade. On the Issues.

40 Senator Bernie Sanders: The Trans-Pacific Trade (TPP) Agreement Must be Defeated. Bernie Sanders: United States Senator for Vermont.

41 Hains, T. (2016, May 9). Hillary Clinton Calls for New "Trade Prosecutor" Position, Opposes TPP "In Its Current Form". *RealClearPolitics*.

42 Browne, A. (2016, May 10). China Faces Its Own Version of Trumpism. *The Wall Street Journal*.

43 Stearns, J. (2016, July 5). Brexit Shocks Hit EU-Canada Trade Deal As New Hurdles Emerge. *Financial Post*.

44 "A waxing negative social mood appears to correlate with a collective increase in discord, exclusion, unhappiness, anger, fear, opposition,

protectionism, depression, defensiveness, somberness, pessimism, restriction, malevolence, dullness of focus, magical thinking, a tendence to criticize, a search for pleasure, an interest in sex over love, destructiveness, a desire for self-deprivation, a desire to separate from others, a desire for power over people, feelings of heterogeneity with others, fuzziness of thinking and emotion, avoidance of effort, and feelings of opposition toward others." — Robert Prechter, *The Wave Principle of Human Social Behavior* (1999), Chapter 14, p. 228.

[45] Tolan, S. (2016, June 30). Brexit's 'Meaning'? Globalization Sucks. *The Daily Beast.*

[46] Tankersley, J. (2016, June 25). Britain Just Killed Globalization As We Know It. *The Washington Post.*

[47] Lee, D. (2016, June 25). Brexit May Mark the Start of a Rebellion Against Globalization. *Providence Journal.*

[48] Schwartz, N.D., & Cohen, P. (2016, June 25). 'Brexit' in America: A Warning Shot Against Globalization. *The New York Times.*

[49] Keane, A.G., & Sink, J. (2016, June 24). Brexit Spawned by Tensions Over Globalization, Obama says. Bloomberg Politics.

[50] Woodruff, J. (2016, June 24). Will Other Countries Follow Brexit Example and Shun Globalization? *PBS Newshour.*

[51] Hutchinson, M. (2016, July 5). Has Globalization Been a Mistake? *Wall Street Daily.*

[52] Kharas, H. (2016, July 5). Does Brexit Mean the End of Globalization? *Newsweek.*

Part VII:

SOCIAL MOOD AND EPIDEMICS

Chapter 52

A Socionomic Study of Epidemic Disease

Alan Hall

May 1 and June 4, 2009 / February 27, 2015 (TS) [excerpts]

According to medical historian David Morens, "The three deadliest events in human history were all infectious diseases. The 1918-1919 flu killed 50 million to 100 million people. The Black Death killed 25 million people, and AIDS has killed 25 million or more."[1]

The first step toward preparing for the increased risk of disease is to understand an important process regulating that risk. It is widely understood that epidemics make people fearful, but only socionomic causality proposes that fearful people are more susceptible to epidemics.

The March 1994 issue of *The Elliott Wave Theorist* observed that epidemic disease is associated with large-degree episodes of negative social mood:

> For whatever reason, disease sometimes plays a prominent role in major corrective periods, with some Cycle and Supercycle degree corrections containing epidemics and larger ones pandemics.

The current study will show that major epidemics tend to break out near negative extremes in social mood—and therefore near significant bottoms in stock prices—and can persist well into the subsequent uptrend.

Epidemics Following Three Multi-Century Bear Markets

Figure 1 shows a long term sociometer in the form of a 1000-year price index for a simple basket of human needs. Periods of negative social mood are indicated by the three sideways moves marked by grey horizontal lines.

During the first period of negative mood, the Crusades that began in 1095 were "turned back by epidemics much more effectively than they were

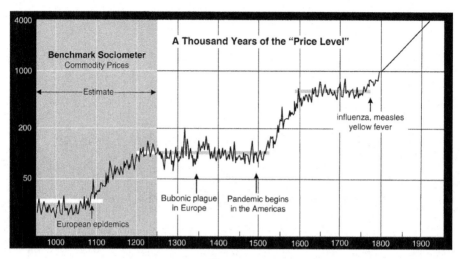

Figure 1

by the armed power of the Saracens," wrote Hans Zinsser in *Rats, Lice and History* (1934).[2] In other words, disease was deadlier than armies. The same thing was true during World War I (see discussion below).

The end of the third period of negative mood from 1600 to the late 1700s, brought not only the American Revolution but also a cluster of contagions: one of the worst worldwide influenza epidemics in 1775-1776, measles in 1788, more influenza in 1793, and yellow fever in 1793-1803.

Consequences of the second period of negative mood are particularly interesting in having brought pandemics to both Europe and America. We will begin our review of this period with Europe, where a modicum of data exists.

The Bubonic Plague in Europe

The Bubonic Plague, a bacterial illness, originated in China. In 1348, it reached Europe, where it found a vulnerable society entrenched in economic contraction. Philip Ziegler, in his book *The Black Death*,[3] described conditions that set the stage for the outbreak:

> Before the Black Death, most of Europe was in recession or, at the very least, had ceased to advance. The cloth trade of Flanders and Brabant stagnated. Colonisation stopped. The great fairs of the Champagne, indices of the economic health of a large and flourishing region, significantly declined. The prices of agricultural produce were falling: agriculture was no longer the easy road to prosperity

which it had been for the past two hundred years. Put in the simplest terms, Europe had outgrown its strength and was now suffering the physical and mental malaise which inevitably follows so intemperate a progress.

These are precisely the conditions that socionomists recognize as being psychological, physiological and economic results of a change toward negative social mood.

Reflecting the depressed social mood of the day, "Europeans were possessed," wrote Ziegler, "by a conviction of their guilt" that they had brought the plague upon themselves. Ziegler also observed that, in accordance with socionomic causality, the European plague was *preceded* by rumors of environmental calamity in Asia and widespread visions of its horror:

Drought, famine, floods, earthquakes, locusts, rains of frogs, serpents, lizards, scorpions and many venomous beasts of that sort, lightning, sheets of fire, huge hailstones, fire from heaven and stinking smoke. The foul blast of wind. This concept of a corrupted atmosphere, visible in the form of mist or smoke, drifting across the world and overwhelming all whom it encountered, was one of the main assumptions on which the physicians of the Middle Ages based their efforts to check the plague.

This notion of noxious air, called "miasma," developed into a crude disease theory that persisted into the mid-nineteenth century.

The plague was accompanied by social hysterias, including "dancing manias," described as frenzied deliriums in which many people reportedly laughed, wept and danced furiously to the point of exhaustion or death. Zinsser[4] observed the possibility that these strange behaviors amid rampant disease could have been partly due to infectious agents:

In great part, no doubt, the outbreaks were hysterical reactions of a terror-stricken and wretched population, which had broken down under the stress of almost incredible hardship and danger. But it seems likely that associated with these were nervous diseases of infectious origin which followed the great epidemics of plague, small pox, and so forth, in the same manner in which neurotropic virus diseases have followed the widespread and severe epidemics which accompanied [World War I].

But Justus Hecker's *Epidemics of the Middle Ages* (1844)[5] ascribed these behaviors to "morbid sympathy" during the widespread pessimism and despair that followed the Black Death, another observation compatible with socionomic theory.

Pandemics in the Americas

Mounting evidence indicates that a massive pandemic erupted in America in the late 1400s at the end of the nearly three-century period of price stagnation depicted around that time in Figure 1. Europe had suffered a massive population collapse from plague and was mired in the political, religious and xenophobic turmoil known as the Crisis of the Late Middle Ages, but the bigger disaster occurred in the Americas.

Charles C. Mann's recently published book, *1491: New Revelations of the Americas before Columbus*,[6] documented this outbreak via written accounts of early European explorers and settlers and with every turn of the archaeologist's spade since that time. Beginning in the late 1400s, disease emptied the Americas of perhaps 95% of an estimated 100 million native people.

Social mood is never the only factor in a pandemic, but it is a precipitating one. As Jared Diamond theorized in his book *Guns, Germs and Steel*,[7] the genetic setup for the Americas' wipeout may have been millennia in the making. As socionomists, we observe that it happened at an accommodating time with respect to social mood as recorded in Europe. Whether the Americas shared in that mood originally we cannot say, but the Europeans surely imported its effects.

Epidemics in London in the 1800s

On the heels of a turn toward negative social mood that brought about the stock market panic of 1825, London experienced cholera epidemics in 1832, 1848, 1854 and 1866. Figure 2 plots the U.K. FTSE All-Share Index along with boxes displaying the time spans and mortality consequences. Notice that each outbreak occurred *after* a stock market decline, a chronology consistent with the socionomic proposal that trends toward negative social mood played a causal role.

London grew increasingly crowded and dirty during this 40-year period of negative social mood, partly because of migration from the impoverished countryside into the city. Sanitary conditions were awful, and they grew worse. London had bad water drainage, open sewers, pigs in most backyards and overflowing cesspits under most houses. As the bear market wore on, people increasingly could not afford to pay to clean or repair these facilities. Drinking water came from private companies via leaky wooden pipes or from hand-pumped shallow wells on the streets.

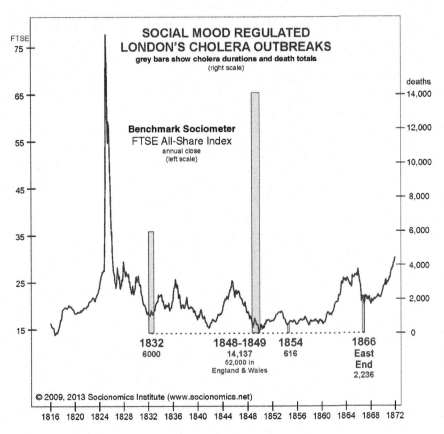

Figure 2

The negative trend in social mood created attitudes and conditions that kept authorities from acting to quell the outbreaks. R.J. Morris, in his 1976 book, *Cholera 1832—The Social Response to an Epidemic,*[8] observed,

> Cholera had demonstrated the relationship between disease and the dirty, ill-drained parts of towns and had shown the need for drainage, sewerage and filtered water supplies. It ought to have been a spur to sanitary reform. Yet little action of this sort followed the [1832] epidemic. In the winter of 1832-3, both government and people seemed to want to forget cholera as quickly as they could.

In October 1849, the London stock market fell to a low that has not been exceeded since. As social mood reached its nadir, society reached peak vulnerability and London suffered the worst among these epidemics.

In 1854, when the third epidemic erupted, social mood had passed its negative extreme and the deaths in London were concomitantly far fewer.

This is when Dr. John Snow's famous map linked cholera to a public water pump on Broad Street. Although Snow had no hard evidence, he managed to convince officials to remove the pump handle, and the epidemic subsided. Afterward, even though no one had identified an infectious agent in the air, the General Board of Health—showing intellectual blindness typical of negative mood periods—stubbornly attacked Snow's waterborne disease theory because he could not identify the "cholera poison" in the water.

The summer of 1858 brought "The Great Stink," when the River Thames became a reeking mess. In 1859, social mood finally began trending strongly positive, and a positive effect resulted: The government began construction of the London Sewer. This remarkable engineering project still functions today. Ironically it was initiated for the wrong reason. As miasma theory was still entrenched, the sewer was built to improve the *air* quality. Bad smells were associated with cholera outbreaks, so doctors thought bad smells must be causing the disease. The unintended consequence of the sewer was that the water supply ceased to be contaminated, a condition that ended both the stink and the epidemics in most of London.

The final epidemic hit in the summer of 1866, at another stock market low. It affected only people in London's East End, which was not connected to the new sewer. This was powerful evidence supporting waterborne transmission of cholera. The East End epidemic killed over 2000 people who drank water supplied by the East London Water Company.[9] The epidemic had a big impact on water treatment policies, but, even then, only a scientific "elite within an elite" believed cholera was spread by water.

Social Mood Coordinated with Seasonality in the Cholera Outbreaks

These cholera outbreaks provide a template on how social mood and seasonality can interact to shape the trajectory of an epidemic. In a March 2011 paper, researchers studied weekly records of cholera deaths in London from 1824-1901. They wrote,

> Three features of the time series stand out: (i) cholera deaths were strongly seasonal, with peak mortality almost always in the summer, (ii) the only non-summer outbreaks occurred in the spring of 1832, the autumn of 1848 and the winter of 1853, and (iii) extraordinarily severe summer outbreaks occurred in 1832, 1849, 1854 and 1866 (the four 'great' cholera years). The non-summer outbreaks of 1832, 1848 and 1853 appear to have been herald waves of newly invading cholera strains.[10]

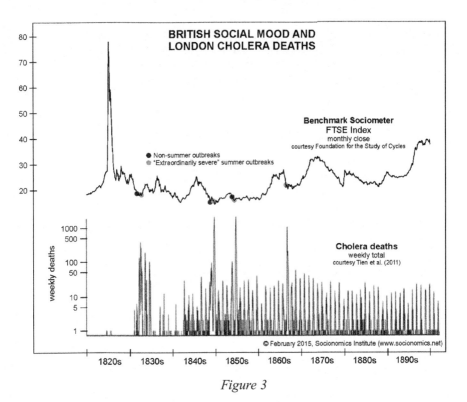

Figure 3

Figure 3 plots weekly cholera deaths in London in the 1800s versus British social mood as reflected in the FTSE All-Share Index. To the FTSE graph we have added black dots and grey dots to mark respectively the "non-summer outbreaks" and "extraordinarily severe summer outbreaks" cited in the previous paragraph. The researchers' data correspond to what we have previously observed: The worst summertime outbreaks occurred after stock declines, and in three of the four cases non-summertime outbreaks preceded them. The deadliest pair coincided with the most negative social mood as indicated by 1849's lowest low for stocks.

Figure 4 shows weekly cholera deaths from 1845 to 1851, which the researchers plotted in order to show seasonal fluctuations in mortality. We added a plot of the FTSE and shaded, vertical bars to mark the seasons. The bars make it easier to see cholera's tendency to be most lethal in the summer and fall. We can now additionally see that overall the seasonal spikes rose as social mood grew more negative, peaked at the 1849 low in stocks, and then returned to less severe levels.

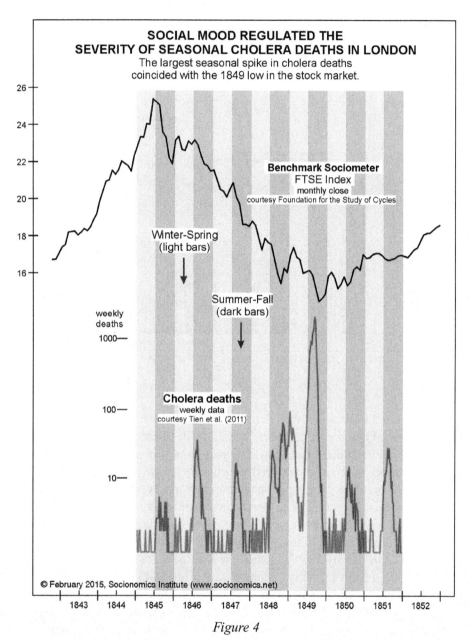

Figure 4

The Death of Miasma Theory

The crisis and the ensuing positive mood trend had another positive effect. It impelled the most important paradigm shift in the history of medical science, from the miasma theory of disease transmission to germ theory.

When cholera first arrived in London in 1832, leading public health figures, including Edwin Chadwick and Florence Nightingale, believed it was spread by miasma. The same theory had held sway during the bubonic plague of 1348, five centuries before.

The first chink in the theory's armor appeared at the negative social mood extreme in 1849, when Snow published his essay, *"On the Mode of Communication of Cholera,"* which described the disease as waterborne. Morris wrote, "The summer of 1849 marked the high noon of miasmatic theory. By the end of the year, confidence in the theory had been weakened by its failure, and by the scientific work of John Snow."[11]

Even after Joseph Lister's success with antiseptics in 1867, it took roughly another 25 years—during which time the trend of social mood was persistently positive—before germ theory fully replaced the miasma paradigm.

Epidemics in the United States in the 1900s

Figure 5 plots a benchmark sociometer, the Dow/PPI, dating from 1888, the year Louis Pasteur opened his laboratory. That time marks the approximate advent of germ theory, which radically improved medicine. Prior to this period, epidemics were far more prevalent overall, although they still occurred mostly during negative trends in social mood.

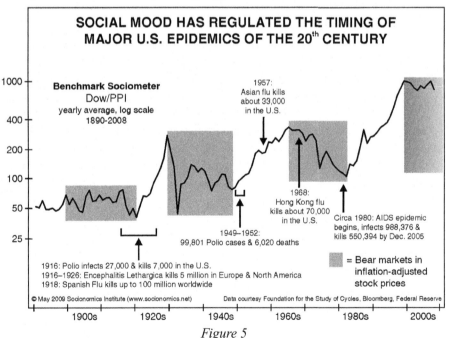

Figure 5

In Figure 5, we have shaded the periods of negative social mood and marked with arrows the major U.S. epidemics since 1888. Seven epidemics breached humans' immune systems near the ends of three periods of negative social mood, each of which lasted about twenty years. The sole exception to socionomic expectations occurred in 1957 during a small-degree pullback within a major positive mood trend.

The Spanish Flu

Figure 6 zooms in on the PPI-adjusted Dow and adds boxes displaying the time spans and mortality consequences of World War I, the 1918 Spanish Flu pandemic and encephalitis lethargica, a deadly neurological disease. Although World War I introduced machine guns and poison gas and caused about 16 million deaths, those casualties were dwarfed by the outbreak of Spanish Flu that followed the war. This epidemic surged right at the bottom of a collapse in stock prices that had signaled a swift change toward intensely negative social mood. The Spanish Flu was 25 times more deadly than ordinary influenza, killed as many as a hundred million people worldwide and reduced by twelve years the average American's lifespan in 1918. Historian Alfred Crosby said the virus "killed more humans than any other disease in a period of similar duration in the history of the world."[12]

The Spanish Flu of 1918 came without warning and killed quickly. Even after excavation of frozen flu victims and decades of research, it is still not completely understood. We know that the virus was associated with encephalitis lethargica[13] as well as a bacterial pneumonia that helped kill the victims, and recent genetic studies show that a specific complex of three genes could have allowed the virus to thrive deep in the lungs. But the 1918 epidemic did not follow the usual progression of contagion. It seemed to spring up out of nowhere—simultaneously across the planet—as if the virus was already in place, waiting for human immunity to weaken.[14] This seeming spontaneity makes sense under the socionomic model but not under any other model of which we are aware. Mechanical models cannot explain it, but a global condition of extremely negative social mood does.

Despite the Spanish Flu's devastating blow to the population, Gina Kolata, author of *Flu—The Story of the Great Influenza Pandemic of 1918*, wrote that she took college microbiology, virology and history courses in the 1970s, and not one of them mentioned the pandemic of 1918. As in the aftermath of London's 1832 cholera outbreak, survivors were in denial and sought to forget the horrific disease. Kolata wrote that the 1918 epidemic

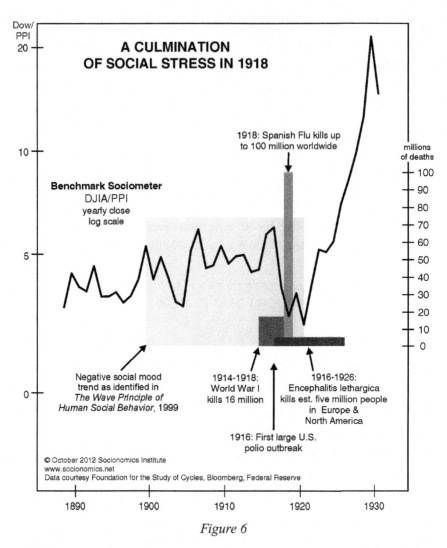

Figure 6

was largely "obliterated from the consciousness of historians."[15] Such for-
getfulness, like waves of social mood, can only be non-rational.

Sleeping Sickness

Other health threats spread while society endured this period of
negative mood and its associated world war. Encephalitis lethargica—an
illness that attacks the brain and leaves many victims speechless and mo-
tionless—emerged in 1916. The disease killed about five million people
in Europe and North America. This number may look small on the chart,

but it is roughly the combined population of Chicago and Houston today. The disease abruptly vanished in 1926, five years into a new trend toward positive social mood.[16]

Polio

Also in 1916, the U.S. suffered its first large outbreak of polio—another neurological disease—with over 9,000 cases reported in New York City alone. The tallest spike in the polio notification rate—as shown on the middle graph in Figure 7—was in 1916, two years before the Spanish flu epidemic. Polio cases jumped again during the 1931 market collapse, and a significant outbreak occurred in Los Angeles in 1934. More polio epidemics occurred in the negative mood period that produced a bear market in 1946-1949 and an average of more than 20,000 polio cases per year from

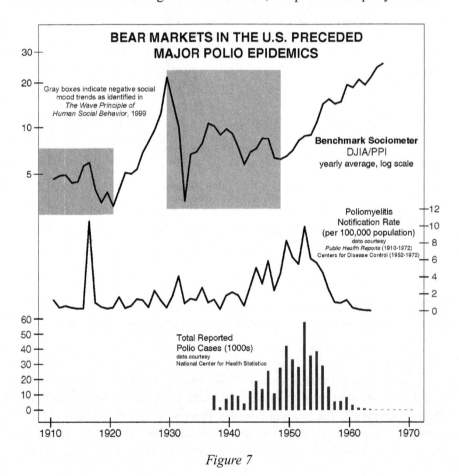

Figure 7

1945 to 1949. The epidemic peaked at 58,000 U.S. cases in 1952, just three years after the 20-year corrective pattern in the Dow/PPI ended (per the second shaded box in Figure 7) and while the Korean War, another result of negative mood, raged. After the Dow exceeded its peak level of 1929, the rate fell to 5,600 in 1957 and shrank to 121 in 1964, near the top of the bull market that signaled a peak in positive social mood.

AIDS

Figure 8 shows the history of the U.S. AIDS epidemic. It began in the early 1980s, right at the end of a 16-year period of increasingly negative social mood, which coincided with that era's low in the Dow/PPI. Chapter 18 of *The Wave Principle of Human Social Behavior* (1999) commented on the AIDS epidemic, which, like polio cases, had started in an environment

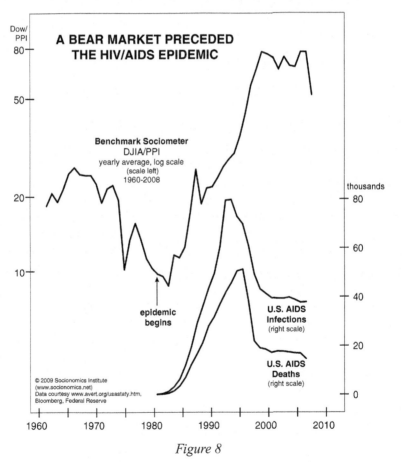

Figure 8

of extremely negative social mood but reached a peak during the subsequent rise in stock prices:

> AIDS might appear to be an exception [to the observation that epidemics occur near negative mood extremes], as this slow-moving epidemic has remained in force during the bull market years of the 1980s and 1990s. However, during this advance, the epidemic has waned significantly, as AIDS today is no longer in the top ten causes of death in the United States, the rate halving in 1997 alone.[17]

The AIDS epidemic peaked near the end of a smaller-degree bear market that lasted from 1987 to 1990 and whose associated recession lasted through 1993, as noted in Figure 1 in Chapter 12 and as explained in Chapter 1 of *Beautiful Pictures*:

> In the early 1990s, extensive layoffs and the biggest collapse in S&P earnings since the early 1940s dogged the economy right through 1993, even though the Bureau of Economic Research declared the recession "officially" over in 1991.[18]

Global Epidemics Since 2000

In the decade of the 2000s, there were two notable epidemics. The SARS epidemic originated in Hong Kong and had its highest incidence rate there. The H1N1 flu outbreak was global in scope. Figure 9 plots the number of cases of each disease versus the most appropriate sociometers: Hong Kong's Hang Seng Index and the World Stock Index, respectively. Most U.S. and European stock indexes show similar trends.

The timing of these flu outbreaks conforms to socionomic theory. Just after the March 2003 low in world stock prices, SARS erupted in Hong Kong and spread to 37 countries. Six years later, beginning at the 2009 low in stock prices, H1N1 flu erupted.

These two negative trends in social mood produced mortality consequences in accord with their sizes. The 2007-2009 declines in our sociometers were larger than the 2000-2003 declines, and the 2009 H1N1 pandemic, accordingly, was far more infectious and killed more people than the 2003 SARS epidemic.

Mechanistic vs. Socionomic Causality

The trend toward negative social mood that took place from 2000 to 2009 produced a number of immediate and lagging effects. Mood manifested

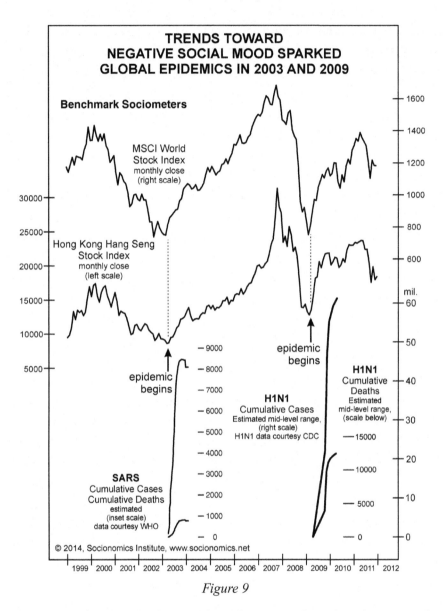

Figure 9

first in stock price declines and credit contraction, then in economic contraction, unemployment, falling incomes, foreclosures and homelessness. As Chapter 53 will relate, each of these effects has been associated with negative health consequences.[19,20,21]

Aware of the connection between the economy and health, researchers have produced numerous academic studies relating the economic contraction of 2007-2009 to public health. They found a decline in men's mental health, increased rates of suicide, more cases of HIV, and reduced access to health care in a number of countries.[22,23,24,25,26] These studies, however, all began with the assumption that economic problems *caused* the adverse health effects. Perhaps someday researchers will begin with the correct assumption: Trends in social mood *precede* and *cause* financial effects, economic effects and health effects, in that order.

Sociometers Can Aid in Forecasting Epidemics

In Figures 5 through 9, we see the effects of infectious diseases with strikingly different modes of transmission:

- Cholera and polio spread through feces-contaminated water or food;
- Encephalitis lethargica spreads by some unknown vector;
- HIV/AIDS spreads through sexual transmission, needle sharing or exposure to body fluids.
- Polio, flu and SARS are air-borne and spread through respiration.

These are *entirely different etiologies*, yet each outbreak shows *the same or similar relationship to the stock market*. The persistence of this connection is *remarkable*. Only socionomic theory explains it.

Information about transmission mechanisms is useful, but researchers who focus only on understanding disease mechanics and proximate causes (see next chapter) will continue to miss the bigger picture. In waiting for outbreaks of disease before reacting, authorities are failing at a game of "whack-a-mole." As soon as they leap to whack the most recent scourge, it dissipates, and later a new one pops up in an unexpected place.

The primary causal factor common to epidemics is a preceding trend toward negative social mood—as indicated by a falling stock market—which produces multiple psychological, physiological and environmental conditions affecting public health. Epidemiologists who want to predict epidemics and prepare for them ahead of time should study their ultimate cause: waves of negative social mood.

Socionomic theory provides an edge even in forecasting which specific diseases are likely to erupt. If the stock market has recently fallen and the lagging economic effects of negative social mood are beginning to manifest, there is an escalating potential for one or more of the *currently active* infectious diseases to become a major epidemic. The socionomic perspective would have been valuable in the early 1980s (see Figure 8) when "the American government completely ignored the emerging AIDS epidemic."[27]

Not until 1986, when infections were skyrocketing and more than half the hemophiliacs in the U.S. were infected, did the government issue its first major statement on preventing the spread of AIDS. If people in the field of public health want to help society in a more timely manner, they should understand socionomic causality and proceed from there.

NOTES AND REFERENCES

[1] Sternberg, S. (2008, October 21). "Experts Predict Next Epidemic Will Start in Animals." *USA Today*.

[2] Zinsser, H. (1934/2008). *Rats, Lice and History*. New Brunswick, NJ: Transaction Publishers.

[3] Ziegler, P. (2009). *The Black Death*. New York, NY: Harper Perennial Modern Classics.

[4] Zinsser, H. (1934/2008). *Rats, Lice and History*. New Brunswick, NJ: Transaction Publishers.

[5] Hecker, J.F.C. (1859). *Epidemics of the Middle Ages*. Translated by B.G. Babington. London, England: Trubner & Co.

[6] Mann, Charles C. (2005). *1491: New Revelations of the Americas before Columbus*. New York: Alfred A. Knopf.

[7] Diamond, Jared M. (1997). *Guns, Germs, and Steel: The Fates of Human Societies*. New York: W.W. Norton & Co.

[8] Morris, R.J. (1976). *Cholera, 1832: The Social Response to an Epidemic*. Teaneck, NJ: Holmes and Meier Publishers.

[9] Luckin, W. (1977). "The Final Catastrophe—Cholera in London, 1866." *Medical History*, 21, 32-42.

[10] Tien, J.H., Poinar, H.N., Fisman, D.N., Earn, D.J.D. (2011, March 22). Herald Waves of Cholera in Nineteenth Century London. Interface. The Royal Society Publishing.

[11] Morris, R.J. (1976). *Cholera, 1832: The Social Response to an Epidemic*. Teaneck, NJ: Holmes and Meier Publishers.

[12] Kolata, G. (2001). *Flu: The Story of the Great Influenza Pandemic of 1918 and the Search for the Virus that Caused It*. New York, NY: Touchstone.

[13] Sacks, O., & Vilensky, J.A. (2005, November 16). "Waking to a New Flu Threat." *The New York Times.*

[14] Loatman, P. (2001, November 7). "West Nile? Meet 'The Mother of All Viruses.'" Mechanicville, New York city website.

[15] Kolata, G. (2001). *Flu: The Story of the Great Influenza Pandemic of 1918 and the Search for the Virus that Caused It.* New York, NY: Touchstone.

[16] Lyons, M. (2002). *The Colonial Disease: A Social History of Sleeping Sickness in Northern Zaire, 1900-1940.* Cambridge, England: Cambridge University Press.

[17] Prechter, Robert R. (1999). *The Wave Principle of Human Social Behavior and the New Science of Socionomics.* Gainesville, GA: New Classics Library.

[18] Prechter, Robert R. (2003). *Beautiful Pictures from the Gallery of Phinance.* Gainesville, GA: New Classics Library.

[19] Marmot, M. (2005). "Social Determinants of Health Inequalities." *Lancet* 365:1099–1104 doi:10.1016/S0140-6736(05)71146-6

[20] Pelletier, D., Frongillo, E., Schroeder, D., Habicht, J. (1995). "The Effects of Malnutrition on Child Mortality in Developing Countries." *Bulletin of the World Health Organization.* 73(4): 443–448.

[21] U.S. Department of Health and Human Services (1999, 2003, 2010). Child Maltreatment Report.

[22] Stuckler, D., Basu, S. (2011). "Effects of the 2008 Recession on Health: A First Look at European Data." *Lancet* 378: 124–125. doi: 10.1016/S0140-6736(11)61079-9

[23] Luo, F., Florence, C., Quispe-Agnoli, M., Ouyang, L., Crosby, A. (2011),\. "Impact of Business Cycles on US Suicide Rates, 1928–2007." *American Journal of Public Health* 101(6), 1139-1146. doi: 10.2105/AJPH.2010.300010

[24] Taylor-Robinson, D., Scott-Samuel, A., McKee, M., Stuckler, D. (2012). "Suicides Associated With The 2008–10 Economic Recession in England: Time Trend Analysis." *BMJ* 345 doi: http://dx.doi.org/10.1136/bmj.e5142

[25] Moore, K., Redd, A., Burkhauser, M., Mbwana, K., Collins, A. (2009-2011). "Children in Poverty: Trends Consequences, and Policy Options." *Child Research Brief.*

[26] Berger, R., Fromkin, J., Stutz, H., Makoroff, K., Scribano, P., Feldman, K., Tu, L.C., Fabio, A. (2011). "Abusive Head Trauma During a Time of Increased Unemployment." *Pediatrics,* 128(4), 637-643. doi: 10.1542/peds.2010-2185

[27] Avert.org (n.d.) "History of HIV and AIDS in the U.S."

Chapter 53

Socionomics Can Help Predict Proximate Causes of Adverse Health Outcomes

Alan Hall

December 2011 / March 2013/April 2013 (TS)

Just as the stock market—our most sensitive sociometer—is a leading indicator of the tone of economic and political news (see Chapter 8 of *The Socionomic Theory of Finance*), it is also a leading indicator of risks to societal health. Positive social mood is a primary cause of favorable public health conditions, and negative social mood is a primary cause of adverse public health conditions. As part of the process, social mood produces many individual and social conditions that can become proximate causes of decreased or increased incidence of disease.

This chapter focuses on those intermediary causes. A few items on our list are from the 2009 study excerpted in the previous chapter, and the rest are from articles in the December 2011, March 2013 and April 2013 issues of *The Socionomist*, which are available to members on the Socionomics Institute's website.

The May 2003 issue of *The Elliott Wave Theorist* reiterated the primary cause of epidemics and proposed possible proximate causes:

> Epidemics and pandemics seem to hit populations during major negative social mood trends. Perhaps it happens that way because people's psychological constitutions are weaker during bear markets. Perhaps it is because people's personal behavior, whether involving hygiene (as in the time of the plague or in recent years with respect to hypodermic needles used to inject drugs) or sexual promiscuity, is more conducive to spreading disease during social mood retrenchments. Perhaps it is because social mood retrenchment brings economic contraction, which makes people less able to afford the creature comforts that ward off disease and more apt to crowd into smaller, more affordable spaces[, thereby increasing susceptibility to contagion].

Social Mood Regulates Social Stresses as Well as People's Responses to Stressful Situations

Two more major factors in susceptibility to disease are *stress* and *feelings of stressfulness*. Many studies find that chronic stress compromises the human immune system. The American Psychological Association reported on a 2004 meta-analysis that reviewed 300 separate studies and found a direct link between stress and disease:

> The most chronic stressors—which change people's identities or social roles, are more beyond their control and seem endless—were associated with the most global suppression of immunity; almost all measures of immune function dropped across the board. The longer the stress, the more the immune system shifted from potentially adaptive changes (such as those in the acute "fight or flight" response) to potentially detrimental changes, at first in cellular immunity and then in broader immune function. Thus, stressors that turn a person's world upside down and appear to offer no "light at the end of the tunnel" could have the greatest psychological and physiological impact.[1]

We propose that an extended trend toward negative social mood not only increases feelings of stressfulness but also impels behavior that creates stressful conditions, both of which weaken human immune systems.

We have also observed that trends in social mood regulate even people's responses to stressful events. The September 2003 issue of *The Elliott Wave Theorist* examined the radically different social responses to the 1965, 1977 and 2003 electrical blackouts in New York City, namely riots in 1977 and amity in 1965 and 2003 (see Chapter 12 in *Pioneering Studies in Socionomics*). These responses can be explained by the differing social mood in those years, as reflected in the PPI-adjusted Dow Jones Industrial Average. As Prechter explained,

> The event was the same each time, so its nature is irrelevant to the behavior. Shared good feelings near the two tops manifested in good behavior, and shared bad feelings near the bottom manifested in destructive behavior.

From this insight, we may further postulate that social mood regulates even when stressful situations lead people to take actions that make things better or worse.

Socionomic theory, then, explains *three aspects* of human stress conditions: When social mood is positive, people (1) *feel less stressed*, (2) act in ways that *produce fewer stressful situations* and (3) *defuse stressful situations when they arise.* When social mood is negative, people (1) *feel more stressed*, (2) act in ways that *produce more stressful situations* and (3) *exacerbate stressful situations when they arise.* The latter situation is a triple whammy to the psyche and the body, making people more susceptible to disease.

Proximate Causes of Epidemics Deriving from Negative Social Mood

Socionomic causality equips us to predict that the next large-degree trend toward negative social mood will cause many psychological, physiological and social changes among humans that will make them more vulnerable to epidemic disease. During the next such time, we would expect the following proximate causes of increased incidence of disease to recur as they have in the past:

- Academic researchers will find evidence of increased feelings of stress, stressful conditions and eventually long-term chronic stress, which compromises immune-system function.

- Increasing pessimism—which researchers have linked to a number of negative public health outcomes—will lead to greater biological susceptibility to disease.

- Aggregate C-reactive protein (CRP) levels, which are associated with a greater risk of psychological stress, clinical depression, heart attacks and cardiovascular illness in the general population, will rise.[2]

- News media will report contemporary versions of the "physical and mental malaise" described by Philip Ziegler in 1300s Europe, as noted in the previous chapter.

- As asset prices fall, the economy will follow, resulting in a decline in the general standard of living due to foreclosures, layoffs, unemployment, homelessness, economic hardship, financial problems and hunger, each of which can foster adverse health conditions. As *The New York Times* put it, "Foreclosure is not just a metaphorical epidemic, but a bona fide public health crisis.... A growing body of research shows that foreclosure itself harms the health of families and communities...."[3]

- Crowding and poor hygiene will increase in cities and elsewhere, and authorities will fail to correct it. Stories about rats, lice, bedbugs, unhygenic practices and other threats to health will be reported in the media.

- Rates of depression, anxiety and mental illness will increase, as will the use of anti-depressant and anti-anxiety drugs.[4]

- Rates of child homelessness and poverty will increase. A report describes one result of the most recent trend toward negative social mood: "The number of homeless children and youth in U.S. public schools increased 41% from 2006 to 2009.... The number of children who fell into poverty between 2008 and 2009 was the largest single-year increase ever recorded."[5]

- Rates of child abuse and abusive head trauma (AHT) will increase. Researchers found that the rate of AHT seen among kids below age five in various U.S. locales rose by 67% from 2004 to 2009, encompassing the onset of the bear market in real-estate-related investments, a bear market in stocks, the Great Recession and massive job losses.[6] An international survey from UNICEF showed substantially lower rates of child abuse in the 1990s vs. the 1970s, a result compatible with the clear difference in the trends of social mood during those two periods.[7]

- Child-abuse fatality rates will increase. The U.S. Department of Health and Human Services reported that child-abuse fatality rates rose by 40% between 1999 and 2008,[8] a period encompassing a major bear market in stocks as revealed by the S&P/PPI and the Dow/gold ratio.

- More infants and toddlers will inherit lasting learning and developmental problems."[9]

- Teen self-harming will increase.[10]

- Public health funding will decline. Following the period of negative social mood of 2007-2011 (as measured by the Dow/gold ratio and real estate prices), the director of the National Center for Disaster Preparedness said in September 2011, "There have been tremendous cuts in virtually every program that has to do with preparedness."[11]

- Funding cuts will result in fears of doctor shortages and perhaps actual doctor shortages. As ABC News reported in November 2012, "Doctor Shortage Could Cause Health Care Crash."[12]

- Drug shortages will increase. Worldwide interest in drug shortages, as recorded in Google searches, recently peaked in November 2011, near the low in the Dow/gold ratio, and in February 2012, at the low in real estate prices.

- Drug providers and outpatient centers will grow laxer about safety.[13,14]

- Dirty hypodermic needles will be blamed for causing preventable infections.[15]

- Suicide rates will increase in civilian society and in the military.[16,17,18]

- Incidences of mosquito-borne diseases will increase.

- Incidences of sexually transmitted diseases will increase.

- Mysticism, denial, fear and authoritarianism will hamper science.[19]

- Military conflict will become more likely. Casualties and shortages will add to the health care burden.

- Any large-degree negative mood trend is likely to be global, which will increase migrant and refugee populations, exacerbating the spread of diseases.[20]

- The potential for use of bioterror pathogens will increase, as might their actual use.[21]

- Fertility rates will decline, reducing the breadth of the family unit and therefore the opportunity of families to care for the elderly.

- All these conditions will increase the possibility of a "syndemic," a combination of ills—such as poverty, hunger, stress, violence, diseases and lack of medical care—that creates what epidemiologists call an "excess disease burden" on the population.

As a result of these factors—all of which will derive from a trend toward negative social mood—epidemics, pandemics and associated neurological diseases will become more common.

Proximate Causes of Disease Inherited from Actions Taken in the Preceding Period of Positive Mood

Some health problems that arise during negative mood trends derive from complacent behavior during the preceding positive mood trend. One example is the cavalier consumption of more sugar during positive mood periods, which in negative mood periods is more likely to lead to cases of diabetes, as discussed in [Chapter 46]. Another example is the current situation following six decades of careless overuse of antibiotics and the consequent emergence of antimicrobial-drug-resistant organisms. In October 2011, *Scientific American* wrote that the 29 million pounds per year of antibiotics administered to U.S. food animals have resulted in "a profitable

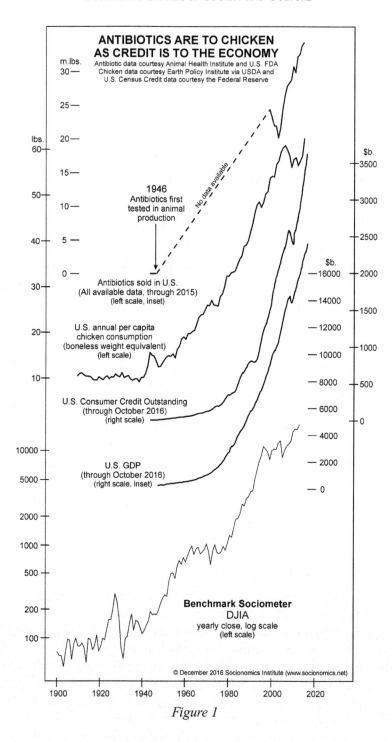

Figure 1

meat industry...but also one of the most effective systems for the evolution and transmission of antibiotic-resistant strains of bacteria that an engineer could devise."[22] The havoc such superbugs will wreak in a "post-antibiotic era"[23] will assuredly increase during periods of negative social mood.

The top graph in Figure 1 plots all available data as of 2016 for agricultural antibiotics sold in the United States, and the next graph plots U.S. chicken consumption per capita. We lack data on antibiotic use prior to 1999, but we deduce that animal feed contained zero added antibiotics prior to 1946, when Moore et al. first reported that streptomycin fed to poultry improved growth.[24] Another clue regarding timing is a quote from a 2011 USDA Food Safety Symposium report: "The variety of antibiotics, the routes of administration and the reasons for their use, expanded during the period between 1950 and 1960."[25] Based on this information, we hypothesize that the extent of the use of antibiotics within the meat industry has roughly paralleled the plot of per-capita chicken consumption since that time. The three lower graphs plot U.S. consumer credit, U.S. GDP and the DJIA. All five graphs parallel exponential growth in a plethora of financial and economic measures, including home prices and average incomes, fitting the socionomic observation of a mostly positive social mood trend since 1932.

As you can see from the chart's title, antibiotics have contributed to expanding meat production much as credit has contributed to an expanding economy. Antibiotics may be considered a form of credit in that health benefits enjoyed in the present may have to be repaid with commensurate health debits in the future. Regardless, unintended adverse consequences from both of these programs will surely wax during the next major trend toward negative social mood.

The trend of social mood is a primary determinant and therefore an excellent predictor of society's aggregate state of financial and physical health. Global health researchers who wish to predict times when proximate causes of epidemics will wax should pay attention to trends in social mood.

NOTES

[1] Stress Affects Immunity in Ways Related to Stress Type and Duration, as Shown by Nearly 300 Studies. (2004, July 4). American Psychological Association.

[2] Elevated Levels of C-reactive Protein Appear Associated with Psychological Distress, Depression. (2012, December 24). *Science Daily.*

[3] Pollack, C.E., & Lynch, J.F. (2011, October 2). Foreclosures are Killing Us. *The New York Times.*

[4] Lloyd, J. (2011, October 20). CDC: Antidepressant Use Skyrockets 400% in Past 20 Years. *USA Today*.

[5] Children's Defense Fund. The State of America's Children. (2011).

[6] Mann, D. (2011, September 19). Recession Tied to Rise in Child Abuse Injuries. HealthDay.

[7] UNICEF. (2003). Child Maltreatment Deaths in Rich Nations. Innocenti Report Card, (5), page 9.

[8] U.S. Department of Health and Human Services, Child Welfare Information Gateway. (2011). Child Maltreatment 2010.

[9] Lazar, K. (2011, July 28). A Rising Hunger Among Children. Boston. com.

[10] Szabo, L. (2011, Feb 21). Teens Share Self-injury, 'Cutting' Videos on YouTube. *USA Today*.

[11] Walsh, B. (2011, September 9). Why Our Public Health System Isn't Ready for Another 9/11. *Time*.

[12] Nathan, N. (2012, November 13). Doctor Shortage Could Cause Health Care Crash. *ABC World News*.

[13] Aleccia, J. (2013, January 30). Sterile Drugs Often Contaminated, Pharmacists Admit. *NBC News*.

[14] Eisler, P. (2012, December 28). Dirty Medical Needles Put Tens of Thousands at Risk in USA. *USA Today*.

[15] *Ibid*.

[16] Dreazen, Y. (2011, August 12). Army Suicides Rise to Record Levels in July. *National Journal*.

[17] Luo, F., Florence, C., Quispe-Agnoli, M., & Ouyang, L. (2011). Impact of Business Cycles on US Suicide Rates, 1928-2007. *American Journal of Public Health*.

[18] Salles, A. (2011, June 27). The Greek Mental-health Crisis: As Economy Implodes, Depression and Suicide Rates Soar. *Time*.

[19] Enserink, M. (2011, November 23). Scientists Brace for Media Storm Around Controversial Flu Studies. Science Insider.

[20] See endnote 12.

[21] Goodman , M. (2011). Attacking the Human Genome: Biological-based Crimes. Future Crimes.

[22] Lloyd, R. (2011, October 16). Drug-resistant Staph Infections in Europe Could Mark Start of a New Epidemic. *Scientific American*.

[23] Eisler, P. (2012, November 29). Deadly 'Superbugs' Invade U.S. Health Care Facilities. *USA Today*.

[24] Gustafson, R., & Bowen, R. (1997). Antibiotic Use in Animal Agriculture. *Journal of Applied Microbiology*.

[25] Hume, M. E. USDA, Agricultural Research Service, (2011). Food Safety Symposium: Potential Impact of Reduced Antibiotic Use and The Roles of Prebiotics, Probiotics, and Other Alternatives in Antibiotic-free Broiler Production.

Chapter 54

Regional Trends in Social Mood Regulate Local Risks of Epidemics

Alan Hall

February 27, 2015 (TS)

Complacency Revived Measles in the U.S.

We reminded readers of measles' resurgence in the August 2014 issue.[1] Three months later, measles erupted in Disneyland and then spread from California to at least 17 other states and Washington DC.[2] The outbreak captured the media's attention, sparking vaccination arguments among potential candidates in the 2016 presidential race. The outbreak reminded us not to underestimate this potentially fatal disease. Dr. Tom Frieden, director of the CDC, said in December that measles is the "most infectious of all infectious diseases."[3]

In the May 2009 issue, we observed that complacency gave measles a foot in the door:

> As recently as 2000, public health officials said measles had been eradicated from the United States, but in 2008, cases resurged to their highest level since 1996. The CDC's most recent U.S. data (through July 31, 2008) show a 68% increase over the number of measles cases reported in all of 2007. The recent "unprecedented" measles outbreak in the U.S., along with similar outbreaks in Switzerland, U.K, Australia, and Vietnam, were fueled by complacency, reduced funding, and importation via travel and immigration—all symptoms of the peak in positive social mood that augured a major trend change.[4]

Figure 1 plots a decade of Google's relative search volume for the term "measles." Searches went ballistic in January 2015, as coverage of the outbreak saturated major media outlets. Reactive fear is a type of societal

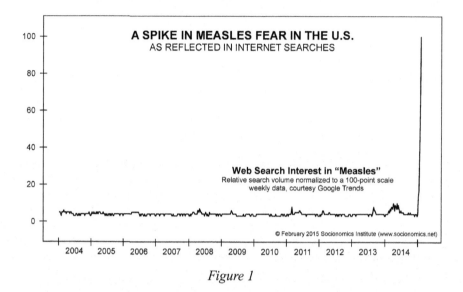

Figure 1

immune response that has enhanced human survival for millennia. The trick is to know when fear is warranted and when it is not. Socionomics and a historical perspective can help.

So far this year, measles has infected only 154 people in the United States.[5] That's a small number in a nation of over 300 million people. It is also small relative to the roughly half-million annual cases documented at the height of the disease's severity in 1958-1960.[6] It is also small relative to the outbreak of 383 cases[7] that began in rural Ohio in the spring of 2014,[8] just months before the Disneyland outbreak. If infections continue at the current rate, they will exceed 2014's total of 644 cases, which was the largest number since measles elimination was declared in the U.S., right at the all-time highest valuation for stock dividends in the year 2000.[9]

So, what are the chances that measles will become a serious epidemic in the U.S. now? We should remember that with infectious disease, almost anything is *possible*. A sufficiently virulent pathogen can overwhelm society's defenses at any time. For example, Asian flu erupted in 1957, a time of relatively positive mood.

But what development is *probable*? As our studies have shown, the most serious epidemics over the past three centuries have tended to come late in major trends toward negative social mood, which impel pessimistic psychology and declines in stock markets as well as increases in economic and social stress, which reduce immunity.

Socionomic theory suggests that a major measles epidemic—or any major epidemic—is unlikely in the U.S. at the current time, because the Dow has rallied strongly for the past six years and stands at an all-time high. Social mood and economic conditions are far more positive than in 2009 when we wrote, "Financial and social stress is reaching levels that most people alive today have never experienced." Much of that pressure is off. We also observe irony in that a positive-mood condition of complacency—like that of 2000—has led to an anti-vaccination movement, which has allowed the measles virus to find small clusters of unvaccinated people.

The same goes for Germany, where a measles outbreak has accompanied all-time highs in its stock market.[10] If U.S. and German stocks continue higher, we expect the current level of measles outbreaks and measles fear to lessen, and vice versa.

A Brief Bout of Negative Social Mood in 2014 Amplified the U.S. Ebola Panic

Measles headlines have been mild compared to last year's Ebola headlines, which carried more than a whiff of panic. On October 15, 2014, the second American nurse to test positive for Ebola violated infection protocol and flew on a commercial jetliner to Dallas. Over the next two days, Ebola fear in the U.S. reached fever pitch. CBS News reported, "Ebola panic spreading much faster than disease in U.S."[11] *The Washington Post* published a headline, "Stop the Ebola panic."[12] *Foreign Policy* advised, "Don't Blame CNN for the Ebola Panic."[13] Politicians called for mandatory quarantines, an idea that was lampooned in a cartoon from the *Los Angeles Times*.[14]

Was the frenzy of concern surrounding Ebola a rational response to the developing news, or did negative social mood amplify the fear? Figure 2 plots the DJIA versus Google's relative search volume for the term "Ebola," a measure of the public's fear of the disease. The two peaks in Ebola searches occurred in the weeks of August 3-9 and October 12-18. The coincident lows in the DJIA were August 7 and October 16, a perfect match.

The latter date happens to be the day I flew to Miami to present the socionomic view of epidemic disease to Harry Dent's Irrational Economic Summit. You might say I had the miasmatic wind at my back. The next morning, near the peak of the Ebola panic, I dramatized the public's outsized concern by walking onstage in a hazmat suit. (See photo insert in Figure 2.)

Ebola fear in the U.S. crystallized precisely at the two stock market lows and quickly dissipated as stock prices recovered. Afterward, the lesser

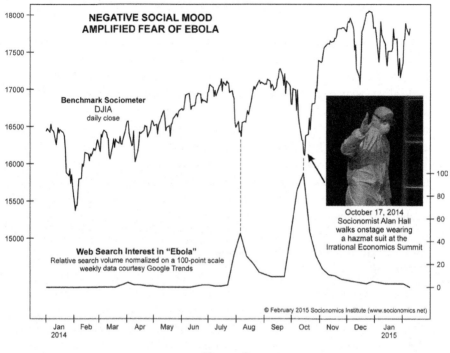

Figure 2

measles story captured the public's interest during the higher-level correction from late December through January.

Trends toward negative social mood generate amorphous feelings of fear in human minds, prompting people to search for a justifying referent. To that end, they will focus on whatever potentially scary news is at hand. The stories about Ebola and measles fit the bill during these recent minor setbacks in our benchmark sociometer. When social mood becomes deeply negative, subjectively generated fear becomes debilitating and leads to adverse health consequences, which are objectively quite frightening.

Six Years of Negative Mood in West Africa Paved the Way for the Ebola Outbreak

Figure 3 updates the Ebola chart from the August 2014 issue.[15] It plots the benchmark West African stock index against monthly Ebola cases and death totals to show that region's social mood trends relative to the timing of the epidemic.

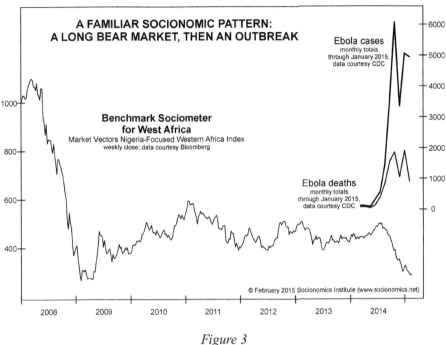

Figure 3

The recent Ebola outbreak has not formed a single peak-and-decline as did the classic epidemics and financial manias [see examples in Chapters 52 and 66]. Rather, the graphs of Ebola cases and deaths so far display a double top as social mood has continued to wax more negative.

Unlike the measles virus, which lives only in human hosts and could therefore theoretically be eliminated, the Ebola virus inhabits animals such as bats, chimpanzees and gorillas. This means it will be difficult if not impossible to eradicate. It is likely to recur. The question is: when?

Key Factors: Social Mood and Seasonality

As we wrote in 2009, "Social mood is never the only factor in a pandemic; but it is a precipitating one." Other factors [see Figure 4 in Chapter 52] include seasonal weather patterns.

In a September 2014 paper, researchers studied a 38-year history of Ebola outbreaks in Africa and found that there were more outbreaks during periods of lower temperatures and greater absolute humidity.[16] If cooler and wetter weather creates conditions conducive to the spread of Ebola, then West Africa's rainy season of May through October represents the next period of heightened seasonal risk for Ebola resurgence.[17] But seasonality describes only one aspect of a disease's tendency to spread. A positive trend in social mood can mitigate that risk.

The recent new low in West Africa's sociometer (see Figure 3) suggest that it is far too early to declare victory over Ebola in that region. If social mood and conditions on the ground do not significantly improve, the potential for another wave of Ebola cases and deaths during the rainy season will be serious. The same goes for other areas where the disease is endemic and social mood is negative.

NOTES AND REFERENCES

[1] Hall, A. (2014, August). Ebola: A Socionomic Booster Shot. *The Socionomist.*

[2] Thompson, D. (2015, February 17). Measles Cases Continue to Rise Across the U.S. WebMD.

[3] Frieden, T. (2013, December 5). The Most Infectious of All Infectious Diseases. CNN.

[4] Hall, A. (2009, May). A Socionomic View of Epidemic Disease: A Looming Season of Susceptibility. Part 1: Epidemics, Markets and a Model Crisis. *The Socionomist.*

[5] 2015 Measles Cases in the U.S. (January 1 to February 20, 2015). Centers for Disease Control and Prevention.

[6] McLean, H.Q., Fiebelkorn, A.P., Temte, J.L., & Wallace, G.S. (2013, June 14). Prevention of Measles, Rubella, Congenital Rubella Syndrome, and Mumps, 2013: Summary Recommendations of the Advisory Committee on Immunization Practices (ACIP). Center for Disease Control and Prevention.

[7] Same as endnote 5.

[8] Tribble, S.J. (2014, June 24). Measles Outbreak in Ohio Leads Amish to Reconsider Vaccines. NPR.

[9] Same as endnote 5.

[10] Moulson, G. (2015, February 24). Toddler Dies of Measles in Berlin, First Death in More Than 570 Cases in German Capital. *U.S. News & World Report.*

[11] Evans, C. (2014, October 18). Ebola Panic Spreading Much Faster Than Disease in U.S. CBS Evening News.

[12] Capehart, J. (2014, October 17). Stop the Ebola Panic. *The Washington Post.*

[13] Leetaru, K. (2014, October 24). Don't Blame CNN for the Ebola Panic. *Foreign Policy.*

[14] Horsey, D. (2014, November 3). Politicians Stoking Ebola Fears are a Bigger Threat Than the Disease. *Los Angeles Times.*

[15] Same as endnote 1.

[16] Ng, S., & Cowling, B.J. (2014). Association Between Temperature, Humidity and Ebolavirus Disease Outbreaks in Africa, 1976 to 2014. Eurosurveillance 19(35).

[17] Average Monthly Temperature and Rainfall for Sierra Leone From 1960-1990. Climate change knowledge portal.

Chapter 55

Disease Erupts after Seven Years of Negative Mood in Brazil

Alan Hall

December 30, 2015 (TS)

Socionomic theory proposes that long trends toward negative social mood produce a number of conditions that make society increasingly susceptible to infectious disease. Figure 1 shows a history of Brazil's social mood as reflected by its Bovespa Index, which topped in 2008, rallied to a lower high in 2010 and has steadily trended lower since. It would be hard to find a better article inadvertently linking disease to negative mood than

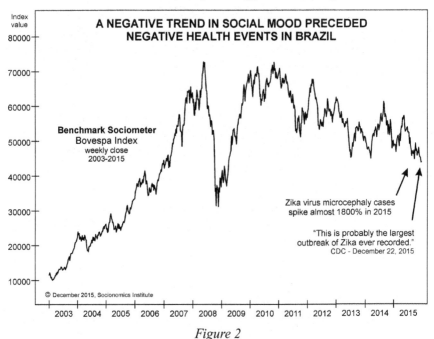

Figure 2

"Spreading Virus Adds to Brazil's Woes," which appeared in the December 22 issue of *The Wall Street Journal*. The article discusses the Zika virus, a mosquito-borne pathogen for which there is no vaccine. It has been around since the 1940s and is now spreading rapidly in Brazil. It has been linked to "an explosion of cases of microcephaly, an extremely rare condition in which babies are born with shrunken skulls because their brains aren't growing properly."[1] Microcephaly cases surged from 147 in 2014 to 2,782 so far in 2015.

Brazil's mosquito population has surged in recent years. The mosquito species that transmit Zika also transmit dengue and chikungunya, diseases that continue to spread in the Americas. *The New York Times* reported, "At least 839 people have died from dengue in Brazil this year, an 80 percent increase from the previous year."[2]

One lesson from our 2009 study [Chapter 52] is that hygiene is related to infrastructure maintenance, and infrastructure maintenance gets neglected in times of negative social mood. Today, negative mood in Brazil is fostering unsanitary conditions, which pose health threats. Authorities are scrambling to "drain water-logged areas and search out and eradicate larvae-filled water supplies." Former state health secretary Dr. Osmar Terra said he "believes Brazil could have as many as 100,000 cases of infection in 2016 if emergency measures aren't taken soon." He based his projections on the handling of the outbreak of the H1N1 virus in 2009. "This is an unprecedented human tragedy," said Dr. Terra, who recommended "a crisis cabinet" to deal with the situation.

Scandals are another feature of negative mood trends. As the article reported,

> With the country mired in its worst economic crisis since the Great Depression and the nation's capital transfixed by a massive corruption scandal and impeachment proceeding against President Dilma Rousseff, some worry that the nation isn't mobilizing fast enough to battle the quick-moving epidemic.

Social mood has so many effects that it is a task to cite them all.

NOTES

[1] Johnson, R., Jelmayer, R., & McKay. B. (2015, December 22). Spreading Virus Adds to Brazil's Woes. *The Wall Street Journal*.

[2] Romero, S. (2015, December 30). Alarm Spreads in Brazil Over a Virus and a Surge in Malformed Infants. *The New York Times*.

Chapter 56

Malaria Erupts in Venezuela
in Accordance with Socionomic Causality

Alan Hall

August 29, 2016 (TS)

Inaugural issues of *The Socionomist* in May and June 2009[1] warned of a looming increase in the prevalence of infectious diseases, including mosquito-borne diseases, in countries suffering from negative social mood. Seven years later, the August 2016 issue reported,

> Some of this prediction has come to pass, and the rest seems more likely each day. A February 2016 *Lancet* article said, "The early part of the 21st century has seen an unparalleled number of emerging infectious disease events.... So many in fact that perhaps we should no longer consider them extraordinary."[2,3]

A recent article in *The Wall Street Journal* tells the same story:

> [T]here is a new normal, seen in the intense, rapid-fire cycle of H1N1 in 2009, MERS in 2012, Ebola in 2014, the reemergence of yellow fever, and Zika. Global epidemics are shifting from rare, historical events to be more like recurring dangers such as hurricanes or tornados.[4]

All of these outbreaks occurred in countries experiencing negative social mood.

Today, mosquito-borne diseases are re-erupting in areas experiencing negative mood. These threats should be on your radar.

In Venezuela, a large-degree trend toward negative mood has produced conditions that have encouraged an ancient plague—malaria—to resurge. On August 15, *The New York Times* published an article titled "Hard Times in Venezuela Breed Malaria as Desperate Flock to Mines." Compelling photos in the article depict the classic negative-mood conditions that have attended many past outbreaks. The article explains why "at least 70,000 people," including many former white-collar workers, now dig for gold in stagnant puddles teeming with malarial mosquitoes:

> [Venezuela] is a society turned upside down, a place where educated people abandon once-comfortable jobs in the city for dangerous, backbreaking work in muddy pits, desperate to make ends meet. And it comes with a steep price: Malaria, long driven to the fringes of the country, is festering in the mines and back with a vengeance.... With the economy in tatters, at least 70,000 people from all walks of life have been streaming into this mining region over the past year.... As they hunt for gold in watery pits, the perfect breeding ground for the mosquitoes that spread the disease, they are catching malaria by the tens of thousands. Then, with the disease in their blood, they return home to Venezuela's cities. But because of the economic collapse, there is often no medicine and little fumigation to prevent mosquitoes there from biting them and passing malaria to others, sickening tens of thousands more people and leaving entire towns desperate for help.[5]

Venezuela's government denies there is a malaria crisis, yet local doctors confirm that cases increased by 72% in the first six months of 2016. Sadly, while the disease is easily treatable with the proper medications, they are unavailable because of the economic collapse and social chaos. Even sadder, Venezuela "was the first nation in the world to be certified by the World Health Organization for eradicating malaria in its most populated areas, beating the United States and other developed countries to that milestone in 1961."[6] The *Times* article elaborated on Venezuela's role reversal and quoted a Brazilian malaria expert:

> Venezuela once trained people throughout the region in malaria prevention. But Venezuela's inability to contain its own outbreak means that it now plays the opposite role: It poses a threat to the countries around it, particularly Brazil, where there are also illegal gold mines. "It's starting to spill over into neighboring countries...."[7]

The trends in Venezuela's social mood are clear in Figure 1, which plots the Caracas Stock Market Index (IBVC) adjusted for inflation via the International Monetary Fund's (IMF) Venezuela Consumer Price Index (CPI). The IMF's CPI data extend only through December 2015, so, we used the IMF's forecast for inflation to increase by 481% in 2016 to produce the remainder of the line extending to the present.

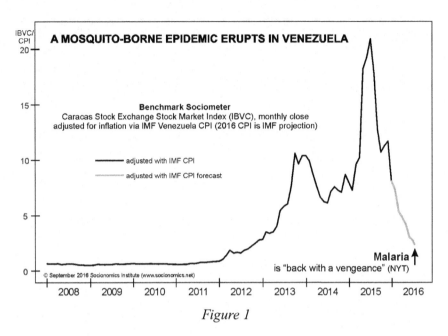

Figure 1

The stunning decline of 2015-2016 to date indicates a social mood that is sufficiently negative to produce adverse public health outcomes. An economist said, "Venezuela is experiencing a very severe economic crisis.... This is not a recession, this is a depression."[8] Malaria, a stock market in freefall, a crumbling economy and pervasive fear are just four among many symptoms of negative social mood in Venezuela. A July 27 CNN article described several others on display in Caracas, the nation's capital:

> Corpses pile up, sometimes for months, at the Bello Monte morgue.... With so many homicide victims arriving every day, the morgue staff can't keep up.... Statistics show Caracas has become one of the most dangerous places in the world.... The chaos is yet another example of societal crumbling in Venezuela, which has been plagued in recent months by unrest, violent crime and shortages of food and electricity.... The resulting indignities and the degradation of humanity are something that have historically been reserved for countries ravaged by war.... "Everybody lives in fear in Venezuela—the poor, the middle class, the rich...."[9]

Look for all these symptoms of negative social mood to dissipate after the IBVC bottoms.

NOTES AND REFERENCES

[1] Hall, A. (2009, May/June). A Socionomic View of Epidemic Disease, Parts I and II. *The Socionomist.*

[2] Hall, A. (2016, August). Still Early in a Season of Susceptibility. *The Socionomist.*

[3] Solomon, T., Baylis, M., & Brown, D. (2016). Zika Virus and Neurological Disease—Approaches to the Unknown. *The Lancet Infectious Diseases,* 16(4), 402-404.

[4] Klain, R. (2016, July 25). Zika Funding: What if Political Gridlock Isn't Why Congress Hasn't Acted. *The Wall Street Journal.*

[5] Casey, N. (2016, August 15). Hard Times in Venezuela Breed Malaria as Desperate Flock to Mines. *The New York Times.*

[6,7] *Ibid.*

[8] Gillespie, P. (2016, April 12). Venezuela: The Land of 500% Inflation. *CNN Money.*

[9] Newton, P. (2016, July 27). Even at the Morgue, Venezuelan Society Unravels. *CNN World.*

Chapter 57

Epidemics in Serial Murder:
Social Mood and Decisions to Kill

Robert Prechter and John Whitney

October 15, 2004 / June 13, 2005 (EWT)

What do Richard Speck, Charles Manson, the Zodiac Killer, John Wayne Gacy, Ted Bundy, David Berkowitz, Jim Jones, Wayne Williams and Gary Ridgway have in common? They are all famous U.S. serial killers who struck during the period of negative social mood lasting from February 1966 to August 1982 as indicated by a bear market in the Dow/PPI over that time.

On July 13-14, 1966, Richard Speck killed 8 nurses in a single night in Chicago. In August 1969, during a sharp decline in stocks following the all-time high in the Value Line Composite index in December 1968, Charles Manson and his followers planned and committed the murder of 7 people in Beverly Hills over two consecutive nights. They had killed once before and were planning more murders. The Zodiac Killer dispatched an estimated 17 to 43 people in the San Francisco area; he began his spree in October 1966, the month of the stock market bottom that year, and continued until 1971, 1974 or 1981 (estimates vary) and was never apprehended. John Wayne Gacy tortured a man in 1968; between January 1972 and December 1978, mostly in the final three years, he tortured and murdered 33 people. Beginning in 1973, at the start of the largest decline in the S&P since 1937-1942, Ted Bundy began a spree, killing an estimated 36 people through February 1978, the month that the DJIA made a daily closing low that has not been exceeded on the downside to this day. David Berkowitz, a.k.a. the Son of Sam, attacked 15 people and killed 6 between December 1975 and August 1977. On November 18, 1978, right at the bottom of what Wall Streeters called the stock market "massacre" of that year, Jim Jones massacred 914 of his followers at Jonestown, Guyana. From 1979 through May 1981, Wayne Williams murdered at least 23 people, mostly children, in Atlanta, Georgia. Gary Ridgway began killing prostitutes on July 8,

1982, one month before the final bottom in the Dow/PPI, and set a record of 48 murders. He voluntarily ended his spree in 1984, the year that stock and bond market sentiment readings registered levels of pessimism nearly equal to those of 1982.

As social mood trended positively thereafter, there were no similarly high-profile serial killings until social mood turned negative from August 1987 to October 1990, producing a classically patterned bear market in the Value Line Industrials [see Figure 3 in Chapter 41 of *The Socionomic Theory of Finance*]. Jeffrey Dahmer had killed just once, in June 1978, in the middle of the 1966-1982 bear market. He killed no one for the next nine years, throughout the rising trend in stocks that topped out in August 1987. The very next month, he began a spree of capturing, killing, dismembering and eating 15 people. (Reflecting the mood of the times, the serial killer/cannibal movie *Silence of the Lambs* won an Oscar in 1990.) Dahmer was captured in July 1991, six months after the bear market ended. Gary Ridgway came out of "retirement" and killed another person in 1990 as the Value Line Industrials broke below their 1987 low. Aileen Wuornos killed 7 people in Florida from December 1989 to November 1990, the month after that period's extreme in negative social mood. (In an interesting coda, a

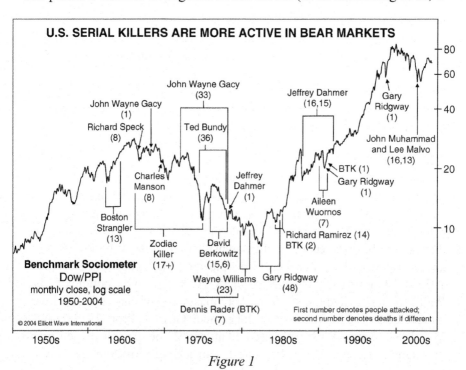

Figure 1

depressed Wuornos requested and was granted execution in October 2002, the month of the next social mood nadir as the S&P bottomed after a 2½-year bear market.)

As social mood resumed its positive trend for the rest of the 1990s, there were few similarly high-profile serial killings. Ted Kaczynski, the Unabomber, was an exception, as he mailed bombs for 18 years through bull and bear markets alike, although his exploits began in 1978, during the negative mood period, as is the case with every serial killer shown in Figure 1. Gary Ridgway returned to kill one person in 1998, when the stock market suffered a brief but sharp setback. There were some lesser killings and also some massacres during the 1991-2000 bull market, such as at Waco in 1993 and Oklahoma City in 1995, although they were committed near the end of the multi-year period of financial pessimism (see Figure 1 in Chapter 12) and economic weakness (see Figure 4-7 of *Beautiful Pictures*) that lagged the bear market bottom of 1990. The massacre at Columbine High School in 1999 was anomalous, although the Value Line Composite index had passed its peak a year earlier. [For more on this topic, see Chapter 60.]

On the very day of the stock market low of September 2001, after the ensuing shift toward negative social mood had been underway for a year and a half, a domestic terrorist began mailing deadly anthrax spores to U.S. citizens. When stocks reached a peak in early 2002, he stopped. [See Figure 10 in Chapter 1 *The Socionomic Theory of Finance*.] As the negative mood trend entered its final months in September-October 2002, Lee Boyd Malvo and John Allen Muhammad conducted a sniping spree in the eastern U.S., shooting 16 people, killing 13. On October 2 and 3, just a week ahead of the low of October 9, 2002, they killed six people in two days.

From reading the histories of these acts, we find three things that most serial killers have in common: (1) they are alcoholics or drug addicts, (2) they have served in the armed forces, and (3) their impulses are activated in periods of increasingly negative social mood, as indicated by a falling stock market. This latter observation is new and useful information.

Most serial killers begin taking action during periods of negative social mood. It is difficult to be sure about when they would naturally cease their activities, because most serial killers are apprehended. But it appears that their actions follow a profile similar to that of lagging sociometers such as the economy [see *Socionomic Theory of Finance*] and wars [see *Socionomic Causality in Politics*]. Generally speaking, our data show that high-profile killing sprees tend to end a year or two after extremes in negative social mood, as represented by bottoms in stock prices. As an additional example, the Boston Strangler began murdering people in June 1962, as the stock market was crashing in a climate of negative mood. He killed his 13th and final victim in January 1964 as the stock market was rising in a climate of positive social mood. A most instructive case is that of Gary Ridgway, who sprung into action at the very bottom of the 16-year trend toward negative social mood, continued until the first setback in the new bull market ended two years later, and then retired except for a couple of single murders during smaller stock market declines. This is further circumstantial evidence that social mood influences the actions of serial killers.

Serial killings—as with many massacres and assassinations—are attacks not on individuals (as in crimes of passion) but on society, by targeting random people, members of specific groups or public representatives. The impersonal, social aspect of these crimes places them under the purview of socionomics.

Not all serial killings occur during or shortly after bear markets in stocks. But preliminary evidence suggests that the pressures of a negative trend or condition in social mood may be part of the reason that many serial killers act when they do or at least when their acts become high-profile events in society. It would be useful to conduct a rigorous statistical study to test this hypothesis. If the hypothesis is borne out, socionomics could help those who are in the role of protecting the public by alerting them to times during which violent actions, including serial killings, are more or less likely.

Serial Killers Redux

The October 2004 issue of *The Elliott Wave Theorist* proposed a link between trends in social mood and the activity and/or publicity of serial killers. Subscriber John Whitney contacted our Message Board to recall an email that he had sent its editor a year ago, proposing almost exactly what my essay discussed. I am printing his email in full to show that socionomics changes the way people think and leads naturally to certain paths of inquiry. I turned over the Message Board to competent hands back in 2000 and did not see his email (which was never posted), but I am more than happy to credit Mr. Whitney with being the first to come up with this idea. The more readers who offer new ideas for socionomic research the better. Be sure to read Whitney's insightful final paragraph, which poses exactly one of the subtle questions I raised in the report.

From: John Whitney
Date: 10/31/2003
Comments: The latest EWFF discussed parallels with 1969 such as the end of Beatlemania, etc. That brought to mind the infamous Charles Manson murders in August of 1969. As I recall, his bizarre motive was to hasten the downfall of capitalism (which he felt was

imminent and had grown impatient waiting for), from which he (and the Beatles) would emerge as saviors. His twisted actions seemed tuned to the transition from wave III to IV. My mind wandered to other famous serial killers and noticed that their crimes tend to occur during 4th waves of some degree, with an especially large number during the 1970s. Ed Gein 1957. Richard Speck 1966. Ted Bundy 1974-76. John Wayne Gacy 1974-1978. David Berkowitz 1976-1977.

Jeffrey Dahmer killed his first victim in 1978 and then lay dormant until 1987 when he began again, only being caught at the tail end of the recession in 1991 as the bull market was beginning.

Interestingly, there are many who believe that Wayne Williams, the Atlanta child murderer (late 1970s to early 1980s) was not the actual murderer, but the murders stopped after his arrest so he must be guilty. On the other hand, they also stopped with the beginning of the bull market of the early '80s.

I'm wondering if there is any chance that these deranged individuals might be tuned somehow to the underlying wave and find themselves compelled to act out during the unsettled times? Or, is it only that the public's fascination with them is piqued during these periods, propelling them to fame?

By the way, we can add Richard Ramirez, "The Night Stalker" of California, to the serial killers chart for 1984-1985. His first known victim was killed on June 28, 1984, as a six-month setback in stock prices was ending; his last known victim was killed on August 18, 1985, one month prior to Market Vane's report of the lowest percentage of bullish stock market advisors for the entire decade. (Ramirez was captured later in 1985 and charged with 14 murders and 31 other felonies involving rape and robbery.) We can also add Dennis L. Rader, the alleged BTK serial killer, to our list. He murdered seven people and nearly killed an eighth from 1974 to 1979 as social mood trended persistently negatively, then one each in 1985, 1986 and 1991. In a letter to Wichita journalists in October 1974 (the month of the bottom in the S&P), he made up his own code word, BTK, meaning "bind, torture, kill." The BTK killer did not communicate with the public again until March 19, 2004, when he sent a letter to the *Wichita Eagle* newspaper claiming responsibility for the murder of 1986. He was arrested on February 25, 2005, 21 years after his first murder.

There is no mechanistic cause and effect between social mood and the acts of serial murderers. But the evidence is strong that, generally speaking, negative mood *inspires* serial killers.

Chapter 58

Epidemics in Self Destruction

Peter Kendall and Mark Galasiewski

October 1, 2004 (EWFF) / January 17, 2007 (EWT)

Suicide (PK, 2004)

Suicide, literally "self-killing," is the ultimate act of social rebellion, the point at which an individual can no longer tolerate his role within the larger social unit. The most straightforward socionomic relationship would be an inverse correlation in which suicides fell with a positive trend in social mood and rose with a negative one. But some of the data don't support such a linkage. In the 1920s, for instance, suicides rose steadily despite a positive mood trend as evidenced by a roaring bull market in stocks, although they did peak in 1932, right at the extreme in negative mood, when the stock market bottomed. Suicides fell from 1937 to 1942 despite a negative mood whose consequences included a decline in stocks, a recession and a war. As the Dow more than doubled from 1980 to 1986, suicides increased slightly. So, suicide rates are not like their opposite, the act of procreation, which in the U.S. has tended to fluctuate more closely with the stock market.

On the other hand, the dominant tendency exhibited in Figure 1 is an overall decline in the suicide rate since the early 1900s as stock prices have risen. The total of 10.4 suicides per every 100,000 people in 2000 was the lowest since 1961. The lowest level on record is 9.8 in 1957, when the bull market of the 1900s was in a powerful third wave, marking the peak rate of change for the advance. So, on the whole, social mood may have some influence over suicidal impulses.

Although prior to the mid-1980s Japanese suicide data are inconsistent with respect to Japanese stock prices, recent data reflect socionomic causality quite well. Japanese social mood trended negatively as stock prices fell more than 80% over fourteen years to a new bear market low in 2003,

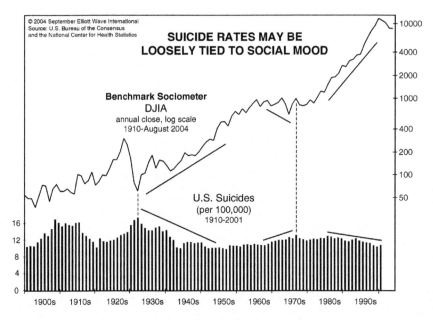

Figure 1

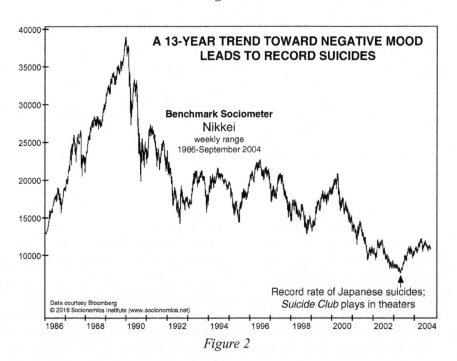

Figure 2

as depicted in Figure 2. That year, Japanese suicides reached 34,427, an average of 94 a day, the highest level ever, with data going back a century. The annual figure was also an all-time high in suicides as a percentage of the population. One could hardly object to calling these statistics evidence of a suicide epidemic. At the bottom in stock prices, a movie called *Suicide Club* played in Tokyo theaters.

Anecdotal evidence from near the end of the 64-year decline in English stock prices from 1720 to 1784 supports the case for a degree of socionomic causality. In 1774, after more than 54 years of a bear market, Johann Wolfgang Von Goethe's novel *The Sorrows of Young Werther*, which ends in the suicide of its protagonist, was a smash hit. According to several sources, it spawned "an epidemic of suicides."

In the wake of the 2000-2003 global bear market, suicide has become an increasingly common hazard of modern-day life. Atlanta recently experienced a spate of attempted suicides in which despondent jumpers positioned themselves atop highway overpasses, bringing traffic to a standstill. Mideast hostilities resumed in late 2000 as the trend of global social mood turned negative, as evidenced by the bear market in the inflation-adjusted World Stock Index [see Figure 5 in Chapter 51]. As part of that dynamic, suicide bombings have become an everyday event. Historically, efforts to gain military or political objectives through self-destruction are almost unheard of. The main precedent is Japanese kamikaze pilots who turned airplanes into guided missiles in the final days of World War II. This is an example of fourth-wave foreshadowing [see Chapter 13], as kamikazes appeared near the end of wave (IV) in the Dow/PPI, and now, 60 years later, Islamic suicide bombers are active.

Suicide has recently become a theme in popular culture. A country song called 'Whiskey Lullaby' tells the story of a dual suicide by drinking: "He/she put the bottle to her/his head and pulled the trigger." For misery, the song beats out the old crying-in-your-beer country hits by a long shot (pun intended). To observe the public's fascination with the song, do a Google search on 'Whiskey Lullaby' lyrics and you will find that Google offers links to 11,000 related sites. Several well-known performers have pretended to kill themselves in music videos. Britney Spears is one, but the death scene in her *Everytime* video was edited out when it came out in March [2004], perhaps due to the influence of a surge in positive mood as evidenced by a one-year advance in the S&P. *Jonestown, The Musical*, a play about the forced suicide of 913 people in Jonestown, Guyana in 1978, made it to the stage in Manhattan in August [2004]. The show was dismissed for being in poor taste, but this type of fare will succeed during times of more negative social mood, when bad taste, mixed morality and complex social issues tend to become entertainment staples.

August 2016 Update: Suicide data for the past quarter century are conforming remarkably well to swings in social mood. Figure 2 extends the data series introduced in Figure 1. It displays a mirror image of trends in suicides and the Dow/PPI since 1989.

Figure 3

Euthanasia (MG, 2007)

Past issues of *The Elliott Wave Theorist* and *The Elliott Wave Financial Forecast* have detailed the fascination with death that increases among the public during periods of negative social mood. Horror movies, suicides and serial killings all tend to increase as social mood turns negative. The debate over euthanasia in the past several decades suggests that negative mood may also raise the public's tolerance for mercy killing. In early 2005, opinions on both sides of the right-to-die debate collided over the case of Terry Schiavo, a brain-damaged, comatose Florida woman who ultimately died after a court ordered her feeding tube removed. One month later, the May 2005 issue of EWFF had this to say about the right-to-die debate:

> In every major stock market decline of the last 30 years, this particular debate has pushed its way to the fore. In the bear market of the 1970s, euthanasia was a prevalent social issue that came to a head with a similarly heated social deliberation over the fate of Karen Ann Quinlan, "the first modern icon of the right-to-die debate." In the wake of the October 1987 stock market crash, the Journal of the American Medical Association printed "It's Over, Debbie," a seminal euthanasia article in which a doctor described his delivery of a lethal injection to a dying cancer patient. In 1990, the year of another major correction, Jack Kevorkian burst onto the scene. The physician known as Dr. Death assisted in the suicide of a middle-aged woman with Alzheimer's. He continued his calling through the early 1990s, but as the bull market wore on, public interest in his exploits faded. In 1999, as the bull market was approaching its peak, he was convicted of murder. At this point, he is largely forgotten, but as the bear market intensifies, the right-to-die forces will make headway. Look for Dr. Death or some other champion of the fatally ill to emerge from oblivion.

Currently, only four governments permit euthanasia. Figure 4 shows that each of them legalized the practice near the end of a major shift toward negative social mood. (Given the lack of stock market data in many European countries prior to 1950, we use the S&P Composite index as a sociometer.) Switzerland legalized the practice in 1942 at the bottom of the 1937-1942

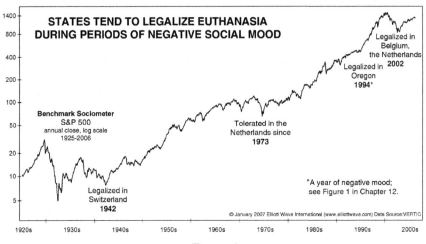

Figure 4

bear market. Courts in the Netherlands tolerated the practice starting in 1973, near the end of the 1966-1974 bear market. Oregon permitted mercy killing in 1994, the final year that financial pessimism reigned in the early 1990s [as depicted in Figure 1 in Chapter 12]. In 2002, as world stock markets neared the low of a three-year decline, the Netherlands officially granted its citizens the right to die, and Belgium followed suit several months later. Though these examples do not constitute a conclusive correlation, they fit socionomic theory.

Post-production update: Mixed social mood in the U.S., as implied by the bear market rally in Dow/gold, has produced mixed feelings about euthanasia. On February 20, 2017, Washington D.C. followed in the footsteps of five left-leaning states in passing a law allowing physician-assisted suicide. But on July 13, the federal Appropriations Committee voted in favor of a measure that, if passed by Congress, will repeal the law in the district it oversees.

Chapter 59

Murder and Mood

Kenneth R. Olson, Ph.D.

July 5, 2009 (TS)

Negative social mood spurs feelings of anger. Murder is usually an expression of anger, which often spurs an urge to destroy. From a socionomic perspective, it seems reasonable to expect murder rates to rise during periods of negative social mood and fall during periods of positive social mood.

An analysis of trends in the annual murder rate from 1942 to 2007[1] accords with that idea. The strong bull market of 1942-1966 in the PPI-adjusted DJIA saw a falling murder rate. Then the rate soared during the bear market from 1966-1982. During the bull market of 1982-2000, the

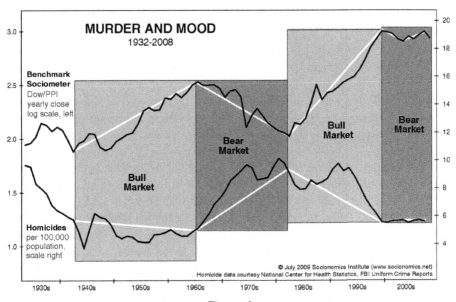

Figure 1

murder rate declined, and there is even an upward interruption in 1987-1992 as the stock market underwent a Primary-degree correction that led to a recession and subsequent heavy job layoffs. When a bear market started in 2000, the decline abruptly ceased and has since been flat. The two sets of fluctuations have moved inversely.

It seems we can now add murder rates to the list of social behaviors that appear to be socionomically influenced. We will see if subsequent data continue to bear out this thesis.

[*Update*: The relationship described above continued to hold over the next seven years of reported data. The flat trend ended in 2008, after which the murder rate fell into 2014 as stock prices soared persistently to new highs. A slight uptick in the 2015 rate fit the stock market's sharp setback that year, which carried into February 2016.—Ed.]

Dr. Ken Olson is professor of psychology at Ft. Hays State University and a contributor to The Socionomic Theory of Finance (2016).

NOTES AND REFERENCES

[1] Murder rate data from the FBI Uniform Crime Reports is used for the years 1950-2007. Pre-1950 homicide data are from the National Center for Health Statistics. The NCHS has data back to 1900, but David McDowall notes in a 2002 Criminology article that these statistics "did not fully cover the nation until 1933." Prof. Ted R. Gurr explains in his book, Violence in America, that U.S. homicide data from the early 20th century can be unreliable. For example, he writes, "Many American police forces treated the fatalities of the auto age as homicides." Due to these concerns, the analysis in this report begins in 1942 at the beginning of the first full Cycle wave in which we are reasonably confident in the data's accuracy.

Chapter 60

Social Mood Regulates Incidences of
Multiple Shootings

Alan Hall
August 23, 2012 (TS)

"Random, multiple-victim shootings make society angry and fearful."
Most people would agree with that statement. But as you are about to see,
new data posit a radical re-ordering of the idea as follows: "An angry and
fearful society is more likely to suffer random, multiple-victim shootings."

As multiple-victim shootings increased in the United States over the
past year, pundits blamed Hollywood, violence-enamored culture and easy
access to guns.

We found data that argue otherwise. Figure 1 shows the NYSE Composite Index—a broad measure of over 2000 stocks—plotted against all
the data compiled by the Brady Campaign to End Gun Violence, a gun-
regulation advocacy group.[1] We carefully examined the data and found two
duplicate entries. After deleting them, we added the August 5 Sikh Temple
attack and the August 13 Texas A&M shooting. We indexed the list and
graphed the daily sum of people killed and wounded in the 432 multiple-
victim shooting incidents since 2005. Finally, we smoothed the graph using
a 40-day moving average.

Social mood trends divide the chart into four main sections, two of
them positive (no shading) and two of them negative (shaded gray). The
chart suggests a strong connection between the trends in social mood, as
indicated by trends in the stock market, and multiple-victim shootings.

Note how closely the shooting data follow the trends in our sociometer. Multiple-victim shootings produced few casualties during most of the
2005-2007 advance in stock prices. As stock prices fell from 2007 to 2009,
the number of victims trended markedly higher. The numbers peaked just
one month after the March 2009 low in stocks. Shootings remained high
for the rest of 2009, lagging in the same fashion as other expressions of

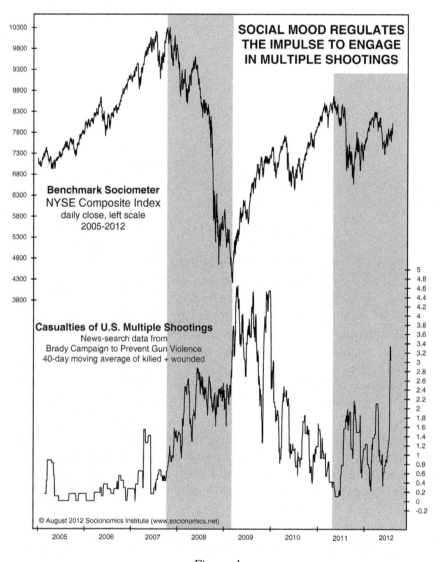

Figure 1

social mood, such as economic statistics and incidents of political unrest. [See Chapter 8 in *The Socionomic Theory of Finance*, Chapters 30 and 31 in *Socionomic Causality in Politics* and Chapter 6 in this book.] As mood continued its positive trend, multiple-victim shooting casualties trended lower, bottoming just a month after the May 2011 stock market peak.

Without the benefit of the socionomic insight, this chart would seem to graph unrelated social activities—stock market fluctuations and multiple-victim shootings—moving in near-parallel trends for no apparent reason. Instead, with the socionomic insight, the chart provides evidence that a third factor—unconscious social mood—drives both data series.

Exogenous vs. Endogenous Cause

Columnist Peggy Noonan wrote about the Aurora shootings in the July 27 [2012] issue of *The Wall Street Journal*:

> [There] are unstable people among us, and they are less defended against dark cultural messages. The borders of the minds of the unstable are more porous. They let the darkness in. You can go to a horror movie and be entertained or amused: "This is scary, I love getting scared, and I love it because I know it isn't real." But the unstable are not entertained by darkness. They let it in. They are inspired by it.[2]

Ms. Noonan went on to blame Hollywood for the shootings and to call for regulations on guns. Yet, mass killers have been around for centuries without movies to inspire them. They find their inspiration and opportunity not in external events but in the prevailing social mood of the time. Dennis Elam, a professor at Texas A&M University and a contributor to *The Socionomist*, explained it well in his response to Noonan's article published in *The Wall Street Journal*:

> Ms. Noonan has the causality reversed.... Her theme is that Hollywood has caused moviegoers to seek the negative side of humanity. But is it possible that people with negative moods seek dark-themed entertainment?...audiences are no longer interested in Jack Nicholson's version of the Joker. His garish, comic figure was in tune with the mood of 1989. Ditto for Dustin Hoffman's Captain Hook in 1991. Both villainous characters appeared during an upbeat social mood from 1984 to 2000.... But Heath Ledger's character [in] "The Dark Knight," tag line "The City Has No Hope" (2008), was all too emblematic of what was about to happen world-wide. Now we have unrest and violence from Syria to Afghanistan, Europe staggers under its social contract and the U.S. is mired in the slowest recovery in decades. Art imitates life rather than drives it.[3]

While many multiple shootings have involved drugs, alcohol, mental illness and/or handy guns, the most notorious and deadly multiple shooters seem to have a "me against the world" mentality. This is an extreme, individual expression of the "us against them" polarization that grips society during large-degree trends toward negative social mood. Norway's Anders Behring Breivik, who said he killed 77 people last year for the purpose of saving his native country from multiculturalism, consciously stated this very motivation.

NOTES AND REFERENCES

[1] Abelson, B., & Keller, M. "Interactive Map: The U.S. Shooting Epidemic." *The Daily Beast.*

[2] Noonan, P. (2012, July 27). "Noonan: The Dark Knight Rises." *The Wall Street Journal.*

[3] Dennis Elam, comment, "Noonan: The Dark Knight Rises." *The Wall Street Journal.*

Chapter 61

Do Australian Bushfires
Have a Socionomic Cause?

Mark Galasiewski

February 27, 2009 (APFF)

Massive bushfires erupted across the Australian state of Victoria in February, resulting in more than 200 deaths. It was Australia's largest loss of life from such an episode. Socionomics provides an interesting perspective on the tragedy, showing that there appears to be a relationship between bushfires in Australia and periods of negative social mood as revealed by bear markets in Australian stocks.

Because humans cause nearly 90% of wildfires (the other 10%, according to the U.S. National Wildfire Coordinating Group, are caused by lightning), we are afforded another chance to test our socionomic hypothesis, which says that positive social mood inspires acts of construction whereas negative social mood inspires acts of destruction. If that's true, then we might expect to find a correlation between Australia's benchmark sociometer and the incidence of deliberately set wildfires.

Figure 1 shows that all eight of Australia's largest bushfires occurred during or shortly after major declines in Australia's All Ordinaries stock index. Not every period of negative mood was followed by a major bushfire, but every major bushfire was preceded by a period of negative mood. The Red Tuesday fires of 1898 and the bushfires of 1944 occurred early in new positive mood periods, after what appear to be small second waves in the stock market. That is when—as *Elliott Wave Principle* first proposed in 1978—pessimism, borne of negative social mood, returns nearly to the extreme of the preceding bottom.

A historic heat wave—the hottest since 1859, when Australia began keeping records—preceded the February 2009 bushfires. Dry conditions are a major factor in wildfires, but the mix of dry conditions and negative social

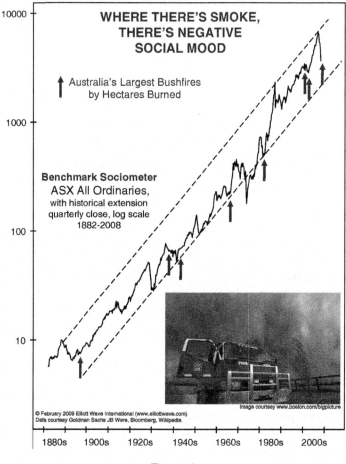

Figure 1

mood appears to have been particularly incendiary this time. Investigators believe that arson was involved in at least some of the fires, and they have arrested suspects. Australia's Prime Minister, Kevin Rudd called the events "mass murder." It seems likely that individuals who deliberately light fires with intent to harm are in a deeply negative mood.

[Global stock prices bottomed just a few days later, in early March, 2009.—Ed.]

Part VIII:

FASHIONS AND PASSIONS

Chapter 62

A Two-Century Strut Down the Catwalk: From Bear Market to Just Plain Bare

Peter Kendall

January 29, 2015 (TS)

In a fascinating video (posted at socionomics.net/skirts), Peter Kendall surveyed more than a century of fashion history to reveal the ubiquitous influence of social mood on hemline heights. This chapter is an edited transcript.—Ed.

Stocks and Skirts: Watch as Peter Kendall explores the connection between social mood trends and hemline heights. Visit www.socionomics.net/skirts. Photo by Jose Goulao.

Wall Street's renowned "hemline indicator" observes that women's hemlines rise and fall with the stock market. University of Pennsylvania economist George Taylor first made the connection between hemlines and stocks in 1926, and market analyst Ralph Rotnem helped to popularize the relationship in the 1960s. Paul Montgomery expanded its scope in the 1990s. Robert Prechter evoked this indicator as far back as 1985 and proposed a basis for its psychological importance. He wrote,

> In my judgment, it is not unreasonable to hypothesize that a rise in both hemlines and stock prices reflects a general increase in friskiness and daring among the population, and a decline in both, a decrease.

Because skirt lengths have limits (the floor and the upper thigh, respectively), the reaching of a limit would imply that a maximum of positive or negative mood had been achieved.

When we happened upon the Fashion Institute of Technology's "Trendology" exhibit during a recent trip to New York, of course we had to go in. The exhibit was billed as "a study of fashion trends and their relationship to the culture." What we found inside led us to conclude that the basic relationship among fashion, culture and social mood as reflected in the stock market has held for at least the past 120 years.

In a video that accompanied the exhibit, fashion experts addressed the idea of trends. In doing so, several of them captured certain manifestations of social mood. Connie Wang, style director of Refinery 29, noted its unifying effect on the character of social expression:

> "Trend" is an interesting word because in some senses it shouldn't exist. If designers have unlimited access to all the resources and touch points, multiple [designers should not come up with the] same thing in one season. It's kind of mind-boggling, right? But I think about trends in that—not the micro trends that happen from season to season—but if you look at trends across the decade, it's just a complete manifestation of...what's happening socially, what's happening politically, what's happening...in pop culture. You can literally see it manifest itself through clothes.[1]

Saul Lopez Silva, Country Manager-Mexico, WGSN, noted a characteristic shared by fashion and stock prices:

> "Trend" is actually a scientific term. It's used either in the financial world or in the fashion world, and it's something that points out the direction. It's something that tells you which direction a term, a concept, an item is going—either going up or going down. Are we talking about the stock going up, going down? Are we talking about motorcycle jackets going up, going down (i.e. the popularity of the market)?

Simon Doonan, Creative Ambassador, Barneys, added,

> Something like "hippie" was very, very much tied into the culture in the broadest, broadest sense, as was "punk." Because England was going through this dire economic period, people had to make clothes out of trash bags. They were angry. Safety pins. It meant something.

The exhibit started with fashions in the late 1700s, near the beginning of a multi-century period of positively trending social mood. As the United States was born and the prior negative social mood trend of 64 years' duration was ending, skirts touched the floor, as shown by the earliest fashion item in the exhibit.

The trend of social mood manifested slowly in fashion during the early stages of the positive mood trend that began in the late 1700s. For its first 100 years, hemlines more or less stayed on the floor. But in about 1895, as the stock market began to approach an interim high, ankle-length skirts appeared (see Figure 1).

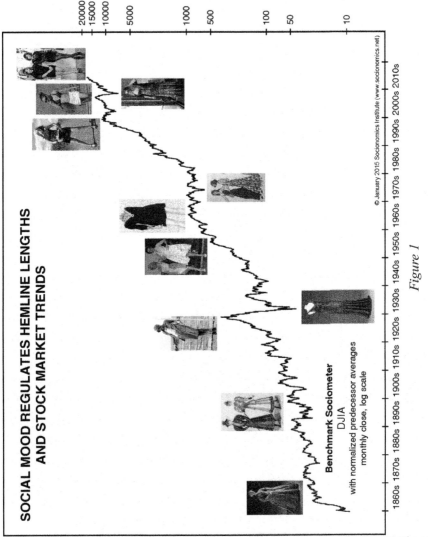

Figure 1 Photo Credits: **Bottom** (l-r) Victoria and Albert Museum, Simplicity (pattern 5349) and Megan Tintari/Flickr. **Top**: All photos Wikimedia Commons with the following attributions: (l-r) Los Angeles County Museum of Art, The Costumer's Manifesto, Infrogmation/Orionist/Beyond My Ken, Los Angeles Times photographic archive, iluvrhinestones, © Raimond Spekking/CC BY-SA4.0 (via Wikimedia Commons), Snowmanradio and Acrofan.

The exhibit's creators noted, "Fashion inhabits the culture." At the beginning of the 20th century, the positively trending social mood produced increased heights in buildings [see Chapter 25] and hemlines, both of which express confidence by saying, "Look at me." In the early 1900s, these two trends came together to give birth to a popular sensation. The Flatiron Building, which opened in 1902, created a serious downdraft at the intersection

Girl-Watcher's Paradise: The Flatiron Building, circa 1903, and (inset) a 1905 postcard poking fun at the building's windy effects. Both photos courtesy of Wikimedia Commons.

of Broadway, Fifth Avenue and 23rd Street. Here's how the book, *The City in Slang: New York Life and Popular Speech*, described the scene:

> The street corner at the prow of the Flatiron Building was famous as the city's best spot for girl-watching. The famous "Flatiron breezes" sometimes blew up women's long skirts to the delight of male gawkers. Cartoons, postcards, photographs, and humor about the spectacle of exposed ankles and knees made the corner famous, even in Europe.

The phenomenon was memorialized in a brief flicker called *The Flatiron Building on a Windy Day*, which came out in 1905, a year before the stock market made a multi-year high [see video, 5:50]. After that peak, the Dow/PPI failed to make headway for another 16 years, during which time hemlines remained relatively stable.

It took the positive trend in mood that facilitated the roaring bull market of the 1920s to elevate skirts to women's knees without the aid of wind power. These designs [see video, 6:20] are from *McCall's* 1929 dress patterns. The revealing new style permeated the culture as flappers became the rage. Flappers put not only their ankles and calves on display but also their bare arms. As historian Kenneth A. Yellis put it, "The flapper was an extreme manifestation of changes in the lifestyles of American women made visible through dress." Journalist Cristen Conger explained that the

Flappers: American actress Alice Joyce (left) and a poster for the 1929 film *Broadway Babies*. Both photos courtesy of Wikimedia Commons.

style "accommodated animated dance styles," such as the foxtrot and the Charleston, the latter an energetic dance with couples dancing apart, a style typical of postive mood periods, notably the first half of the 1960s.

High hemlines found expression in various pop culture outlets as positive mood reached a major extreme in the late 1920s. *Bare Knees*, the story of a flapper who causes a scandal in town with her bobbed hair and short skirts, came out in February 1928. By 1929, the flapper pic was a genre unto itself. This clip [see video, 7:09] from the film *Broadway Babies* shows how revealing the flapper look became. The "flapper look" flamed out in the wake of the 1929 stock market crash as an intensely negative mood trend pushed hemlines, stock prices and the heights of new buildings all lower in concert.

Hemlines eventually rebounded in the early 1950s as positive mood brought stock prices to new all-time highs. This display [see video, 7:40] of an evening dress from around 1950 and a silk number from 1954 show how skirts moved higher with the DJIA.

The birth date of the mini-skirt is open to debate, but the name is credited to Mary Quant, whose designs pushed hemlines several inches above the knee. Quant credited the look to everyday girls on the street. She took the name from her favorite car—the Austin Mini Cooper—in 1965, a few months before the DJIA reached 1000 in February 1966.

More shocking fashion displays appeared as the positive mood trend continued through 1968, when the Dow returned to 1000 and speculative shares tracked by the Value Line Composite index soared to new all-time highs. The mini-skirt then gave way to the micro. This [see video, 8:58] is *McCall's'* sewing pattern circa 1968.

As in the late 1920s, the high hemlines of the late 1960s were more than just a fashion; they were a social phenomenon. Short skirts again figured in the plot lines of some feature-length films, although these cinematic offerings were fewer in number and lower in quality than their 1929 counterparts. 1967's *Scorpions and Mini-Skirts* is a good example of the B-movie fare. Another long-forgotten drama, *Mini-Skirt Love*, was billed as a "shocking glimpse into the warped morals of the mod world." *The Mini-Skirt Mob* came out in May 1968 as the Value Line Composite index advanced to record highs.

As social mood turned negative and stock prices subsequently plunged, so did hemlines. The maxi skirt appeared near each of the next two lows of the negative social mood trend, in 1970 [see video, 9:56] and 1974.

A positive mood trend resumed in 1975. The Dow was making new highs when society re-embraced short skirts in 1987—right before another stock market crash. An even bigger mini-skirt revival occurred as a stock mania took the Dow to record heights in the 1990s. This black rayon dress [see video, 10:17] is from Calvin Klein in 1996.

As sociometers headed to all-time highs in 2000, mini-skirts became a standard look for the first time since the 1960s. Over the ensuing decade, hemlines vacillated rapidly with the wild fluctuations in the stock market, as this display representing the years 2000 to 2013 from the Trend-ology exhibit illustrates [see video, 10:35].

Sometimes the mixed trends of this net-sideways period are evident within the same dress; the high-low skirt, with hemlines low in back and high in front, has had its moments in recent years. The seeming fickleness has been so widespread that the exhibit's experts concluded by considering whether fashion trends themselves are a thing of the past. Simon Doonan, Creative Ambassador of Barneys said, "Social media, the Internet, online shopping are a part of this vast, confusing landscape of fashion, and if you try to understand it all and make sense of it, you really are going to lose your mind. ...I think everyone now in fashion is a little trend-skeptical."[2] Elizabeth Cline, author of *Overdressed: The Shockingly High Cost of Cheap Fashion*, added, "Trends absolutely exist. I think what's happening now is they move so fast that they seem to not exist. ...They're moving so rapidly that they're kind of hard to pin down and talk about in any individual way."[3]

But, through the lens of social mood, we *can* pin them down, year by year. This camo maxi, for instance [see video, 11:56], from the Trend-ology exhibit makes perfect sense; it reveals that some designers were quick to spot the emerging negative mood trend. The Christian Dior design appeared in 2001 following the initial turn toward negative social mood, which reached its nadir in late 2002.

The mini won out again as stocks made new highs in 2007. The victory was short-lived. As sociometers plummeted, the maxi returned to prominence in late 2008. Since the stock market low of 2009 and especially the low in real estate prices of 2012, an unequivocal trend toward positive mood has led to the re-emergence of frisky clothing designs. At 2014's spring fashion shows, mini-skirts [see video, 13:15] once again dominated the catwalks.

These media headlines [displayed in Figure 7 of Chapter 10 in *The Socionomic Theory of Finance*] show how faithfully long and short hemline dominance has coincided with key highs and lows in the stock market from the late 1990s through 2014.

As in 1929 and 1968, the mini in 2015 has once again invaded the culture at large. As the Dow moved past 17,000 through the spring, summer and fall of 2014, the roster of celebrity mini-skirt sightings got longer and longer. This photo essay [see video, 14:02] was posted on InStyle.com on May 28, 2014. On November 21, *The New York Post* ran a piece highlighting an array of celebrities sporting ultra-short looks. It was titled, "Where's the rest of your dress?" The trend is evident even here on Main Street in the small town of Gainesville, Georgia. A block from our offices, short skirts became a hot item this summer at the Dress Up fashion boutique. Here's the display that appeared out front in mid-July. And here [see video, 14:44] are some more minis that the shop used to lure customers through the rest of the summer and fall. Even as temperatures plunged, stocks continued to advance into the new year, so hemlines stayed high as well. This one [see video, 14:55] is from January 8th, [2015] after the Dow crossed 18,000.

In some ways, the mini-skirt is more mainstream than ever. As the director of the Fashion Institute of Technology told the *Daily News*, "Today, the mini-skirt can be worn by anyone. It used to be a very young-person style, but that concept has disappeared." The BBC cited a recent study by a British department store reporting that whereas data from 1980 showed that on average women stopped buying minis when they reached their early 30s, women today are happy to wear mini-skirts up to the age of 40. Women of 1800 would be appalled.

Since the 1990s, minis have become more fashionable among plus-size women as well. For instance, the fashion website Polyvore offers more than 100 different styles of plus-size mini-skirts. It may be tempting to agree with the *Liverpool Echo*'s headline from 2014 that proclaimed, "The Mini-skirt Will Live on Forever." A similar sentiment surfaced in the late 1960s. But the broad, seemingly-permanent acceptance of the mini is actually another sign of an approaching extreme in the trend toward positive social mood. The Trend-ology exhibit quotes novelist Marie von Ebner-Eschenbach saying, "As soon as fashion is universal, it is out of date." The fractal structure of social mood changes explains why this is so.

Another sign that the positive mood trend is reaching an extreme is that in some cases the style is so revealing it covers hardly anything at all. At extremes in positive social mood, little is left to the imagination. In 1968 and 1969, designer Yves Saint Laurent rang the bell with see-through dresses.

In November 2013, a similar extreme was established when a fashion commentator stated, "Stars are under a lot of pressure to show off their bodies. Expect to see plenty of celebrity skin. It's picking up." In June, pop star Rihanna showed up in New York in this see-through dress [see video] to receive the "Fashion Icon Award." In October 2014, designer Tom Ford took a page out of Saint Laurent's 1968 design book and clothed Rihanna and Miley Cyrus in an ultra-revealing style that was dubbed "Viva Glam." In November, Kim Kardashian made a big splash with this cover [see video, 17:16] for *Paper* magazine.

The latest bout of mini-skirt mania diverges from its predecessors in one important respect: It has yet to inspire any motion pictures. The closest it seems to have come is an adult film called *Miniskirt Madness*, which came out in 2000, and a 2013 short film by Stuart Weitzman, "Made for Walking," which features Kate Moss. The music in the film, "These Boots Are Made for Walking," was a #1 hit in 1967 by a mini-skirted Nancy Sinatra. On June 16, there was a free screening of 1968's *Mini-Skirt Mob* at the Social Club in Miami. On New Year's Eve 2014, the Queen of England celebrated the late 1960s by honoring Mary Quant, now Dame Mary, as a pioneer of the mini-skirt.

There are some signs that the fervor surrounding the latest mini-skirt mania is losing steam. On August 10, controversial clothing retailer American Apparel came under fire for an ad in its new "Back to School" line. The ad featured a model bending over in a plaid mini-skirt with her underwear visible. On August 11, *Time* magazine labeled the scandal "boring" and said, "These ploys have gotten tiresome." The mini-skirt's inability to generate the cultural excitement of prior eras is an early signal of the cover-up to come.

There are other hints of change. Designer Tom Ford paired his barely-there tops in his latest fashion statements with skirts that fall straight to the floor. Also, more recently, Kardashian covered her legs—or, at least, most of them. [In February 2015, however, as the Dow reached another new all-time high, Kardashian continued to reflect extremes in social mood by going fully naked for a photo shoot.] Using 120 years of history as our guide, we expect hemlines to stay high as long as the social mood trend is positive and to fall deeply again whenever mood turns decisively negative.

NOTES AND REFERENCES

[1] YouTube.
[2] *Ibid.*
[3] *Ibid.*

Chapter 63

Stocks & Sex in Europe and Japan

Mark Galasiewski

February 15, 2008 (EWT)

In September 1999 [see Chapter 9 of *Pioneering Studies in Socionomics*], *The Elliott Wave Theorist* showed how long term trends in social mood have tended to correlate with U.S. conception rates, plotted as annual birth rates minus a year to approximate a pregnancy term. Stock market bottoms in 1932 and 1974 perfectly matched lows in conception rates prior to the two major baby booms of the 20th century. That correlation suggested a

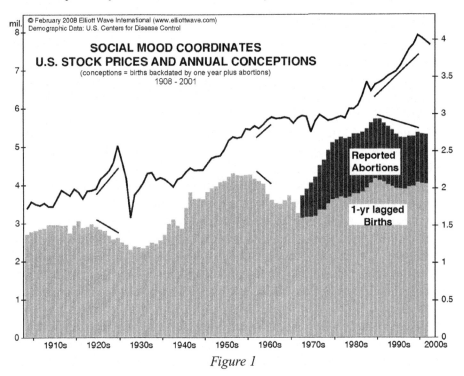

Figure 1

socionomic explanation: that social mood simultaneously motivates trends in conceptions and in stock prices. The data have repeatedly diverged in a fifth wave (the last advance in a bull market), as you can see by the six lines on the chart. We speculated, not entirely with tongue-in-cheek, that in fifth waves the population is too distracted chasing investment profits to care as much about conceiving children.

The correlation we offer is far better than the one associated with the idea that demographic trends drive the stock market, an assumption commonly held in the investment world even today. As we stated at the time, there were not enough data to be certain that our explanation was correct, but at that time all available data fit the hypothesis.

[Subsequent data have continued along socionomic lines. The December 2, 2010 issue of *The Socionomist* quoted a source saying that the birth rate for 2009 was "the lowest rate of the century." That year's 4,136,000 births was 200,000 fewer than just two years prior. As AP reported, "The situation is a striking turnabout from 2007, when more babies were born in the United States than any other year in the nation's history." Not coincidentally, the stock market experienced a striking turnabout at the very same time.]

Adding Abortion Data

We have since considered the impact of abortion data on the profile of conceptions. Abortions hide conceptions from the birth-rate data. The decriminalization of abortion in 1973 in the U.S. allowed doctors openly to collect data on abortions, whereas its criminalization prior to that time had kept them from keeping data at all.

Since doctors and others did perform abortions prior to 1973, adding abortion figures to our graph from 1973 forward biases the conception rate upward for that period by an unknown amount. We do not even know for sure whether abortions increased after the law was passed, though one would suspect that they did.

Another question is whether we should include abortion data in our tally at all. Perhaps a positive trend in social mood should lead not only to conceptions but also to decisions to carry to term. But there is reason to doubt this line of reasoning. Through most of human history, an influence that regulated conceptions would pretty much have equated to one regulating births.

Regardless of whether we include abortion data, the correlation in the U.S. still holds up well. Figure 1 updates the 1999 study for the U.S. by including reported abortions in our calculation of total annual conceptions.

Each total comprises births backdated by one year plus abortions, which are not backdated, since the legal—and therefore reported—ones occur within the first trimester. The additional data have the result of pushing conceptions to a new high in the 1980s along with the stock market, making this aspect of the data even more compatible with our hypothesis. But it also either wipes out or simply obscures the low in conceptions of 1974, when the stock market bottomed. Regardless, the overall ebb and flow of the two trends remains fairly close.

Data from the UK, Germany and Japan

Further research shows that data from some other countries seem to support, though not as well, the connection between benchmark sociometers and the conception rate, at least as far as we can determine. Figure 2 charts the record of annual conceptions in England and Wales against an index of U.K. stocks back to 1838. While there is a rough fit between the peaks and troughs in these two measures, the overall correlation is not as tight as that in the United States.

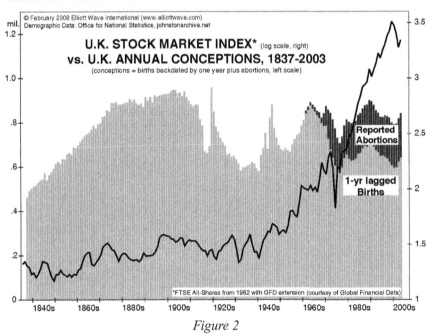

Figure 2

In ages of inflation, nominal stock indexes are usually not the best sociometers. As we have noted [see Chapter 7 of *The Socionomic Theory of Finance*], measures of stock prices normalized to the value of things

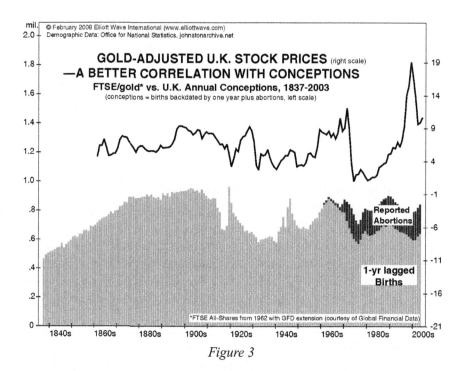

Figure 3

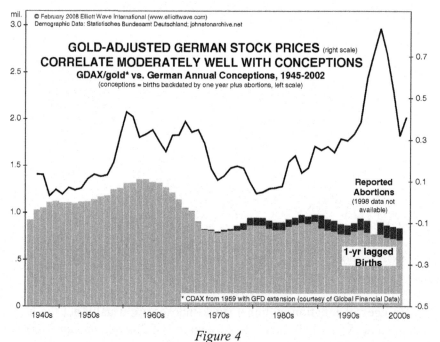

Figure 4

(the PPI) or to real money (gold), typically track more closely with other mood-influenced social activities. Figure 3 shows that the gold-adjusted index of U.K. stocks tracks conceptions better than the nominal index used in Figure 2.

Figure 4 shows German conceptions against a long term, gold-adjusted index of German stock prices. The trends are fairly close through 1992, and then they diverge against the final stock-market advance, as we saw in the U.S. data.

Japan's birth data also show a measure of support for our hypothesis. Figure 5 shows that Japanese conceptions peaked in 1954 and remained elevated right into the 1972 high in the gold-adjusted Nikkei stock index. Japan experienced a decline in conceptions during its fifth wave in the 1980s—denoted by the white area on the chart—just as the United States, the UK and Germany experienced during its fifth wave in the 1990s.

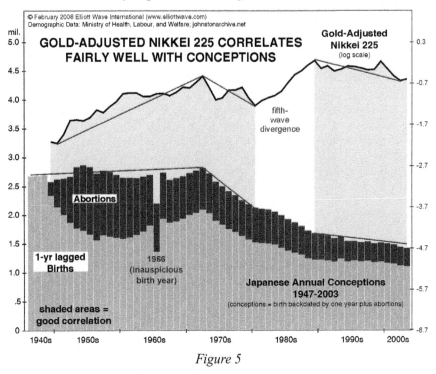

Figure 5

We would be remiss if we were to overlook the possible role of some aspects of culture in regulating conception trends. There is, for example, a precipitous decline in pregnancies in Japan during the year 1966 because it was deemed an inauspicious year for female births according to Japanese superstition. What other cultural influences may be at work in all these measures we are not equipped to speculate.

We cautioned in 1999 that U.S. data were too limited statistically to prove a correlation. Although all these new data are highly suggestive of socionomic causality, whether social mood regulates conception rates remains an open question.

Chapter 64

A Socionomic Perspective on Transgender Expressions in Popular Culture

Chuck Thompson
June 1, 2014 (TS)

In "Popular Culture and the Stock Market" (1985), Robert Prechter observed that the early position of a trend toward positive social mood produces gender idols that are clearly defined. In such times, masculine men and feminine women are the norm, as were John Wayne and Marilyn Monroe in the 1950s and Arnold Schwarzenegger and Madonna in the 1980s.

Positive-mood gender idols tend to be "sexually distinct and stereotypical," whereas the sexuality of negative-mood gender idols is often "mixed and blurred," as Prechter elaborated in the December 1994 *Elliott Wave Theorist*. The extent of negatively trending mood within a society regulates its acceptance of mixed and blurred gender expressions, including androgynous fashions and transgender people.

In recent decades, mixed gender expressions hark back to the negative mood period of the 1970s, "arguably the last time sartorial gender blending was as pervasive in the culture," said *The New York Times*[1] in 2009, the year of a major bottom in stocks following a nine-year trend toward negative social mood. In 2010, the *Times* followed up with an article titled "Bold Crossings of the Gender Line," which featured cross-dressing photos of actor James Franco and designer Marc Jacobs. The article, which also drew comparisons to 40 years ago, said, "Not since the glam era of the 1970s has gender-bending so saturated the news media."[2] Even *Time* magazine has become hip to the transgender boom. Its June 9 [2014] cover story, "The

Transgender Tipping Point," includes a full-length photo of transgender actress Laverne Cox.

To contextualize the recent rise in transgender expressions, it is helpful to review the past 60 years from a socionomic perspective, beginning with the first transsexual to go public in the U.S.

1942-1966: Waxing Positive Mood Limits Public Acceptance of Transgender Expressions

In 1950, the year after a twenty-year bear market formation in the Dow/PPI ended, George William Jorgensen, Jr. traveled to Denmark to begin the transition from a man to a woman, known thereafter as Christine Jorgensen. News about her broke in 1952 as the Korean War, a belated expression of the preceding period of negative social mood, occupied the U.S. armed forces.

According to *The New York Times*, Jorgensen was "sensationalized in the daily tabloids."[3] She was the object of headlines such as, "Bronx 'Boy' Is Now a Girl" and "Dear Mum and Dad, Son Wrote, Have Now Become Your Daughter." And, when she returned to the U.S. in 1953, she faced a barrage of questions from the media, which made her an object of ridicule.[4] She was denied a marriage license in 1959, and her male fiancé lost his job when his engagement to Jorgensen was made public.[5]

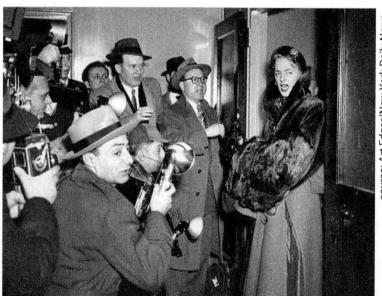

source: Art Edger/New York Daily News

Under Fire: Christine Jorgensen (right) is accosted by reporters.

Two years later, transsexual model April Ashley was rising through the ranks of the fashion world, appearing in magazines such as *Vogue* and becoming a female sex symbol and lingerie model. But in 1961, when a friend told the British media that Ashley had once been a man, the news amounted to a scandal that forced her out of the fashion industry.[6] The black-and-white morality attending the positive trend in social mood did not welcome transexuality.

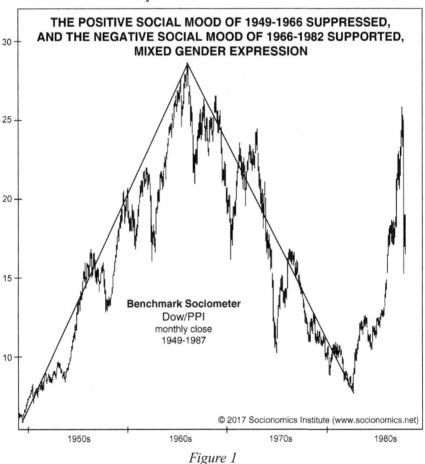

Figure 1

1966-1982: Negative Mood Opens Doors for Transgender Celebrities

As social mood began trending negatively in the late 1960s, acceptance of blurred gender expressions increased. Unlike the reception given to Christine Jorgensen and April Ashley, cross-dressers Jackie Curtis, Candy Darling and Holly Woodlawn were featured in films and sung about in popular music. The three caught the attention of artist and filmmaker Andy Warhol, who cast them in movie roles and included them in a group of celebrities known as "Warhol Superstars."[7]

Superstars: Filmmaker Andy Warhol with Holly Woodlawn (l), and Candy Darling (r).

Darling was the inspiration for the 1969 Velvet Underground song "Candy Says"[8] and was mentioned along with Woodlawn and Curtis in Lou Reed's 1972 hit, 'Walk on the Wild Side'.[9]

All three Warhol Superstars were cast in the 1971 film *Women in Revolt*,[10] for which Warhol was cinematographer. He was the producer of *Flesh* (1968), which featured Darling and Curtis,[11] and of *Trash* (1970), which featured Woodlawn.[12]

Curtis wrote poetry and plays and went on to appear in *Cabaret in the Sky—An Evening with Holly Woodlawn and Jackie Curtis* (1973) at the New York Cultural Center. Curtis's drag performances, which included lipstick, glitter, bright red hair and ripped dresses and stockings, have prompted some assertions that they inspired the shimmering costumes and extravagant makeup of the 1970s Glitter Rock movement.[13] David Bowie, one of Glitter Rock's most renowned stars, introduced his androgynous alter ego Ziggy Stardust in 1972.[14]

In 1970, Hollywood released *The Christine Jorgensen Story* and *Myra Breckenridge*, a movie about a transsexual who goes to Hollywood. In 1972, the cross-dressing actor Divine gained recognition in the movie *Pink Flamingos*, in which he played the "filthiest person alive." Divine starred in other taboo-breaking cult films, performed in a solo cabaret act and made 11 recordings of disco music. 1975 saw the release of *Dog Day Afternoon*, about a man who tries to rob a bank in order to finance sex reassignment surgery for his lover. *Dressed to Kill* hit theaters in 1980 and became "one of the early entries in the extremely problematic 'trans women as dangerous psychotics' category," according to BuzzFeed writer Rafe Posey.[15] And in 1982, *The World According to Garp* told the story of a transgender former football player.

In sports, tennis player Renee Richards became the first transsexual to compete in competitive sports after transitioning. The United States Tennis Association barred her from entering the 1976 U.S. Open tournament, but the New York Supreme Court granted her the right to compete in the following year's event.[16]

Despite the negative mood trend, some transgender celebrities nevertheless encountered encumbrances to their stardom. For example, Darling sought the lead role in *Myra Breckenridge* in hopes of breaking into mainstream movies,[17] but the role went to Hollywood pin-up girl Raquel Welch. "They decided Raquel Welch would make a more believable transvestite," Darling complained.[18] Transsexual models also continued to struggle to find a foothold in the fashion world. Tracy Africa and Tula faced challenges similar to those experienced by April Ashley in the 1960s. Both were successful until they were discovered to be transsexual.

1982-2000: Transgender Celebrities Capitalize on Brief Windows of Opportunity Within the Large-Degree Positive Mood Trend

The negative mood trend that began in 1966 came to an end in 1982, when mood began to trend positively. The fashion world again proved to be a difficult one for transgender people. Transsexual model Lauren Foster was working extensively in Europe, South America and the U.S. With journalists on her trail, Foster's agent advised her to grant an interview in an attempt to control the details of her story. She described what happened next:

> The story was then sold by the original interviewer and picked up by Reuters, tabloids like Bunte, Globe and other international press ran the story, with the headline, "Revealed: Vogue Model Was a Man!".... It was tough. My modeling career slowed down and the only jobs I was offered were in countries that had never heard of me. This was in the 80s, before the Internet, so I could play the "stealth game" in my career. I moved to Greece, Paris and anywhere they didn't know who I was.[19]

Transsexual Teri Toye modeled for designer and "punk glamour god" Stephen Sprouse, who was known for wearing eyeliner, black nail polish, garage-band hair and graffiti on his arms.[20] Toye did not come under scrutiny as Foster did, but she left the modeling profession after three years to work in historic preservation and real estate.[21]

Glitter Rock's Inspiration? Jackie Curtis (left) and David Bowie as Ziggy Stardust.

The positive mood trend was interrupted briefly in the early 1990s, a period marked by a recession, the Gulf War, a reelection loss for incumbent U.S. President George H.W. Bush and four years of pessimism on Wall Street (see Figure 1 of Chapter 12). This small-degree negative mood trend showed up clearly in the sharp declines of 1989-90 in the Dow Jones Transportation Average, the Value Line Composite index (not shown) and the Consumer Confidence Index (see Figure 2). This period offered a brief window of opportunity for transgender expression to reach the mainstream.

The 1990 movie *Paris is Burning*—issued the year the 1987-1990 bear market ended—chronicled New York's 1980s drag scene. The film's cast included

Drag Scene: The 1990 film *Paris is Burning* was released during a small-degree negative mood trend.

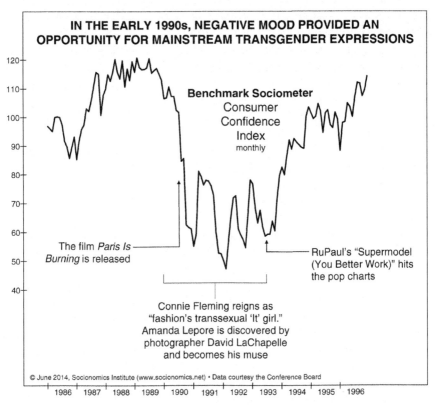

IN THE EARLY 1990s, NEGATIVE MOOD PROVIDED AN OPPORTUNITY FOR MAINSTREAM TRANSGENDER EXPRESSIONS

Benchmark Sociometer
Consumer
Confidence
Index
monthly

The film *Paris Is Burning* is released

RuPaul's "Supermodel (You Better Work)" hits the pop charts

Connie Fleming reigns as "fashion's transsexual 'It' girl." Amanda Lepore is discovered by photographer David LaChapelle and becomes his muse

© June 2014, Socionomics Institute (www.socionomics.net) • Data courtesy the Conference Board

Figure 2

transgender performer Octavia St. Laurent.[22] Transgender model Connie Fleming ("Connie Girl") had a short reign as what *The New York Times* called "fashion's transsexual 'It' girl."[23] Meanwhile, transsexual New York nightlife personality Amanda Lepore met photographer David LaChapelle, who brought her international exposure as his muse.[24] In 1993, cross-dresser RuPaul's song "Supermodel (You Better Work)" hit the pop charts. RuPaul parlayed that success into two #1 hits on the U.S. dance charts, a spot on the MTV Video Music Awards, a duet with Elton John that landed in the top 10 on the UK singles chart, a modeling contract with a major cosmetics firm, a gig co-hosting the BRIT Awards (the UK's Grammys) and a short-lived show on VH1.

Once the positive mood trend resumed in earnest, it mostly shut down opportunities for mainstream transgender expression. Then, in 1998, shortly after the Value Line Composite index peaked for that era, Julie Hesmond-halgh joined the cast of Britain's longest-running television soap, *Coronation*

St. and portrayed the first transsexual character on a British serial.[25] One year later, Hollywood released *Boys Don't Cry*, a film about the murder of Brandon Teena, a transgender person, in Nebraska. Hilary Swank won an Academy Award for her work in the film's lead role.[26]

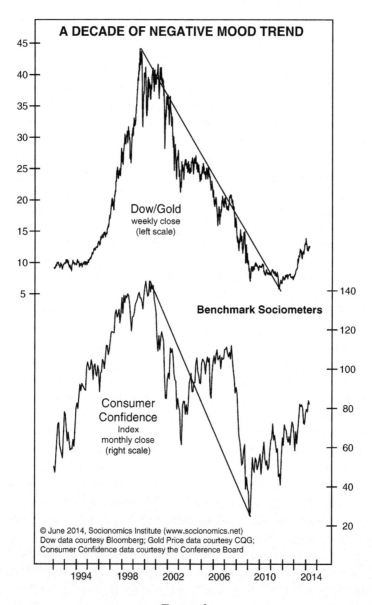

Figure 3

2000-2012: Transgender Expressions Proliferate as Mood Trends Negatively at Large Degree

The trend of the Dow/gold ratio reversed from up to down in 1999, marking the beginning of a negative trend in social mood. Declines lasted until 2009 in the nominal DJIA and Dow/PPI, until 2011 in the Dow/gold ratio and until 2012 in real estate prices. The negative trend was also manifest in the Consumer Confidence Index (Figure 3).

This large-degree negative mood trend created a correspondingly large window of opportunity for mainstream transgender expressions in sports, entertainment, culture and, most notably, fashion. For two decades, revelations of being transgender had been career-killers for people in the fashion industry. Since 2000, openly transgender models have been featured in publications such as *Vanity Fair*, *Vogue*, *Love*, *W* and *ELLE* and in ad campaigns for brands such as Kenneth Cole and Barneys New York.

2000-2012 Transgender and Related Expressions

2003—HBO releases *Normal*, a movie about a Midwestern factory worker who comes out as transgender. Bravo launches *Queer Eye for the Straight Guy*, a reality show featuring an all-gay cast; it becomes a hit.

2004—The International Olympic Committee adopts policies for trans-sexual and transgender athletes. Other sports later adopt the same policies, allowing players such as golfer Mianne Bagger and soccer player Martine Delaney to compete.[27]

2005—The movie *TransAmerica* tells the story of a transgender woman who learns she has a runaway son she never knew about. The film *Kinky Boots*, about a shoe company catering to drag queens, is released.

2007—The television show *Ugly Betty* introduces a transgender character.[28] Transgender actress Candis Cayne begins a two-year stint as a transgender woman on ABC's *Dirty Sexy Money*, becoming the first openly transgender actress to play a recurring transgender character on primetime American television.[29]

2008—Transsexual model Nina Poon is featured in fashion designer Kenneth Cole's international fall advertising campaign.[30] Poon becomes the first transgender female to model in full-page ads featured in *Vanity Fair*, *Vogue* and *The New York Times*.[31]

2009—Chaz Bono, formerly Chastity Bono, daughter of entertainers Sonny and Cher, makes his transgender status public. ABC's prime-time sitcom *Modern Family* features a gay male couple. Logo TV begins airing *RuPaul's Drag Race*, a reality television series in which the performer searches for America's next drag super-star.[32] *The New York Times* reports that twenty-something urban Americans are "revising standard notions of gender-appropriate dressing," noting that men are "making unabashed forays into mom's closet, some for fashion's sake, others for fit." The *Times* says gender blending was so entrenched that

source: Three Dollar Bill Cinema

> mainstream purveyors of hip, including Urban Outfitters and American Apparel, are offering clothing and jewelry meant to be worn by either sex. American Apparel has no fewer than 724 unisex items—hoodies, cardigans, blazers and bow ties, among them—on its Web site, simply because, as Marsha Brady, the company's creative director, put it, "that's the way people wear clothes."[33]

Success: Negative mood made a success of RuPaul's *Drag Race*, which launched in 2009.

The year also marks the launch of *Candy* magazine, named for Candy Darling, which bills itself as "The First Transversal Style Magazine."

2011—Andrej Pejic, a man who models both men's and women's clothes, is the face for designer Marc Jacobs' Spring/Summer Marc line of clothing. Pejic also appears in women's as well as men's runway shows for designer Jean Paul Gaultier. *FHM* magazine names him among the "100 Sexiest Women in the World."[34] Chaz Bono becomes a competitor on the U.S. version of *Dancing With the Stars*. Australia joins the U.S. and Britain in allowing three gender choices on passport applications: male, female and indeterminate.[35]

2012—The online version of Sweden's National Encyclopedia adds a gender-neutral pronoun, "hen," that

source: Serbia In

Andrej Pejic: The 22-year-old has successfully modeled both men's and women's clothes.

citizens can substitute for "han" (he) and "hon" (she). *Kinky Boots* debutes as a live theatre production. Transsexual Jenna Talackova enters the Miss Universe Canada pageant and is dismissed when organizers discover she had been born a boy. She is later reinstated and finishes as one of the twelve final contestants. *Archie* comics features an issue in which boys become girls and vice versa. A banner at the top of the issue reads, "What if everything were reversed?"[36] The May 2012 issue of *The Elliott Wave Financial Forecast* notes that the speed of society's "gender blender [had] bumped up a notch":

> While men are crossing over with "Manlashes, Manscara and Mantyhose" as well as bikini waxes, the new "it trend for women is tomboy fashion." Australian designer Kym Ellery credits the trend "to a greater acceptance of blurred gender identity. 'Everyone's really open to it.'"

Transgender model Connie Fleming poses on the front of *Candy* magazine as Michelle Obama being sworn into office. *Candy* publisher Luis Venegas says his motivation for the cover came from the idea that someday, a black, transsexual woman might become president of the United States.[37]

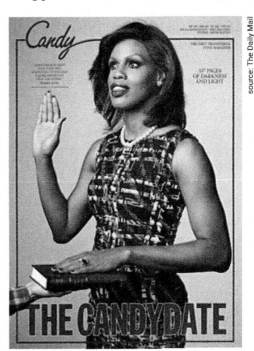

source: The Daily Mail

Sworn In: Transgender model Connie Fleming poses as Michelle Obama.

Post-2012 Expressions

Although all sociometers have been trending upward since 2012, non-traditional gender expressions have so far been more aligned with the unfinished bear market formation that began in 1999 in the Dow/gold ratio than with the nominal and PPI-adjusted Dow. They include the following events:

2013—Fashionising.com notes that masculine-feminine boundaries have blurred:

> the time has become right for the outliers to become the mainstream. Androgyny is now an evolving, large-scale fashion trend and one we've continued to observe as we move into the fashion trends for spring 2014.[38]

Germany becomes the first country in continental Europe to introduce a third, "indeterminate," gender designation on birth certificates.[39] Retired Navy SEAL Kristin Beck publishes the book *Warrior Princess*, describing a lifelong struggle with sexual identity. Three months before the book's release, Beck begins hormone treatments, receives laser treatment to remove facial hair and publishes a new LinkedIn profile picture dressed as a woman.[40] The Associated Press reports that on high school and college campuses, young people who identify as genderqueer are pushing to be called by pronouns other than "he" or "she" and instead are opting for alternatives such as "they" or "ze."[41] According to the Huffington Post, transgender model Nicole Gibson "wowed audiences on the catwalk at London's Fashion Week." The event occurs two years after Gibson began hormone-replacement therapy.[42] Transgender model Jenna Talackova appears in a major fashion spread in *ELLE Canada*'s January 2014 issue.[43] *USA Today* reports that more children are challenging traditional gender boundaries and going public at younger ages. Although their numbers are "relatively small," they are creating challenges for schools, such as which bathrooms they use and where they change for gym class.[44]

2014—In India, the Supreme Court recognizes transgender people as a third gender who are eligible for minority rights, including job quotas, education and amenities. An estimated 2 million people among India's population of 1.2 billion identify themselves as transgender.[45] In the U.S., a Health and Human Services review board determines that transgender Medicare recipients cannot automatically be denied coverage for sex reassignment surgeries.[46] La Leche League International removes gender language from its leadership requirements and now acknowledges that men can breastfeed.[47] In the fashion world, photographer Bruce Weber features almost 20 transgender models in a catalog and magazine campaign for Barneys New York.[48] Model Geena Rocero, who has been in the fashion business for a decade, uses a TED Talk to announce she is transgender.[49] Reversing an image from Robert Palmer's 1988 music video "Simply Irresistible," in which he is surrounded by "heavily made-up, scantily-clad ladies," singer Ingrid

Michaelson releases a music video for 'Girls Chase Boys', which features "an equally made-up, scantily-clad group of guys."[50] The Huffington Post notes that, with the song, Michaelson has "joined the gender-bending coterie."[51] In Europe, cross-dresser Conchita Wurst wins the 2014 Eurovision Song Contest in Copenhagen, Denmark. The event draws a television audience of about 180 million in 45 countries.[52] Television actor Hoon Lee plays a cross-dressing computer hacker on the Cinemax action series *Banshee*.[53] Other television shows, such as *Orange Is the New Black*, *House of Lies*, *Glee* and *Transparent*, have featured main characters who are transgender or genderqueer.[54]

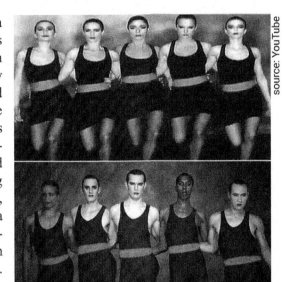

Turning the Tables: Robert Palmer's girls (above) and Ingrid Michaelson's boys.

Eurovision Song Contest: This year's winner was cross-dresser Conchita Wurst.

2015-2016 Update: Television personality and Olympic gold medalist Bruce Jenner reveals his new identity as transgender woman Caitlyn Jenner, who becomes the most famous transgender woman in the world. Jenner receives widespread publicity and in 2016 becomes the first openly transgender person to be featured on the cover of *Sports Illustrated*.

As social mood becomes even more positive, some backlash appears. In May 2016, the governor of North Carolina signs the state's "bathroom law," barring transexuals from using bathrooms incompatible with their sex at birth, although the law is repealed ten months later. On June 12, 2016, an ISIS sympathizer kills 50 people and wounds 53 more at a gay nightclub in

Orlando in the country's deadliest mass shooting. *Post-production update*: On May 12, 2017, the media report that in 2016 "Caitlyn" plummeted in popularity as a name for newborns. An article from June 30, 2017 states, "killings of trans women have soared in past 3 years."[55]

Transgender Expressions Through a Socionomic Lens

It has been 30 years since socionomist Robert Prechter observed the tendency for gender lines to blur during times of negatively trending social mood. Over the latest negative mood trend at large degree, we have witnessed manifold incidences of transgender expression. Clothing designers, entertainers, musicians and many other people have capitalized on a trend that socionomists forecast three decades ago.

When negative social mood next prompts all sociometers to turn south in unison, expressions of less mainstream sexual identities will become more extreme, if not bizarre. Backlash will increase near the low, and as social mood turns more positive, non-traditional sexual expression will likely be pushed back into the closet.

The socionomic insight continues to provide a basis for assessing and understanding social attitudes and actions of all kinds. The present review adds further credence to the use of socionomics as a tool for understanding, explaining and anticipating social trends.

NOTES AND REFERENCES

[1] La Ferla, R. (2009, November 19). It's All a Blur to Them. *The New York Times*.

[2] Van Meter, W. (2010, December 8). Bold Crossings of the Gender Line. *The New York Times*.

[3] McQuiston, J.T. (1989, May 4). Christine Jorgensen, 62 is dead; Was First to Have a Sex Change. *The New York Times*.

[4] Christine Jorgensen Biography. Biography.com.

[5] Reed, T. (2013, February 25). History of Transgenderism—part 2 (1900-1969). Examiner.com.

[6] Brooks, K. (2013, September 30). 'April Ashley: Portrait of a Lady' explores the life of Britain's first transgender icon. *The Huffington Post*.

[7] Warhol Stars. Warholstars.org.

[8] Darling, Candy. Warholstars.org.

[9] "Walk on the Wild Side." Lou Reed lyrics. AZLyrics.com.

[10] *Women in Revolt* (1971). IMDb.

[11] *Flesh* (1968). IMDb.

[12] *Trash* (1970). IMDb.

[13] Curtis, Jackie. Wikipedia.org.

[14] Lynskey, D. (2012, March 27). Ziggy Stardust—It Was All Worthwhile. *The Guardian*.

[15] Posey, R. (2013, September 4). 21 Times Actors Who Aren't Actually Transgender Have Played Trans Characters. *BuzzFeed LGBT*.

[16] Jacques, J. (2013, April 16). Sport is Slowly Catching Up With Transgender Realities. *The Guardian*.

[17] Colacello, B. (1990). *Holy Terror: Andy Warhol Close Up*. New York, NY: Vintage Books.

[18] See endnote 13.

[19] Lauren Foster, transgender model, and Alex Davis, transgender musician, discuss trans issues. (2012, July 12). *The Huffington Post*.

[20] Stephen Sprouse. Voguepedia.

[21] Lance, G. (2011, December 11). Teri Toye. *TG Reporter*.

[22] Octavia St. Laurent (1970-2009). IMDb.

[23] See endnote 2

[24] Whitelocks, S. (2014, January 21). 'I've Got The Most Expensive Body On Earth': Celebrated Transsexual Party-goer Speaks Out About Her 'Painful Transformation-Including Breaking Her Lower Ribs to Look Thinner. *Daily Mail*.

[25] Reed. T. (2013, February 27). History of Transgenderism—Part 4 (1990-1999). Examiner.com.

[26] Fairyington, S. (2013, December 31). Two Decades After Brandon Teena's Murder, a Look Back at Falls City. *The Atlantic*.

[27] See endnote 16.

[28] Kane, M. (2013, November 12). Transgender Characters That Changed Film and Television. GLAAD.org.

[29] Reed, T. (2014, March 30). History of Transgenderism—Part 6. *The Examiner*.

[30] Reed, T. (2014, March 30). History of Transgenderism—Part 6 (2006-2009). *The Examiner.*

[31] Cast bios, Transform Me. VH1.

[32] RuPaul's Drag Race (2009). IMDb.

[33] See endnote 1.

[34] LeTrent, S. (2012, September 7). High Fashion, Minus the Labels. CNN.

[35] Australian Passports to Have Third Gender Option. (2011, September 15). *The Guardian*.

[36] Gregorian, D. (2012, April 23). Gender 'Issues'. *New York Post*.

[37] O'hare, S. (2012, December 18). Outrage as Magazine Uses Transgender Model to Pose as Michelle Obama. *The Daily Mail*.

[38] Braukamper, T. (2013, March 14). Androgynous Fashion: Spring's Evolution. Fashionising.com.

[39] Heine, F. (2013, August 16). M, F or Blank: 'Third Gender' Official in Germany from November. *Spiegel*.

[40] Stanglin, D. (2013, June 5). A Navy SEAL's Biggest Secret: Life as a Transgender. *USA Today*.

[41] 'Genderqueer' rising: Colleges Welcome Kids Who Identify as Neither Male Nor Female. (2013, November 30). Associated Press/*The Washington Times*.

[42] Nichols, J. (2013, September 18). Nicole Gibson, Transgender Model, Walks in London Fashion Week. *The Huffington Post*.

[43] Murray, R. (2013, December 19). Transgender Model Jenna Talackova Scores Fashion Spread in ELLE Magazine. *New York Daily News*.

[44] Irvine, M. (2013, May 28). Boy or Girl? Gender a New Challenge for Schools. *USA Today*.

[45] India Court Recognizes Transgender People as Third Gender. (2014, April 15). *BBC News*.

[46] Associated Press. (2014, May 30). HHS Board Rules Transgender Medicare Recipients Can Seek Coverage for Sex-change Surgery. *Fox News*.

[47] Tapper, J. (2014, April 25). Transgender Man Can Be Breastfeeding Coach. *Toronto Star*.

[48] Bernstein, J. (2014, January 29). A Barneys Campaign Embraces a Gender Identity Issue. *The New York Times*.

[49] Vingan, A. (2014, April 1). Transgender Model Geena Rocero Gives Inspiring TED Talk About Coming Out. *Fashionista*.

[50] Ross, J. (2014, February 5). In a Brilliant New Video, Ingrid Michaelson Perfectly Parodies Sexism in Pop Music. *PolicyMic*.

[51] Ingrid Michaelson Bends Gender Both Ways in 'Girls Chase Boys'. (2014, February 11). *The Huffington Post*.

[52] Coleman, M. (2014, May 11). Bearded Drag Queen Conchita Wurst Wins Eurovision Song Contest. *Rolling Stone*.

[53] Rathe, A. (2014, January 8). *Banshee's* Hoon Lee On What It Takes To Play a Beauty. *Out*.

[54] Ulaby, N. (2014, April 23). On Television, More Transgender Characters Come Into Focus. NPR.

[55] Johnson, Kevin. (2017, June 30). Sessions to Review Transgender Murders. *USA Today*.

Chapter 65

Negative Mood Supports
Transgender Expressions in Brazil

Chuck Thompson

March 26, 2015 (TS)

The South American nation of Brazil has a cultural legacy of gender-bending. As *The New York Times* reported,

> public cross-dressing peaks each year with the pre-Lenten Carnival celebrations. The participation of boisterous men in women's clothing and crude makeup is as much a tradition as samba competitions. Drag shows by transgender and gay performers became a fad in Rio nightclubs in the 1950s and '60s, and in subsequent decades some transgender women began using hormonal treatments and silicone to feminize their bodies....[1]

Aside from a brief respite from late 2008 through 2009, Brazil has been undergoing a negative social mood trend for the past eight years (Figure 1). During that time, transgender expressions have become even more visible in the country's popular culture.

Currently, there is a transgender trend in Brazil's fashion industry. It is spearheaded by supermodel Lea T, who was born as Leandro (Leo) Cerezo, the son of soccer hero Toninho Cerezo. Activists in Lea's hometown of Belo Horizonte, Brazil's third largest city, view her popularity as a step toward tolerance.[2]

Ms. T and other trans models have "added a pinch of

Source: Wikimedia Commons/Ambev Brasil

In the Spotlight: *Transgender supermodel Lea T.*

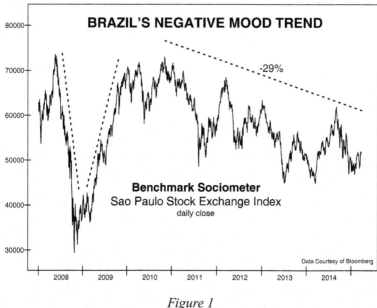

Figure 1

exoticism to the country's showcase modeling sector."[3] Sergio Mattos, head of a Brazilian modeling agency, said one advantage of trans models is their "long, sinewy limbs." He added, "Once they've lasered away facial or body hair, they can sometimes look more feminine even than models who were born female."

One of Mattos' top trans models is Carol Marra, who has opened her own lingerie line and filmed two mini-series for major Brazilian television stations.[4] Marra has completed a "whirlwind of commercial work," enjoyed well-publicized appearances at Fashion Rio and Sao Paulo fashion week and posed nearly nude on the cover of the popular men's magazine, *Trip*.[5]

As Brazil's negative social mood trend has continued, crossing gender lines has become more common in the country's most populous cities, and more trans models have come to the fore. They include Melissa Paixão, Camila Ribeiro and Felipa Tavares, who are doing runway and catalog work in Brazil's national fashion market.

Increases in transgender expressions are evident beyond the country's fashion industry. In 2011, the highly rated reality show *Big Brother Brazil* featured its first transgender contestant. The following year, a transgender person competed in the second annual Miss Bumbum competition, "a beauty contest that focuses exclusively on Brazil's most obsessed-over part of the female anatomy."[6] In November 2014, at a low in the Sao Paulo index, Rio de Janeiro held the "largest collective same-sex civil wedding ceremony in the world," in which 160 homosexual and transgender couples exchanged vows.[7] Sao Paulo, Brazil's largest city, now offers payments of 840 Brazilian reals (US $266) to transgender youth who attend 30 hours of middle school or high school classes per week in hopes that they will finish their education and avoid prostitution.[8]

Brazil is regarded as a haven for transgender people. Its government now pays for gender reassignment surgery,[9] and it allows people who have undergone the procedure to change their name and gender on their birth certificates.[10]

Yet even in Brazil, transgender people are occasionally victims of violence, which is another trait of negative-mood times. According to the *Rio Times*, Brazil is "the seventh most violent nation in the world, behind war-torn countries such as Somalia, Iraq and Afghanistan."[11] Total murders in the country numbered 47,136 in 2012, and 114 of those murders were of transgender people. Some of the killings were especially grisly and involved machetes and multiple stabbings.

In the face of these risks, transgender expressions continue to rise in Brazil, where the "newfound prominence" of transgender models in the country is said to point to a "seismic shift" in the nation's society.[12] But such shifts are never permanent. We can expect the trend to continue as long as Brazil's negative social mood trend persists. Those who benefit from greater transgender acceptance should capitalize on this window of opportunity, as the window will likely begin to close when the social mood trend turns back toward the positive.

NOTES AND REFERENCES

[1] Barnes, T. (2014, March 15). Transgender Models Prosper in Brazil, Where Carnival and Faith Reign. *The New York Times*.

[2] Phillips, T., & Davies, L. (2010, July 31). Lea T and the Loneliness of the Fashion World's First Transsexual Supermodel. *The Guardian*.

[3] Barchfield, J. (2012, December 6). Transgenders Break into Brazil's Modeling Sector. Associated Press/*Yahoo! News*.

[4] Carol Marra: Transgender Model Making Waves in Brazilian Fashion World. *Inquisitr*.

[5] See endnote 3.

[6] See endnote 4.

[7] Hearst, C. (2014, November 24). Rio Holds Mass Same-sex Wedding Ceremony. *The Rio Times*.

[8] Associated Press. (2015, January 29). Brazil's Largest City to Pay Transgender Youth to Finish School. *LGBTQ Nation*.

[9] Brazil, Cuba to Provide Free Sex-change Surgery. (2008, June 7). *IBN Live*.

[10] Changing Legal Gender Assignment in Brazil. Wikipedia.

[11] Conde, M.L. (2013, November 12). Murder Rate Up Nearly 8 Percent in Brazil. *The Rio Times*.

[12] See endnote 3.

Chapter 66

Socionomics Can Benefit Sociology—
Case in Point: Baby Names

Alan Hall

May 21, 2010 (TS)

Time after time, sociological studies are hindered by mysteries that socionomics can explain. Socionomics can resolve certain questions because it seeks answers from a fundamental cause: waves of unconsciously shared mood that impel society's choices.

Three recent, related studies offer a concise example. All three studies analyze the same expression of social behavior: babies' names. The first one spots boom-and-crash behavior in the popularity of certain non-traditional names. The second mentions similarities to the stock market and cycles of boom and bust. The third reveals comprehensive societal swings from individualism to conformism and back. All three studies uncover clues whose value is crystal clear to a socionomist, and all three verge on the socionomic insight. Yet none of them compare naming data to sociometers such as stock price data. Had they done so, they might have discovered that social mood regulates changes in both categories of decisions. We will examine the three studies in chronological order.

1. The Faster They Rise, the Faster They Fall

In March 2009, Jonah Berger and Gael Le Mens published a paper titled, "How Adoption Speed Affects the Abandonment of Cultural Tastes." The authors examined baby naming in the United States and France and found that the popularity of unusual names—much like the popularity of fads such as Hula Hoops, Lava Lamps or Pet Rocks—rises and falls rapidly:

> Things that catch on more quickly are more likely to be seen as fads and decline more quickly. We can show that things that catch on

quickly are less successful over all. That dynamic could be at play in everything from music and fashion to cars and hair styles.[1]

Unusual names—monikers that barely make it into the top 1,000 popular names of a decade—are the most prone to boom and bust. Charts of the popularity of unusual names—available at BabyNameWizard.com—are remarkably similar to graphs of history's prominent financial manias and their aftermaths as well as death tolls from epidemics, as shown in "A Socionomic View of Epidemic Disease" (*The Socionomist,* June 2009) [Chapter 52].

Figure 1 shows the rise and fall of a sample unusual name (left), a stock index (middle) and the death rate during an epidemic (right). Each history reflects a rapid growth and decay process. Chapter 9 of *The Wave Principle of Human Social Behavior* includes this passage: "Says Oxford zoologist Richard Dawkins, 'When a craze, say for pogo sticks, paper darts, Slinkies or jacks sweeps through a school, it follows a history just like a measles epidemic.'"[2] A similar dynamic of social interaction drives all these activities.

Similar Dynamics at Work

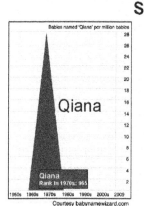 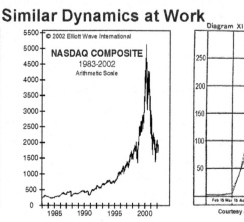 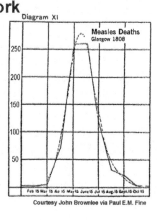

Figure 1

2. Parents Choose Names Much as Investors Choose Stocks

Todd Gureckis and Robert Goldstone published the study, "How You Named Your Child…" in August 2009. The authors used the Social Security Administration's database to analyze the naming of children throughout the entire U.S. population from 1880 to 2007. They found that although naming is an expression of individual preference, it is also "fundamentally linked to the behavior and decisions of others." They elaborated,

> We will ultimately argue that the perceived value of a name is deter-
> mined not by some intrinsic property of the name itself, but is rather
> an emergent property of the behavior of other parents.... Like the
> stock market, cycles of boom and bust appear to arise out of the
> interactions of a large set of agents who are continually influencing
> one another.[3]

The authors attempted to link these cycles to a positive feedback loop:

> In the more recent data (1981-2007)...names seemed to carry with
> them a "momentum" that tends to push changes in popularity in
> the same direction year after year. Parents in the United States are
> increasingly sensitive to the change in frequency of a name in recent
> time, such that names that are gaining in popularity are seen as more
> desirable than those that have fallen in popularity in the recent past.[4]

Such loops, however, do not account for the reversals. As the authors intimate, parents sometimes herd when they choose baby names, much as
investors herd when they move stock prices up and down. Prechter and
Parker linked human interdependence to an Elliott-wave-based herding
dynamic in their paper, "The Financial/Economic Dichotomy" [reproduced
as Chapter 15 in *The Socionomic Theory of Finance*, 2016], and the fractal
form of the Elliott wave model *does* account for reversals.

3. Social Mood Governs Conformity in Naming

A study from 2010 ventures closer to socionomic causality. "Fitting
In or Standing Out: Trends in American Parents' Choices for Children's
Names, 1880-2007," by Jean M. Twenge, Emodish M. Abebe and W. Keith
Campbell, explores the individualism vs. conformism expressed in baby
naming. The authors explained,

> We gathered naming data from the Social Security Administration's
> database of baby names from 1880 to 2007, recording the percent-
> age of babies given the most popular name or a name among the
> 10, 25 or 50 most popular for each year and sex. Higher percentages
> of babies receiving common names correspond to fewer parents
> giving unusual names and thus presumably an emphasis on fitting
> in; lower percentages of babies with common names mean more
> emphasis on standing out.[5]

The authors also observed that from "1880 to 2007, parents have increasingly given their children less common names, suggesting a growing
interest in uniqueness and individualism." The increase in unique names,
however, is not a straight line:

Common names decreased in use from 1880 to 1919 and increased slightly from 1920 to 1949 before becoming steadily less popular from 1950 to 2007, with an unremitting decrease after 1983 and the greatest rate of change during the 1990s.[6]

We decided to compare the authors' commonness-of-names data to one of our benchmark sociometers. In Figure 2, we plot the commonness of baby names in the U.S. from 1935 to 2007 against social mood as reflected by the Dow/PPI. We find a moderate relationship prior to 1935 and a strong correlation thereafter. Note that each major turn in stocks preceded a major turn in naming trends. The chart shows that parents tend to give their children increasingly unusual, if not unique, names during and shortly after positive mood trends and increasingly ordinary names during and shortly after negative mood trends. The authors of the third study noted, "After 1950, fewer and fewer babies received common names." This observation perfectly fits our socionometer, because the year 1949 marked the end of a 20-year bear market in the Dow/PPI and the kickoff of a major bull market. The authors also observed that the fastest decrease in the use of common names occurred in the 1990s. This trend coincided with the highest positive rate of change in stock prices on the chart.

Socionomics proposes that naturally shared, unconscious impulses to herd produce social mood trends. A positive mood trend imbues society with increasing certainty, confidence and optimism, which are feelings that propel bull markets and foster creativity, individualism, diversity, friskiness and flamboyance in areas as varied as fashion, automobile design, housing design, body art and baby names. A negative mood trend imbues society with increasing doubt, fear and pessimism, which are feelings that drive bear markets and foster conformity and conservatism in fashion, automobile design, house design and baby names.

Prechter's early socionomic research observed that people tend to be individualistic during positive mood periods and conformist during negative mood periods. His August 1985 Special Report, "Popular Culture and the Stock Market," noted people's tendency to flaunt their individuality in the former environment and to blend in with the crowd in the latter:

> Bright colors have been associated with market tops and dull, dark colors with bottoms. It is not coincidence, then, that the smaller the skirt or swimsuit, the brighter the color(s); floor-length fashions, in turn, are more associated with dull, dark colors such as brown,

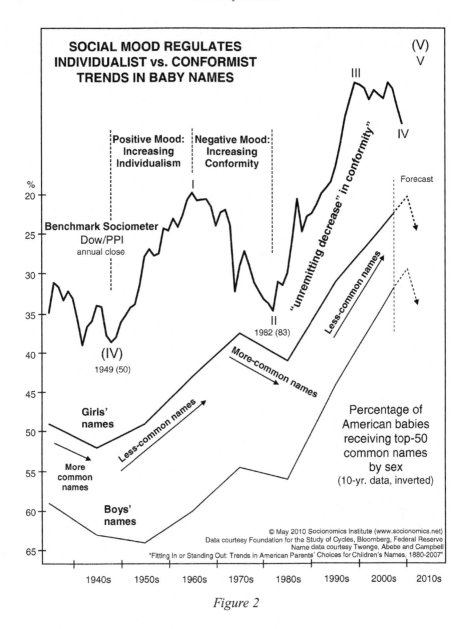

Figure 2

black and grey. All these fashion elements reflect the same general mood. Tie width, heel height, pants leg style, and flamboyance or conservatism in men's fashions also fit the trends in the stock market.[7]

A table in that report listed 25 areas of cultural expression that manifest differently depending on the trend in social mood. In the areas of politics and fashion, positive social mood trends produce individualism, and negative mood trends produce social conformity, as noted in bold in the portion of the table reproduced below:

	RISING TRANSITION	PEAK POSITIVE MOOD	FALLING TRANSITION	PEAK NEGATIVE MOOD
Fashion (style)	"Correctness" is stressed	**Flamboyant individuality** For men and women	Anti-fashion Fashions	**Conservative** dress returns
Politics	**Individualism** increasingly popular	**Individualism** reigns	**Collectivism** increasingly popular	**Collectivism** reigns

We can now add trends in choices for babies' names to the list.

Parents' tendency to choose ordinary names during times of negative social mood probably reflects an evolutionary tactic to aid surviving and thriving. People choose to blend in with the herd in times of fear and uncertainty, and stand out for advantage when it's safe to do so. When social mood trends negatively, parents unconsciously feel that an unusual name could hurt their children's prospects in society or even endanger them. When mood trends positively, parents feel that an unusual name will help their children get noticed for their special qualities. Baby naming, then, may simply reflect unconscious perceptions of risk (see Chapter 19 of *Socionomic Theory of Finance*), which are regulated by social mood.

Cultural Signals of Extremity and Reversal

Baby names hitch rides on pop culture's currents. Two of the most uniquely named individuals in America are Moon Unit and Dweezil, so named by father Frank Zappa in 1967 and 1969, right at a major extreme in positive social mood. In the latter year, Johnny Cash signaled a reversal in the trend when he recorded Shel Silverstein's 'A Boy Named Sue'. It became Cash's biggest hit, spending three weeks at #2 on the Billboard Hot 100 chart and topping the country-music and adult-contemporary charts, and it earned Silverstein a Grammy Award in 1970. The song ends like this:

> And if I ever have a son, I think I'm gonna name him Bill or George! Anything but Sue! I still hate that name![8]

Our Forecast: A Continuation of Socionomic Causality

The relationship between social mood and baby naming demonstrated in Figure 2 allows us to forecast that negative social mood will continue to produce more-conformist baby names in coming bear market years, and positive social mood will continue to produce less-conformist baby names in future bull market years. As a corollary, we should see compatible trends of expression in everything from fashion to architecture.

The Socionomic Perspective Can Help Sociologists

Sociologists often uncover behaviors they can't fully explain. The authors of the second study, "How You Named Your Child," wrote, "As yet we do not have a complete explanation for why the situational factors contribute to peaks and reversals in the actual name data." The authors of the third study, "Fitting In…" lamented that data on the "cultural practices, social behaviors, and psychological processes linked to individualism [are] historically limited because psychological measures are relatively recent, often not beginning until the 1970s." But socionomists propose that aggregate stock prices are a reliable psychological measure—of social mood—and they have been recorded for over 300 years.

Socionomics can help social scientists who do great work yet are hindered by lack of the proper causal paradigm. The three naming studies described above pointed us to a new sociometer. More sociometers await discovery. Any broad data that track emotionally charged, non-rational social activity are likely to parallel benchmark sociometers such as stock prices. We also expect to see an increasing number of academic studies skirt the edges of socionomics. Perhaps someday they will start there.

Post-production update: As the Dow continued to trend positively, an article from July 2017 titled "Baby Names Have Got Out of Hand—Use Numbers Instead"[9] poked fun at the recent rash of celebrities saddling their children with extremely unusual names and cited 18 real-life monikers (last names excluded): Moxie CrimeFighter, Audio Science, Bronx Mowgli, Pilot Inspektor, Sixtus Dominic Boniface Christopher, Tom Wentworth Somerset Dunstan, Peter Theodore Alphege, Anselm Charles Fitzwilliam, Alfred Wulfric Leyson Pius, Poppy Honey Rosie, Daisy Boo Pamela, Petal Blossom Rainbow, Buddy Bear Maurice, River Rocket, Nell Marmalade, Eric Mustard, Vincent Mash and DeNiro. The trend is enough in people's consciousness that Sweden updated its anti-weird-baby-naming law on July 1. We expect that some expressions of baby-name regret will accompany the next big trend toward negative social mood.

NOTES AND REFERENCES

[1] Dotinga, R. (2009, May 5). Fad Baby Names Tend to Fizzle Fast. *Healthday News*.

[2] Prechter, R. (1999). *The Wave Principle of Human Social Behavior and the New Science of Socionomics*. Gainesville, GA, USA: New Classics Library.

[3,4] Gureckis, T. Goldstone, R. (2009). How You Named Your Child: Understanding the Relationship Between Individual Decision-making and Collective Outcomes. *Topics in Cognitive Science*, 1 (2009), 651, 652, 668.

[5,6] Twenge, J. Abebe, E. Campbell, K. (2010). Fitting In or Standing Out: Trends in American Parents' Choices for Children's Names, 1880-2007. *Social Psychological and Personality Science*, 1(1) 19-25, 20-21.

[7] Prechter, R. (1985, August). *The Elliott Wave Theorist* special report, "Popular Culture and the Stock Market", 17.

[8] Silverstein, S. (1969). *A Boy Named Sue*.

[9] Dawson, A. (2017, July 7). Baby Names Have Got Out of Hand. Use Numbers Instead. *The Guardian*.

Chapter 67

"Like, Ew! Grody to the Max!" Social Mood Influences the Tone of Popular Slang

Alan Hall

November 29, 2016 (TS)

A number of researchers have examined the frequencies of word-occurrence in relation to social behavior, and we have reported on many of their findings in past issues of *The Socionomist*. As examples, University of Houston professor Alex Bentley and colleagues found that changes in the frequencies of emotion-laden words in U.S., U.K. and German literature reflected changes in social mood.[1] Thomas Lansdall-Welfare, Vasileios Lampos and Nello Cristianini of the University of Bristol's Intelligent Systems Laboratory discovered that Londoners' Tweets became increasingly negative leading up to the 2011 riots in London [see Chapter 28 in *Socionomic Causality in Politics*].[2] The RAND Corporation released similar findings about the 2012 protests in Iran [see Chapter 33 in *Socionomic Causality in Politics*].[3] And Warwick Business School professor Suzy Moat's research group found that Google searches for finance-focused terms predicted changes in the Dow Jones Industrial Average.[4]

Popular slang has received less attention from academic researchers. We wondered if social mood might influence the tenor of popular slang words and phrases that emerge over time. We found evidence that mood alternately lightens and darkens the "swank"[5] of popular slang. We selected the terms cited in this article from several crowd-sourced lists of slang words by decade.[6,7,8]

Figure 1 illustrates a few slang words and phrases that became popular at positive and negative social mood extremes in the second half of the 20th century. The late 1960s produced slang that fit the positive mood extreme

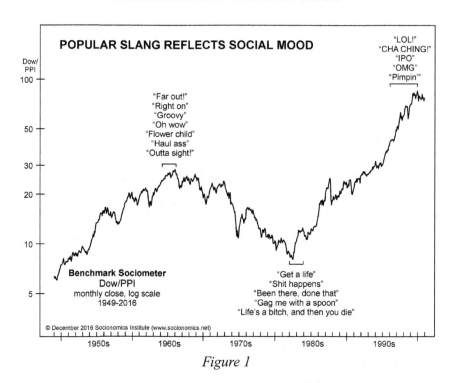

Figure 1

of those times, as noted in Figure 1. Popular phrases included enthusiastic exclamations, "Far out!" "Right on!" and "Outta sight!"

The negative social mood extreme of 1982 produced several slang phrases that were primarily negative in tone. A February 2007 *New Yorker* article, "Notable Quotables," mentions four of them:

> It is extremely interesting to know, for instance, that the phrase "Shit happens" was introduced to print by one Connie Eble, in a publication identified as "UNC–CH Slang" (presumably the University of North Carolina at Chapel Hill), in 1983. "Life's a bitch, and then you die," a closely related reflection, dates from 1982, the year it appeared in the *Washington Post*. "Been there, done that" entered the public discourse in 1983, via the *Union Recorder*, a publication out of the University of Sydney. "Get a life": *The Washington Post*, 1983. (What is it about the nineteen-eighties, anyway?)[9]

It is not, however, "about the nineteen-eighties"; it is about the extremely negative social mood that manifested at the 1982 bottom in the PPI-adjusted Dow Jones Industrial Average.

At the bottom of Figure 1, we added "Gag me with a spoon"—an expression of disgust derived from Valspeak, an "obnoxious form of

Californian English"[10]—to *The New Yorker*'s list. The phrase "gag me with a spoon" boomed in popularity after Frank Zappa released the song 'Valley Girl' in 1982, in which his 14-year-old daughter, Moon Unit Zappa, spoke phrases stereotypical of the Southern California Valley Girl. What's that, you ask? According to a 1982 article in *Time* magazine, Valley Girl was a new subspecies, "*puella americana vallensis*." *Time* explained,

> All of a sudden, from Tarzana, Calif., to Tarrytown, N.Y., everyone with a teen-age daughter is wondering: Is she one? A Valley Girl, that is. If she's from a fairly well-to-do family, and between the ages of 13 and 17, chances are she is. If her passions are shopping, popularity, pigging out on junk food and piling on cosmetics, the answer is probably "fer shurr." If she is almost unintelligible, the verdict can only be: "Totally." Particularly if she pronounces the word "Toe-dully."... Like Zappa, puts it:

> > Last idea to cross her mind
> > Had something to do with where to find
> > A pair of jeans to fit her butt
> > And where to get her toenails cut.[11]

Zappa intended to lampoon the Valley Girl, a stereotype with "many negative connotations…including low intelligence, uncertainty, vanity, and immaturity."[12] But his song struck the negative social-mood nerve, and the popularity of Valspeak slang skyrocketed, spawning a 1982-83 TV show, *Square Pegs*, and a 1983 movie, *Valley Girl*. The slang had staying power. In 2015, actress Drew Barrymore, who grew up in SoCal, wrote,

> As if I had been lobotomized, we packed our things and moved into our new home, indeed in Sherman Oaks, in 1983. It's why I still talk like a valley girl. That cadence snuck into my life at that spongelike age of eight and never left.[13]

You can still hear that distinctive cadence today, which, as *Time* pointed out, is peppered with the word "like":

> "Shopping is the funnest thing to do, 'cause, O.K., clothes? They're important. Like for your image and stuff. Like I'm sure. Everything has to match. Like everything. And you don't want to wear stuff that people don't wear. People'd look at you and just go, 'Ew, she's a zod,' like get away."[14]

From now on, when you hear the word "like" used repeatedly in one sentence, you will probably remember that Valspeak sprang from the social-mood valley of 1982. Socionomics changes the way one observes social behavior, and that insight will stick better than slang.

The bouncy materialism of the late 1990s differed from the "peace and love" ethic of the late 1960s, but popular slang was equally positive, featuring "Cha-ching!" and such texting favorites as "LOL" ("laugh out loud") and "OMG" ("oh my god"). The slang of both eras reflected the friskiness, optimism and wondrous amazement generated by peak positive mood.

An Area for Further Research

Slang remains under-researched by academics, although some sociologists, anthropologists and linguists are beginning to realize its importance as a window into social dynamics. Robert L. Moore of Rollins College proposed that slang reflects shifts in generational values.[15] Connie C. Eble of the University of North Carolina at Chapel Hill discovered that slang cements group identity.[16]

We think slang is a groovy topic for future social mood research. It would be fun, for instance, to extend our study back further in time. Evidence suggests that a well-known expression suggestive of negative-mood origins—"Life is one damn thing after another'—first appeared in print in March 1909,[17] suggesting that it originated shortly after the Panic of 1907, which ended that year in November. The ebullient 1920s produced such cheery gems as "And how!" "Attaboy!" and "It's the bees' knees." A 2012 paper titled "Increases in Individualistic Words and Phrases in American Books, 1960–2008" addresses some other ideas that we think are ripe for further exploration. Authors Jean M. Twenge, W. Keith Campbell and Brittany Gentile (along with editor R. Alexander Bentley) found that in general, "individualistic words and phrases increased in use between 1960 and 2008."[18] We would like to see the study divided into times before and after 1982, when the trend of social mood changed. The researchers did find that

> individualistic words and phrases emphasizing standing alone (such as independence, self reliance, self sufficient, solitary, and sole) were among the few that decreased or did not change. [Also,] the modern communal words and phrases prominently featured the words "community" and "team," constructions of communalism that were apparently used less often in previous decades. This is a potentially interesting avenue for future research.[19]

We're cool with that.

NOTES AND REFERENCES

[1] Bentley, R.A., Acerbi, A., & Hall, A. (2015, January). Word Choices in 20th Century US, UK, German and Russian Literature Reflect Social Mood. *The Socionomist.*

[2] Thompson, C. (2012, September). Twitter Study Shows an Increase in Negative Mood Leading Up to Last Year's London Riots. *The Socionomist.*

[3] Wilson, E. (2013, February). When Emotions Ran High: Study Finds That Twitter Swearing Predicted Iranian Protests. *The Socionomist.*

[4] Thompson, C. (2014, February). Suzy Moat Tracks Correlations Between Internet Data and Human Decision-making. *The Socionomist.*

[5] Thefreedictionary.com defines "swank" as "stylishness, elegance, swagger or pretension."

[6] Do You Remember the 60s Slang? The60sofficialsite.com

[7] Glossary of Eighties Terms. *In the 80s.* Inthe80s.com

[8] Terms of the 90s, Slang of the Nineties. *In the 90s.* Inthe90s.com

[9] Menand, L. (2007, February 19). Notable Quotables. *The New Yorker.*

[10] What Is the Origin of the Phrase "Gag me with a spoon"? *English Language & Usage Stack Exchange.*

[11] Demarest, M. (1982, September 27). How Toe-dully Max is Their Valley (1 of 2). *Time.*

[12] Whitmire, A. Slang and Intonation Used by Young Americans. *Conversations Direct.*

[13] Barrymore, D. (2015). *Wildflower* (pp. 2; 7). New York: Dutton. ISB N 9781101983799. OCLC 904421431

[14] Demarest, M. (1982, September 27). How Toe-dully Max is Their Valley (2 of 2). *Time.*

[15] Moore, R.L. (2004). We're Cool, Mom and Dad Are Swell: Basic Slang and Generational Shifts in Values. *American Speech*, 79(1), 59-86. *Project Muse.*

[16] Connie C. Eble. English & Comparative Literature. College of Arts & Sciences. The University of North Carolina at Chapel Hill.

[17] "Life is just one damn thing after another," Quote Investigator. quoteinvestigator.com.

[18] Twenge, J.M., Campbell, W.K., & Gentile, B. (2012). Increases in Individualistic Words and Phrases in American Books, 1960-2008. *PLoS ONE* 7(7): e40181. doi:10.1371/journal.pone.0040181.

[19] *Ibid.*

Chapter 68

More Golf Links to Social Mood

Peter Kendall on a study by Kevin Armstrong

May 16, 2013 (TS)

In October 1997, my article in *The Elliott Wave Theorist* [reprinted as Chapter 17 in *Pioneering Studies in Socionomics*] documented "golf's pedigree as one of the great bull market games" and traced its rise from an initial boom in the Roaring '20s up through the 1990s. Its waves of greatest success have been coincident with every major upward surge in stock prices. At the time of that report, a mania for stocks was in full swing, and its alignment with the booming popularity of golf was so tight that many business publications, including *The Wall Street Journal*, *Business Week* and *Barron's*, actually added golfing supplements to their issues. The October 1, 1997 issue of *Barron's* stated outright, "We can now report that there appears to be a definite connection between golf and stocks."

When demand for "golf shares" developed into "a legitimate stock market sector with no less than 29 issues," EWT argued that the mania for stocks and golf had become literally one and the same.

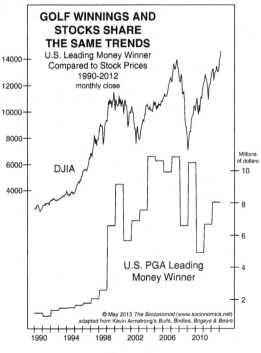

Figure 1

At the 2013 Socionomics Summit, financial professional and author Kevin Armstrong expanded upon the "remarkable and revealing relationship between golf and investment markets." Armstrong updated this relationship with data on the prize money awarded annually by the Professional Golfers Association. Figure 1 shows just how closely the amount of money won by the PGA's top winner each year has tracked trends in stocks since 1990. Figure 2 confirms that relationship all the way back to the mid-1930s. Armstrong calculated that if the 1936 money leader had invested his winnings in U.S. stocks, "his wealth would have grown to almost exactly the amount that each year's leading money winner accumulated."

Figure 2

Armstrong's findings extend to more nuanced socionomic insights as well. *Prechter's Perspective* (1996) had noted, "In every field, women gain dominance in bear market periods." Armstrong compared the total amount of money earned by the men's top golfer to that earned by players in the Ladies Professional Golf Association tour over a period of 60 years. His chart of the PGA/LPGA earnings ratio revealed a consistently more dominant role of women in negative-mood environments (see Figure 3). As the nominal DJIA triple-topped near 1000 from 1966 to 1973, male supremacy, represented by a higher PGA/LPGA winnings ratio, resulted in the leading male golfer earning six times that of the LPGA leading money winner. By the end of the bear market in 1982, on the other hand, the ratio approached parity. As stocks rose again, the ratio rose dramatically to between four and six times.

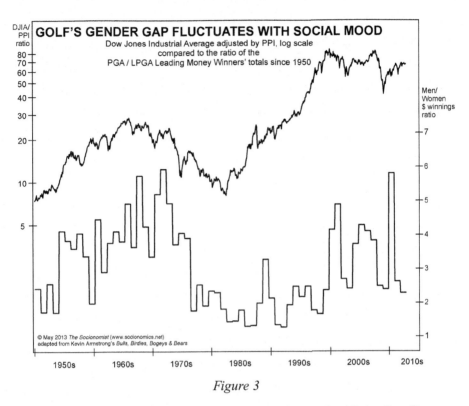

Figure 3

Back in 1997, EWT established the ascendance of golf's leading figures in times of positive social mood. It showed that Tiger Woods had assumed a "top athlete" mantle, "just as Jack Nicklaus did in the mid-1960s and Bobby Jones did in the late 1920s." In his recently released book, *Bulls, Birdies, Bogeys & Bears*, Armstrong extended that observation with a broad array of comparisons showing how "incredibly, the ebb and flow of Tiger's fortunes" reflect the "ups and downs of the stock market during one of its most tumultuous fifteen-year periods."

Chapter 69

Social Mood and the
Ryder and Solheim Cups

Kevin Armstrong
October 17, 2013 (TS)

The May issue of *The Socionomist* mentioned my recently released book, *Bulls, Birdies, Bogeys and Bears: The Remarkable and Revealing Relationship Between Golf and Investment Markets*, and my presentation at the 2013 Socionomics Summit. Since then, the thesis behind the book—that social mood and professional golf are inextricably linked—has been put to the test in real time.

Trends in golf, particularly professional golf, as well as the fortunes of professional golfers, have mirrored trends in the stock market for more than a century. We now find that stock market trends have had an uncanny correspondence to the subsequent results of professional team competitions such as the Ryder Cup, awarded to male professionals of Europe, and the Solheim Cup, the females' equivalent.

If success in golf is a reflection of social mood, and if a region's social mood is more positive, making its stock market perform better, then that region's professional male golfers should do better. For the Ryder Cup, that has indeed been the case. Throughout the Ryder Cup's early history—before World War II—the relative performances of the stock markets on the two sides of the Atlantic were very even, as were the relative results of the golfers' teams. This situation changed after the war, when both American golfers and the American stock market dominated. This domination continued until the early 1980s.

The trend of American dominance began to weaken in 1983, when America prevailed by only the narrowest of margins. It ended two years later when America lost the cup for the first time in 28 years. This shift is clearly seen in the relative performance of the stock markets on the two sides of the Atlantic.

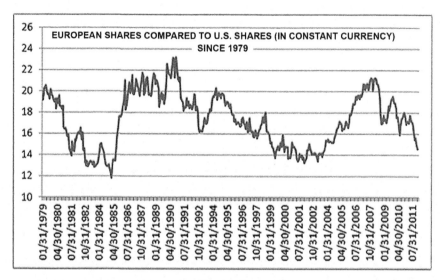

Figure 1

Figure 1, from *Bulls, Birdies, Bogeys and Bears*, shows the performance of the European market relative to the U.S. market since 1979. When the line is rising, the European market is performing better, and when it is falling, the U.S. market is superior.

The low in relative performance for the U.S. market just prior to the 1985 Ryder Cup is clear. It was an indication that social mood in Europe had been more positive than in the U.S. over that period. Against that backdrop, Europe went on to win the Cup. Ever since, whichever side's stock market has performed the best since the last contest has gone on to win the cup 83% of the time. These results have frequently been at odds with the pre-match forecasts of sports experts and the expectations of bookmakers.

The Gender Gap

In *Popular Culture and the Stock Market* (1985), Robert Prechter observed that during times of negative social mood, more women are elected to office, whereas the reverse is true during periods of positive social mood. Is a similar social-mood-driven effect seen in other areas, such as golf?

The first Solheim Cup competition was in 1990, the final year of a four-year bear market in the Value Line Composite stock index. Through 2012, there had been 12 contests. Of those 12, the winning team on 10 occasions (83%) represented the side of the Atlantic whose stock market had been the *poorer* performer during the prior two years—the *inverse* of the relationship found in the Ryder Cup.

Source: Golf Week

Defying the Odds: *The European Team's win was contrary to the forecasts of golf analysts and bookmakers, but not socionomists.*

Ahead of this year's 13th staging of the Solheim Cup in Colorado (August 16-18), that insight led me to a non-consensus forecast. On August 6, I informed my subscribers that since the 2011 victory by the European ladies in Ireland, the European market had risen by about 40%, whereas during the same period the U.S. market had risen 50%. The euro had also slipped a couple of percentage points against the dollar. All this added up to out-performance on the part of the U.S. markets, reflecting a more upbeat social mood in the U.S. as compared to that in Europe. It also indicated that the European ladies should win the Solheim Cup, just as they did two years earlier when the European Union appeared on the verge of collapse.

Few anticipated such an outcome. In early August, the media and bookmakers expected the "All Star" American team to comfortably maintain its 100% home win record. The U.S. team included Stacy Lewis, the world's second-ranked player at the time, who had just secured victory in the British Open. Bookmakers placed the odds of a European victory at an almost insulting 11-4. Such confidence for an American home win presented an opportunity to anyone wishing to place a wager based upon a socionomically inspired forecast.

I concluded my note to subscribers with this comment:

> In some ways, the situation in the Solheim Cup now is very similar to that in the Ryder Cup in 1987. Then the Europeans were defending the trophy in America, and the markets strongly favoured an unlikely first European victory on American soil. The Europeans delivered then, and don't be too surprised if their female counterparts pull off

a surprise victory in Colorado the weekend after next. With odds of
11-4 against such an outcome it may just be worth an "investment."

Such an "investment" proved worthwhile. The European ladies stunned
their American counterparts and the majority of commentators. They led
after the first day, whitewashed the Americans in the afternoon round of
the second day and then dominated on the final day to eventually win by
a convincing 18-10 margin. Laura Davies, a veteran English golfer and
longtime stalwart of the European Solheim Cup team, said, "If you were
having a bet on this event you'd never have picked 18-10 in a million years."

Social mood as reflected in the markets may not have indicated the
magnitude of the victory, but unlike the vast majority of forecasts, it did
signal the counter-intuitive outcome.

Chapter 70

Success *vs.* Scandal—Real-Time Socionomic Analyses of Tiger Woods' Fortunes, 2009-2013

Gary Grimes with Ben Hall and Alan Hall

December 16, 2009 / January 20, 2010 /
January 31, 2012 / May 7, 2012 / March 28, 2013 (TS)

12/16/09 (BH)

Positive-mood personalities had better tread carefully when social mood is negative, because given the chance, the media will pounce on any misstep. Consider golfer Tiger Woods. Woods turned pro in 1996 and quickly became the world's most respected golfer and the youngest player ever to achieve a Grand Slam. Woods has the most PGA and other major tournament wins among active players and received the PGA's Player of the Year award a record ten times.

Woods' prodigious career accomplishments now seem undone by— what? —an exceedingly minor one-car auto accident that has mushroomed into allegations including serial infidelity, alcoholism, drug abuse and more. Members of the media have attacked Tiger Woods, and the public can't get enough of the scandal. Woods' popularity 13 years after he turned pro is in a nosedive. Rasmussen's survey found that just 38% of Americans now have a favorable opinion of the golf superstar. That's down from 56% the week after the accident and 83% in 2007, when the public's love of stocks also peaked.

1/20/10 (GG)

When negative mood intensifies, society scrutinizes its figureheads from the former period of positive mood and often tears them down. Heroes from the field of athletics are no exception.

In 1997, Peter Kendall demonstrated that golf is a positive-mood game. It is gentlemanly as opposed to rough-and-tumble. It is a pastime for people with means, as equipment, greens fees and annual club dues cost thousands of dollars. The game possesses a clear code of ethics, sharp geometry, objective scorekeeping and a connection with the manicured outdoors. Tiger Woods is this positive-mood game's figurehead.

Woods' steamy affairs reportedly amounted to about a baker's dozen (*The New York Post* made a calendar) over the course of his five-year marriage. But *when* the news broke is what catches a socionomist's eye.

The *Post* first intimated at Woods' infidelity in 2004. A column reported that Tiger, baseball star Derek Jeter and basketball great Michael Jordan left a Manhattan night club with a trio of girls en route to Jeter's apartment. With social mood over a year into a newly positive trend, the story failed to gain traction. A U.K. golf columnist wrote, "We all knew about Tiger's secret life," saying it was common knowledge around the PGA Tour clubhouse. Several media reports say that the *National Enquirer* had photographic evidence of his infidelity two years ago. The tabloid supposedly used it as leverage to gain a cover story with Tiger for its sister publication, *Men's Fitness Magazine*. Other reports say that Tiger's wife had confronted him about the affairs and talked to other players' wives about her husband's partying. So, again: Why did no scandal erupt before now? Socionomics suggests an answer.

Rasmussen Reports has conducted phone surveys on Woods' popularity. "Just 38 percent of Americans now have a favorable opinion of the golf superstar," the service stated on December 9, 2009. "That's down from 56 percent a week ago, shortly after the story first broke about Woods' auto accident." But the sentence that follows is the most revealing: "Two years ago," i.e. in 2007, "83 percent had a favorable opinion of Woods."

Thus, as social mood turned from extremely positive in 2007 to extremely negative in 2009, so did Woods' popularity. Tiger Woods' star status began to fade even before his alleged playboy lifestyle became news. Two of his biggest sponsors dropped long-held endorsement deals with the golfer more than a year ago—American Express in August 2007, after ten years, and GM in December 2008, after nine years. Based on the polls and these actions, we infer that Woods' popularity reached its zenith in the months between his latest major wins, the PGA Championship in August 2007 and the U.S. Open in June 2008. Stock indexes, reflecting social mood, made all-time highs in July and October, 2007.

Long-time readers of our analysis may see a similarity between the Woods scandal and others like it. Bill Clinton, Martha Stewart and "The Donald" Trump all blew up when benchmark sociometers indicated that society was in a foul mood. The fortunes of all three of these public figures later recovered in step with equities.

Woods turned 34 years old on December 30. He is young enough to enjoy a rebound in popularity, much like his Nike counterpart Kobe Bryant, who only recently reappeared in prominent ads after his own infidelity scandal in 2003, the year of a global stock market low. If Tiger returns to golf and remains healthy, he can compete for the next 20 to 30 years. That's good, because it might take five to ten years for positive mood to restore his badly tarnished star.

1/31/12 (GG)

When Tiger Woods launched his professional career in 1996, social mood was overwhelmingly positive. In 1997, one sports writer was so wowed by the young player that he said there was no one in the field who could beat Woods over the next 30 tournaments. Many other sports writers made similar predictions. Woods went on to sign a five-year endorsement contract with Buick in 1999, and the following year he signed a $100 million contract extension with Nike.[1] Beginning in 1999 and continuing through 2008, Woods won 14 major golf championships. He continued his winning ways in 2009 with 8 more victories, and when he finished first in the non-major Australian Masters on November 15, 2009, it "looked as though he would rule golf for as long as he played,"[2] according to the Golf Channel.

As *The Wave Principle of Human Social Behavior* (1999) noted, however, "Mainstream social and economic forecasting has forever been a practice of extrapolating present and recent conditions into the future."[3] Linear predictions overlook the influence of waves of social mood.

Prechter also observed, "negative social moods are a natural chemical for ripening scandals, and the taste for them."[4] Just two weeks after Woods' win in November 2009, his sex scandal broke. The January 2010 issue of *The Socionomist* described the role that social mood seemed to be playing in a longer-term fall from grace. After we wrote that analysis, Woods went on a 26-tournament skid. In October 2010, he lost his global #1 ranking. In July 2011, he came under heavy criticism for firing the caddy who had guided him to 13 of his 14 major championships. In August 2011, he missed the cut for the PGA championship; it was only the seventh missed cut of his career on the PGA tour. In October 2011, he fell out of the Top 50 rankings for the first time in 15 years.

More recently, Woods did emerge victorious at the Chevron World Challenge in December 2011, giving him his first win in 27 attempts spanning more than two years. It moved Woods from #52 to #21 in the world ranking.[5]

So, is Tiger back? We asserted in January 2010 that based on EWI's forecasts, "it might take five to ten years for positive mood to restore his badly tarnished star." He is not there yet.

5/7/12 (AH)

In March, Tiger Woods won the Arnold Palmer Invitational—his first PGA Tour victory in 30 months—and the Tour's website proclaimed, "Tiger's back." Pundits expected Woods to perform well at the 2012 Master's Tournament held April 5-8, but his play was marred by multiple "what-the-heck-was-that?" shots and his worst four-round score in any tournament in almost two decades. Spectators also saw him curse, throw clubs and, on one occasion, kick his 9-iron about 15 yards.

One observer said that Woods' behavior was "startlingly indicative of a man whose state of mind won't soon allow him to get back to winning at the highest level of his sport."[6] Paul Azinger, former Ryder Cup captain, said about Woods, "In the 28 years I've played golf for a living I've never been as lost as he looked out there."[7]

Woods' behavior meant he faced the possibility of disciplinary action by the PGA Tour. We may never know

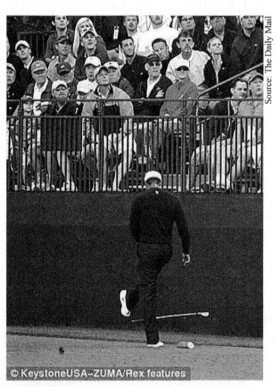

Source: The Daily Mail

© KeystoneUSA–ZUMA/Rex features

Bitter Boot: Woods kicks his club after another failed shot at the Masters.

whether the organization fined Woods, however, as the Tour "does not disclose its dispensation of fines and suspensions."[8] In any case, Woods faces an uphill battle. He is a positive-mood performer struggling to recover from a negative mood setback. [Note: The Case-Shiller Home Price Index bottomed that very month—Ed.]

3/28/13 (GG)

We thought it would take at least five years, but it took only three. Less than a month after the Dow Jones Industrial Average scored a new all-time high, Tiger Woods reclaimed the No. 1 spot in professional golf "with a game that looks as good as ever."[9]

As Tiger and the Dow jointly reclaimed their lofty positions, their symbiotic relationship has come to the attention of a golf-minded market watcher. A March 26 *Wall Street Journal* article plotted Woods' on-course performance alongside the Dow (see Figure 1). Author Matthew Futterman wrote, "Pay particular attention to the period between 2004-2009 and from late 2011 to the present. The trend lines are eerily similar." Not to mention the fact that the Dow/gold ratio bottomed in 2011 in sync with Woods' professional nadir. Futterman chronicled the transition:

> As the U.S. economy fattened on the strength of an illusory real-estate boom, Woods was ascendant on the golf course and seemingly off of it too—a fourth Masters in 2005, wins at the PGA Championship and the British Open in 2006, a fourth PGA Championship in 2007 and a third US Open in 2008, plus a beautiful wife and a baby girl.
>
> But the second half of 2008 brought the subprime mortgage and banking crises that sent the markets reeling. Woods broke his leg and had to call it quits for the season. Then came 2009, a DJIA dipping below 7000 and revelations of a series of extramarital affairs that doomed Woods's marriage.[10]

Tiger's comeback surprised people who penned the "Tiger Woods is Finished" headlines from a few years ago. But his fall and subsequent return to the top are consistent with our forecast three years ago for the worst period of his career *and* for his eventual recovery along with social mood and stocks. We expect this symbiotic relationship to continue.

A Tale of Two Averages

The last decade has produced a strange synchronicity between Tiger Woods's performance on the golf course and the Dow Jones Industrial Average.

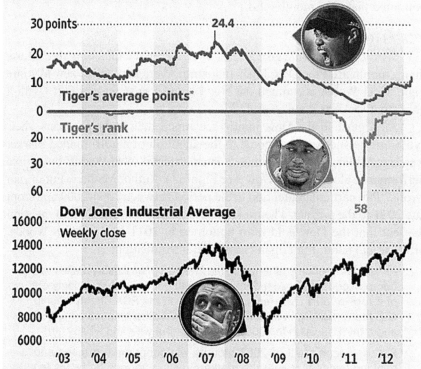

*Points are awarded based on tournament performance during previous two-year period. The average is determined by dividing total points by the number of events played, with a minimum divisor of 40 and a maximum of 52.

Photos top to bottom: Agence France-Presse/Getty Images, Getty Images

Sources: Official World Golf Ranking, WSJ Market Data Group   The Wall Street Journal

Figure 1

NOTES AND REFERENCES

[1] DiCarlo, L. (2004, March 18). Six degrees of Tiger Woods. *Forbes.*

[2] Ferguson, D. (2011, December 4). Skid Snapper: Tiger Finally Wins Again. Golf Channel.

[3] Prechter, R. (1999). *The Wave Principle of Human Social Behavior* (pp. 371-372). Gainesville, Georgia: New Classics Library.

[4] *The Wave Principle of Human Social Behavior* (p. 310).

[5] Lamport-Stokes, M. (2011, December 5). Tiger Woods Wins Chevron: Did Tiger Get His Groove Back? *The Christian Science Monitor.*

[6] Martin, J. (2012, April 9). Tiger Woods: Possible punishment for behavior at Masters marks another low. BleacherReport.com.

[7] Cherner, R. (2012, April 11). Azinger: Tiger acted like south end of a northbound mule. *USA Today.*

[8] See endnote 6.

[9] Associated Press. (2013, March 25). Tiger Woods is No.1 Again After Victory at Bay Hill.

[10] Futterman, Matthew. (2013, March 26). The Dow of Tiger Woods. *Wall Street Journal.*

Chapter 71

Academic Scandals,
Once Unthinkable, Have Erupted

Alan Hall

March 2012 (TS)

In February 2011, as the Dow/gold ratio continued its deep downtrend, we anticipated more fallout from negative social mood and wrote, "we may see academic versions of the Madoff scandal." Just five months later, the *Christian Science Monitor* ran the headline, "America's biggest teacher and principal cheating scandal unfolds in Atlanta." The Atlanta scheme proved to be only "the largest of dozens of major cheating scandals unearthed across the country...an ongoing problem for U.S. education."[1]

The cheating is not confined to high-school grading. In August 2011, four states and the Department of Justice filed an $11 billion fraud suit against the Education Management Corporation—the nation's second-largest for-profit college company—charging that it was ineligible for the state and federal financial aid it had received from July 2003 through June 2011. "The depth and breadth of the fraud laid out in the complaint are astonishing," said a former federal prosecutor. *The New York Times* reported that the lawsuit is one of many filed against the for-profit college industry.[2]

In our June 2011 issue, Ted Solley described the emerging backlash against U.S. law schools. The furor continues to heat up. In October, Congress began inquiries into "'the confluence of growing enrollments, steadily increasing tuition rates and allegedly sluggish job placement at American law schools.'"[3] In February of this year, two professors from Atlanta's Emory University published a 77-page paper, "Law Deans in Jail." They wrote,

> [Law] schools, their deans, *U.S. News & World Report* and its employees may have committed felonies by publishing false information as part of *U.S. News'* ranking of law schools. The possible federal felonies include mail and wire fraud, conspiracy, racketeering, and making false statements...crimes affecting the lives and careers of thousands of people.[4]

By March 2012, some fifteen law schools faced class action lawsuits over allegedly deceptive employment data.[5]

[Q1 2012 marked the low in the last sociometer to bottom out in that period: the Case-Shiller index of real estate prices. As sociometers trended uniformly upward from there, the pressure on all these educational sectors eased.—Ed.]

NOTES AND REFERENCES

[1] Jonsson, P. (2011, July 5). America's Biggest Teacher and Principal Cheating Scandal Unfolds in Atlanta. Yahoo! News.

[2] Lewin, T. (2011, August 8). For-profit College Group Sued as U.S. Lays Out Wide Fraud. *The New York Times*.

[3] Marklein, B. (2011, October 25). Law Schools Pressed to Tell the Truth on Job Placement, Debt. *USA Today*.

[4] Cloud, M., & Shepherd, G.B. (2012, February 24). Law Deans in Jail. Social Science Research Network.

[5] Zaretsky, S. (2012, February 1). Twelve More Law Schools Slapped With Class Action Lawsuits Over Employment Data. Above the Law.

Chapter 72

The Ebb and Flow of Outrage
in the Penn State Scandal

Lynda Edwards

September 24, 2012 (TS)

The ancient Greeks could have concocted an epic tragedy based on the Penn State scandal. It would involve assistant coach Jerry Sandusky's abuse of underage boys; America's hero worship; football's "winning-est coach," Joe Paterno; and mounds of hubris. The play would illuminate the dark impulses hidden in the human soul and show how pride in an institution can drive otherwise respectable people to ignore wicked behavior and pleas for justice.

Socionomists offer an added perspective about such human mysteries. They examine social mood and its influence on social events.

The Dates

Police were investigating accusations about Sandusky showering nude with pre-teen boys as early as 1998, but the district attorney decided not to prosecute (Figure 1). Then, in 2002, graduate assistant Mike McQueary told Paterno that he had seen Sandusky abusing a boy in a Penn State locker room shower. But it wasn't until 2008, when social mood waxed strongly negative, that one mother's complaints about Sandusky victimizing her son suddenly found traction with the media and the public. In response, the school district banned Sandusky from children's programs. In the first week of March 2009, the very week that the stock market bottomed, *The Patriot-News* broke the story that a grand jury was investigating sexual misconduct allegations against Sandusky. In November 2011, a few months after the Dow/gold ratio hit bottom, the legendary Paterno was fired and the grand jury summoned him and other university leaders.

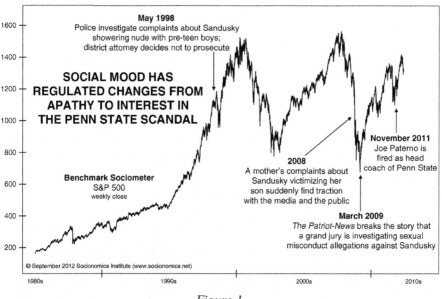

Figure 1

"Positive-mood stars tend to be more revered, because positive mood encourages more love and loyalty than does negative mood," Robert Prechter wrote in his 2010 study on the Beatles [Chapter 1]. "Almost no person or ensemble is consistently popular through positive and negative trends in mood. [W]hen mood changes, so does the focus of people's adoration or vilification."

Paterno died before he was stripped of all the trappings of a hero. His 900-pound statue was removed from campus, and 111 of his football victories were vacated from the record.

Socionomic theory holds that when a society is in a positive mood, it tolerates flawed heroes, whereas when it is in a negative mood, it scandalizes and punishes them. As Figure 1 shows, only when mood darkened severely in 2008 did accountability and punishment finally follow.

Severing Ties: Workers at Penn State remove a statue of Joe Paterno.

Chapter 73

Europe Hosts Another Scandal in the Catholic Church

Chuck Thompson

November 2015 (TS)

With the Euro Stoxx 50 still down 36% from its all-time high in 2000, Europe is becoming a hotbed of scandals. Last month's issue of *The Socionomist* detailed a scandal involving the suspensions of top officials of FIFA, the International Federation of Association Football. This month, the Vatican is the focus of scandal after the release of books by two Italian journalists. Revelations in the books are based on stolen documents, and two members of a financial reform commission appointed by Pope Francis in 2013 have been arrested as part of an investigation into the theft.[1]

One of the books, *Merchants in the Temple*, alleges that the Vatican is a "black hole" where millions of euros disappear as a result of waste and mismanagement. The other book, *Avarice*, alleges that the €378,000 which churches gave in 2013 to help the poor went into a secret account for Vatican expenses instead.[2]

This month also brings the release of the film *Spotlight*, about *Boston Globe* journalists who uncovered sexual abuse of children by priests in Massachusetts and a long-standing policy of cover-up by the Boston Archdiocese. The team uncovered the abuses as the negative mood trend from 2000 unfolded. It began publishing articles on the subject in 2002, the year of a multi-year low in U.S. stock prices, and it was awarded the Pulitzer Prize for Public Service in 2003, the year of the associated low in global stock prices.

In a speech in St. Peter's Square on November 8, Pope Francis said he plans to continue his effort to bring financial reform to the Vatican bureaucracy.[3]

NOTES AND REFERENCES

[1] Associated Press. (2015, November 8). Pope Pledges to Continue Reforms in Face of Leaks. *Business Insider.*

[2] Samuel, H. (2015, November 3). Vatican is a "Black Hole" of Mismanagement and Greed, Claims New Book. *The Telegraph.*

[3] See endnote 1.

Chapter 74

Climate and Herding

Robert Prechter

June 15, 2007 (EWT)

On May 9, NASA issued a press release, which appeared in different forms throughout the national media. *USA Today* introduced the report as follows: "Warnings about global warming may not be dire enough." If you are wondering how it would be possible for warnings about global warming to be any more strident, here is an excerpt from the agency's press release:

> A new study by NASA scientists suggests that greenhouse-gas warming may raise average summer temperatures in the eastern United States nearly 10 degrees Fahrenheit by the 2080s.

> "There is the potential for extremely hot summertime temperatures in the future, especially during summers with less-than-average frequent rainfall," said lead author Barry Lynn of NASA's Goddard Institute for Space Studies and Columbia University, New York.

> The research found that eastern U.S. summer daily high temperatures that currently average in the low-to-mid-80s (degrees Fahrenheit) will most likely soar into the low-to-mid-90s during typical summers by the 2080s. In extreme seasons—when precipitation falls infrequently—July and August daily high temperatures could average between 100 and 110 degrees Fahrenheit in cities such as Chicago, Washington, and Atlanta.

> To reach their conclusions, the researchers analyzed nearly 30 years of observational temperature and precipitation data and also used computer model simulations that considered soil, atmospheric, and oceanic conditions and projected changes in greenhouse gases. The simulations were produced using a widely-used weather prediction model coupled to a global model developed by NASA's Goddard Institute for Space Studies.

> The global model, one of the models used in the recently issued climate report by the Intergovernmental Panel on Climate Change

(IPCC), was utilized in this study to identify future changes in large-scale atmospheric circulation patterns due to the build up of greenhouse gases. This information was then fed into the weather prediction model to forecast summer-to-summer temperature variability in the eastern United States during the 2080s.

"Since the weather prediction model simulated the frequency and timing of summer precipitation more reliably than the global model, its daily high temperature predictions for the future are also believed to be more accurate," added co-author Leonard Druyan, NASA Goddard Institute for Space Studies and Columbia University.

"Using high-resolution weather prediction models, we were able to show how greenhouse gases enhance feedbacks between precipitation, radiation, and atmospheric circulations that will likely lead to extreme temperatures in our not so distant future," said Lynn.

The study is published in the April 2007 issue of the American Meteorological Society's *Journal of Climate*.

According to the researchers, this is just the good news. Citing one of the authors of the study, AP reported as follows:

But Druyan said the problem is most computer models, especially when compared to their predictions of past observations, underestimate how bad global warming is. That's because they see too many rainy days, which tends to cool temperatures off, he said. "I'm sorry for the bad news," Druyan said. "It gets worse everywhere."[1]

The chief peer reviewer endorsed it:

Andrew Weaver of the University of Victoria, editor of the journal *Climate* but not of this study, praised the paper, saying "it makes perfect sense."[2]

This study uses 30 centuries...no, 30 decades...no, less than 30 years of data to make predictions of an unprecedented temperature rise over the next 63 years. As they say, extraordinary claims require extraordinary evidence. Extrapolating 30 years' worth of data to make conclusions about cycles taking millennia does not seem to meet that standard. It does not make "perfect sense."

Evidence for man-made global warming falls short of delineating the idea from pure myth, and the hysteria over it may turn out to be little more than herding. Sometimes scientists herd as much as investors do, and this study appears to be a case of extreme expression following a long-established trend. I would be willing to bet that Chicago, Washington and Atlanta's average peak daily summer temperature—recently running about

95 degrees—will not be 110 degrees, 105 degrees or even 100 degrees in the year 2080. I am not a climatologist, but I am a student of manias and herding, and that is what the man-made-global-warming craze appears to be about.

The researchers who make dire global-warming claims tend to be either dependent upon government grants, haters of humanity or power grabbers. The study came from NASA, an oft-criticized agency desperate for funding and survival. The documentary is produced by a presidential candidate. A publicly funded political conglomeration called Intergovernmental Panel on Climate Change (IPCC) is heavily involved.

The crowd fearing catastrophic global warming due to human activity rejects as heretics professors and scientists who challenge all these methods and conclusions, whether they be at MIT[3] or Stanford.[4] Such rejection is akin to what happens near the end of a financial mania, such as the peak of the real estate mania a year ago, when bears were dismissed as delusional. As evidence of this attitude, after NASA's own chief administrator, Michael Griffin, expressed doubt about catastrophic global warming on NPR on May 31, he was viciously attacked. The Associated Press reported the next day that he was "under fire" because he "should know better." The article quotes critics calling him "a deep anti-global warming ideologue," not to mention "ignorant," "arrogant" and "totally clueless." One of Griffin's critics predicted "hundreds of millions of refugees" from future global warming. No hysteria there. Griffin, in contrast, was polite and sober.[5]

A big clue to the nature of today's panic over catastrophic man-made global warming is its lack of support from, and at times contradiction to, important data. For example:

1. There have been much warmer times in centuries and millennia past. The earth is not at some new level of high temperature.[6] The Industrial Revolution was not a factor in earlier ages.

2. Current average temperature is in the middle of its range of the past 3000 years, as measured at sea level over the Sargasso Sea.[7]

3. If the latest rise in temperature has reached a peak, it is a lower peak than previous cycles of like duration. One might just as easily make a scare case for long term global cooling. People feared just that, by the way, in the mid-1970s.

4. Greenland's ice cores show that in past millennia the earth has seen brief eruptions of carbon dioxide into the air that were nine times as great as all the CO_2 produced by the Industrial Revolution to date.

Yet they created temperature rises of only 2 degrees Fahrenheit, challenging the CO_2 causality theory.[8]

5. Alarmists have fudged data or sidestepped full explanations. For example, the claim that the snowpack in the Cascade mountains of Washington state had shrunk by 50% turned out to be a statistical trick, based on using 1950, a year with an "unusually high level of snowpack."[9] Blaming global warming for changes in the snow cover on Kilimanjaro is also proving highly questionable, as the latest issue of *American Scientist* demonstrated.[10] Many times, published graphs show only the most recent centuries of climate data and then add "extrapolation" lines. When people rationalize, they resort to any method of thought that will bring about the conclusion they want. Rigor and full honesty are not part of the deal.

You can find all these facts listed and graphed on the Internet and a pretty good summary of what some view as "the most expensive pseudo-scientific hoax ever implemented."[11]

Then there is the fact that government is involved. From the starch-heavy "food pyramid" to ethanol fuel, the government adopts programs not because they are right but because they gain votes, money or political power or because they solve problems that politics has already created, such as silos full of subsidized wheat or a shortage of gasoline due to the maze of controls on drilling and refining. Sometimes, as with government-mandated recycling programs, they are due significantly to economic ignorance.

My purpose here is not primarily to make a case against man-made global warming. My primary intent is to take a look at the question from the point of view of a social psychologist to decide whether the level of concern appears to be the result of hysteria. The points above establish that there are two sides to the manmade-global-warming question. Yet only one has captured the public's imagination (and I choose that word consciously). The global-warming scare is highly reminiscent of the Alar scare, in which Congress called upon the expertise of movie stars; the claim that pesticides were making frogs lame (it turned out to be a virus); the rash of reports of devil worshippers, who were never found; the national child-care molestation hysteria, which turned out to be entirely contrived; the panic in Europe over poison in Coca-Cola; and any number of like manias. [On the other hand, the ozone-depletion scare and the acid-rain scare were real and man-made, and political action helped curtail those problems.]

Although there is little reason to believe so, global warming might be a real trend. But there is no good evidence that it is a man-made trend. There is even a case (see the "Stanford" link [endnote#4] above) that increased CO_2 will be good for plants, upon which higher forms of life depend, and that global warming would be a good thing, not bad, meaning that panic is the opposite of the correct response. But panic is everywhere.

Ironically, environmentalists, who seem the most concerned about global warming, have blocked the construction of nuclear power plants for three decades. Nuclear plants release no so-called "greenhouse gases" into the atmosphere,[12] so blocking their construction has caused the release of tons more of such emissions over a period of decades. It's tough when one myth battles another.

We must not confuse weather with climate, but it is rather interesting to be experiencing a cool spring this year. Locally the cool temperatures have occurred in the midst of a drought, which according to the global-warming advocates is supposed to correspond to higher temperatures. So, if their logic is correct, temperatures would have been even lower had it rained. In April and May, freezes destroyed crops and even disrupted rallies against global warming. Here are some headlines over a six-week period, courtesy of the Drudge Report. June has been cool, too.

April 13, 2007   *Snow won't dampen global-warming rallies*

April 15, 2007   *Global warming rally in the snow*

April 17, 2007   *Global warming activists urged to focus on Earth Day rallies and ignore snow as it "piles up outside our windows"*

April 18, 2007   *Northeast storm leaves remarkable wake, breaks April snow & rain records*

May 23, 2007   *S. Africa sets 54 cold weather records as snow and ice continue*

May 23, 2007   *Colorado mountains under Memorial Day snow advisory, up to 8 inches expected*

May 28, 2007   *Spring snow breaks 1911 Canadian record*

May 28, 2007   *Britain hit with arctic air, snow*

Hysteria often signals the end of a trend. I would guess that the most likely film image sometime in the next two decades is Al Gore wrapped up in a parka in June talking about global warming.

NOTES AND REFERENCES

[1] Associated Press (2007, May 10). "Eastern U.S. Summers to be Hotter, NASA finds."

[2] *Ibid.*

[3] Morano, Marc (2004, December 2). "Meteorologist Likens Fear of Global Warming to 'Religious Belief.'"

[4] Moore, Thomas Gale (1995). "Global Warming: A Boon to Humans and Other Animals."

[5] NPR (2007, May 31). "NASA Chief Questions Urgency of Global Warming."

[6] Whitehouse, David (2007, December 5). "Can the Sun Save Us from Global Warming?" *Belfast Telegraph.*

[7] Civil Defense Perspectives (2007, March). "Global Warming Primer,"

[8] Zarembo, Alan (2007, May 11). "Ancient Eruptions of Carbon Dioxide Traced to Oceans," *Los Angeles Times.*

[9] Cornwall, Warren (2007, March 15). "How One Number Touched Off Big Climate-Change Fight at UW," *Seattle Times.*

[10] Mote, Phillip and Georg Kaser (2007, Jul-Aug). "The Shrinking Glaciers of Kilimanjaro: Can Global Warming Be Blamed?" *American Scientist*, Vol. 95, No. 4, p. 318.

[11] Correa, Paulo N. and Alexandra N. Correa (2005, November). "Global Warming: An Official Pseudoscience," *Journal of Aetherometric Research* 1,5:1-58.

[12] Lipper, Ilan and Jon Stone. "Nuclear Energy and Society."

Chapter 75

Global Warming Redux

Robert Prechter

July 13, 2007 (EWT)

The piece in the June EWT on herding with respect to the global warming issue [Chapter 74] garnered a lot of response, ranging from "great,"
"terrific" and "brilliant" to "disappointed," "ignorant" and "wacko." The
latter adjectives are not without merit. Because my interest lay in the herding
phenomenon, I gave short shrift to the scientific case for man-made global
warming and fell short of my usual standards in expressing the issues. I did
not cover the evidence in favor of the possible effects of man-made CO_2,
and I did not take the time to locate fully credible references for the opposition. As I said in the piece, "My purpose here is not primarily to make
a case against man-made global warming," and my lack of interest in the
underlying issue showed. If you want to read the advocates' case, a good
site is www.realclimate.org.

It is also true, however, that professors, PhDs and lifelong climatolo-
gists who attempt to raise objections to the evidence for man-made global
warming are ridiculed, shouted down, exiled and dismissed from their posts
(there is a short list in Wikipedia under "Richard Lindzen"). Perhaps this
tactic can attend good theories, but it is a notorious aspect of dominant yet
flawed theories whose advocates feel personally threatened by opposition.
When Timothy Patterson, professor of geology and director of the Ottawa-
Carleton Geoscience Centre at Canada's Carleton University, says that his
work with cores of mud from Western Canada's fjords covering 5000 years
shows "a direct correlation between variations in the brightness of the sun
and earthly climate indicators"; when Reid Bryson, Emeritus Professor
and founding chairman of the University of Wisconsin's Department of
Meteorology, citing historical and archeological records of the warmth of
Greenland in Medieval times, says it's warming "because we're coming
out of the Little Ice Age, not because we're putting more carbon dioxide
into the air"; when Dr. William Gray, professor emeritus of the atmospheric

SOCIONOMIC STUDIES OF SOCIETY AND CULTURE

department at Colorado State University, says, "fluctuations in hurricane intensity and frequency have nothing to do with carbon dioxide levels or human activity but with natural variations in ocean currents, [and] the ocean circulation pattern [is] a major cause of climate change"; when Richard Lindzen, professor of meteorology at M.I.T., notes that despite increasing carbon emissions, the rise in earth's temperature has been less than theory would predict (GW theorists blame the inconvenient cooling period in the last century on another atmospheric chemical reaction caused by humans); when Freeman Dyson, physicist at Princeton, calls the GW threat "grossly exaggerated" and says that existing climate prediction models "do a very good job of describing the fluid motions of the atmosphere and the oceans [but] a very poor job of describing the clouds, the dust, the chemistry and the biology of fields, farms and forests [and] do not begin to describe the real world that we live in; when "Solar scientists predict that, by 2020, the sun will be starting into its weakest Schwabe cycle of the past two centuries, likely leading to unusually cool conditions on earth" (*Investors Business Daily*, April 9, June 26; Wikipedia; Internet); GW advocates, aside from labeling such people as "stooges for the oil companies" and such, say, quite accurately, that these people's research has not been peer-reviewed.

Let us address this latter point. GW advocates who contacted me all said pretty much the same thing: "Man-made global warming is a fact; no credible scientist disputes it; no peer-reviewed literature makes a case against it." In the 1970s and 1980s, economists said the same thing about the Efficient Market Hypothesis and Random Walk in the stock market. On two points they were right: No credible economist disputed it, and no peer-reviewed literature made a case against it. One reason is that the club door was shut so tightly that no learned opposition was allowed. Our group heard recently from an MIT professor who said that his paper on stock market cycles was "blackballed" in the early 1980s by the powerful proponents of EMH. A key word that GW supporters omitted about the lack of peer-reviewed research is *yet*. No one has amassed a counter-attack in academic literature *yet*. Today Random Walk is discredited and EMH is on the run. But it took a whole new way of looking at data, and new hypotheses, to bring about the change. Before that shift, many people had evidence contradicting EMH and RW, but its presentation was not yet up to academic standards. Likewise, evidence exists that there are climatic cycles millennia long and that there were rapid temperature changes in short periods of time prior to the Industrial Revolution. Perhaps it has not made it into scientific journals yet, but from what I read about ongoing research and theory-building, I expect that it will. It takes time to mount a defense to initially accepted theories, and it will take time to build a credible case for why temperature can move up and down over 30 years whether man is present or not. EMH survived unchallenged at the academic level for 20 years, and after 40 years it is still the dominant theory, awaiting a replacement. We don't know whether socionomics will help boot EMH into the closet of formerly accepted theories, but we hope so. [For a suggested alternative, see *The Socionomic Theory of Finance* (2016).]

The Herding Aspect

Now back to my main point: The fact remains that there is powerful evidence of herding at the social level on the global warming issue. Commentary on the subject is even selling theater tickets. Like all social trends that are ending, there is a rush to extrapolate. The temperature data from which modelers at NASA derive their extrapolation are scant, the projection is extreme and their tone is strident. When any writers, including scientists, extrapolate 29 years' worth of temperature data to predict an imminent apocalypse of biblical proportions in an environment of waxing social focus, rising panic and calls for government obstruction, one must acknowledge the likelihood of social-psychological forces behind such a report and investigate whether the data support the prediction.

It's fine to describe chemistry. It's fine to offer a theory of atmospheric and temperature change. But there seems to be a degree of statistical selectivity behind the specific prediction from NASA.

GW advocates told me that doubting man-made global warming was akin to denying evolution. But the GW movement has not a little taste of old-time religion in its accompanying admonition of humanity: Man is evil; he is destroying the earth; he is "fouling his own nest," as one scientist on the web says. Scientists are usually good at their fields but not necessarily at recognizing their own political, moral and economic biases.

As I said, "My primary intent is to take a look at the question from the point of view of a social psychologist to decide whether it appears to be the result of hysteria." One thoughtful scientist took issue with the term *hysteria*. But the term applies here to social activity, not the overt behavior of any particular individual. In 2005, when I was speaking about that year's real estate hysteria and warning people against investing in property [see Chapter 13 of *The Socionomic Theory of Finance*], some people got emotional, but others, sporting a rather bemused expression, would coolly respond—as if instructing an alien who lacked understanding of the way things worked on Earth—"Listen, they are not making any more land" and "Relax, it's all about location." They were not hysterical but rational and thoughtful. At least, that was the appearance of their behavior at the individual level. At the collective level, something else was going on. The number of people participating in the real estate market was unprecedented, and their borrowing, building and bidding activities, collectively, were extreme. Likewise, some advocates of man-made global warming may appear sober as judges individually, but they are participating in a mass movement, complete with press releases, student rallies, pop concerts, movie documentaries and an underlying tone of moral crusade.

As one advocate for GW admitted, the issue does become problematic when politics enters the picture. That is an understatement. Collective fears come and go, but public policy in response to them usually causes real horrors. The U.S. pays foreigners for oil and emits more greenhouse gasses into the atmosphere thanks to government bans on building nuclear energy plants, which could have powered a nationwide rail system producing no air pollution whatsoever. [Whatever programs the government creates in trying to stop global warming will surely increase people's misery and may harm the environment as well, for example by impoverishing society enough to delay the technology of hydrogen fuel cells, which would solve the automobile pollution problem.]

Perhaps catastrophic global warming will prove to be an exception to the overwhelming tendency of mass fears to prove unfounded. Perhaps NASA's spectacular extrapolation of more than a 10% rise in temperature in the span of a single lifetime is accurate. But the advocates of government restrictions on productive activity had better be right, or they will once again have to answer for the collateral damage they will do with their proposals.

So, would I call man-made global warming a hoax, as a recent television program did? Definitely not; it has a strong scientific basis. Is the social environment with respect to the issue one of mass herding in an emotional state? It most definitely is. Should you believe predictions that climate change will usher in mass doom in coming decades? I don't. I think the current frenzy over the subject is probably a symptom of peaking trends in both climatic temperature and social psychology.

What I expect, based upon observing mass movements, is that this fear, too, will go away. Like a sweeping prison-yard spotlight that catches glimpses of purported external causes for stock-market behavior and then abandons them to darkness, crescendos of commentary on various foci of social fear come briefly into view and then almost always retreat to black. Before my lifetime ends, catastrophic global warming will probably fade as a focus of concern, and some new mass fear will be on the front page of *USA Today*. Nevertheless, I caution that only my views on the social aspects of the matter—not the meteorological aspects—are adequately informed.

Chapter 76

Elliott Waves Simultaneously Regulate Commodity Prices and Expressions of Environmentalism

Alan Hall

April 11, 2008 (EWT)

Fear characterizes C waves of bear markets in stocks as well as fifth waves of bull markets in commodities. Both types of waves are in progress today at fairly high degrees. The War on Terror, broad-based environmental fear, and worries about the end of cheap oil and food all express the negative mood that supports these simultaneous wave patterns. This excerpt from chapter 6 of *Elliott Wave Principle* describes fifth waves in commodities:

> Also in contrast to the stock market, commodities most commonly develop extensions in fifth waves within Primary or Cycle degree bull markets. This tendency is entirely consistent with the Wave Principle, which reflects the reality of human emotions. Fifth wave advances in the stock market are propelled by hope, while fifth wave advances in commodities are propelled by a comparatively dramatic emotion, fear: fear of inflation, fear of drought, fear of war. Hope and fear look different on a chart, which is one of the reasons that commodity market tops often look like stock market bottoms.

Figure 1 is an updated chart of commodity prices since 1260. In 1995's *At the Crest of the Tidal Wave*, Robert Prechter made a two-part prediction using this chart:

> A Fibonacci 21-year bear market in commodities from the 1980 high would produce a price low in 2001. [T]he bear market now in progress may prove ultimately to be only a temporary, if deep, interruption of the larger trend toward higher prices.

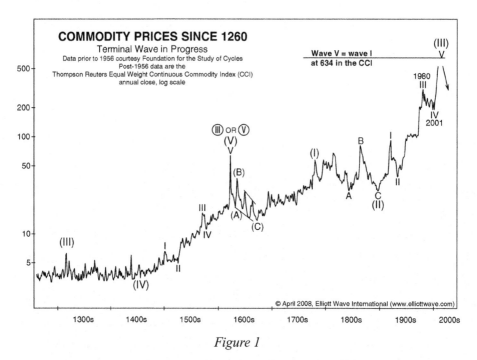

Figure 1

That was a great call in 1995, and today, seven years after the low of 2001, the Thompson Reuters Equal Weight Continuous Commodity Index (CCI) finally shows a clear five waves up from the bottom in 1897, suggesting that the largest reversal of the past hundred years is due. Based on the guideline of price equality between waves one and five when wave three is extended—a common Elliott wave relationship within impulse waves; see *Elliott Wave Principle* (1978)—a target for the CCI's peak using annual closing data is 634, as indicated on the chart. The CCI has already registered a daily closing high of 576, which is within 12% of the target. Since then, it has fallen almost 20% and may already be in a bear market. The bear market should carry prices to the normal retracement level near the low of 2001—a drop of about 60%.

Ironically, some food price rises have resulted directly from fears of global warming and peak oil. The stated aims of government-mandated biofuel standards are to reduce greenhouse-gas emissions and dependence on foreign oil. The forced adoption of ethanol as a gasoline additive has resulted in a corn shortage that has starved the poorest Mexicans and pushed up prices for grain-fed animals.

Today's commodity-related fear is more than just concern over high prices. A *New York Times* article published on April 6 quotes from a new book, *Wealth, War and Wisdom,* by Barton M. Biggs, formerly the chief global strategist at Morgan Stanley. Biggs encourages stockpiling food and seeds, and says people should "assume the possibility of a breakdown of the civilized infrastructure.... Think Swiss Family Robinson." In the same article, the editor of a survivalist blog says his web traffic has doubled in the past eleven months and reports that interest in the survivalist movement is spreading to "stridently green and left-of-center readers [and] is experiencing its largest growth since the late 1970s." These are just two examples of manifestations of today's climate of commodity-related fear, which springs from the most negative social mood since the late 1970s.

Fear Motivates Environmentalism

Negative social mood produces other fear-related behaviors, including the advocacy of environmentalism. Figure 2 relates commodity prices to a key-events history of the environmental movement since 1920. As you can see, important actions favorable to the environmental movement—legislation, government regulation, and group actions that require a broad consensus—have occurred mostly during commodity price rises, whereas acts of disregard for the environment are more common during commodity price declines. Commodity prices languished for two decades prior to the 1970s and for two decades thereafter. In between those times was a major advance in commodity prices, which corresponded with numerous public actions to protect the environment. *Environmental Politics in Japan, Germany and the United States* confirmed, "The 1970s were the environmental decade in the U.S.... Congress continued to pass one major new environmental law after the next." The last gasp of that trend happened in December 1980, when Congress belatedly responded to the groundswell of environmental fear by passing legislation for a Superfund for the purpose of cleaning up the environment. President Ronald Reagan's appointment of anti-environmentalist James Watt as Secretary of the Interior in 1981 occurred the year of a major price peak that led to a twenty-year stall in the environmental movement as commodity prices declined. These histories demonstrate that price advances in commodities coincide with widespread environmental activism and price declines do not.

The correspondence between pro-environmental actions and commodity bull markets over the past century is no accident. From the birth of the modern conservation movement in the 1940s to the large-scale legislative efforts undertaken in the 1970s to the global warming hysteria of recent years, we see an Elliott wave progression of rising environmental fear. It is hard to imagine a more fitting expression of the type of fear we should expect to see at a major top in commodity prices than the recent worldwide panic over a catastrophic shortage of life-sustaining climate. For the first time in human history, a large percentage of people are afraid that humans have

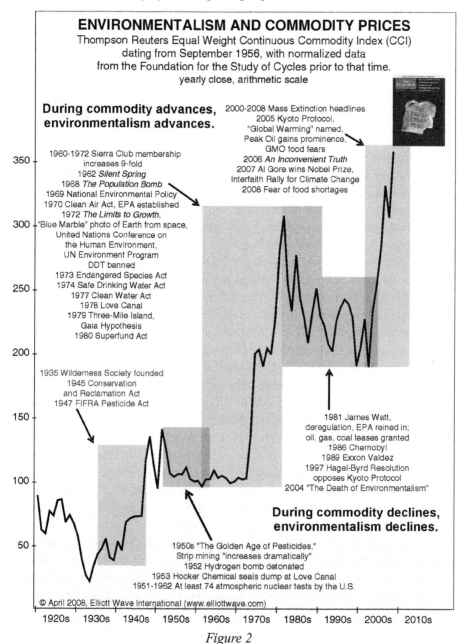

Figure 2

ruined Spaceship Earth. This extreme fear signals the looming exhaustion of the century-long bull market in commodities and is a logical prelude to a commodity price collapse and a period of setback for the environmental movement.

To a socionomist, it is a natural step to connect environmental fear with commodities booms, because one mood trend fuels them both. The socionomic perspective explains why contemporaneous extremes in fears about climate, food shortages and monetary inflation signal an approaching price collapse for commodities. These fears simultaneously serve to generate collective blindness to the potential for reversal.

On December 6, 2007, *The Economist* ran a cover titled "The End of Cheap Food." As Paul Montgomery of Universal Economics has repeatedly shown, magazine covers often reflect sentiment extremes shortly ahead of turning points in markets. *The Economist*'s cover may mark just such a sentiment extreme. It certainly reflects the fear that is characteristic of terminating fifth waves in commodities.

The looming downturn in the CCI implies an upcoming period of lessening popular concern about the environment as well as material setbacks for the environmental movement. The primary cause will be a change in mood.

June 2009 Update: The CCI topped three months later, on July 2, 2008, at a daily closing high of 615, and dropped in half by year's end. Accordingly, the popularity of environmentalism has waned, oil exploration and drilling have increased, and the power of the EPA is being challenged. In June 2009, *The Socionomist* cited a year's worth of news headlines that chronicled the dramatic shift in attitudes:

Global Warming as Mass Neurosis
—*The Wall Street Journal*, July 1, 2008

Financial Crisis Tests Industry's Green Priorities
"Industry has seized on the slowdown to lobby for delayed or watered down regulations…. This crisis changes priorities…."
—*The Financial Times*, October 6, 2008

European Nations Seek to Revise Agreement on Emissions Cuts
—*The New York Times*, October 17, 2008

EU Agency Warns About Damage from Biofuels
"…may cause adverse effects on the environment…."
—*European Voice*, November 13, 2008

In Bad Economy, Boat Owners Abandon Their Vessels
"Oil, gasoline and sewage from these boats leak into the aquatic environment."
—AP, November 13, 2008

Tennessee Ash Flood Larger Than Initial Estimate
"...largest environmental disaster of its kind in the United States."
—The New York Times, December 27, 2008

Dark Days for Green Energy
"Installation of wind and solar power is plummeting."
—The New York Times, February 4, 2009

Ethanol, Just Recently a Savior, Is Struggling
"Plants are shutting down virtually every week."
—The New York Times, February 12, 2009

Is Global Warming Passé?
—MarketWatch, February 27, 2009

Increased Number Think Global Warming Is "Exaggerated"
"...record high 41 percent...the highest level in a decade....[global warming] urgency has stalled."
—Gallup, March 11, 2009

Tonnes of Oil Blanket Queensland Beaches
"...turned the sand black 'as far as the eye can see.'"
—ABC, March 12, 2009

The Ethanol Bubble Pops in Iowa
"...a business model built on fantasies...."
—The Wall Street Journal, April 18, 2009

Seeking to Save the Planet, with a Thesaurus
"...oil companies, utilities and coal mining concerns...are trying to 'green' their images.... global warming [is] last among 20 voter concerns."
—The New York Times, May 2, 2009

Sarkozy in Climate Row Over Reshuffle
"Sarkozy's desire to appoint an outspoken climate-change sceptic [is a] terribly bad signal...tantamount to giving the finger to scientists...like putting organic farming alongside Chernobyl."
—The Financial Times, May 27, 2009

[Another widely used index of commodity prices, the Reuters-Jeffries CRB index, made its final high on July 2, 2008 and has been in a bear market ever since. The CCI managed a new high in 2010, and its annual close for that year occurred at 630, four points shy of the target cited in this article.—Ed.]

Chapter 77

Passion over
Man-Made Global Warming Subsides

Robert Prechter

July 17, 2009 (EWT)

The June and July 2007 issues of *The Elliott Wave Theorist* [Chapters 74 and 75] called for a peak in the hysteria over man-made global warming. The April 2008 issue [Chapter 76] called for a peak in commodity prices and with their reversal a reduction in the intensity of fear relating to the environment. Both of these forecasts, made at the pinnacle of their respective frenzies, have come to pass.

Although I have been skeptical toward the alarmists' claims, I made it clear at the time that my primary purpose was not to judge the scientific case but to make a prediction regarding the social process of what one might call a fear bubble, not unlike those that occur in commodity markets. As befits a bubble, there was an *accelerating trend*, fueled by *credit* (in the sense that much of the science was bad and would be refuted) and many signs of emotionally charged *herding*.

Sure enough, in the ensuing two years the passion has cooled. The following report and chart reveal the trend change. Note Gallup's comment on the *specificity* of this change, which is exactly what one would expect given that we had diagnosed a narrowly focused bubble of social concern.

PRINCETON, NJ — Although a majority of Americans believe the seriousness of global warming is either correctly portrayed in the news or underestimated, a record-high 41% now say it is exaggerated. This represents the highest level of public skepticism about mainstream reporting on global warming seen in more than a decade of Gallup polling on the subject.

As recently as 2006, significantly more Americans thought the news underestimated the seriousness of global warming than said it exaggerated it, 38% vs. 30%. Now, according to Gallup's 2009 Environment

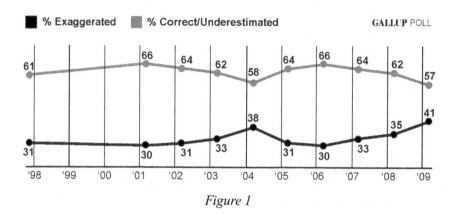

Figure 1

survey, more Americans say the problem is exaggerated rather than underestimated, 41% vs. 28%.

Importantly, Gallup's annual March update on the environment shows a drop in public concern about global warming across several different measures, suggesting that the global warming message may have lost some footing with Americans over the past year. Gallup has documented declines in public concern about the environment at times when other issues, such as a major economic downturn or a national crisis like 9/11, absorbed Americans' attention. To some extent that may be true today, given the troubling state of the U.S. economy. However, the solitary drop in concern this year about global warming, among the eight specific environmental issues Gallup tested, suggests that something unique may be happening with the issue. (Gallup, 3/11)

Despite receiving one of the most vehement responses to anything I have written, Gallup's chart in Figure 1 shows that the breadth of global-warming fears had in fact begun to moderate sometime in 2006. Yet if memory serves, the *intensity* of conviction that man-made GW was a scientific fact was greater in 2007 than in 2006, even if the number of people expressing it was receding. Perhaps the most extreme event demonstrating the extremity of the consensus was the "interfaith rally for climate change," which took place on September 12, 2007, a month before the stock market topped out:

Surrounded by icebergs, Sunni, Shiite, Buddhist, Hindu, Jewish, Christian, and Shinto leaders committed themselves last Friday to leave the planet "in all its wisdom and beauty to the generations to come." They included the Grand Rabbi of Paris, René-Samuel Sirat, Bishop Sofie Petersen of Greenland, Cardinal Theodore McCarrick of Washington, and the Rev. Jim Ball, founder of the Evangelical Environmental

Network.... Carl Pope, executive director of the Sierra Club, says the
event was indicative of the progress that was being made bridging
the divide between environmentalism and faith." (UNEP, 9/12/07)

Gallup took its latest poll in March, and the trend away from fear of
catastrophe seems to have continued. On June 26, *The Wall Street Journal*
reported, "The number of skeptics is swelling everywhere," and detailed a
rapidly growing scientific challenge to the idea of man-made global warming that it dubbed "The Climate Change Climate Change."

The only sector left that is still expanding the man-made GW agenda
is government, which is always the last institution to express or to abandon
a trend. On June 26, the House passed a massive tax called "cap and trade,"
and the Senate will vote on it next. One may justifiably wonder whether
government really cares about global warming or simply cannot pass up
the chance to enact a grand license to reap monetary benefits from selling privilege. I think politicians are clever, so the latter reason rings truer
to me. If this bill passes, it should be the last overt public expression of
global-warming fear; if it doesn't pass, its failure will confirm the end of a
remarkable period of social hysteria.

[An update of Figure 1 appears as Figure 23 of Chapter 21 in *The Socionomic Theory of Finance* (2016). It shows that the two lines converged
in 2010.]

Chapter 78

Social Mood Is Evident in Facial Expressions

Alan Hall

November 29, 2013 (TS)

This month, *The Socionomist* presents a special 18-minute video[1] that explores an emerging idea that may lead to new benchmark sociometers. This article offers an edited transcript that includes only the most important visuals.

When he addressed the April 2013 Social Mood Conference, Robert Prechter mentioned the idea of communication via facial expressions:

> We are not really sure how social mood is communicated. It is communicated by what people say, surely, but there are probably many things…that are more unconscious: The way facial muscles change, for example. We might be hearing content on television, but we are also getting messages [from] facial expressions.[2]

Social mood is unconscious, but its effect is visible in facial expressions. According to a 1980 study, "The face is one of the richest sources of communicating affective and cognitive information."[3] We postulate that scanning and evaluating faces to gauge the emotional states of individuals and groups is deeply ingrained survival behavior. Because of technology, reading faces is about to become even more refined, automated and useful.

Facial recognition technology is a hot topic and getting hotter. With cameras and image-analysis software proliferating across the planet, people are increasingly worried about vanishing privacy. But faces are far more than just "the new fingerprints," as National Public Radio put it.[4] Eventually, the collective mood revealed in faces may constitute a useful sociometer and improve predictions of crowd behavior.

Legislators' Facial Expressions Reveal Social Mood

Chapter 14 of *The Wave Principle of Human Social Behavior* (1999) listed many behaviors and emotions that people tend to display when expressing social mood. Let's look at the two poles of one of those categories in particular, *confidence* versus *fear*. Do people who feel fearful due to negative social mood display different facial expressions than do people who feel confident due to positive mood? If so, how reliably do they do so?

To explore that question, let's start with two iconic photographs. Subscriber William Lauber, Portfolio Manager at Sterling Capital Management, posted a Reuters story[5] to the Socionomics Institute's group page on LinkedIn. The story read like this:

> Here's a snapshot of FDR & Co. in 1933 as they signed Glass-Steagall, which separated the financial sector into safer, deposit-taking commercial banks and risk-taking investment banks.

Negative Emotions: FDR & Co. in 1933 as they signed the Glass-Steagall Act

And here's a photo of Bill Clinton & Co. repealing Glass-Steagall in 1999, with the passage of the Graham-Leach-Bliley Act, also known as the Financial Services Modernization Act.

Positive Emotions: Bill Clinton & Co. repealing the Glass-Steagall Act in 1999

It's a simple story: The two groups display opposite demeanors. The first group was in the grip of extremely negative social mood in 1933. Their negative mood was plain on their faces and in their action. They were grim, unenthusiastic, fearful, risk-averse, seeking safety and signing regulation—four years too late—to rein in financial speculation.

Of the nine visible faces in the first group, the tallest man in the center is the only one who *might* have been smiling; that's 11% of the group. Sitting front and center, President Roosevelt "had the look of one who had drunk the cup of life and found a dead beetle at the bottom," to quote the 1930s humorist, P.G. Wodehouse.

The second group was enjoying extremely positive social mood in 1999. Their positive mood was plain on their faces and in their action. They were ebullient, confident, risk-embracing, seeking adventure and signing deregulation to *allow and encourage* speculation—17 long years after the financial mania had begun. Members of the second group are *unanimously* smiling; it's clear on 100% of the visible faces.

The change in social mood from 1932 to 1999 was evident in (1) stock prices, (2) the radical shift from restrictive financial regulation to permissive deregulation and (3) legislators' facial expressions.

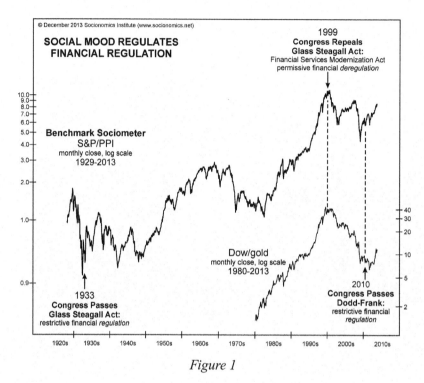

Figure 1

Figure 1 shows the nearly pinpoint accuracy of the socionomic timing of these two regulatory actions. In 1933, Congress passed laws designed to prevent the contraction that had already happened. In 1999, Congress passed laws designed to encourage the expansion that had already happened. (For a fuller history of this tendency, see Chapter 31 of *Pioneering Studies in Socionomics*.)

So, we see some reasons to believe that social mood is reflected in people's facial expressions. Let's consider a more recent example, in which lawmakers once again signed restrictive financial regulation.[6]

The Dodd–Frank Wall Street Reform and Consumer Protection Act of July 21, 2010 was a reaction to the largest financial crisis since the Great Depression, and it contained the most significant financial regulatory reform since that time. As the third arrow in Figure 1 shows, at the time of the signing, social mood—as reflected in the deep decline in Dow/gold—was approaching a negative extreme at major degree, while the Dow Jones Industrial Average had recovered somewhat but was still down almost 30% from its October 2007 high. The mixed expressions on the faces of the group at this bill's signing (see photo) are just what a socionomist would expect. Most of these legislators sport neutral expressions, few are grinning, and the President looks stern.

Mixed Mood: Mixed facial expressions at the signing of the Dodd-Frank Wall Street Reform and Consumer Protection Act.

A Series of Photographs Suggests the Influence of Social Mood

We wondered how well the association between social mood and facial expressions would hold up in a regular series of photographs. To find out, we did a quick, informal survey via Google image searches.

We looked for the best-quality photos from the United States that showed a lot of faces from one organization over a long period of time. One particular group-photo series stood out: those taken at the semi-annual meetings of the American Astronomical Society.[7] Two pictures [omitted from this book] reveal how the group's facial expressions changed over time. Granted, the analysis is qualitative and imprecise, but it is not too hard to differentiate smiling, happy faces from those that are not.

In the photo of the August 1929 meeting, of the 103 members whose faces are visible, 49% of them are smiling. The Dow Jones Industrial Average collapsed during the next three years, indicating that social mood was close to a historic negative extreme. In the photo of the December 1932 meeting, only 8% of the group's members are smiling. The contrast between the 1929 and 1932 facial expressions is stark. From 1929 to 1932, there was an 84% drop in smiling within the group, commensurate with the 89% drop in the Dow. At the same group's December 1933 meeting, the year that included the worst economic news of the Great Depression, only 6% of the astronomers were smiling. That is an 88% decline from 1929.

Next we did a larger, informal analysis of all 73 of the American Astronomical Society's annual group photos, which began in 1908 and ended in 1950. The top line in Figure 2 plots the PPI-adjusted Dow Jones Industrial Average, and the bottom line graphs the percentage of people smiling in each photo.

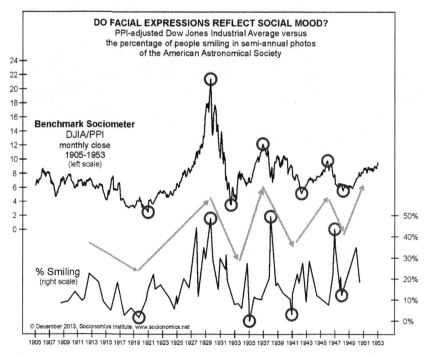

Figure 2

There are some resemblances between the graphs: The three highest peaks in smiling occur near or soon after the three highest peaks in stock prices (see top circles). Four of the lows in each graph somewhat coincide (see bottom circles), though they are not as well aligned. And the general trend of each graph is somewhat similar, as suggested by the grey arrows.

We looked at numerous other group photos and concluded that even though such snapshots have some potential for socionomic analysis, they do not reflect broader social mood as well as the stock market does, for at least four reasons: Group photos show only a tiny fraction of society, in a contrived setting, at a moment in time; long term, periodic photo series of members of the same organization are too rarely available for a statistical study; and there is always the possibility that someone will crack a joke, or something else, just before the photographer trips the shutter, triggering laughter and producing false results.

Facial Expressions in Unposed Photos

The people in the pictures we have discussed so far knew that they were posing for a group photo, yet the influence of social mood still seems evident. Photos of unaware subjects in crowds should reflect social mood even more faithfully.

Two hours before Game 7 of the Stanley Cup Final ended, Ronnie Miranda took a GigaPixel image of many of the 100,000 hockey fans that crowded into the streets of Vancouver, Canada in June 2011. Miranda assembled his massive image from 216 high-resolution photographs taken over a 15-minute span near 5:46 PM on June 15, 2011. You can type http:// bit.ly/lC53TG into your browser to view the entire, amazing image and zoom into almost every one of the thousands of faces in it.

The next three displays show different, tiny portions of his photo. Although these three zooms come from different places in the crowd and were taken seconds or minutes apart, the faces express similar emotion. In all of them, 0% of the people are smiling. While it is possible to find people smiling in the larger image, a careful count would find a very low percentage of them doing so.

That no one is smiling in these pictures suggests that the crowd's mood was predominantly negative that day. What happened next confirms this assessment. Just two hours later, after Game 7 of the 2011 Stanley Cup Final ended at 7:45 PM, the 2011 Stanley Cup Riot erupted.

At least 140 people and nine police officers were injured in the melee. At least four people were stabbed.[8] Rioters overturned and burned cars, smashed storefronts and looted stores. Property damage estimates exceeded $4 million.[9]

We think negative social mood played a role in the riot, because it took place after a 9% decline in the middle of a larger 22% bear market in Canada's TSX Composite Index (see Figure 3). The unreasoning, impulsive nature of the melee was evident in an observation from the Vancouver Police Chief, who said, "[Most] of the people who joined in the riot and who have now been charged represent a wider spectrum of young people, many of whom do not have criminal records."[10]

Generally Unhappy Facial Expressions: Less-than-positive emotions suggest the crowd's social mood was predominantly negative.

This photo, from another part of the crowd, shows no people smiling.

Again, no smiles.

Figure 3

Riot: The gathering ended in vandalism and violence.

Seventeen years earlier, the Vancouver Stanley Cup Riot of June 14, 1994 likewise occurred after Game 7 of the Finals. In similar fashion, it followed a 12% drop in the TSX Composite Index, as shown in Figure 4. Property damage was about $1.73 million in today's dollars.[11]

What makes the near-term declines in Figures 3 and 4 more important than others is that they occurred during the late stages of much larger trends toward negative social mood. The year 1994 was the last year of a negative mood period that started in 1987, as indicated by the pessimism toward stocks exhibited in [Figure 1 of Chapter 12]. The year 2011 was the final full year of a six-year decline in global real estate prices (see Figure 1 in Chapter 48), and the month of June was just two months before the low in the Dow/gold ratio, as shown in Figure 5. No wonder so many members of that soccer crowd were somber: Two major sociometers had fallen more than at any time in nearly 80 years and were grinding their ways to a bottom. The riot expressed the public's negative mood and marked its temporary end.

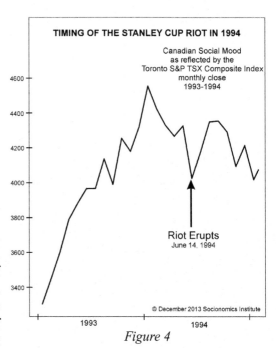

Figure 4

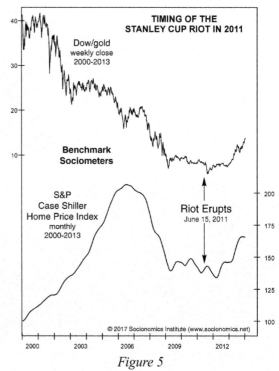

Figure 5

Crowds' Facial Expressions Could Become a Useful Sociometer

Here is a prediction: Facial recognition and analysis technology will be a boon to applied socionomics by providing new benchmark sociometers that can operate even when stock exchanges are closed or absent. People, companies and governments are already recording and storing digital images today that will provide rich data bases for future analysis. Our small-scale studies of the facial expressions in photographs offer only a tiny hint of what will be possible with computer algorithms that automatically analyze hundreds of thousands—or even hundreds of millions—of facial expressions over time.

As you can already see in Miranda's ocean of faces, photographic technology is progressing rapidly. The robotic camera mount that automates this gigapixel photography process and the software to assemble the image cost less than $1,000.[12]

The technology for facial expression analysis is also making huge strides. For example, Affectiva, which began in MIT's Media Lab, has developed software that can "recognize human emotions[13] based on facial cues or physiological responses."[14] RealEyes is another emotion-detection software company,[15] as is Emotient, which describes itself as "the leading authority on facial expression recognition and analysis technologies that are enabling a future of emotion aware computing."[16]

The advertising industry has been driving much of this technology, as retailers seek feedback to improve their sales. Academia is interested, too. For example, a recent study from North Carolina State University used software that analyzed facial expressions of students and allowed researchers to recognize when they were either having trouble with the work or finding it too easy.[17]

On August 21, *The New York Times* reported that the U.S. government is stepping up its facial recognition capabilities, too, although it seems concerned mostly about identification for now:

> The federal government is making progress on developing a surveillance system that would pair computers with video cameras to scan crowds and automatically identify people by their faces.... The Department of Homeland Security tested a crowd-scanning project called the Biometric Optical Surveillance System—or BOSS—last fall after two years of government-financed development.[18]

A September 2012 paper, "Mood Meter: Counting Smiles in the Wild," from a group of researchers at MIT, comes closest to the applications we envision. The team installed cameras and video screens in four locations across the campus and used algorithms that recognized faces, evaluated whether people were smiling, and estimated on a scale from 0 to 100 how big their smiles were. They then averaged the expressions into a "happiness barometer."[19] The barometer fluctuated over time. The researchers reported, "Quantitative analysis of the interactions revealed periodic patterns... reflecting the emotional responses of a large community."[20]

The researchers added, "With the development of computer vision technology, now it is possible to capture spontaneous moments of individuals with their emotional footprints at various time units." The recording of millions of facial expressions over time, which is happening now on streets and in stores around the world, will eventually produce enough data to allow rigorous statistical analysis. We expect that eventually there will be enough data to reveal a statistically significant association between trends in social mood as reflected in stock market trends and in people's facial expressions in the aggregate. Since facial expressions and stock market trends express social mood nearly simultaneously, we expect future data on facial expressions among the public to change more or less coincidentally with trends in the stock market. They may even prove to shift in accordance with Elliott waves. The Socionomics Institute is happy to support any related studies.

NOTES AND REFERENCES

[1] The video is available to members on the Socionomics Institute's website.

[2] www.socialmoodconference.com.

[3] Ekman, P., Freisen, W., & Ancoli, S. (1980). Facial Signs of Emotional Experience. *Journal of Personality and Social Psychology*, 39(6), 1125.

[4] O'Brien, M. (2013, May 29). Are Faces the New Fingerprints? *PBS Newshour*.

[5] Da Costa, P. (2012, October 25). A Picture is Worth a Thousand Pages of Financial Reform. Reuters.

[6] Remarks by the president at signing of Dodd-Frank Wall Street Reform and Consumer Protection Act. (2010, July 21). Office of the Press Secretary. The White House.

[7] Sponberg, B., Routly, P., & Tenn, J.S. *History of the American Astronomical Society. Meetings of the Society 1908-1915.* History Astronomy Division. American Astronomical Society.

[8] A Tale of Two Riots: Comparing the 1994 and 2011 Stanley Cup Riots in Vancouver. (2011, June 16). *CBC News*.

[9] Bill for Damages to be Much Higher Than for the 1994 Vancouver Riot. (2011, June 23). *The Globe and Mail*.

[10] Vancouver Police Shift Blame for Riot. (2011, June 20). *CBC News*.

[11] See endnote 8.

[12] Introducing the New GigaPan EPIC series. Active Computer Services.

[13] How Affdex Works. Affdex.com.

[14] Bosker, B. (2013, January 2). Affectiva's Emotion Recognition Tech: When Machines Know What You're Feeling. *The Huffington Post*.

[15] Dorrier, J. (2013, July 6). Realeyes Emotion Detection Software Knows How You're Feeling About Their Clients' Ads. SingularityHUB.

[16] www.emotient.com..

[17] Knight, W. (2013, July 1). Facial Analysis Software Spots Struggling Students. *MIT Technology Review*.

[18] Savage, C. (2013, August 21). Facial Scanning is Making Gains in Surveillance. *The New York Times*.

[19] Locke, S.F. (2011, November 10). MIT Meter Measures the Mood of Passers-by. *Popular Science*.

[20] Hernandez, J., Hoque, M., Drevo, W., & Picard, R.W. Mood Meter: Counting Smiles in the Wild. *Media Lab*. Massachusetts Institute of Technology.

Chapter 79

Losing Nemo:
Herding Suppresses Individual
Personality in Fish

Alan Hall

December 23, 2016 (TS)

In the animated film *Finding Nemo* (2003), a baby clownfish named Nemo swims away from home, takes phenomenal risks, has amazing adventures and survives. Nemo's exciting and risky behavior helped make *Finding Nemo* the best-selling DVD of all time.[1] But that was a cartoon, and Nemo was definitely not schooling, as fish do.

That observation brings up the question: Do individuals behave the same when they are alone as they do in social settings? For people, the answer is "no." But what about animals such as fish?

New evidence in a September 2016 paper titled "Consensus and Experience Trump Leadership, Suppressing Individual Personality during Social Foraging" suggests that even fish behave differently in social settings than they do when swimming solo.[2]

For the study, researchers at the University of Bristol's School of Biological Sciences caught eighty of the UK's smallest freshwater fish, the three-spined stickleback, and placed them in aquarium tanks. They tested the fish individually and in groups of ten as they risked venturing from safe cover to cross an open area to reach

Three-Spined Stickleback: The United Kingdom's smallest freshwater fish lost their individual personalities when in a group.

Swimming With the Herd: Blackside Dace in a mountain stream in Tennessee.

food. The authors observed both leaders and followers among the fish, but they found that "the individual personalities of fish were lost when in a group. [T]he fish stuck together when making a risky decision."[3]

Dr. Christos C. Ioannou, one of the researchers, said, "This is the first time that the suppression of personality in groups has been linked to its underlying cause, which is conformity in group decision making."[4] When schooling, it seems, Nemo is no longer an individual.

The authors said it is highly significant to find such herding behavior in a tiny fish that is

> not the most social of animals [and] uses less social information compared to closely related species. Thus, our results should apply more strongly to animals where group cohesion is even more important and, therefore, apply to a wide range of social species.[5]

The authors added, "The suppression of personality in groups suggests that individual risktaking tendency may rarely represent actual risk in social settings...."[6] We think this is also true of humans. As postulated in detail in *The Socionomic Theory of Finance*, herding may lead individuals both to embrace higher investment risks and to reject lower investment risks than they would if they were to make investment decisions independently of social influence.

NOTES AND REFERENCES

[1] Dutta, S. (2015, September 25). 12 Bestselling DVDs of All Time. *Insider Monkey*.

[2] McDonald, N.D., Rands, S.A., Hill, F., Elder, C., & Ioannou, C.C. (2016). Consensus and Experience Trump Leadership, Suppressing Individual Personality During Social Foraging. *Science Advances*, 2(9).

[3] Fish Lose Their Unique Personality When They Go to 'School'. (2016, September 16). *Science Daily*.

[4] *Ibid*.

[5,6] See endnote 2.

Chapter 80

Independent Elliott Waves
in Data on Social Trends

Robert Prechter and Alan Hall

August 31, 2011 (TS) / February 13, 2015 (EWT) / expanded December 2016

Some social activities wax and wane in Elliott waves yet are substantially independent of financial markets and overall social mood. Graphs of these activities support the utility of the Elliott wave model for depicting human herding but pose a question for socionomic theory: Are such activities independent of overall social mood, or do they function as parts of a tapestry of shared moods whose woven parts constitute the larger expression of social mood? Chapter 19 of *The Socionomic Theory of Finance* comes down of the side of the former explanation.

Figure 17-1 in *The Wave Principle of Human Social Behavior* presented a chart of the annual per capita sales of cigarettes in the United States. It traced out a "classic Elliott wave advance" over six decades and then reversed. Figure 1 shows an update.

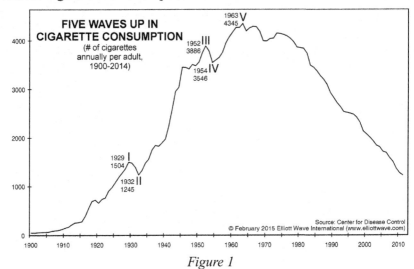

Figure 1

We have found the same five-wave structure in other non-financial data series. Look at Figure 2 and see how much the rise depicted there looks like that in Figure 1. This nearly identical formation occurs over a period of eight decades in the annual total number of union members in the United States.

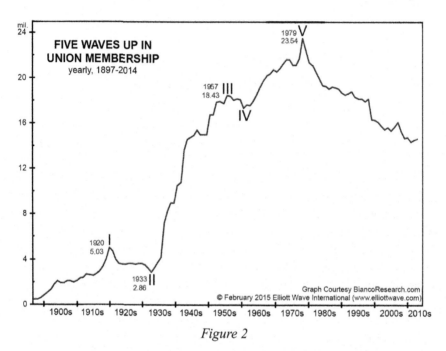

Figure 2

Figure 3 displays another excellent five-wave form, this one in the annual tally of homicides in New York City over a period of two centuries. The fifth wave in that series sports a clear five-wave subdivision, too.

A recent study made available ten-year totals of the number of slaves embarking on ships sailing under the flags of about ten countries over a period of 360 years. To create their "Atlas of the Transatlantic Slave Trade," David Eltis of Emory University and David Richardson of the University of Hull, England drew upon "five decades of research in archives around the north and south Atlantic." The authors' online database is extensive, as "almost every port in the early modern Atlantic world organized and sent out a slave voyage, and…the bigger the port, the greater the number it sent out."[1] The database is also easily searchable and contains the names, ages and genders of almost 92,000 captive people.[2] The authors reported,

> **The trans-Atlantic slave trade was the largest long-distance coerced movement of people in history and, prior to the mid-nineteenth century,**

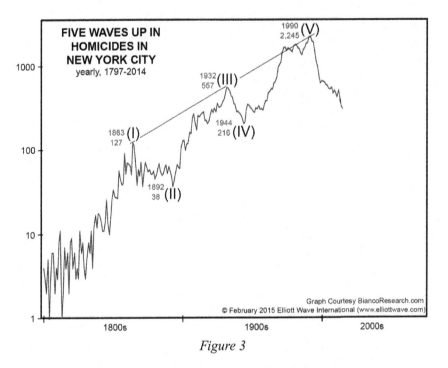

Figure 3

formed the major demographic wellspring for the re-peopling of the Americas following the collapse of the Amerindian population.[3]

It is remarkable that we have numerical data pertaining to a practice as reviled as slavery. The authors offer two reasons why we do: (1) "The African slave trade reduced people to commodities, but commodities generated profits, and where there were profits there was generally good record-keeping." (2) Slavery was both legal and "widely accepted in the mid-eighteenth century among both Europeans and Africans."[4] As a result, there was no moral outrage and no reason to hide such records.

We plotted the authors' data in Figure 4 and added labels to reveal a textbook Elliott wave—five waves up, three waves down—in the volume of transatlantic slave traffic over this period. Taking the most common form, the middle wave of the rise is the longest.

Many slaves died in the horrid conditions during passage, so, as the Atlas reveals, the numbers of slaves who disembarked at their destination were significantly lower than the numbers of those who had boarded. Nonetheless, those data (not shown) display exactly the same wave structure.

Consider that a vast variety of forces—wind, current, weather, seasons, economic changes, market conditions, moral objections and political forces—buffeted the transatlantic slave trade throughout its history. Yet,

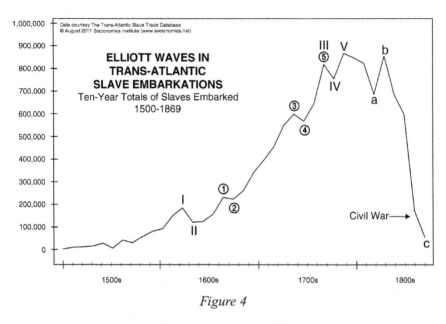

Figure 4

these figures reveal the very same fractal growth-and-decay pattern found in many other graphs of social activity, including those of financial markets.

None of the data series shown in Figures 1 through 4 seems causal to any of the others, and none of them corresponds to waves of overall social mood as recorded by the stock market. Each one traveled its own path.

Sociologists' Ad-Hoc, Mechanistic, Retrospective Explanations vs. the Socionomic Explanation

Economists and sociologists have attempted numerous retrospective explanations for each of these trend reversals. The text in Chapter 17 of *The Wave Principle of Human Social Behavior* accompanying the first version of Figure 1 cited an article offering no fewer than six retrospective hypotheses for why people were smoking less.

Stuck in full mechanical-cause mode, analysts in November 2015 attempted to explain a slight *uptick* in cigarette smoking for the year, the first in a decade. They blamed it on four things: a good economy, rising employment, lower gasoline prices and industry advertising. This is an absurd list. For the past six years, the economy has been good and employment has been rising, and the tobacco industry always advertises. This leaves falling gas prices as the culprit: "Smokers…are using the money they're saving at the gas pump to buy cigarettes."[5] The experts, however, did not bother to offer any data linking cigarette consumption to changes in gasoline prices. Their reason just felt good, thanks to their mental default to mechanical cause and its equally non-rational facilitator, rationalization. In keeping with the mechanics paradigm, experts also recommended a solution: even higher taxes on cigarettes.

An online article reports that economists have offered five different hypotheses of the same ilk to explain the decline of union membership (per Figure 2) that began nearly half a century ago. They are: company opposition to unions; self-destructive union demands that force hiring to go elsewhere; a rise in the percentage of employed women, teenagers and immigrants; a shift away from factory jobs to service jobs; and government mandates on employer behavior that have reduced the need for unions. The first four of these purported causes have been around to some degree for the past hundred years, and government has been involved in labor legislation for nearly as long.

Observers have credited the decrease in New York City's murder rate to get-tough police programs and an increase in abortions among the poor. A mechanistic cause in this case would be no serious challenge to socionomics, as everyday murderers do not participate in murdering herds (unless they join armies). We nevertheless suspect that some kind of socionomic causality is behind the trend and its reversal, because that is the only way to account for the clear Elliott wave in Figure 3. As Kenneth Olson has demonstrated, moreover [see Chapter 59], the national murder rate does seem to ebb and flow with overall social mood.

No doubt many professors of American history would credit the Civil War with abolishing the transatlantic slave trade. But Figure 4 reveals that the slave trade had been shrinking sharply for 30 years prior to the war, which erupted not at the beginning of the downtrend but near its end. That attitudes toward slavery had changed so extensively is what allowed anti-slavery to become a major theme of the war. The war was not a cause of that shift but a result.

To a socionomist, none of the supposed external or mechanistic causes offered for the trend changes depicted in Figures 1 through 4 actually explains them. Some of the reasons cited are results, not causes, while others are just coincidental events. Consider that none of the actions cited by sociologists in any of these cases either occurred or became plausible as causes until after the uptrend completed five waves and the trend had reversed. Once that happened, people's attitudes and behavior changed in ways that fit the new trend. As the new trend progressed, people cast about to identify events that they thought would explain it.

Figures 1 through 4 imply that the form of the progress and regress of attitudes resulting from the unconscious interaction of human minds in social settings does not change. While the specifics of recurring social expressions often differ, their pattern of growth and decay remains consistent.

568 SOCIONOMIC STUDIES OF SOCIETY AND CULTURE

More broadly, it seems safe to hypothesize that the primary causality behind any particular social trend or change is either socionomic or mechanistic. If the data are tied to overall social mood and/or display evidence of Elliott-wave regulation, then we can presume the primary causality is socionomic. If both of those signs are absent, the cause is likely to be mechanistic, i.e. sociological, political or economic.

Singular Waves of Social Activity?

The five-wave advances displayed in Figures 1–4 need not be part of larger wave structures. I had thought that tobacco consumption might increase again after a partial retracement of the rising wave, but this social activity is not tied to overall social mood, so it need never recover. Perhaps cigarette smoking will go the way of snuff boxes. Neither is union membership tied to overall social mood. The multi-decade decline could resolve with a resumption of increased union activity, or unionism might simply disappear as a social construct as did guild membership by the early 1800s. Many states still have laws forcing certain workers to join unions and pay dues, no doubt because unions donate to political campaigns. But any structure whose maintenance requires government force is a candidate for eventual extinction. Homicide is not likely to disappear in New York City, but it *could*, because unlike, say, economic production, murder is not a necessary human pursuit. Trends in many social activities follow Elliott waves, but some social activities are in effect only temporarily, in which cases only the five-wave rise and the ensuing decline to extinction will show on the graph. As for the slave trade, it, too, could disappear completely, although since political practices seem to make little, if any, discernible long term progress, such a benign future seems doubtful. Even the aggregate degree of concern over nuclear war (see Figure 1 in Chapter 35 of *Socionomic Causality in Politics*) has followed independent Elliott waves of rise and fall since the early 1940s. It could likewise either fade entirely or develop into a larger wave.

Charts such as these raise the question of whether humanity itself and its shared mood should be considered perpetual. Overall social mood, as revealed by benchmark sociometers, fluctuates in Elliott wave form and will continue to do so as long as human societies exist. If the human species is ever to go extinct, I would expect its decline toward that end would begin only after a five-wave advance of the highest degree up to that time is completed. Fortunately, no such wave appears anywhere near ending.

In the meantime, graphs such as these display a highly practical tool. Sociologists would benefit from learning the Elliott wave model. They could make some good predictions with it.

NOTES AND REFERENCES

[1] Eltis, D., & Richardson, D. (2011, January 5). New Revelations About Slaves and Slave Trade. CNN.

[2] Eltis, D., & Richardson, D. The Trans-Atlantic Slave Trade Database.

[3] Eltis, D., & Richardson, D. (2007). A Brief Overview of the Trans-Atlantic Slave trade. The Trans-Atlantic Slave Trade Database.

[4] Eltis, D., & Richardson, D. (2011, January 5). New Revelations About Slaves and Slave Trade. CNN.

[5] Kaplan, Jennifer, "Why Are Some Americans Smoking More?" Bloomberg, November 6, 2015.

Keep up with every development in socionomics.
Become an SI member now at www.socionomics.net/membership.

Socionomics Institute

CPSIA information can be obtained
at www.ICGtesting.com
Printed in the USA
LVOW03*1910111017
552066LV00003B/6/P